MERIWETHER LEWIS

WILLIAM CLARK

From paintings by Charles Willson Peale.
Courtesy of Independence National
Historical Park Collection.

The Men of the
Lewis and Clark Expedition

a biographical roster of
the fifty-one members

and

a composite diary of their activities
from all known sources

by

CHARLES G. CLARKE

INTRODUCTION TO THE BISON BOOKS EDITION BY
Dayton Duncan

UNIVERSITY OF NEBRASKA PRESS
LINCOLN AND LONDON

Library of Congress Cataloging-in-Publication Data
Clarke, Charles G.
The Men of the Lewis and Clark Expedition: a biographical roster of the fifty-one
members and a composite diary of their activities from all the known sources / by
Charles G. Clarke; introduction to the Bison Books edition by Dayton Duncan.
p.   cm.
"Bison book editions"
Originally published: Glendale, Calif., A.H. Clark Co., 1970.
ISBN 0-8032-6419-4 (alk. paper)
1. Lewis and Clark Expedition (1804-1806)—Biography. 2. Explorers—West
(U.S.)—Biography. 3. Lewis and Clark Expedition (1804-1806) 4. West (U.S.)—
Discovery and exploration. 5. West (U.S.)—Description and travel. I. Title
F592.7 .C57 2002
917.804'2'0922—dc21
[B]
2002017974

This Bison Books edition follows the original book, in which the introduction
begins on arabic page 13 and pages 74–75, 140–41, and 322–23 are blank; no
material has been omitted.

DAYTON DUNCAN

Introduction to the Bison Books Edition

A few years ago I was helping my friend Stephen Ambrose lead a group of people along some of the most scenic stretches of the Lewis and Clark Trail. On a warm summer evening, after a pleasant day of paddling canoes on the Missouri River, we camped amid the eerie and majestic White Cliffs of north-central Montana, close to the exact spot where, on 31 May 1805, Meriwether Lewis wrote one of his most lyrical journal passages about the wondrous landscape he and his men were encountering with such fresh eyes. "As we passed on," Lewis concluded, "it seemed as if those seens of visionary inchantment would never have an end."

Nearly two centuries later we found the enchantment equally palpable as we sat around the campfire and gazed at the silent cliffs reflected in the river, tinged pink by the setting sun. There were about thirty of us in the group, roughly the same number as in the original Corps of Discovery. Beyond that one feature of our trip—and our geographical location—most of the similarities between the two expeditions ended. On average our group's members were about thirty years older than the young men under the command of Lewis and Clark (along with one teenaged Indian woman and her infant son). We had paddled *down*stream to our camp (which was tiring enough for people our age), but nothing we did could be compared to dragging bulky dugouts day in and day out against the Missouri's relentless current. Unlike the Corps of Discovery, we felt no concerns about grizzly bears (they disappeared from the river a century ago), getting lost (we had precise maps and an experienced outfitter), or finding horses when the canoe portion of our journey ended (a chartered bus was hired to take us back to our parked cars). Having studied the history of the expedition in some detail, we also had made sure of another important difference: unlike the Corps of Discovery, we were absolutely *not* going to run out of whiskey.

That evening, after Steve and I took turns reading aloud from the journals, he spoke for a few minutes about teamwork. It's a point he had eloquently made three years earlier in the documentary film Ken Burns and I produced for public television: how after so many days together in their struggle to cross the continent, members of the Corps of Discovery eventually became so close to one another that they could hear a cough in the night and know who it was; they could recognize the sound of each other's footsteps; they knew who was best at hunting, at starting a fire, or at any other task; they even knew who liked salt on his meat and who didn't. Such detailed knowledge about everyone else's personal habits and strengths—a simultaneous acknowledgment of individuality within a group that itself has begun to act as a single, organic unit—is the natural byproduct of the intimate bond of teamwork so crucial to the success of any expedition.

Everyone around the campfire nodded in agreement, then headed for their sleeping bags. The next morning I told Steve he could add another item of familiarity to his list. After only one night of camping together, I said, we already knew who snored and who didn't—and we would be pitching our tents accordingly for the remainder of the trip.

Did any members of the Lewis and Clark expedition snore? If so, which ones? Was it a gentle sawing sound that encouraged the others to sleep, like the croaking of frogs on a riverbank? Or was it a series of erratically erupting snorts and rasps, perhaps even a grand anvil chorus of a dozen or more men that reverberated out of the tents, echoed over the hills, and alarmed the wild beasts of the Plains? Did their non-snoring campmates ponder (as that other great American adventurer Huckleberry Finn would have) the age-old conundrum, the "curiosest thing in the world": why is the snorer, the person closest to the sound, the only one left undisturbed by his snoring? Did they kick or shove or toss sticks at the offender? Or did they simply lie there, wide awake and murderously sleep deprived, silently calculating how hard it would be to slip a few doses of Rush's Thunderbolts (that super-powered laxative) into someone's breakfast?

We don't know the answers to these questions because the primary source of information, the expedition's journals, doesn't provide them. But it's a safe bet that every single member of the Corps of Discovery could have answered them, and probably in elaborate detail.

The men considered some specific disruptions of their slumber important enough to mention in their journals. The night before the expedition entered the White Cliffs, for instance, a buffalo bull stampeded into the sleeping camp, rampaged around the four fires, bent a rifle and one of the blunderbusses with its pounding hooves, and, according to

Sgt. John Ordway, came "within a fiew Inches of Several mens heads" before Lewis's dog, Seaman, chased it away. "It was Supposed," Ordway added, that "if he had trod on a man it would have killed him dead."[1] This puts the issue of being awakened by snoring in a different perspective. Or consider the night of 26 July 1806, on the Corps's return trip, when a vicious wolf sank its fangs into the hand of Sgt. Nathaniel Pryor— the kind of disturbance that might rouse anyone from even the deepest of dreams.

Both captains reported times when the worries of leadership prevented them from sleeping: William Clark, when the entire crew was required to spend the night on their keelboat, surrounded by hundreds of Teton warriors; Lewis, when he camped near Lemhi Pass with a band of Shoshones, whom he feared were about to abandon him before he could purchase any of their desperately needed horses. Seaman the dog had his own share of what Lewis called "wristless nights"—constantly patrolling the campsites after dark in bear country to warn the men of approaching grizzlies, as if the responsibility to allow others some well-earned rest was his alone.

Most other recorded bouts with insomnia, though far less dramatic, are nonetheless helpful in providing a fuller picture of the expedition's experience. At a site west of the Yellowstone River the beaver were so numerous that the slapping of their tails on the water kept some men from nodding off; near the mouth of the Columbia the huge and noisy flocks of geese and brants had done the same thing. Along the Missouri mosquitoes caused at least two sleepless nights (and probably innumerable others unrecorded); fleas were the problem at Fort Clatsop. Among the Nez Percés in Idaho, after the nearly starved men had unadvisedly gorged themselves on salmon and camas root, Clark dutifully noted in his journal that the feast "filled us so full of wind, that we were scercely able to Breathe all night" (and then, thankfully, he left additional details of the evening to the imagination).

But nowhere in the journals—among the hundreds of thousands of words that chronicle every day of the historic two-and-a-half-year expedition that brim with a remarkable accumulation of information—do we learn who among the Corps of Discovery snored his way across the continent and back.

Obviously the issues of sleep and snoring are not the most critical points of consideration in the epic journey of Lewis and Clark and their fellow explorers. But they do lead to larger, more important ones.

First, despite the incredible wealth of detail in the expedition's journals, much went unrecorded for posterity. (This is not so much a complaint as an observation.) Embarked as they were on an arduous trek into unmapped territory, where every bend in the river and every new horizon might spell discouragement, disaster, or defeat, the insistent priorities of mere survival could easily have overwhelmed the more prosaic task of taking pen to paper every evening. That they wrote at all—let alone created such an enduring classic among the annals of exploration—stands as a stunning achievement in itself, a testament both to President Jefferson's farsighted instructions that "your observations are to be taken with great pains & accuracy, to be entered distinctly & intelligibly for others as well as yourself," and to their diligence in carrying out those orders, even in the most difficult situations.

Journals from six men have survived: those of Captains Meriwether Lewis and William Clark, Sergeants John Ordway, Patrick Gass, and Charles Floyd, and Private Joseph Whitehouse. Taken together their commentaries leave no day of the expedition unrecorded, and for most days provide multiple perspectives from which to triangulate events. In addition, Sergeant Pryor and Private Robert Frazer are presumed to have kept journals as well, as yet unrecovered. What has been lost from not hearing their voices? How much more would we learn from the personal accounts of others on the expedition, such as York, Clark's black slave; or Sacagawea, the young Shoshone woman, and Charbonneau, her French Canadian husband; or the other enlisted men? It's impossible to tell.

This leads to a second issue: the nature of the journals themselves. These are not the diaries of teenage girls, full of emotion and juicy gossip, meant as an outlet for personal feelings and destined to be kept under lock and key for fear of embarrassment. Nor are they the journals of mature adults as we might expect them to be written today, recording a day's activities as a springboard for someone's innermost thoughts and contemplations. These are the journals of busy military men writing under orders from the president of the United States, recording information meant to be useful to him and the rest of the "civilized world," and fully anticipating that what they set down would be published in some form or another. In other words, the more personal the information— from the trivial (naming names about snoring habits) to the profound (private desires and misgivings, or frank assessments of another expedition member's strengths and weaknesses)—the less likely the Corps of Discovery's chroniclers are to reveal it.

On a few occasions Lewis displays a histrionic yearning for glory or alternately provides brief glimpses into the darker recesses of his soul. Clark sometimes whines about his health or exhibits a fatherly concern for the welfare of his men. Ordway's descriptions of the most dangerous moments come the closest to expressing outright fear, just as his entries about Christmas and his longing to return home seem the most heartfelt. In general, though, the information the journals provide exists within a fairly narrow range: miles traveled, the day's weather, locations of campsites, new species and new landscapes encountered, Indian tribes met and the prospects for trade, brief accountings of the day's highlights, and so on. All the things, in other words, that Mr. Jefferson so anxiously awaited. He wasn't interested in reading a novel of western adventure, he wanted facts. The Corps of Discovery obeyed by returning with a prodigious number of them.

If Jefferson had added in his instructions to "Take equal pains to tell us more about yourselves and your traveling companions, your own habits, beliefs, and customs, &c.," the journalists might possibly have taken a soldierly stab at it—though it is as difficult to imagine them doing so with much enthusiasm as it is to imagine the shy and secretive president wanting that kind of information in the first place. His priorities were clear: he wanted facts, not story.

Nevertheless, from the unelaborated facts alone a dramatic narrative emerges, one that is chock full of more heart-pounding near misses than most novels of the day would have dared attempt: a crumbling riverbank nearly overwhelms the keelboat; Lewis nearly falls to his death from a cliff; a confrontation with the Teton Sioux nearly turns deadly for both sides; men nearly freeze to death on the northern Plains; buffaloes nearly trample them and grizzly bears nearly catch them; a pirogue containing the most valuable cargo nearly capsizes; the expedition nearly takes a disastrous turn up the wrong river; a violent hailstorm nearly kills some of the men, while a flash flood nearly sweeps Clark to his death; Sacagawea nearly dies from sickness; her people, the Shoshones (with their all-important horses), nearly abandon Lewis; while crossing the Bitterroot Range, nearly lost, everyone nearly starves; the Nez Percés nearly decide to kill rather than befriend the weak and starving strangers; Columbia River cascades and then ocean swells nearly swamp the small flotilla of dugout canoes; Blackfeet warriors nearly leave Lewis and a few companions horseless and gunless in hostile territory; Lewis is shot and nearly killed in a hunting accident. (And, unbeknownst to the expedition, Spanish war parties dispatched for their destruction nearly intercept them.)

Just as facts overshadow feelings and personalities in the journals, the repetitive drumbeat of dramatic moments eventually drowns out the details of the more mundane day-to-day routines and the quiet heroics of getting up each morning for yet another exhausting day of moving only a few miles more across a seemingly endless continent. What is captured in the bargain is undoubtedly the most important information, as well as the most stirring moments. But what is lost is a fuller sense of the participants in this historic event, and perhaps some greater insights into how they succeeded so spectacularly. It's like reading an intricately plotted, action-packed, and highly informative novel that is sadly populated by rather featureless characters, or embarking on an epic adventure without really getting to know everyone else along on the trip.

Exacerbating the problem with all this lost potential is the way in which the captains overshadow everyone else. From the very start the historic enterprise tended to be viewed from the top down. President Jefferson, for instance, always considered it the "Lewis Expedition," reflecting his notion that Lewis was the only one to whom he had delegated authority and who therefore was solely responsible for the journey's outcome. Lewis knew better. He was the first to add Clark to the expedition's name, and always insisted that his trusted friend shared in the fame (just as he had shared in the decision making throughout the hard journey). So successful were these two remarkable leaders at melding their talents that they now seem historically joined at the hip, two quite different men who cast an even larger shadow because they stand together. They are unquestionably the "stars" of the story and the ones we most easily recognize, not only because they were the leaders but also because they are the story's principal narrators. Despite the existence of other journals, we turn to the captains' version of events first.

From time to time in the story a few other members of the expedition threaten to emerge as personalities in their own right, however fleetingly. The lavish attentions and honor which Indians paid to York because of his black skin prompt the journalists to take note of it, too, although for most of the expedition his presence—and its social ramifications—goes unremarked. Did some of the men (many from slave-holding states) resent those attentions? Did any consider him their friend and equal? What were York's thoughts? As they all paddled furiously down the Missouri toward home in 1806, did he expect that whatever newly found freedoms he had gained from the journey (if indeed any were gained) would be extended to him once they reached St. Louis?

Similar questions could be asked—and left unanswered—about Sacagawea, the only woman, mother, and full-blood Indian on the expedition. She figures prominently in some of the more dramatic moments (such as the near capsizing of the white pirogue and, of course, the Shoshone negotiations with a chief who miraculously turns out to be her brother), and we get a few hints at her character (such as when she insists on being taken to see the beached whale on the Oregon coast, or when she presents Clark with a Christmas present of two dozen white weasel tails). But she is absent from the recorded story as often as she is in it, and her point of view is available only through speculation.

What Sacagawea and York have in common—and, to a lesser extent, what Charbonneau, George Drouillard (a mixed-blood of French and Shawnee descent), the baby Jean Baptiste, and even what the dog, Seaman, also share—is what sets them apart from those we call simply "the men." That's merely another way of saying "everyone else." While these few stand out as individual characters in the saga, most often "the men" come across as an undifferentiated whole, a single unit comprised of interchangeable parts rather than a collection of individuals, each one with his own distinct personality, his own foibles and strengths, his own role to play, his own unique perspective on the larger experience. History has tended to lump them all together as "the men" and left it at that.

Clearly *they* didn't see it that way. As military men they recognized the authority and leadership of their captains and no doubt accepted the enterprise as the "Lewis and Clark Expedition." But as human beings (and, equally pertinent, as Americans in the first generation of independence), each man surely considered it *his* expedition—in experience if not in name. "The men" were individuals with individual names, individual attributes, and individual stories to tell.

Charles Clarke's *Men of the Lewis & Clark Expedition*, first published in 1970, was one of the first to remind the world of that self-evident but too-often-overlooked fact. As he wrote in his introduction,

Clarke's purpose was to "bring these men into being again and to rescue them from oblivion so far as is possible at this late date." *So far as is possible at this late date.* Unfortunately, for the many reasons mentioned—the missing voices, the circumscribed nature of the journals' focus, the dominance of the captains (and a few others) as individual characters—what is "possible at this late date" carries special weight and places severe constraints on a noble (and eloquently stated) goal. If "the men" have not exactly been fully brought back into being again in these pages, the reason is a simple lack of documentary raw material.

But they can be rescued from complete oblivion. By providing biographical sketches of fifty-one expedition members and then arranging a synopsis of each day's events with an emphasis on those things directly relating to each of the members, Charles Clarke performed a valuable service. One by one "the men" struggle to emerge as the individuals they surely must have been. Yet the facts—or, more precisely, the lack of enough facts—constantly limit their complete resuscitation. Enough exists to reassemble a skeleton and perhaps a bit of flesh, but, *so far as is possible at this late date,* breathing real life and blood into them is now probably best left to historical novelists. As for the rest of us, we can string together the available facts about an individual expedition member to hint at a fuller portrait and, with a little imagination, at least point ourselves toward a fuller understanding of what it must have been like to be a member of the greatest expedition in American history.

Consider, for instance, one of my personal favorites, Alexander Hamilton Willard, one of the many men about whom there is more that we don't know than what we do know. Born along the Connecticut River in Charlestown, New Hampshire (just a few miles from my home), Willard was twenty-five years old, apparently a skilled blacksmith, and a private in the army when he joined the Corps of Discovery at its camp in Illinois during the winter of 1803–1804. What prompted Willard to volunteer for the expedition? How did he fit in with the other young men who tended toward rabble-rousing that first winter? What did he expect for the journey? (Fevered excitement? foreboding? feigned ambivalence?) These are all unknown. Aside from a few passing references—a jumbled list of recruits, a notation of who got drunk on New Year's Eve, the mention of bringing in a pair of hinges—Willard's name rarely appears in the early months of the journals.

As the expedition began its ascent up the Missouri, it appears Willard spent at least some days on shore riding horseback with George Drouillard, the expedition's chief scout and best hunter, which suggests that the captains recognized in him some level of competence with a gun and horses. Someone raised along the Connecticut would have been familiar with rivers, but the mighty Missouri's size, power, and soon-to-be-legendary treachery must have amazed Willard. Perhaps he was thankful to be assigned to hunting duty rather than fighting the Big Muddy with the others. Did he and Drouillard exchange stories from their very different backgrounds? Was there an implicit competition between them over who supplied the most fresh meat to the hungry men? Did the primeval hardwood forests of Missouri, with their majestic stands of hickory and oak, hearken him back to the gentle hills of New Hampshire, blanketed with trees as they might have been when Willard's ancestors first arrived in New England? We can speculate but we cannot know. The journals only report for certain that he and Drouillard were responsible for the horses in late May, that on at least one occasion he and other hunters killed three fat elk bulls, and that, in the organization of the party, he was assigned to the squad of Sergeant Ordway, a fellow New Hampshire native. It takes a careful reading of the early journals to be even aware of Willard's presence.

But on 12 July 1804, at Camp New Island, just north of what is now the Kansas-Nebraska line, Willard burst onto center stage in the expedition's narrative. He did it, ironically enough, by sleeping. During the first months of the expedition the captains had worked to instill military discipline on a group of young men who seem to have been particularly reluctant to accept it. There were cases of drunkenness (Willard's had been but one of many such infractions), open disobedience, men going AWOL, and night guards helping themselves to supplies (that is, the whiskey). In each case Lewis and Clark had convened a court-martial of enlisted men to hear the charges, judge the facts, and mete out punishments, usually consisting of fifty lashes.

On 12 July, however, the captains themselves composed the court-martial because of the seriousness of the offense: falling asleep while on night guard duty, the kind of lapse that might endanger the entire expedition's survival in the wrong circumstance and obviously something Lewis and Clark wanted to make sure never happened again. The few facts we know of the incident are confined to the four terse paragraphs Lewis and Clark entered in the expedition's orderly book: Willard had been assigned as night sentinel the previous evening; his sergeant, Ordway, accused him of "lying down and Sleeping on his post"; the offense was considered *"Capatol Crimes,* and under the rules and articles of *War* punishable by *Death.*" Acting in his own defense, the report says, Willard made what I would consider to be the first attempt at a plea bargain west of the Mississippi River: *"Guilty of Lying Down, and not Guilty of Going to Sleep."*

Whether he had actually been asleep a few hours earlier (as charged) or not (as he claimed), Willard must surely have been fully alert during these proceedings. His life potentially hung in the balance as the captains weighed their decision and then announced it: guilty of both charges. An extra jolt of adrenaline must have rushed through his system in the brief moment between verdict and sentencing: not execution (obvious relief) but one hundred lashes on the bare back (a quick, reflexive tensing of shoulder muscles) to be administered in equal amounts over four nights.

It would be interesting—and informative—to know the other men's reaction to the trial, the verdict, and the next four evenings at each successive campsite, when Willard would have stepped forward to strip down his shirt and turn his face away to receive his nightly dose of twenty-five lashes. Perhaps some of the men, by now friends since spending seven months together, turned their faces away too. Maybe others relished the sight, harboring either some personal grudge against Willard or a belief that he truly had endangered their survival and deserved a stricter punishment. Once again the journals are of no help in creating a complete sense of the event. Gass, Whitehouse, and Floyd make no mention whatsoever of the court martial, let alone the nightly lashings. Ordway devotes only a single sentence to the incident ("one Sentinel a Sleep on his post last night, and tried by court martial this day"), omitting not only that Willard was the accused but that Ordway himself was the accuser. Is the near silence about the matter in the enlisted men's diaries significant? It's impossible to say.

Equally lost to history is Willard's point of view. If wrongly accused he could have been justifiably resentful toward his sergeant and commanding officers; if caught "fair and square" he might have considered himself properly chastised, perhaps even lucky to have escaped with whatever skin was left on his back at the end of the fourth evening. Did

Lewis (the chief dispenser of medicine) treat Willard's wounds each night? Did the floggings leave lasting scars? Was Willard comforted or shunned by his mates during the next few days? Was he brought back into the company of men with, perhaps, a few jokes, a friendly word, a helping hand during a task made difficult by a sore back? Answers to those questions would explain much about the dynamics of the Corps of Discovery—between the commanders and their men, between noncommissioned officers and their squads, within the group as a whole, or between individual members—but we could answer them only if we had more details. Instead we are left to wonder, extrapolate, speculate, yearn for fuller information, and, in the end, be thankful for the few facts we do have from which to populate this epic expedition with more than simply names on a list.

We know with certainty that July 1804 was not a good month for Private Willard, because he surfaces next in the journals on 29 July when he was dispatched back to the previous night's campsite to retrieve a tomahawk he had forgotten, and then, while crossing a creek on a log, had lost his balance and dropped his rifle into the deep water. We know also that Reuben Field was sent out to rescue the gun from the creek's muddy bottom. Willard probably never forgot that humiliating day: the look in the captains' eyes or the sounds of their voices after he admitted to misplacing his tomahawk; the long walk to retrieve it; the moment on the log when he thought he would fall in, and the next moment, right after dropping his rifle, when he probably wished he had; the sight of Reuben Field disappearing underwater and his reappearance moments later with the prize; the talk and the looks of the other men when he and his sodden companion returned to camp and retold the story; the sinking feeling that perhaps he shouldn't have volunteered for the expedition in the first place. Regardless of how memorable that day was for Willard, the journals' mention of his part in it slides by in a few short sentences. We are told more about the weather (dark with occasional rain, cold wind from the WNW, the state of the river (more bends and slower current north of the Platte, the banks lined mostly with cottonwoods now, many of them ravaged and broken by a storm of sometime in the recent past), and the day's provisions (some huge catfish and jerked meat from Drouillard's fresh kills) than we are told about any particular person.

And so it goes for the remainder of the "Willard Expedition." For the rest of the journey he sporadically appears in tantalizing shards of information—the DNA of a fuller story, suggesting (but only suggesting) the unique quality of one man's unforgettable experience—and through him a better knowledge of the larger organism known as the Corps of Discovery. He appears, then just as quickly disappears, leaving us to fill in the blanks or connect the dots.

And what dots there are to connect!

• 14 SEPTEMBER 1804.   Willard accompanies Clark in a vain attempt to locate a volcano (a volcano!) rumored to exist somewhere nearby (they are in South Dakota); along the way Clark kills their first antelope, an animal unknown to science at the time, and Willard hauls it back.

• WINTER, 1804–1805.   Willard and John Shields become indispensable to the expedition's survival by trading their blacksmithing work for corn and meat from the Mandans.

• 18 JUNE 1805.   Dispatched to bring in a load of freshly killed buffalo meat during the portage of the Great Falls, Willard is attacked and nearly caught by a grizzly bear, which chases him to within forty yards of the camp.

• 15 AUGUST 1805.   Clark names a creek in southwestern Montana "Willard's Creek." (A special moment of pride, perhaps? Or even less than a matter-of-fact occurrence, since during the preceding four months so many other creeks had been named for other expedition members?)

• 18 SEPTEMBER 1805.   During the terrible ordeal in the Bitterroot Mountains, Willard's "negligence" (Lewis's words) causes a delay in the morning's start: his unattended horse is missing. Lewis sends Willard back to find the horse and marches off with everyone else. Late in the afternoon Willard finally catches up with the expedition, without the horse.

• 10 February 1806.   Willard returns to Fort Clatsop from the salt works on the seashore with a serious injury. While butchering some elk he had killed, he "had cut his knee very badly with his tommahawk," according to Lewis.

• 20 FEBRUARY 1806.   Like a number of the other men, Willard is reported sick: "a high fever and complains of the pain in his head and want of appetite," writes Lewis, who treats him with "Scott's pills" the next day. On 27 February he is still reported as "very unwell;" on 8 March he is "yet complaining and is low Spirited;" on 20 March, "remain[s] weak;" and on 21 March still does "not seem to recover" and now taken by a "violent pain in his leg and thye." Not until 29 March, nearly a week after the expedition has departed for home from Fort Clatsop, is Willard considered "quit well" by his captains.

• 19 APRIL 1806.   Halfway up the Columbia River, near the Dalles of Oregon, Willard once more allows his horse to wander off. "I repremanded him more severely for this peice of negligence than had been usual with me," a piqued Lewis writes. (Can words sting as much as a physical lashing?) But by 9 May, back with the Nez Percés, Willard has apparently regained his captain's confidence and is sent with Chief Twisted Hair to retrieve the expedition's large horse herd (which the Indians had kept over the winter). By the end of May it appears that Willard is one of the few privates entrusted with the all-important trade for food going on with the Nez Percés.

• 4 AUGUST 1806.   In eastern Montana, where Willard has once more become one of the regular hunters, he and Ordway kill two deer and a large grizzly (revenge from the near-death experience of a year earlier?) and set out in their canoe to catch up with the others. Darkness falls but they decide to continue down the Missouri by moonlight, only to be pushed by the current into a thick tangle of driftwood, which knocks Willard into the rushing water. As Ordway frantically maneuvers the dugout to safety, Willard clings to a limb. Somehow he grabs two small logs, ties them together, places his clothes on them, and then floats with them about a mile downstream and finally to shore. "It was fortunate for Willard," Lewis writes of the accident, that, unlike many of the other men on the expedition, "he could swim tolerably well."

• 28 AUGUST 1806.   In South Dakota Willard is among a small group dispatched by Clark to kill an antelope so its skeleton and skin can be preserved for President Jefferson (others are sent out for prairie dogs and magpies). On the 29 August he returns empty-handed, but tells Clark he did manage to measure the White River a few miles upstream from its mouth: two feet deep, two hundred yards wide. His method of measurement: wading.

• 30 AUGUST 1806.   Just before midnight a violent thunderstorm erupts, whipping up such ferocious winds and waves that the men are ordered to hold onto the canoes to prevent them from being blown off the sandbar where the expedition is encamped. Two canoes that had been lashed together nonetheless break loose— with Willard and Private Peter Weiser in them, powerless to do anything but hang on for dear life—and are blown across the river. Ordway and six men set out in the small pirogue to effect a rescue. By 2:00 A.M., during a lull in the storm, they all finally make it back to camp, where it rains until daylight, leaving everyone, in Clark's words, "wet and disagreeable."

     With that notation Willard exits from the journals forever. What a pity because, as this brief outline suggests, *The Adventures of Private Alexander Hamilton Willard* would have been an epic in itself, if only he could be brought back to life to tell it in detail from his own point of view. Part *Pilgrim's Progress,* complete with valuable lessons learned on the road, and part *Perils of Pauline,* full of close calls and comic mishaps, it would also add immeasurable depth to the larger story of the Corps of Discovery. If fully fleshed out, Willard's tale—of a lowly and sometimes hapless private who suffered lashings, injuries, illnesses, and accidents, yet persevered to earn his commanders' trust and his nation's thanks—would humanize the expedition in a way that the existing accounts never will.

Lacking that, the mere outline of Willard's journey (and of everyone else's brought forth in this book) at the very least demands that we resist the temptation to think of "the men" of the Lewis and Clark expedition only in passing or predominantly as a single entity. *So far as is possible at this late date,* they should be remembered in the way their captains thought of them and in the way they knew each other: as distinct and fallible human beings. In realizing their individuality, the key to their success—their unity—appears even more remarkable. By admitting their fallibility their heroic achievement becomes that much more inspiring.

Alexander Willard lived to the ripe old age of eighty-seven—long enough to serve his country several times more (as a government blacksmith for the Sauk, Fox, Delaware, and Shawnee Indians, and in the War of 1812); long enough to marry and raise twelve children (one given the name Lewis, another Clark); long enough to be alive during the invention of photography and have his picture taken, his back proud and erect, his eyes confidently fixed straight ahead; long enough to play his part in yet another national transcontinental endeavor, the covered wagon migrations to the gold fields of California, where he died in 1865.[2]

There is a faint suspicion that he did, in fact, keep a journal during his expedition with Lewis and Clark and the Corps of Discovery. Certainly he must have told and retold his adventures to his children and grandchildren in the many years that followed. How I wish that journal could be found in someone's attic or that one of Willard's descendants had transcribed his reminiscences.[3]

But even if such accounts were miraculously discovered, I doubt they would settle a question which, in the absence of conclusive facts to the contrary, I've decided to believe about Alexander Willard. I believe he *was* asleep during night guard duty back on Camp New Island in 1804.

And I think I know how Sergeant Ordway discovered him and then knew immediately that Willard was both lying down *and* sleeping. He was snoring.

NOTES

1. All quotations herein are taken from *The Journals of the Lewis & Clark Expedition,* edited by Gary E. Moulton and published by the University of Nebraska Press. In cases of factual differences between that work and *The Men of the Lewis and Clark Expedition,* which was published much earlier, I have relied on Moulton.

2. Recent efforts have turned up two photos of Willard, one in addition to the one Clarke published in 1970. Furthermore, a photo of Sgt. Patrick Gass has also been subsequently discovered.

3. There is always hope: segments of Whitehouse's journal came to light in 1903 and 1966; Ordway's journal wasn't discovered until 1916; and Clark's field notes were uncovered in 1953.

Contents

Illustrations

To my dear wife
MARIAN
who let me buy all those books
on Lewis and Clark, and who has been
a good scout when we covered their trail

Acknowledgment

This work would not have been possible without the help of many people and organizations who have so generously put their records at my disposal. I am particularly indebted to the Missouri Historical Society; the St. Charles Historical Society and the Oregon Historical Society for the many favors shown me by the staffs of these wonderful deposits of manuscripts and documents. The Newberry Library of Chicago has graciously allowed me to extract data from the recently discovered and as yet unpublished *Private Joseph Whitehouse Journal*. This is a new version and continuation of his published journal.

The Dodd, Mead & Company, publishers of *The Original Journals of the Lewis and Clark Expedition;* The State Historical Society of Wisconsin, publishers of *The Journals of Meriwether Lewis and John Ordway;* the University of Illinois Press, publishers of the *Letters of the Lewis and Clark Expedition with Related Documents 1783-1854,* and the Yale University Press, publishers of *The Field Notes of Captain William Clark,* have kindly allowed me to quote from their most valuable publications. All these sources have been used to compile the "Personnel Diary" which follows.

I am happy to acknowledge the great aid given me by Miss Anna M. Cartlidge of Baltimore for new data on the Floyd-Pryor families. To Mrs. Edna McElhiney Olson of St. Charles, Missouri, I am indebted for the St. Charles and Millington family data. To Rev. Frederick Weiser for the Weiser family material and to Mrs. Lois More of Sonoma, California, for the lineage of Alexander Hamilton Willard. To them I express my gratitude.

Many others have sent encouragement and biographical details, but the list is so long that I cannot acknowledge them all here. I ask that they accept my sincere appreciation for their interest and valuable help.

I cannot close however, without mention of one more who has been of great assistance. Mrs. Dorothy Shields Lollier of Carlsbad, California, has researched the Shields family and has brought to my attention most of the information regarding that most valuable man to the expedition – John Shields.

Mr. Anton J. Pregaldin of Clayton, Missouri, has generously supplied me with his research on those unsung members of the expedition, the French-Canadian engagés. His findings, in a most difficult field, throw a helpful glimmer of light on those heretofore obscure watermen.

Last, but far from least, I express deep gratitude to Anna Marie and Everett G. Hager for preparing the fine index. I am most fortunate in having all such outstanding experts on my team.

Now I can only hope that my own research and arrangement of all this scattered material will be helpful to future students of the Expedition.

CHARLES G. CLARKE

Beverly Hills, California, 1970

Introduction

The Lewis and Clark Expedition to the Pacific and return
by way of the Missouri River in 1804-1806 was probably the
best written and officially documented of all such govern-
mental undertakings. Certainly its captains and several of
its members made copious mention in their journals of the
daily travels and notable sights encountered along the way.
We have complete records of the material and supplies
carried, details of the boats and medicines taken, and full
reports on the Indians and strange animals and plants discovered. But a complete roster of all the men who set out
with the expedition was never made.[1]

---

[1] The journals as written by various members of the expedition are: Reuben G.
Thwaites, editor, *The Original Journals of the Lewis and Clark Expedition,* also
containing the journal of Sgt. Charles Floyd and the journal of Pvt. Joseph Whitehouse. Seven volumes. Dodd, Mead & Co., New York, 1904. (Hereafter cited as
Thwaites.)

Milo M. Quaife, editor, *The Journals of Captain Meriwether Lewis and Sergeant
John Ordway,* State Historical Society of Wisconsin, Madison, 1916. (Hereafter
cited as Quaife.)

Ernest S. Osgood, editor, *The Field Notes of Captain William Clark, 1803-1805,*
Yale University Press, New Haven, 1964. (Hereafter cited as Osgood.)

In addition to the two-volume edition *(History of the Expedition . . .)* edited
by Nicholas Biddle, and published in Philadelphia in 1814, which is a condensation
of the original journals, with occasional assistance and clarification from George
Shannon (one of the members), there is the reprint of the text:

Elliott Coues, *History of the Expedition under the Command of Lewis and Clark.*
Four volumes. Francis P. Harper, New York, 1893. This edition is valuable for the
notes of Dr. Coues. (Hereafter cited as Coues, *Lewis and Clark.*)

Patrick Gass' journal was published in Pittsburgh in 1807 under the title, *Journal
of the Voyages and Travels of a Corps of Discovery, under the Command of Captain
Lewis and Captain Clarke. . .* As edited by David McKeehan, Gass' journal is
so polished as to have little value to this study. However in a few cases Gass is
mentioned and he adds to some points which have been incorporated in my "Diary."

Though not properly a journal of the expedition, Donald Jackson, editor, *Letters
of the Lewis and Clark Expedition with Related Documents, 1783-1854,* University
of Illinois Press, Urbana, 1962, is a most valuable work, for in it are collected under

Unfortunately, they omitted to mention much about themselves in their journals, for they were innocently unaware that they were creating history. True, the captains do mention a member now and then, but that is about all. They were certainly convinced that no biographical data was necessary, for this was a military command.

After the expedition successfully returned in 1806, there was a long delay before the publication of their journals in 1814.[2] The War of 1812 occupied the nation's attention, and for a long lapse of years the members of the expedition were forgotten.

The purpose of this study is an attempt to bring these men into being again and to rescue them from oblivion so far as is possible at this late date. Therefore, it is not the purpose here to discuss the reasons that brought the Lewis and Clark Expedition into being. However, I think it pertinent to recall that an investigation of what lay beyond the Mississippi had for many years been in Thomas Jefferson's mind.

At least two of his previous plans to cross the continent – that of John Ledyard and Andrew Michaux – had come to naught. Jefferson knew of the recently published account of Alexander Mackenzie's journal which contained a detailed plan of how Great Britain might set up posts at the mouth of the Columbia River, and at other suitable ports. These were to control the ever increasing numbers of American ships that were then dominating the sea-otter trade to the Orient. These plans also included control of the fur trade and fisheries of that part of Western America.

These international schemes were plain to Jefferson, and

one cover all the letters and documents relative to the expedition. Dr. Jackson's notes are of real interest to explain some of the statements made in the journals. (Hereafter cited as Jackson.)

2 Thwaites, I, p. xxxvi, relates the many problems encountered before the journals were published.

they had to be averted before they became permanently established. The United States had a claim to the Oregon country because Captain Robert Gray was the first to discover and enter the mouth of the Columbia River in 1792. This claim could be strengthened by an overland expedition to, and exploration of, the lands bordering the upper waters of the Columbia – and by descending that river to the sea.

In the winter of 1802, Jefferson instructed his private secretary, Meriwether Lewis, who was skilled at frontier living and who had recently served in several campaigns with the army, to study botany, zoology, medicine, and celestial navigation in preparation for leading an expedition to the Pacific.

In a secret appeal to Congress on January 18, 1803, the sum of "Twenty-five Hundred Dollars" was appropriated for "An intelligent officer with ten or twelve chosen men, fit for the enterprise and willing to undertake it, taken from our military posts, where they may be spared without inconvenience, might explore the whole line, even to the Western Ocean." To further cinch the argument, Jefferson mentioned that "The soldiers pay would be going on, whether here or there" and that "the appropriation of Twenty-five Hundred Dollars for the purpose of extending the external commerce of the United States – would cover the undertaking."[3]

In the light of recent study, it appears that Congress was privy to an understanding, not openly admitted, of the "official" request for appropriations. In early 1803, the jealousies of England, France, and Spain were not to be aroused by a large military party snooping around in disputed domains. Furthermore, the influential fur trading companies did not look with favor on this constant probing into their lands. The inevitable settlement which followed was contrary to the source of their income.

---

[3] Excellent accounts of the origin of the expedition are found in Thwaites, I, p. xvii; and in Bernard DeVoto, *Journals of Lewis and Clark,* p. xv.

But before the year 1803 was finished, it became evident that such a small party as ten or twelve men could never overcome the Indians who zealously contested the passage to the upper Missouri River. The British traders already in that country did not desire competition from traders coming up the Missouri from the south, and they did all in their power to prevent it.

In the fall of 1803, Captain Lewis was firmly convinced by Auguste Chouteau, Manuel Lisa and other experienced traders, who had for many years been familiar with the lower Missouri – that a stronger, and hence, larger party, would be necessary to command respect, and safe traverse of the Missouri waters.

Captain Lewis kept Jefferson advised of these developments, and the latter adroitly managed the additional funds required. Historians may never learn how this was done, but the fact remains that it was. To help matters, he had as we say today, "something special going for him" in 1803. Louisiana, which in those days was about all the lands west of the Mississippi to the western mountains (wherever they were), changed hands from Spain to France to the United States in that year. That transaction removed some of the sticky diplomatic difficulties, although Spain remained convinced that the Lewis and Clark party really intended to take over the Spanish establishments. Spain actually sent out from Santa Fe in 1804 an overland expedition to cut Lewis and Clark off.[4] Fortunately it could not find them.

During the summer and fall of 1803, Lewis and his co-leader, William Clark, were recruiting and testing men as possible prospects for the rigorous adventures that lay ahead. While the men were selected with great care, Captain Lewis was authorized to offer the following inducements to those enlisting:[5]

---

[4] A. P. Nasatir, *Before Lewis and Clark,* vol. II, p. 752.
[5] Document in Missouri Historical Society Collections, reprinted in Jackson, 60.

FIRST: The bounty (if not a soldier) but in both cases, six months pay in advance. Pay of $10.00 per month, plus clothing and subsistence.

SECOND: To discharge them from service if they wish it, immediately on their return from the expedition, giving them their arrears of pay, clothing, etc.

THIRD: To secure to them a portion of land equal to that given by the United States to the officers and soldiers who served in the Revolutionary War.

Captain Lewis was authorized to select by voluntary engagement, men from the companies of Captains Russell and Daniel Bissell, and of Captain Amos Stoddard now occupying the posts of Fort Massac and Fort Kaskaskia. Captain Lewis was also authorized to engage any other men, not soldiers, whom he thought useful in promoting the objects or success of the expedition. They were to recruit "some good hunters; stout, healthy, unmarried men, accustomed to the woods, and capable of bearing bodily fatigues to a considerable degree. The hunters were to be engaged with the understanding that they were to bear the common labor of the party and not to engage in hunting exclusively."

With William Clark's agreement to join Captain Lewis in the expedition, Clark was furnished with these instructions, and Lewis advised him to be on the lookout for suitable men. Several young gentlemen's sons applied to Clark, but as he felt they were not accustomed to labor, he had to diplomatically offer them no encouragement. He did temporarily engage some men who later became known as "The nine young men from Kentucky."

Major William MacRae, Commandant at South West Point, Kentucky, was instructed to send six or eight soldiers as likely candidates from Tennessee to Fort Massac to await Captain Lewis's arrival.

With this help and inducements, Captain Lewis wrote Clark on September 28, 1803, that he felt "we shall be able to form our party without much difficulty; four or five French water-men I conceive will be essential, this we can do I presume very readily at St. Louis." In the same letter Lewis wrote, "I have two young men with me whom I have taken on trial and not yet engaged them, but conditionally only, though I think they will answer tolerably well."[6]

Thus when Captain Lewis came down the Ohio River and was joined by Clark at Louisville, some twelve temporary recruits also came along. At Pittsburgh, Pennsylvania; in Kentucky, and at the frontier military posts of Fort Massac, Vincennes and Kaskaskia, other volunteers were recruited and transferred to Lewis and Clark's command.

They formed a camp at Wood River (Camp du Bois) in Illinois, which in 1803 was about opposite the mouth of the Missouri River.[7] This location was not too far from St. Louis, but sufficiently removed from its wine shops and women, and, most importantly, was *not* in Spanish territory. Here during the winter and spring, Captain Clark and Sergeant Ordway observed and drilled the men who had been chosen thus far. All of them had been selected for their special talents and experiences as backwoods men. All were of a resourceful nature, and a few, such as one Mr. Leakins, who were overly resourceful, were rejected as being too undisciplined to serve under a military command.

During the cold winter the men built huts, hunted deer, rabbits, racoons and turkeys for their sustenance. They had to build a sled in order to haul in enough firewood. Compatibility was established, and a pattern of camp life was begun which would prevail over the next two years.

Whiskey peddlers soon found the camp, which caused some trouble. Discipline had to be enforced. Court-martial rules were set up for dealing with the red-blooded, rugged recruits who were frequently drunk. It is worthy of note

---

6 Jackson, 124. Though Lewis mentions "two young men" with him, he actually was accompanied by three – Charles Floyd, Reuben Fields and Joseph Fields.

7 See 1796 map by Collet, reprinted in Osgood, 2.

that some of the men who later turned out to be the most valuable men of the party, were among those who had to be punished while at Camp Woods, as the following orders will show:

March 3rd, 1804.

The Commanding officer feels himself mortified and disappointed at the disorderly conduct of Reubin Fields in refusing to mount guard when in the due roteen of duty he was regularly warned; nor is he less surprised at the want of discretion in those who urged his opposition to the faithful discharge of his duty, particularly (John) Shields, whose sense of propryety he had every reason to believe would have induced him rather to have promoted good order, than to have excited disorder and faction among the party, particularly in the absence of Capt. Clark and himself.

The Commanding officer is also sorry to find any man, who has been engaged by himself and Capt. Clark for the expedition on which they have entered, so destitute of understanding, as not to be able to draw the distinction between being placed under the command of another officer, whose will in such case would be their law, and that of obeying the orders of Capt. Clark and himself communicated to them through Sergt. Ordway, who, as one of the party, has during their necessary absence been charged with the execution of their orders; acting from those orders expressly, and not from his own caprice, and who, is in all respects accountable to us for the faithful observance of the same.

A moments reflection must convince every man of our party, that were we to neglect the more important and necessary arrangements in relation to the voyage we are now entering on, for the purpose merely of remaining at camp in order to communicate our orders in person to the individuals of the party on mere points of policy, they would have too much reason to complain; nay, even to fear the ultimate success of the enterprise in which we are all embarked. The abuse of some of the party in respect with privilege heretofore granted them of going into the country, is not less displeasing; to such therefore as have made hunting or other business a pretext to cover their design of visiting a neighboring Whiskey shop, he cannot for the present extend this privilege; and does therefore most positively direct that Colter, Bolye, Wiser and Robinson do not receive permission to leave camp under any pretext whatever for *ten days,* after this order is read on the parade, unless otherwise directed hereafter by Capt. Clark or himself. The Commanding officers highly approve of the conduct of Sergt. Ordway.

The Carpenters, Blacksmiths, and in short the whole party (except Floyd, who has been specially directed to perform other duties) are to obey implicity the orders of Sergt. Ordway, who has received our instructions and is held accountable to us for their due execution.

MERIWETHER LEWIS,
Capt. 1st U.S. Regt. Infty.
Comdg. Detatchment.[8]

This order obviously produced the desired effect, for we find all the men mentioned to be members of the party when it started out, and John Shields, Reuben Fields, John Colter and Peter Weiser became members of the permanent party that went on to the Pacific.

Captain Clark, as he was always recognized by the party, though when his commission arrived was only as a second lieutenant in the Artillery, spent most of the time at Camp Woods. He pondered the provisions needed for the expedition, the loading of the three boats, and gave considerable attention to those men who would be selected as permanent members who were to cross the continent, and to those which would comprise the extra force needed to get the equipment and provisions beyond the Indians who dominated the lower Missouri. Try as he would, the total number always came out to be around fifty men. In one of his notes he lists "Our party: 2 Captains; 4 Sergeants; 3 interpreters; 22 Americans; 9 or 10 Frenchmen, and York, his slave. Plus 1 Corporal and 6 soldiers in a canoe with provisions for the party as far as these provisions last."[9] This totals 48 men if there were nine Frenchmen, or 49 if there were ten.

This is a point to remember when later the journalists all state the total number of the party consisted of only forty-five men.

---

[8] Original in Voorhis Collection, Missouri Hist. Soc., printed in Thwaites, I, p. 9.
[9] Thwaites, I, p. 16.

George Drouillard had been engaged to act as interpreter for the party. He was dispatched to Tennessee to recruit men, and he returned on December 16, 1803, with eight men. One was a blacksmith and another was a "Housejoiner." Captain Clark wrote to Captain Lewis in St. Louis "that he did not know how they will answer our experiment, but I am a little disappointed in finding them not possessed of more of the requisite qualifications. There is not a hunter among them. Drouillard nor myself have made no particular bargain with them. I have offered Drouillard $25.00 per month for as long as he may choose to continue with us."

Captain Lewis spent most of the time in St. Louis, procuring maps and every bit of information he could gather regarding the land and natives resident up river. Additional medicines and provisions for the voyage were obtained. He was advised that the best men for propelling the boats were those French-Canadian water-men who lived at Kaskaskia and Cahokia. These were villages on the Illinois side of the Mississippi near St. Louis where these boatmen resided when not off on some trading adventure up the Missouri or Mississippi rivers. With Mr. Chouteau's help, the most capable and reliable men were engaged to man the boats as far as the Mandan Nation. Lewis wrote Clark that "Mr. Chouteau has procured seven engagés to go as far as the Mandans but they will not agree to go further, and I found it impossible to reduce them to any other engagement than that usually made with these people."[10] Probably meaning that they would not enlist in a military organization.

Some of these engagés may have been former employees of the North West Company of Canada. John McDonnell, about the year 1795, wrote an account found in Masson's *Les Bourgeois de la Compagnie du Nord-Ouest* (vol. I, p.

---

[10] Jackson, 178.

272) : "Many of the Company's servants (have been) deserting from the Mandan country with an intention of going to the Illinois and other places on the Mississippi. . ." It is possible that "La Liberte" (Jo Barter), Joseph Collin and Jean Baptiste DeChamps were former members of the North West Company. Likewise, Francois Rivet, Paul Primeau, Peter Roi and others could have originated from that source, for the same, or variants of the name, appear in the rosters of the North West Company for the years just prior to the formation of the Lewis and Clark Expedition. See for example, above citation, pages 396-411.

John Francis McDermott [11] reprints an apt description of the engagé:

> These men carried out the necessary work of the trade; cordelling, poling or rowing up the Missouri to operational headquarters, seeking out and trading with the Indian villages; trapping the beaver and other fur-bearers; hunting meat animals; maintaining the equipment, conveying the messages through the unknown country; cooking; keeping camp; tending horses; and performing a score of other regular and extra duties. Some of them were sons and grandsons of the men who had come up the Mississippi River from New Orleans with Laclede and Auguste Chouteau, and of this group some were native St. Lousians and many more came from the settlements such as Fort Chartres, Kaskaskia, Cahokia and St. Genevieve.

The number of men now deemed necessary was a considerable advance over that understood by Congress. In view of this situation, there could possibly have been an understanding with President Jefferson that the "official" figure would be acceptable if the total number did not exceed forty-five, including the two captains. This could be one of the reasons that no complete roster was compiled by the captains at the outset of the expedition.

At any rate, all those who kept journals – Lewis, Clark, Gass, Ordway, Floyd, and Whitehouse – dutifully record

---

[11] John Francis McDermott, editor, *The French in the Mississippi Valley,* 94-95.

that the total number was about forty-five men. They do not all agree on the number, but none exceeds forty-five.

So for over a hundred and fifty years this number has been accepted. As the names of the entire roster had never been published, no one seemed to question it. Of course, the names of the thirty men who had gone on to the Pacific were known and recorded in the journals, but what of those twenty or so who had helped the party up to the Mandan villages, had wintered there, and had returned to St. Louis in the early summer of 1805? They brought back the maps and reports that had been made thus far, as well as many crates of new animal, mineral and botanical specimens. They saw to it that all this material was dispatched to Jefferson in Washington, and several of them conducted those Indians who had been prevailed upon to visit the Great White Father, and had acted as interpreters between them and President Jefferson. All this was part and plan of the expedition from its original conception.

To many students of the expedition, these men *were* important to the success of the enterprise. It has since been felt that more should be known of the entire party – just who they were – and as much biographical information should be collected as is possible.

As the journals were studied, it also became evident that more men returned from the expedition than the forty-five that were stated to have gone at its start.

In the December 1944, issue of the *Oregon Historical Quarterly,*[12] I submitted a roster and made the suggestion that the number should be forty-seven including the captains. I presented a list of forty-five, plus additional names that merited consideration. At that time I felt it presumptuous for a mere student to fly into the face of the scholars and historians who had edited the journals. Since 1944,

[12] Volume XLV, no. 4, pp. 289-305.

much new material has been published which substantiates, and even elaborates on that thinking.

In 1964, *The Field Notes of William Clark, 1803-1804,* edited by Ernest S. Osgood, were published by the Yale University Press. *The Letters of the Lewis and Clark Expedition, with Related Documents 1783-1854,* edited by Donald Jackson, were published in 1962 by the University of Illinois Press. Each adds bits of additional information regarding the personnel. It now appears that Captain Clark was right when he noted a party of about fifty men.

But even if we accept this new figure, we are still far from an easy solution as to the names of the men, for the captains, especially Clark, had a charming disregard for the accuracy of spelling. When it came to proper names, almost any combination of letters seemed to suffice. Take the name of Corporal Richard Warfington for example. We find it rendered *Warfington, Worthington, Worbington, Worthyton* and even more exotic variations. George Drouillard was nearly always *Drewyer.* But those are the easy ones. In another case we have *Carrn, Carr, Cane* or *Cann,* all apparently meant to represent one person. I need not here show what happened to the spelling of the French names. That will be found in the roster.

As though this were not problem enough, we also have those who, following the success of the expedition, attempted to climb on the band-wagon and publicly claim that they had been members of the party. There are many examples, of which it is sufficient to cite only one:

> Benjamin Jones was a noted hunter, trapper and surveyor of early times in Missouri. His father was an Englishman who settled in Virginia at an early date. He had two sons, Lewis and Benjamin. The latter ran away from home when he was sixteen years of age, and came to St. Louis, where he joined the Indians and engaged in trapping, until Lewis and Clark started on their expedition, when he joined their party in the capacity of a scout. Before the expedition reached the

Pacific Ocean, he and one or two others were sent back to St. Louis with dispatches. They fell into an Indian ambuscade, lost their horses, and had to perform the journey on foot, which occupied six months but they arrived safely and delivered the dispatches.[13]

Now the first part of this notice could be true, for this Benjamin Jones *was* on the Missouri in 1809-1810, and was a hunter with the government service on the Santa Fe trail in 1825. But we find no other documented mention of where Jones was ever a member of the Lewis and Clark Expedition.

The student can only sift these momentarily exciting bits of data, and present those which seem to contain honest pay-dirt. My roster which follows, has been compiled from the researchers who were on the scene some sixty-five years ago, such as Reuben G. Thwaites, Elliott Coues, Eva Emery Dye,[14] Olin D. Wheeler,[15] James K. Hosmer[16] and others. They all gave an account of the men, as far as they knew at the time. In addition we have the works of Bradbury,[17] Brackenridge,[18] Henry,[19] and others who lived in, and wrote

[13] Wm. S. Bryan and Robert Rose, *A History of Pioneer Families of Missouri*, p. 504.

[14] Though Mrs. Dye is sometimes dismissed as a "novelist," she did extensive research for her books some seventy years ago, and interviewed the families of Clark, Shannon, Drouillard and others of the expedition. Her papers are now in the Oregon Historical Society, Portland, and are worthy of study. She used this material in *The Conquest: the True Story of Lewis and Clark*, 1902, published at the time Thwaites and Coues were editing the journals. (Hereafter cited as Dye.)

[15] Olin D. Wheeler, *The Trail of Lewis and Clark, 1804-1806*. Two volumes. Valuable for its maps and illustrations. The reprint edition of 1926 adds extra material.

[16] James Kendall Hosmer, editor, *The Expedition of Lewis and Clark*. Hosmer also edited Gass' *Journal of the Lewis and Clark Expedition*. The latter work contains a good life of Gass and also some data on the personnel.

[17] John Bradbury, *Travels in the Interior of America in the Years 1809, 1810, and 1811*, London, 1819. I have used the reprint edition in *Early Western Travels* series, vol. 5. (Hereafter cited as Bradbury.)

[18] H. M. Brackenridge. *A Journal of a Voyage up the River Missouri*, Baltimore, 1815; reprinted in *Early Western Travels*, vol. 6.

[19] Elliott Coues, editor, *New Light on the History of the Greater Northwest: the Manuscript Journals of Alexander Henry and David Thompson, 1799-1814*. Three volumes. (Hereafter cited as Coues, *New Light*.)

of the days when some of these men were still living. Army records and considerable genealogical research have also added details for a more complete picture. I have used them all as sources in compiling my roster.

Probably not all historians and researchers will ever agree on exactly which men actually started out with Lewis and Clark. A few of the French engagés seem to have disappeared from the records, so further data on them is completely lacking. Just when a solution seems to be reached, a new name will crop up. For example, we find a new one in *The Field Notes of William Clark* previously mentioned. On page 244 of that work we find in a tentative list of engagés, a very legible "E. Cann" written in someone's hand. It is interesting to note in the same reproduction of the original document that two of the engagés' names are joined together in one: William Labiece Mallat. These are surely William Labiche and Etienne Malboeuf. On page 278 Cann is written out in what appears to my perhaps prejudiced eye as "Carn," though on page 118 Dr. Osgood deciphers the word as "Cane." In all my many years of study and research "Cann" and "Cane" are new names to me. To my knowledge none of the journals, nor the vast literature of the fur trade which followed the expedition, even suggests this name.

On the other hand, one of the spellings in the original journals under date of August 13, 1804, is *Carrn*. In the *Field Notes,* page 48, there is the word *Carseux* written over an entry. This is not singular, for on the entry for July 5, 1804, we find the name of Howard – one of the members – written over it. In *The Territorial Papers of the United States,*[20] under date of December 28, 1805, we find that Alexander Carson, along with Manuel Lisa, Joseph Robidoux, Pierre Chouteau, John Carson, John Robertson and hundreds of others, were signers of a memorial attesting to

---

20 Vol. XIII, p. 344.

the good conduct of Governor Wilkinson. John Bradbury[21] states that Alexander Carson was near the head of the Missouri in 1807-1808. In 1809 Alexander Carson was engaged by William Clark – as were also a few other former members of the expedition, to try to return the Mandan chief, Shahaka, back to his home on the upper Missouri.

In a letter in the collection of the Oregon Historical Society we learn:[22]

Fairfield, Oregon,
Sept. 24, 1858.

[James W. Nesmith, Indian Commissioner]

Dear Sir: . . . You desire to know the particulars of the murder of Alexander Carson, a Virginian (I think) who was murdered in April, or May, 1836, at a place called Ellick's [Alec's] Butte, about six miles north of Lafayette, Yam Hill County, by an Indian, who was called Boney, of the Nefalitin Tribe.

This Boney had been in Carson's employ for several years, trapping, and had always been treated with the utmost kindness and regard, by Carson, he had great confidence in the Indian.

Whatever led to the crime, is more than anyone knows. Carson had been stopping at my house two or three weeks, this Boney, his wife, and son with him. Carson was sick. When he thought he was able to travel, left my house accompanied by Boney, Boney's wife and son. The first night after leaving my house (he) camped at Ellick's Butte, the whole tribe camped there. Boney arose in the night, stole out of Carson's tent his (Carson's) rifle, which he held in reserve and holding up the curtain of the tent so that the light of the fire might shine on Carson, compelled his son (a lad of twelve or fourteen years) to shoot him in the head with a shot-gun, blowing his brains all over the tent.

The body was thrown in a small stream, and the plunder distributed out amongst the tribe. I may mention here an Indian by the name of Click-kowin who was said to be a half Killamook, and was with the Killamooks a portion of his time, was accessory to the murder, and shared in the plunder.

---

21 Bradbury, 93.

22 Original on file in Nesmith papers, Oregon Historical Society. James Nesmith was an early collector of Oregon historical material which was obtained by interviews and correspondence with pioneer settlers. Thomas J. Hubbard was a gunsmith who came to Oregon with the Wyeth Expedition in 1832.

Boney, and his son, died soon after the murder was committed, and Click-kowin was shot after the murder, by Waaninkapah, the Chief of the Nefalitin tribe.

Those Indians have never atoned for the crime, they were compelled to give up a portion of the plunder which was delivered over to William Cannin, a cousin of Carsons. Boney's son confessed the crime and went with us and showed where all the plunder had been cached, as far as he knew of.

Carson came out to the Mountains with Lewis & Clark and after returning to the States, engaged with Hunt in 1811 and returned to this country, and remained here.

Yours in haste,
T. J. HUBBARD.

I quote this letter in full, except for some irrelevant matter at the opening, because Alexander Carson, along with Joseph Collins, Charles Hebert, Charles Caugee and "Rokey," have no official record of any wages paid for service. Heretofore, historians have questioned that they were members of the expedition.

As I have shown above, Lewis was authorized to hire, rather than enlist, extra men, which he apparently did and paid some of them off at Fort Mandan in the spring of 1805. Note the entry under date of August 22, 1806, where we read:

At this nation we found Rokey who was one of our engagés as high as the Mandans. This man had spent all his wages and requested to return with us. We agreed to give him passage down [to St. Louis].[23]

This would seem to be proof that a few of the men were not enlisted, but were hired for the trip up the Missouri only, and were paid wages out of funds in hand. The others were paid by Captain Amos Stoddard, Capt. Lewis's agent in St. Louis. For this reason they do not appear on the muster rolls and were not entitled to extra pay and land warrants as the enlisted men later were. This may also be a reason why the journalists list only forty-five men, for they

---

[23] Thwaites, v, p. 356.

might not have considered the hired, extra men as technically a part of the expedition.

In the revised *Private Joseph Whitehouse Journal,* as yet unpublished, there is found a partial list of the members who set out and adds "8 Canadians who were only to proceed with us to the Mandans."

Alexander Carson could have been one of these extra men, for with the evidence I have shown, and the entry in the journals for August 18, 1804,[24] where it is stated: "Detached Sgt. Oderway, Peter Crusatt, George Shannon, Werner and *Carrn* to the Mahar Village with a flag. . ." [italics mine], we know that such a man *was* with the expedition. Thwaites appears to have had some evidence, for on page 109 he notes after the word Carrn "(Carson-editor)."

The above evidence, while not conclusive, is the best we have at present. However, I believe it is strong enough that Alexander Carson should be considered as one of the party until such time as we have positive contrary evidence.

In connection with these "alleged members," it may be of interest to report a sidelight that is of record. As shown, the previously mentioned Alexander Carson, in his last years, was living in the Willamette Valley in Oregon. A companion of his trapping days, William Canning, was living on a farm nearby. William Canning was a bona fide mountain man, and had been with Wilson P. Hunt's Astorian party of 1810.[25] When Charles Wilkes, U.S.N., wrote of his Oregon explorations of 1841 [26] he stated:

---

[24] *Ibid.,* I, p. 109.

[25] Coues, *New Light,* 857, 868.

Carl P. Russell, *Firearms, Traps, & Tools of the Mountain Men,* p. 140. William Cannon, a Kentuckian who came to Oregon in 1811 with the Astorians, was a blacksmith at Astoria, and Fort Vancouver for the Hudson's Bay Co. for thirty years and died about 1865 at French Prairie, Oregon. This valuable book describes the guns, blacksmith tools and traps carried by the expedition.

[26] Charles Wilkes, U.S.N., *Narrative of the United States Exploring Expedition 1838-1842,* IV, p. 348.

At Champoeg, Willamette Valley, was an old man by the name of
Cannon [there goes that spelling again – author] who had been one of
the party with Lewis and Clark, and from his own account, the only
remaining one in the country. . .

Now Canning should have been aware that Francois
Rivet, who was a member of the party as far as the Mandans, was living on a farm nearby. We can forgive him
that he may not have known that Patrick Gass was living in
West Virginia at the time. But he may just be bragging
about himself. Mountain men had a bad habit of doing that.

Wilkes of course did not mention the fact that Alexander
Carson had, in 1829, made a will in favor of Canning, and
that after Carson had been murdered in 1836, Canning had
claimed from the Hudson's Bay Company, the balance of
accounts that were due Carson.[27] It appears that in his relation to Wilkes, Canning was also trying to claim Carson's
role as a Lewis and Clark member.

There is ample documentary evidence to show that Carson and Canning were two different men. It is tempting to
speculate that Captain Clark could have been referring to
Canning when he rendered the name as *Cann* and *Cane*. But
it is difficult to imagine that the clearly legible E. of *E.
Cann* could be taken to mean an initial for *William*. "G"
for the French spelling of William perhaps, but hardly an
"E". We have already seen that Ellick is one of the spellings, along with Alec., as a nickname for Alexander.

In any event, neither Canning, Cannin, nor Cannon is
ever mentioned in conection with Lewis and Clark until
Wilkes quotes him in 1845.

I have given all this Carson material as a typical example
of the research done to arrive at the most complete and
correct roster possible. In an attempt to gather further information, I appended additional data to my 1944 roster,

[27] Alice B. Maloney, "Alexander Carson: Wilhamot Freeman," in *Ore. Hist.
Quar.*, XXXIX, 1938, p. 21.

and it was published in the *DAR Magazine* for November, 1965.[28] The idea for submitting the story to that magazine was to solicit the aid of the members of the DAR who may be descended from some of these men, and who would furnish genealogical information. I am happy to acknowledge that quite a bit of new information has been acquired, and is collected here for the first time. In no case have I used "family tradition," but only include data that is fully documented. I am particularly pleased that some of the members who heretofore have had the notation after their names — "Nothing more known of him" — have been rescued from oblivion.

By the time the winter of 1803 had passed into the spring of 1804, Captain Clark had decided on which of the men would be taken along on the expedition. Many of them had been transferred from their former military units as of January 1, 1804, onto the muster rolls of the Lewis and Clark Expedition. Later, some of the French water-men had been enlisted, but others were hired as extra hands. The provisions and Indian trade goods were divided so that some of each were placed in separate boxes in order that all would not be lost in case of accident. The air gun was mounted on the keel-boat and the arms checked and put in order. The powder was contained in cannisters of lead which could later be melted and molded into bullets when the cannisters were empty. A hundred other details had to be thought out and arranged, for once the expedition set out, no other supplies could be obtained in the frontier country into which they were going.

At long last, spring arrived, and the Missouri was showing signs of becoming navigable. Captain Lewis was in St. Louis winding up the many last minute details, including a conference with a delegation of Osage Indians. George Drouillard was with him most of the time.

---

[28] *Daughters of the American Revolution Magazine,* vol. 99, no. 9.

Captain Clark, at Camp Woods (Camp du Bois):

. . determined to go as far as St. Charles, a french Village 7 Leags.
up the Missourie, and wait at that place untill Capt. Lewis could finish
the business in which he was obliged to attend to at St. Louis and join
me by Land from that place 24 miles; by this movement I calculated
that if any alterations in the loading of the Vestles or other Changes
necessary, that they might be made at St. Charles.[29]

So at 4 o'clock on the afternoon of May 14, 1804, the
shake-down cruise began. They easily could have made St.
Charles in one day, but Captain Clark took all of two, for
there was no hurry, and much had to be learned about the
men, the boats, and the loading. They soon found out that
the keel-boat was too heavily loaded in the stern. On the
nights of the 14th and 15th, they camped along the river, for
this presented an opportunity to test the arrangement of the
men into messes, or groups, where each prepared its own
meals. This pre-arrangement was continued until May 26th
of the voyage when a few changes were made. On the 16th
of May, the party arrived at St. Charles, where, during the
following four days, the cargoes were reloaded. On the 19th,
Drouillard came over from St. Louis with $99.00 which was
apparently used to purchase supplies which Clark thought
necessary.[30]

Captain Clark had warned the members:

That they should act with true respect for their own dignity, and not
make it necessary for him to leave the comforts of the town for a more
retired situation.[31]

Nevertheless, William Werner, Hugh Hall and John
Collins went absent-without-leave, and furthermore, Collins
behaved in an unbecoming manner at the ball, and after his
return to the keel-boat, had uttered disrespectful statements
in regard to the orders of Captain Clark. Clark had been
over to Portage des Sioux to talk and trade with the Indians

---

[29] Thwaites, I, p. 16.   [30] Ibid., 21.   [31] Ibid., 18.

at that place, and the three men had taken advantage of his absence. This sort of behavior had to be stopped, so Captain Clark appointed a court-martial, headed by Sgt. John Ordway, with Reuben Fields, Richard Windsor, Joseph Whitehouse and John Potts as members. The court sentenced each of the culprits to receive twenty-five lashes on their bare-backs, but because of the former good conduct of Werner and Hall, they recommended mercy from Captain Clark. The punishment was remitted for them, but John Collins received his punishment at sunset that evening.

On Sunday, May 20th, the men were given leave to enjoy themselves and to hear a sermon at the Catholic Church on Main Street. That afternoon at six-thirty, Captain Lewis arrived from St. Louis with a group of friends to help send the expedition off. He was accompanied by Capt. Amos Stoddard (who was to act as his agent while he was away), Lt. Clarence Mulford, Lt. Stephen Worrall and the Messrs. Auguste Chouteau, Charles Gratiot, David Delaunay, Sylvestre Labadie, James Rankin and Doctor Antoine Francois Saugrain. Captain Lewis made some additional purchases such as sugar, and castor-oil was obtained from Doctors Jeremiah and Seth Millington. These were two American doctors who had arrived in St. Charles in January 1799 and were now raising medicinal plants on their farms located above the town.[32]

The gentlemen of the village gave a banquet and a ball for the party. It was the last taste of civilization before their departure. The next day, May 21, 1804, the orders were given for departure, and despite the rain, a farewell parade was given. The band played all the way down the mile long main street fronting the Missouri River, and there was singing and fiddle playing.[33] By four o'clock all the men were aboard who were to sail at the time, and the expedition left

---

[32] Records on file in St. Charles Historical Society, St. Charles, Mo.

[33] *Idem.*

St. Charles under a salute and three cheers from the dignitaries and citizens. In honor of their warm hospitality, three cheers were returned and three guns were fired from the boats as a salute. Under the joint command of Captains Lewis and Clark, the expedition officially started up the Missouri.

Since that fateful day some one hundred and sixty years ago when the expedition faded off into the dim distance, the following facts have been gathered about the men who comprised it, and who set off on this historic voyage of exploration.

The Men of the Expedition

Biographical Roster of
the Corps of Discovery[1]

1. CAPTAIN MERIWETHER LEWIS, U.S. INFANTRY.

Born, August 18, 1774, near Ivy, seven miles west of Charlottesville, Virginia, of Welsh parentage. Son of William and Lucy (Meriwether) Lewis. Well educated, blond-sunny hair; bowlegged, particular, precise, serious, reserved and inclined to melancholia and hypochondria. He served in the 1st Infantry, U.S. Army and in Gen. Wayne's northwestern campaigns. In 1801 he was appointed Pres. Jefferson's private secretary. After the expedition, he was appointed the Governor of Louisiana Territory. Clerks in Washington protested some of his drafts – some of which were connected with the expedition – which caused him emotional strain. He decided to go to Washington to explain the drafts, and while enroute on the Natchez Trace, he died, either by murder or suicide, on October 11, 1809. A monument stands at his burial place on the Trace near Nashville, Tennessee. He never married.[2]

2. SECOND LIEUTENANT WILLIAM CLARK, U.S. ARTILLERY.

Born, August 1, 1770, near Charlottesville, Virginia, of Scottish ancestry. Son of John and Ann (Rogers) Clark. Six feet tall, red-haired, a popular leader of men. He was promised a captaincy by Lewis, and received the same pay and recognition as a captain, though when the commission was received, it was for a second lieutenant. When the ex-

---

[1] As I have cited, in the preceding chapter, the sources for much of the material gathered here, further citation seems unnecessary. Where statements are made enclosed in quotes, that material is from Thwaites' edition. Where other sources, not mentioned before, are used, citations are given to the source.

[2] The best biography of Lewis is: Richard Dillon, *Meriwether Lewis*, 1965.

pedition returned to St. Louis he promptly returned the commission on October 10, 1806. After the expedition he was appointed Indian Agent, and after Lewis' death, the Governor of Missouri.

He married first, on January 5, 1808, Miss Julia Hancock of Fincastle, Virginia. She died June 27, 1820, leaving four sons and a daughter. He married second, Mrs. Harriet Kennerly, widow of Dr. John Radford. One son survived this marriage. William Clark died in St. Louis on September 1, 1838, and is buried in Bellefontaine Cemetery near St. Louis.[3]

3.   (BEN?) YORK.[4]

Clark's negro servant who was willed to him by Clark's father on July 24, 1799. Since their childhood, a life-long companion of Clark. York was the son of "Old York" and "Rose," slaves who had been with the Clark family all their lives.

York was kinky-haired, jet-black, large sized, and of herculean strength. A wag, wit and delight of the party and Indians, who considered him Great Medicine. After the expedition he was freed by Clark, and he returned to Louisville, Kentucky, where he married. He was furnished a dray and six horses by Clark who was concerned for his welfare for as long as he lived. He engaged in the draying business between Nashville, Tennessee, and Richmond, Kentucky. He took to drink and entertained with stories about his adventures with the expedition, which became taller with each telling. He died of cholera in Tennessee.

---

[3] William Clark has not been the subject of a biography solely devoted to himself. The best work on Clark is: John Bakeless, *Lewis and Clark, Partners in Discovery*, 1947.

[4] The first name of York, "Ben," is printed in the *National Geographic Magazine* for November 1965, p. 647, based on information given by Mr. Jack E. Hodge, once connected with the Amon Carter Museum of Western Art, at Fort Worth, Texas. The Museum informs me that they have no records that confirm this statement, and that Mr. Hodge made it on his own authority. The balance of the data on York is from documents in the Missouri Hist. Soc.

4. SERGEANT CHARLES FLOYD.

Born in Kentucky, son of Robert Clark Floyd, and a grandson of William and Abadiah (Davis) Floyd. He was one of the first to enlist in the party, which he did on August 1, 1803, in Kentucky, and is therefore listed as one of the "Nine young men from Kentucky." He was a cousin of Nathaniel Pryor, also one of the party. Captain Clark called him "A man of much merit." He kept a journal which is published in Thwaites' edition of the Lewis and Clark journals. He died on August 20, 1804, of what has since been diagnosed as a ruptured appendix – the only man to die on the expedition. He is buried at Floyd's Bluff, on the Missouri near Sioux City, Iowa. He was posthumously awarded a land grant, which was deeded to his brother, Davis, and two sisters, Elisabeth and Mary Lee Floyd.[5]

5. PRIVATE (later Sergeant) PATRICK GASS.

Born, July 12, 1771, at Falling Springs, near Chambersburg, Pennsylvania, of Irish descent. He was a son of Benjamin and Mary (McLene) Gass. Dark complexion, grey eyes, dark hair, short, burley, barrel-chested. "His talk unconventional – better suited for the camp than the parlor." He was recruited from Capt. Russell Bissell's 1st Infantry at Kaskaskia, and his pay started with Lewis and Clark as of January 1, 1804. He had enlisted in the 10th U.S. Infantry in 1799 at Carlisle, Pennsylvania, after having served in a Ranger Company in 1792. He was a fine carpenter, boat builder, woodsman and great wit. After Charles Floyd's death, he was elected sergeant. After the expedition, he served in the War of 1812 under Capt. Kingsly of Nashville, Tennessee. In March 1813, he was at Fort Massac, Kentucky, then at Bellefontaine, Missouri. In 1814, he ascended the Ohio to Pittsburgh, then on to Fort Erie. He was in the battle of Lundy's Lane; then to Sackett's Harbor.

---

[5] Anna Margaret Cartlidge, compiler, *Children and Grandchildren of William and Abadiah Floyd.*

He lost his left eye at Fort Independence in June 1815, and was discharged and pensioned in the same month for total disability. He married at the age of sixty, in 1831, to Maria Hamilton, aged twenty. They were the parents of six children: Benjamin, William, James, Sarah, Annie and Rachel.

He died April 2, 1870, aged almost ninety-nine years — the sole survivor of the expedition. He is buried at Brooke County Cemetery, at Wellsburg, West Virginia. He was the first to publish a journal of the expedition in 1807, seven years before the official Lewis and Clark journals were finally printed in 1814.[6] (See his portrait at page 58.)

6. SERGEANT JOHN ORDWAY.

Born about 1775 at Dumbarton, New Hampshire. His parents and a brother, Stephen, lived near Hebron, New Hampshire, in the spring of 1804. He was recruited from Capt. Bissell's 1st Infantry Company at Kaskaskia and went on Lewis and Clark's payroll as of January 1, 1804, though he was in charge of Camp du Bois much of the time before this date. He was educated and kept a journal which, after being lost for over a hundred years, was published in 1916. He was held in high esteem by his commanders. He kept the orderly books and held other important duties while on the expedition.

After the expedition returned in 1806, he witnessed the sale on September 29, 1806, of John Collins and Joseph Whitehouse's land warrants. He purchased the land warrants of his fellow members, William Werner and Jean Baptiste La Page. He went to Washington with Captain Lewis and a party of Indians to show to the President, then he returned to New Hampshire for a time. In 1809 he returned to Missouri and settled in the Tywappity Bottom, near New Madrid, Missouri. He became an owner of extensive lands and attained some prosperity — having two

---

[6] James Kendall Hosmer, editor, *Gass' Journal of the Lewis and Clark Expedition*, p. xiv; and Earle R. Forrest, *Patrick Gass*.

plantations of peach and apple orchards. He married in Missouri, and he and his wife, Gracy, died in Missouri about 1817. They left no survivors.[7]

7. SERGEANT NATHANIEL HALE PRYOR.

Born in 1772, probably in Amherst County, Virginia. He was a son of John and Nancy (Floyd) Pryor. She was a sister of Robert Floyd, and Robert was the father of Charles Floyd – also a member of the expedition. Therefore, Pryor and Floyd were cousins. He moved with his parents in 1783 to Kentucky, and was recruited by Captain Clark on October 20, 1803. He is usually listed as one of the "Nine young men from Kentucky." He married on May 17, 1798, Miss Peggy Patton, so was one of the few married men of the expedition. His leaders stated, "He was a man of character and ability." He probably kept a journal, but it has not yet been discovered. His journal is said to have been lost while enroute to France for publication. After the expedition returned, he was one of the party who in 1807 attempted to return the Mandan Chief, Shahaka, to his homeland, but was prevented from doing so by the Arikara Indians. Nathaniel H. Pryor remained in the army and was a second lieutenant until 1810. He then entered the Indian trade on the upper Mississippi. In 1812 he was attacked at Fort Madison where he nearly lost his life. Two of his men were slain, but he escaped by crossing the ice of the Mississippi. He re-entered the army in 1813, and in 1814 he became a captain. He served in the Battle of New Orleans. Later, he was discharged and he then set up a trading post on the Arkansas River. He married an Osage girl, and they had several children who were all given Indian names. They lived among the Osages until his death on June 1, 1831. He is buried at Pryor, Mayes County, Oklahoma, where a

[7] Olin D. Wheeler, *The Trail of Lewis and Clark*, 1926, p. 92, gives a short life of Ordway. Other details are found in Missouri Hist. Collections, II, p. 282.

monument has been erected to his honor. He is not the same Nathaniel Pryor of *Pattie's Narrative*. This was Nathaniel "Miguel" Pryor, born in Kentucky in 1798, and died in Los Angeles in 1850. The family relationship, if any, is not clear, for there were several other Nathaniel Pryors at this time.[8]

8. INTERPRETER, GEORGE DROUILLARD (DREWER; DREWYER).

Probably born at Sandwich, Canada, son of Pierre Drouillard of Detroit, and a Shawnee mother. His father had served with Kenton and as interpreter for George Rogers Clark at Fort McIntosh and at the Great Miami. George was in the U.S. Army at Fort Massac when he was transferred to Captain Lewis on November 11, 1803, after some resistance on the part of his commander who did not want to lose him. He was tall, straight, and had black hair and dark eyes. He was adept in the Indian sign language. He was always with one captain or the other in most emergencies and situations of danger where skill, nerve, endurance and cool judgement were needed.

After the expedition he lived for a few years at Cape Girardeau, Missouri. He bought the land warrants of John Collins and Joseph Whitehouse, which, with other land, he sold on April 3, 1807 for $1300.00. As he received $25.00 per month while he served with the expedition, he had the funds to make land purchases. He made a return trip to the Rocky Mountains and gave William Clark considerable topographical details of the mountain country which Clark incorporated into his map of the Northwest. He was killed by the Blackfeet Indians in 1810, not far from the area in which he had the scrape with these Indians while he was with Captain Lewis when they made the exploration to the upper Maria's River. He was with the Manuel Lisa party when he met his death.[9]

---

[8] Cartlidge, *op. cit.*

9. PRIVATE WILLIAM E. BRATTON (BRATTEN).

Born, July 27, 1778, in Augusta County, Virginia, of Irish parentage. He probably is a son of George Bratton, or of George's brother, James, who were sons of Capt. Robert Bratton and his wife, Mrs. Annie (McFarland) Dunlap. Robert Bratton came to America from Donegal, Ireland, about 1740, and later settled in Cowpasture, Augusta County, Virginia. I give these clues to William's ancestry because there is yet some confusion as to just which of the brothers was William's father.

It is reported William's family migrated to Kentucky about 1790, and on October 20, 1803, William enlisted under William Clark for the expedition. Hence he is usually listed as one of the "Nine young men from Kentucky." His middle name may be Elliott, for it appears this was his mother's name. This "E" was adopted during his Indiana

---

[9] M. O. Skarsten, *George Drouillard, Hunter and Interpreter for Lewis and Clark;* also in LeRoy R. Hafen, editor, *The Mountain Men and the Fur Trade of the Far West,* vol, IV, pp. 69-82.

A tantalizing bit of information is contained in a letter to me from Milo M. Quaife, dated Detroit, January 19, 1945, from which I quote in part: "As recently as 1929, a member of the Drouillard family at Windsor, Canada, brought me two letters. One of them was George Drouillard's last letter written at St. Louis, May 23, 1809, and addressed to his half-sister, Mary Louise, wife of Lambert Parent of Detroit. – When Miss Drouillard brought me these two letters just noted, I of course proceeded to inquire whether she had any more of the family letters. She answered that some years before her parents had moved from Windsor to Hollywood, California, and had died there. Miss Drouillard herself before returning to Windsor, had placed the family furniture in storage with some storage company, and it was still in their possession in 1929. Meanwhile, the charges which had accrued upon it had become so large that she was unable to pay them and recover possession of the furniture. The pertinent point in this connection was that she stated there was a box of family papers included among her parents' possessions. Of course I wanted to recover the box but saw no way to do it in view of the circumstances recited. Fifteen years have passed and I have no present knowledge of Miss Drouillard's whereabouts. It is perhaps a fair supposition that more of George Drouillard's letters and family papers were dumped into the rubbish heap by the storage company in Hollywood, at some date subsequent to 1929. Sincerely Yours, M. M. Quaife."

I am advised that the storage companies usually auction off such goods held for delinquent payments. There is the remote possibility that some second hand furniture dealer may yet have this box of papers.

years to distinguish him from another William Bratton, probably his cousin, who also lived near Waynetown, Indiana, and with whom he has often been confused.

William E. Bratton was over six feet tall, square of build, very straight and erect, rather reserved, economical, of fine intelligence and the strictest morals. At an early age he was apprenticed to a blacksmith, possibly his father, or uncle, James, and later became an excellent gunsmith and blacksmith on the expedition. In these capacities, and as a hunter, he was a useful man.

After the expedition had reached the mouth of the Columbia River in November 1805, Bratton and four companions were assigned to salt making at the seashore. They produced enough salt for the expedition's winter requirements as well as enough to last them for the return trip to the states. While working at this exposed task, Bratton became seriously ill of lumbago. He became so weak that he could hardly walk, although the captains did everything in their power to help him. At long last, on May 24, 1806, an Indian steam bath was constructed as a forlorn hope of saving his life. This proved effective, and soon Bratton was able to resume his duties. Bratton's conscientious service was attested to by the discharge he received at the end of the expedition.

After the expedition, Bratton returned to Kentucky. He lived there for a time, but returned to Missouri where he lived near John Ordway for a few years. He enlisted from Kentucky for the War of 1812, and was one of those surrendered at Frenchtown (now Monroe, Michigan) on January 22, 1813. He sold his warrant for land to a Mr. Samuel Barclay in 1816.

When aged forty-one, he married on November 25, 1819, Miss Mary H. Maxwell (1796-1875) and they resided for a time at Greenville, Ohio. By the year 1822, in June, William located on some land at Waynetown, Indiana. They were the parents of eight sons and two daughters, one of whom, Griselda Ann, married a Mr. Stephen Fields. It was she who gave the first brief biographical data to Olin D. Wheeler, who incorporated this data into his roster found in his *The Trail of Lewis and Clark.*

William E. Bratton was elected the first justice of the peace of Wayne township in June 1824, and he served in that capacity for five years. Meanwhile he raised his large family, and now the many Bratton descendants are spread over the United States. Apparently one of the sons, S. Bratton, came to California during the gold rush of 1849.

William E. Bratton died November 11, 1841, at Waynetown, Indiana, and is buried in the pioneer cemetery there. A monument marks the final resting place of this important man.[10]

10. PRIVATE JOHN COLLINS.

Collins was born in Frederick County, Maryland. His army unit is unknown, but as he went on the muster roll as of January 1, 1804, he was possibly transferred from Capt. Russell Bissell's Company. He was one of the best hunters of the party. While at Camp du Bois, Captain Clark once noted him as a "blackguard," perhaps because he killed a farmer's pig, and then claimed it was "bear meat." Later this cloud was removed by most excellent service throughout the voyage. He sold his warrant for land to George Drouillard, in September 1806, for $300.00 in cash. He was killed while with Ashley in a fight with the Arikara on June 2, 1823. He may be the John Collins who married Elisabeth Yager of Madison County, Virginia, and who later returned to Missouri.[11]

---

[10] Genealogical research from Mrs. Harold Walters and Mrs. Mabel V. Shanklin, both of Indiana, and Mrs. G. Hal Burnett of Grants Pass, Oregon, form the base for the material used here.

[11] Missouri Hist. Soc. Coll.

11.   PRIVATE JOHN COLTER   (COALTER; COUL-
        TER).

Born about 1774, near Staunton, Augusta County, Virginia. He was a son of Joseph and Ellen (Shields) Colter
and a grandson of Micajah Coalter. When he was about five
years old, his parents moved to Maysville, Kentucky. John
spent his boyhood in Maysville and as a young man he probably served as a Ranger under Simon Kenton.

He was five feet ten inches tall; rather shy; had blue eyes;
an open pleasing countenance; was quick minded, coura-
geous and a fine hunter. He was recruited by Captain Lewis
at Maysville on October 15, 1803 – one of the "Nine young
men from Kentucky" and a permanent member of the expedition. He was trusted with many special missions while
with the party.

When the expedition was enroute home, Colter was hon-
orably discharged on August 13, 1806. He returned to the
Yellowstone with Forest Handcock and Joseph Dickson,
free trappers from Missouri and Illinois. Colter had probably known both men during his Maysville days. The partnership with Handcock and Dickson lasted only some six
weeks, for a falling out had occurred. Colter and Handcock
returned to the Mandans during October 1806, and they
spent the winter there. In the spring of 1807, Colter started
for St. Louis alone, and by July he was at the mouth of the
Platte River when he encountered, and joined, Manuel
Lisa's trapping party bound for the Yellowstone. They arrived there in October 1807, and Lisa immediately dispatched Colter to the Crow Indians then on the Bighorn
River. During 1808-1809, Colter trapped the area around
the Stinking Water (Shoshoni) River.

By May 1809, Colter had returned to St. Louis. He sold
his military warrant for land, probably to the land specula-
tor, John G. Comegys. Colter soon signed up with Andrew
Henry whose trapping expedition was headed for the upper

Missouri. Colter was sent with a party to trap the rich beaver country of the Blackfeet Indians. Because of his past friendship with the Crows – mortal enemies of the Blackfeet – Colter was forced into a conflict with the latter. He escaped from the Blackfeet in the famous encounter in which another Lewis and Clark member, John Potts, was killed.

Colter now had enough of the mountains and returned to St. Louis. Back in Missouri, probably in early 1811, he married a woman named "Sallie." Mrs. Dye, in *The Conquest,* page 311, states, "Coalter – married a squaw." Other traditions say she was a white woman. Whichever, they settled on a farm near Charette, Franklin County, Missouri. They had a son, Hiram Colter, who became the father of eight children.

John Colter died about November 22, 1813. Dr. E. B. Trail writes that according to local tradition, Colter was buried in a cemetery near Dundee, Missouri, on Tunnel Hill, which was located between the Big and Little Bucui creeks. A railroad cut was later made which eliminated all trace of this cemetery. The remains were said to have been scattered along the railroad fill. However, in the collections of the St. Charles Historical Society are the books of the Fee Fee Baptist Church Records. An entry is written, "John Colter – a fur trader with Manuel Lisa." A tombstone, said to have been in the church cemetery, read:

Here lies John Colter
of Lewis and Clark Expedition
Born in 1775 in Va.
Died 1813 of jaundice

This church and cemetery are at Bridgeton, Missouri, not far from Colter's farm at Charette. No trace of the tombstone has yet been found.

While William Clark was putting finishing touches to his map of the Northwest to accompany the long delayed publication of the Lewis and Clark journals, John Colter supplied many new details gleaned from his travels into the Yellowstone, Wind River and other mountain areas not known to Clark.

On May 28, 1811, Colter sought, but could not collect, $377.60 from the insolvent estate of Meriwether Lewis, deceased. This amount was probably due Colter as extra pay for service during the expedition. After Colter died, his household furnishings were auctioned on December 10, 1813, and brought $124.44½. Sallie, his wife, received an additional $69.00 on January 9, 1815. She had remarried, but died after 1822.[12]

12.   PRIVATE JOSEPH FIELDS   (FIELD).

Born about 1774, perhaps in Culpeper County, Virginia. He may have been a grandson of Abraham Field, Jr., who married a Miss Byrd and lived in Culpeper County. One of the sons of Abraham was Col. John Field, born in Culpeper. John married, Anna Rogers Clark, an older sister of William Clark. Colonel Field served under George Washington in the Braddock campaign. He lost his life in the Battle of Point Pleasant in October 1774, for which services his heirs were granted a large tract of land in Bourbon County, Kentucky. Another brother, Reuben, served in the 8th and 4th Virginia Regiments, and was present at the surrender of Cornwallis. John had eleven children, and our Joseph and Reuben may have been his sons, or the sons of the brother, Reuben.[13]

Joseph and Reuben Fields therefore may have been known to Captain Lewis before their enlistment with him on August 1, 1803 – two of the very earliest. They were probably raised in Kentucky and each is listed as one of the

---

[12] Burton Harris, *John Colter;* and Thomas James, *Three Years among the Indians and Mexicans,* St. Louis, 1916, p. 278. New data from research of Dr. Frank H. Dickson of Des Moines, Iowa, and Mrs. Edna McElhiney Olson of St. Charles, Missouri.

[13] Rev. N. M. Woods, *The Woods-McAfee Memorial,* Richmond, 1905, p. 298.

"Nine young men from Kentucky." They served the expedition as two of its most valuable men until discharge on October 10, 1806. Both were excellent woodsmen-hunters and were usually involved in every duty of exploration and trust while on the expedition. Joseph was in charge of a small party which explored the lower Yellowstone River.

After the expedition, Joseph received a warrant for land located in Franklin County, Missouri. William Clark noted he was dead by 1825-28.[14]

13. PRIVATE REUBEN FIELDS (FIELD).

Born about 1772, probably in Culpeper County, Virginia. A brother of Joseph, above. Much of the same biographical data applies.

After the expedition, Captain Clark recommended Reuben for a lieutenancy in the army, which suggests that Reuben was older than Joseph. Reuben also received a warrant for land in Missouri, but he returned to Kentucky to live. In 1808, in Indiana, he married Mary Myrtle, daughter of John and Phoebe Myrtle of Jefferson County, Kentucky. Reuben died in late 1822 in Jefferson County, Kentucky, his will being probated on January 14, 1823.[15]

14. PRIVATE GEORGE GIBSON.

Born in Mercer County, Pennsylvania, but was probably raised in Kentucky for he is listed as one of the "Nine young men from Kentucky." He was a fine hunter, horseman and also played the violin. Sgt. Ordway states that he was an interpreter and there was some rivalry between him and Drouillard in this capacity. He married after the expedition, but died in St. Louis in 1809. He may have been one of the party under Sgt. Pryor who attempted to return Chief Shahaka to his home in 1807, and may have been wounded then by the Arikara.

---

[14] Gen. William Clark made a list of expedition members about 1825-1828 with some terse comment regarding them. Printed in Jackson, *op. cit.*, 638.

[15] *Kentucky Court and other Records*, Keystone Co., Lexington, Ky., v. 2, p. 56-125.

15. PRIVATE SILAS GOODRICH (GUTHRICH).

Born in Massachusetts. He may have been related to the Elisha Goodrich who was a land owner in St. Charles, Missouri, in 1799. His army unit is unknown, but he was transferred as of January 1, 1804, to the Lewis and Clark command. He was the fisherman of the party whose efforts very often supplied a change of diet for the men. After the expedition, he re-enlisted in the army. Clark notes he was dead by 1825-1828.

16. PRIVATE HUGH HALL.

Born about 1772 in Carlisle, Pennsylvania. He was recruited from Capt. John Campbell's 2nd Infantry Company. He was five feet eight inches in height, had grey eyes, fair hair and a sandy complexion. Clark notes that he drank and was one of the more adventuresome of the party. He is reported in St. Louis in 1809 and was living in 1828.

17. PRIVATE THOMAS PROCTOR HOWARD.

Born in 1779 and raised in Brimfield, Massachusetts. He had blue eyes, fair hair and complexion. Clark says "he never drank water." He was recruited from Capt. John Campbell's 2nd Infantry Company and was entered on the Lewis and Clark muster as of January 1, 1804. A private named Thomas Howard, served as boatman, and left Fort Adams in May 1808, under Capt. H. Stark, U.S. 1st Infantry. He served for a time at Fort Adams. He married Genevieve Roy in St. Louis and had a son, Joseph, who was in the fur trade with Ashley in 1827. During the years 1834 to 1849, Joseph Howard was on the upper Missouri.

18. PRIVATE HUGH McNEAL (NEEL; NIEL; O'NALL).

He was born and raised in Pennsylvania, but probably lived in Kentucky at time of enlistment. He was an excellent hunter and a faithful man to the expedition. A man of this name was in the 1st Infantry in August 1803, when that unit went up the Mississippi to establish Fort Madison. Hugh McNeal apparently remained in the army for he is on the muster rolls as of September 1811. Clark lists him as dead by 1825-1828.

19. PRIVATE JOHN NEWMAN.

Born in Pennsylvania, son of Walter N. and Catherine (Zimmerman) Newman. He was recruited from Capt. Daniel Bissell's 1st Infantry Company. He was powerful, strong willed and quick tempered. While enroute up the Missouri with the expedition, he made mutinous remarks, but afterwards did all he could to atone. He was with the return party in 1805 and was of valuable help in handling the keel-boat. After the expedition he married, on July 5, 1832, Olympia Dubreuil, daughter of Antoine and Elisabeth (Paran) Dubreuil of St. Louis. He traded on the upper Missouri during the years 1834 to 1838. He was killed by the Yankton Sioux in the spring of 1838.

20. PRIVATE JOHN POTTS.

Born about 1776 in Dillenburg, Germany. He had been a miller. Had black hair, blue eyes, and a fair complexion. He was recruited from Capt. Purdey's Company and joined the expedition on November 24, 1803. After the expedition he joined Manuel Lisa's trapping party of 1807 to the upper Missouri. At Fort Raymond on July 6, 1808, he with Peter Weiser and Forest Handcock, signed a note promising to pay Manuel Lisa the amount of $424.50, apparently for trapping supplies furnished by Lisa. In 1810 he was a member of Andrew Henry's party to the Three Forks of the Missouri. Here he again met John Colter, where they were attacked by the Blackfeet, and John Potts was killed. His estate was sued by Lisa, Menard and Morrison Fur Company for $1,000.00 past debts.

21. Private MOSES B. REED (READ).

Not much known of this man. Apparently he was not
valued for he once deserted while enroute up the Missouri,
and as a result he was transferred to the return party of 1805.
He drew extra pay from January 1 to February 13, 1805,
for $7.00, which was in addition to his pay for service from
date of enlistment. In the original manuscript of the Lewis
and Clark journals someone has written "Moses B. Reed?"
after the name of John Boley, but it is evident that these
were two different men.

22. Private GEORGE SHANNON.

Born in 1785 in Pennsylvania, hence only eighteen when
he joined Captain Lewis at Maysville, Kentucky, on October 19, 1803. His family had moved to Belmont County,
Ohio, in 1800. He is listed as one of the "Nine young men
from Kentucky." His brother, William, later was a member
of Congress from Ohio. George was Protestant-Irish, a good
singer, hunter and horseman. He frequently was lost, but
always managed to get back to the main party.

After the expedition, in 1807, he was one of the force
under Ensign Nathaniel Pryor which attempted to return
Chief Shahaka to his home among the Mandans. While the
party was halted by the Arikara, Shannon was shot in the
leg, which, after much suffering, had to be amputated at St.
Charles, Missouri. In 1809 he was in St. Louis, and in 1813,
by an act of Congress, was pensioned for the loss of his leg.
During 1810 he assisted Nicholas Biddle edit the Lewis and
Clark journals, and undoubtedly added some details to their
notes. In 1813 he married Miss Ruth Snowden Price of
Lexington, Kentucky. Clark offered him an opportunity to
go into the fur business with him and others, and suggested
that the firm be known as "George Shannon & Company."
Shannon, however, elected to study law at Transylvania
University of Kentucky – and also at Philadelphia. By 1818

he was practicing law at Lexington, Kentucky. He was elected a member of the Kentucky House of Representatives in 1820 and 1822. He sold his land warrants for 320 acres to Hon. Henry Clay, who later helped him on many occasions. After his Kentucky years, he practised law in Missouri. He was a senator from Missouri for a time, then returned to law. He died suddenly in court at Palmyra, Missouri, in 1836, aged forty-nine, and is buried in that city.[16]

23. PRIVATE JOHN SHIELDS.

Born in 1769 near Harrisonburg, Augusta County, Virginia. Being aged thirty-five, he appears to be the oldest man of the round-trip party. He was the son of Robert and Nancy (Stockton) Shields, the sixth son and one of ten brothers and an older sister. In 1784, his parents emigrated to Pidgeon Forge in what is now Sevier County, Tennessee. Here John ran a mill and a blacksmith shop for his brother-in-law, Samuel Wilson. About 1790, he married Nancy ————, and they had a daughter, Janette. John Shields enlisted in the expedition on October 19, 1803, in Kentucky, and is considered one of the "Nine young men from Kentucky." He was one of the most valuable men on the expedition, as he was the head blacksmith, gunsmith, boat builder and general repair man for anything needed. His blacksmith work helped keep the party in corn and other food-stuffs for much of the winter and spring of 1804-05.

When the expedition returned, Captain Lewis wrote: "Shields had received the pay of only a private. Nothing was more particularly useful to us, in various situations, in repairing the guns, accoutrements, etc., and should it be thought proper to allow him something [extra] as an artificer, he has well deserved it." In 1806 he received $180.00 in back pay, and in 1807, $178.50 in extra pay (as did the others), plus a warrant for land located in Franklin County, Missouri.

---

[16] Frederick L. Billon, *Annals of St. Louis,* 271.

After the expedition, he spent a year trapping with his kinsman, Daniel Boone, in Missouri, and the following year with Squire Boone in Indiana. He died in December 1809, and is probably buried among some of his brothers in "Little Flock Baptist Burying Grounds," south of Corydon, Harrison County, Indiana. His wife Nancy, survived him. Their only daughter, Janette, married her cousin, John Tipton, and they left descendants. John Tipton was an executor of his will.[17]

24.   PRIVATE JOHN B. THOMPSON.

Place of birth unknown, but he lived in Indiana. He was a former surveyor at Vincennes, Indiana, and it can be imagined that he was of some assistance to Captain Lewis' celestial observations, and of Captain Clark's map-making. In addition to other duties, he often served as a cook while on the expedition. Clark notes that he was dead by the years 1825-1828.

25.   PRIVATE WILLIAM WERNER   (WARNER).

He was probably born in Kentucky and enlisted from an unknown army unit. He was one of the salt makers and cooks of the party. After the expedition, on March 11, 1807, Governor Lewis advanced him $30.75, and a horse, saddle, etc., valued at $44.50, which Lewis directs Gen. Clark to deduct from the extra pay due Werner "if he has sold or given the horse away. If the horse died not through his negligence – then do not deduct." He assisted General Clark for a time as Indian Agent in Missouri. In 1828 he is reported to be in Virginia.

26.   PRIVATE JOSEPH WHITEHOUSE.

Joseph Whitehouse was born about 1775, probably in Fairfax County, Virginia. About 1784, he and his family

---

[17] John A. Shields, editor, *Shields Family 1600-1780*. Also Bible and court records furnished me by Mrs. Dorothy Shields Lollier, Carlsbad, California. Also, "Original Probate Records," Box 64, Corydon Court House, Harrison County, Indiana.

migrated to Kentucky. They seem to have located in Boyle and Mercer counties, Kentucky. Captain Clark lists him as one of the "Nine young men from Kentucky" which would indicate that he grew up in that state.

As a young man, he enlisted in the U.S. Army and during one period was stationed at Kaskaskia, Illinois Territory, where he had frequent contact with the traders who trafficked with the Indians on the lower Missouri River. This was a favorite subject of interest to Whitehouse, so when he heard that recruits for the Lewis and Clark expedition were sought, he located the captains with the hope of joining them.

He was transferred from Capt. Daniel Bissell's Company, then at Fort Massac, to the expedition and was entered on the rolls of Lewis and Clark as of January 1, 1804. This would appear to mean that Whitehouse, and the other members recruited from other military commands, had remained on the pay-roll of their former units until December 31, 1803, when they were entered upon the pay-roll of the Lewis and Clark Expedition.

The Lewis and Clark journals frequently mention Whitehouse as a "hide-curer" and a "tailor," and record that he often made and repaired the clothes of the men.

After the expedition returned, Whitehouse sold his warrant for land of 160 acres to George Drouillard for $280.00. In 1807, a St. Louis court ordered him arrested for debt. Clark, in his account of the members made during the years 1825-1828, lists the name, Joseph Whitehouse, without comment. This could mean that Clark did not then know the whereabouts of Whitehouse – or that he may still have been living then.

Joseph Whitehouse kept a journal while on the expedition. A portion, apparently the field notes, or actual diary, is printed in Thwaites' edition of the Lewis and Clark journals. Recently a revised version of Whitehouse's journal has been found and now is in the Newberry Library of Chicago. This version has an entry for November 17, 1803, but properly begins with the date, May 14, 1804, when the expedition set out, and ends on April 6, 1806 when the expedition was on the lower Columbia, homeward bound. It would appear that Whitehouse, during the fall of 1806, prepared, or had prepared for him, a new, expanded journal with the thought of having it published. He included a preface and announced that his volume would contain a map. This new version is to be published under the able editorship of Dr. Donald Jackson.

27. PRIVATE ALEXANDER HAMILTON WILLARD.

Born August 24, 1778, at Charlestown, New Hampshire. He was an only son of Jonathan and Betty (Caswell) Willard. Five feet ten inches tall, brown hair, dark eyes, dark complexion and of fine physique. He was living in Kentucky at time of enlistment from Capt. Amos Stoddard's Artillery Company. He went on Lewis and Clark's payroll as of January 1, 1804. He was a good blacksmith, gunsmith and fine hunter. He may have kept a journal, yet to be located. He married in 1807, Eleanor McDonald of Shelbyville, Kentucky, and they were the parents of seven sons (one of whom was named Lewis, and another Clark), and five daughters. They have left many descendants. In 1808 he worked as a blacksmith in Missouri. He served in the War of 1812. From 1824 to 1852 he lived at Plattesville and at Elk Grove, Wisconsin. In 1852 he and his family migrated by covered wagon to California, where he died in 1865, aged eighty-seven. He is buried at Franklin, near Sacramento, California. His wife, Eleanor, died June 11, 1868, aged seventy-eight. He and Sgt. Gass lived during the discovery of photography, and is the only member of whom a photographic likeness is known.[18]

Alexander Hamilton Willard and wife, Eleanor.
From the only known photograph of any member of the Expedition.
Courtesy of G.P. Putnam's Sons.

PATRICK GASS IN HIS OLD AGE, LONG AFTER HE HAD
LOST THE SIGHT OF HIS LEFT EYE
A woodcut made from an Ambrotype taken by E.G. Moore of
Wellsburg, West Virginia, as it appeared in *The Life
and Times of Patrick Gass*.

28. PRIVATE RICHARD WINDSOR (WINSER; WINSOR).

Place of birth unknown. He enlisted in Kentucky and was on the Lewis and Clark muster roll as of January 1, 1804, which suggests that he was recruited from some military unit, perhaps that of Capt. Russell Bissell. He was a useful man on the expedition and was usually with the hunting parties. After the expedition, he settled for a time in Missouri, but later re-enlisted in the army where he served until 1819. From 1825 to 1829 he was living on the Sangamon River in Illinois.

29. PRIVATE PETER M. WEISER (WISER; WYSER; WYZER).

Born, October 3, 1781, in Pennsylvania of German descent and probably a descendant of the noted Conrad Weiser. His father was John Phillip Weiser, born 1755; and grandfather, Peter, born 1730, was a son of Conrad. He was enlisted as of January 1, 1804, probably recruited from Capt. Russell Bissell's Company. He was often a quartermaster, cook and hunter on the expedition. After the expedition returned, he, with John Colter and John Potts, joined Manuel Lisa's party in 1807 to the upper Missouri. In July 1808, he was in Fort Raymond, where, with John Potts and Forest Handcock, they executed a note for $424.50 payable to Manuel Lisa. Between 1808 and 1810 he was on the Three Forks of the Missouri, and on the Snake River. He was killed prior to the years 1825-1828. The town of Weiser, and the Weiser River in Idaho, are named for him.[19]

30. CORPORAL RICHARD WARFINGTON (WORTHINGTON; WORBINGTON; etc.).

He was born in 1777 at Louisburg, North Carolina, and was transferred from Capt. John Campbell's 2nd Infantry

[18] Additional data furnished by Mr. Stephen F. Willard, Wollaston, Mass., and Mrs. Lois More, Sonoma, Calif.

[19] Rev. Frederick S. Weiser, editor, *The Weiser Family*, 706.

Company on May 14, 1804. He was on Lewis and Clark's payroll until June 1, 1805, when he had returned to St. Louis in charge of the "return" party members from Fort Mandan. He was five feet ten inches tall, had brown hair, black eyes, fair complexion. After the expedition he returned to his original military company. Some time later he was discharged after serving his enlistment agreement.

31. PRIVATE JOHN BOLEY (BOLEYE; BOYLEY; BOLYE).

He was probably born at Pittsburgh, Pennsylvania, but at time of enlistment was living at Kaskaskia, Illinois. His father, John Boley, Sr., came to St. Louis in 1794 from Pittsburgh. His mother, Sophia (Shaffer) Boley, had six children: John, Henry, William, Elisabeth, Marian and Sarah. John Jr., was a highly spirited young man and was one of those cited for misconduct while at Camp du Bois. He was one of the return party of 1805. On August 9, 1805 he joined Zebulon Pike's expedition to the sources of the Mississippi, and went again with him in 1806 to the Rocky Mountains. He was with the party that descended the Arkansas River and arrived in New Orleans in February 1807. His parents home place at Meramac, Missouri, became his property at their death. He is said to have been with the Bissell brothers expedition to the mountains. He and his wife were living at Carondelet in October 1823.[20]

32. PRIVATE JOHN DAME.

Born in 1784 at Pallingham, New Hampshire. Five feet nine inches in height, blue eyes, light hair and fair complexion. He was recruited from Capt. Amos Stoddard's Company at Kaskaskia. He was mentioned in the journals because he killed a pelican on August 7, while enroute up the Missouri.

---

[20] Billon, *op. cit.*, pp. 10, 282-3.

33. PRIVATE ROBERT FRAZIER   (FRASURE;
     FRAZURE; FRAZER).

For many years Robert Frazier has been reported as being
born in Vermont, and was a former fencing master. There
was a Robert Frazier living in Brattleboro, Vermont, in
1834. However, recent research indicates that our Robert
Frazier was born in Augusta County, Virginia, a descendant
of the Frazier family long resident in that and Rockingham
County.

He was a valuable man on the expedition, and was transferred from the extra party to the permanent party in the
spring of 1805. He kept a journal which he intended to
publish, but it has become lost. His map of the Northwest,
which was intended to be issued with his journal, is now in
the Library of Congress – a small section of which is published in this work.

After the expedition he accompanied Captain Lewis to
Washington and Virginia, and then returned to St. Louis.
On October 6, 1806, the captains gave him a bond for land
with the citation: "That said Robert Frazier, having faithfully complied with the several stipulations of his agreement, the undersigned, . . ." He served with the Louisiana Militia against the Aaron Burr plotters in St. Louis
and New Orleans. He was reported in several scrapes with
the law in St. Louis until the year 1815. From 1825 to 1829
he was living on or near the Gasconade River in Missouri.
He died in Franklin County, Missouri, in 1837.[21]

34. PRIVATE JOHN G. ROBERTSON (ROBINSON).

Born about 1780 in New Hampshire. He was a shoe-
maker and was transferred from Capt. Amos Stoddard's
Company at Kaskaskia on October 1, 1803. He was cited
for disorderly conduct while at Camp du Bois. He started
with the expedition but was dismissed on June 12, 1804, less

---

[21] Missouri Hist. Soc. Coll.

than a month after it had started. He was returned to St. Louis and he probably rejoined his original unit in Capt. Stoddard's Infantry. Later, he may have been the same John G. (Jack) Robertson, "an old Ashley man and whisky peddler," and partner with Antoine Robidoux in the 1830s. He is reported to have been a fur trader for forty years – from 1825 to 1865. On August 3, 1837, he wrote to his mother, Mrs. S. Robertson, then living at Owens Station, Missouri, from Green River (Wyoming). In this letter he states that he had intended to come home, but had re-engaged with William Sublette and Andrew Drips as a partner in a trading company. In another letter dated Fort John (Laramie), May 24, 1849, from Andrew Drips to Bruce Husband, Robertson is reported at that place.[22]

35. PRIVATE EBENEZER TUTTLE.

Born in 1774 at New Haven, Connecticut. He was recruited from Capt. Amos Stoddard's Company. Five feet seven inches tall, blue eyes, brown hair and of fair complexion. Before his army service he had been a farmer.

36. PRIVATE ISAAC WHITE.

Born in 1777 at Holliston, Massachusetts. He was recruited from Capt. Amos Stoddard's Company. Five feet seven and a half inches tall, sandy hair and fair complexion.

37. PRIVATE PIERRE CRUZATTE (CRUZAT; CRUSATTE; CROUZATT; CROISETTE).

Half French and half Omaha, he probably was a descendant from the Cruzatte family who were early settlers of St. Louis. Obviously his father had lived among the Omaha at an early date. He enlisted with Lewis and Clark

---

[22] Missouri Hist. Soc. Collections, *Drips Papers*. Since the above was written, vol. VII of Hafen, *The Mountain Men* . . . . , has been published. On page 247 therein appears a biography of John Robertson, the Ashley man, wherein Dr. Hafen gives this man's birth as circa 1805. Obviously this man could not be the same Jack Robertson who started out as a member of the Lewis and Clark Expedition. One is tempted to speculate if he could have been the father?

on May 16, 1804. Pierre had formerly been a trader on the Missouri for the Chouteaus before enlisting. He could speak the Omaha language and was skilled in sign-talk, so was of valuable assistance to the captains at the Indian councils and encounters with the tribes on the lower Missouri. He was a small man, wiry, had but one eye and was nearsighted. He was called "St. Peter" by the men as a nickname. Like the other regular men, he was awarded extra pay and a land grant after the expedition's return. He was killed by 1825-1828.

38. Private JEAN BAPTISTE DeCHAMPS (DESCHAMPS).

Probably a son of Jean Baptiste Deschamps and Marie Pinot. He may be the same Jean Baptiste Deschamps, Jr., who with his wife, Marie Anne Baguette, dit Langevin, were the parents of Jean Baptiste, III, baptized at St. Charles, August 15, 1792.[23]

Our Jean seems to have been recruited at Kaskaskia and was the patron, or head waterman of one of the pirogues.

39. Private JOSEPH BARTER   (LA LIBERTE; LE BARTEE; JO BARTER).

He was recruited at Kaskaskia. He deserted the expedition early on the voyage and was not found thereafter. He probably remained among the Otoe for a few years. Andrew Henry,[24] lists a "La Liberte" at Fort Gage, Canada, in

---

[23] While this book was being prepared for the printer, I received a most informative communication from Mr. Anton J. Pregaldin of Clayton, Missouri, in answer to an earlier request of mine for data regarding the French-Canadian engagee members of the Expedition. Mr. Pregaldin has been researching and compiling the genealogies of the French pioneer families from the Catholic parish registers and other records for many years. He has kindly allowed me to incorporate his material into my biographies of these men. I am most grateful for such data, as it throws more light upon these men, long lost in the darkness of time and neglect. Mr. Pregaldin states: "Research on the voyagers is difficult because many of the Frenchmen on the rivers came from Canada and either returned there after a time, or died in the Indian country. These, of course, would not be likely to leave much trace in the Parish registers."   [24] Coues, *New Light*, p. 561.

September 1799. If this is the same man, he may have drifted down the Missouri and lived among the Otoe Indians a year or two before joining Lewis and Clark.

Milo Quaife, editor of the Ordway journal, suggests that he may be the Joab Barton who died near Jefferson City, Missouri, about 1820. Mr. Anton J. Pregaldin informs me "that a Canadian named Joseph La Liberte married a colored woman called Julie Village at St. Louis, January 11, 1835. La Liberte, aged 60, probably the same man, was buried at St. Louis, May 31, 1837."

40. PRIVATE FRANCOIS (WILLIAM) LABICHE (LA BUCHE; LA BEICHE; LA BUISH).

He was recruited at Kaskaskia and was half-French and half-Omaha. He served as interpreter and as patron of one of the pirogues. Adept in French, English and several Indian languages, he was of considerable value to the expedition. As he was also an excellent tracker, hunter and waterman, he was elected to be one of the permanent party.

After the expedition, he went to Washington as interpreter to the group of Indians accompanying Captain Lewis.

A Francois Labuche and his wife, Genevieve Flore, baptized seven children at St. Louis between 1811 and 1834. It appears that Labiche and Labuche were both nicknames. The proper family name is probably Milhomme. Among other things, Labiche meant "the doe," while Labuche meant "the log" or a "heavy fall." Most of the family around St. Louis used Labuche.[25] Our Francois was alive in St. Louis, or nearby, after 1828.

41. PRIVATE JEAN BAPTISTE LA JEUNNESSE (LA GUNESS; LA JUENESS).

Probably a son of Ambrose and Marie (Boyet) La Jeunnesse of St. Rose, Quebec, Canada. He had married at St.

---

[25] See nootnote no. 23.

Louis, July 9, 1797, Elisabeth Malbeuf and they were the parents of: Reine, born 1801; Jean Baptiste, Jr., born 1803; and Marie Louise, born 1807. All were baptized at St. Charles. He apparently died in late 1806, for his wife married a Mr. Poirier of St. Charles on September 19, 1807. It may be his son, Jean Baptiste, Jr., who is buried in St. Paul Parish, Oregon.

As shown above, La Jeunnesse was another of the married men of the expedition. There were several other La Jeunnesse families but it probably was his nephew, Basil, born June 25, 1814, at St. Louis, son of Jacques and Helene Le Vasseur, who accompanied Frémont on his first and second expeditions to the west in 1842-1843.[26]

42. ENGAGE ETIENNE MALBOEUF (MABBAUF; MALBEUF; MALLAT).

He was from Lac de Sable, Canada – a brother-in-law of La Jeunnesse, above. His father, Francois Malbeuf, baptized at least seven children by two or three Indian women. Elisabeth, his daughter by Angelique, a Mandan woman, was baptized at St. Charles in 1797 and married Jean Baptiste La Jeunnesse two months later on July 9, 1797. Etienne was baptized at St. Charles on December 26, 1792, but no age nor date of birth is given in the Parish Register. He must have been born about 1775 as he was old enough to serve as godfather to a child of his sister, Elisabeth, and her husband, Jean Baptiste La Jeunnesse, in 1802. By 1804 Etienne was living in Kaskaskia where he was hired for the expedition. Wages were paid for this employment under Captain Lewis on October 4, 1805.[27]

43. ENGAGE PETER PINAUT (CHARLES PINEAU?).

Probably a son of Joseph Pineau and a Missouri Indian woman. He was born "in the woods" about 1776, and was

---

[26] Missouri Hist. Soc. Coll., Fur Trade Papers.   [27] See footnote no. 23.

baptized at St. Louis in 1790.[28] He was listed on May 26, 1804, as a member of the party and did start with the expedition. He may have been sent back to St. Louis on June 13, 1804, along with John Robertson, in Pierre Dorion's returning raft crew, as he is not mentioned as being with the expedition thereafter.

44. ENGAGE PAUL PRIMEAU (PRIMAUT).

He was from Chateauguay, Canada, son of Joseph and Louise (Lalumiere) Primeau. He married Pelagie Bissonet at St. Louis on November 18, 1799.[29] Among their five sons and five daughters they had: Joseph Endlion and Charles, both of whom were later traders on the upper Missouri.

Paul was hired for the expedition at Kaskaskia, and is mentioned as a member on May 26, 1804. In 1807 he was in debt to George Drouillard and Manuel Lisa in the amount of $292.05, which seems to have been paid back in 1808.

45. ENGAGE FRANCOIS RIVET (REVEE; RIVES; RIVEY; REEVEY, etc.).

Born near Montreal, Canada, in 1757, he was hired at Kaskaskia. Rivet was the man who "danced on his head" at the Mandan parties. He, with three others, DeChamps, Malboeuf and Carson, seem to be the four engagees who, after being discharged, built a hut of their own next to Fort Mandan, and remained there under the protection of the expedition during the winter of 1804-05. (Thwaites, vol. I, p. 254.)

In the spring of 1805, Rivet and Philippe Degie – who had attached himself to the party on October 18, 1804 – built a canoe of their own and descended the Missouri with Warfington's return party as far as the Arikara nation.

When Lewis and Clark returned from the Pacific in 1806,

---

28 See footnote no. 23.   29 See footnote no. 23.

they found Francois Rivet among the Mandans. He was in the Flathead country in March 1810, and may have gone with the Charles Courtin party to the upper Columbia River country a few years before that date.

He was an interpreter for Alexander Ross on the Snake Expedition of 1824, and was at Flathead Post in 1825. He is reported to have been at Fort Colville for "forty years as a sort of confidential man and blacksmith" where he worked for the Hudson's Bay Company. "Here I found an old man, who thirty years before had accompanied Lewis and Clark across the continent, and for several years past, resided here at Fort Colville. He is in the employ of the Fur Company and acts as an interpreter to the neighboring Indians."[30]

He did not accompany Lewis and Clark across the continent but only as far as the Mandans. In later life, Francois Rivet lived in the Willamette Valley, Oregon, where he died September 16 or 26, 1852, at St. Paul Parish, aged ninety-five.

46. ENGAGE PETER (PIERRE?) ROI (ROY; ROIE; LE ROY; etc.).

The identity of this man is difficult to define as there were so many of the same name (Roi and Roy) among the early settlers. In fact, this family was descended from a line of pioneers of French and Indian blood who had settled in the Illinois country even before Laclede had founded St. Louis in 1764. These adventuresome people came from Montreal and Quebec. One was Pierre Roy who married Marie Jeanne La Lande at Ste. Genevieve (later Missouri) on January 27, 1776. They had a son, Pierre, born April 27, 1786. This could be our man, though not yet proven.[31]

---

[30] Samuel Parker, *Journal of an Exploring Tour, 1835-1837*, p. 294. A more extended biography of Rivet appears in Hafen, *The Mountain Men*, vol. VII, p. 237.

[31] St. Charles Hist. Soc. Collections, and data from Mr. Anton J. Pregaldin.

47. ENGAGE CHARLES CAUGEE.

Listed by Captain Clark in his *Field Notes* on July 4, 1804, as one of the nine engagees hired. Unfortunately nothing more has been found regarding him.

48. ENGAGE ALEXANDER CARSON (CARRN; CARSN; CARN; CARR; CANE; E. CANN).

Born about 1775, possibly in Mississippi. He was a son of Alexander Carson, Sr., who probably was an older brother of Lindsey, father of the famous "Kit" Carson. His grandparents were William and Eleanor (McDuff) Carson who, with their family, came to Pennsylvania about 1755 and to North Carolina in 1760. His father settled in Mississippi in 1760 and it is possible that his son, in his formative years, lived so long among the French that he became known as a "French" engagee. This theory may account for the variants in the spelling of his name.

"Carrn" and "Carr" are mentioned in the journals of Lewis and Clark on August 13 and 25, 1804, which definitely places someone of like name as a member of the party. He is of record as being in St. Louis in December 1805, having had time to return with Warfington's party.

Alexander Carson and the Ben Jones, mentioned in my introduction, wintered with the Arikara Indians in 1809-10. Thwaites notes that "Alex. Carson was probably one of the party of expert riflemen who escorted back to his home in 1810, the Mandan chief, Shahaka, who three years before had accompanied Lewis and Clark to the east." Other ex-members of Lewis and Clark also were of the Shahaka party – such as Shannon and Pryor.

He was one of the earliest settlers at Chemaway, Oregon, and is recorded as having been at Fort George and Fort Vancouver in the Hudson's Bay Company account books of 1820-21. Alexander Ross calls him a "gunsmith." He was killed by Indians there in 1836 as previously related. An isolated hill known as "Aleck's Butte," located near Carlton, Oregon, is named for him.[32]

49. ENGAGE CHARLES HEBERT (HEBERT dit CADIEN).

Perhaps a son of Charle Hebért and Ursule Forest, and a native of Prairie de la Madeleine, Canada. He married Julie Hubert dit La Croix, at St. Louis on September 11, 1792. Their eleven children were baptized either at St. Charles or at Portage des Sioux.[33]

Charles Hebért's name appears on Captain Lewis' list of engagees as of May 26, 1804. There is no record of wages paid him, so he was probably one of those hired, rather than enlisted, in the party, and was paid in cash by Captain Lewis when discharged at the Mandans in the winter of 1804.

50. ENGAGE JOSEPH COLLIN.

There was a Joseph Collin, a son of Joseph and Marie (Dier) Collin of St. Genevievc de Montreal, Canada, who married Marie Louise Denis dit La Pierre, at Portage des Sioux, on July 15, 1818. She was a widow, having been married in 1790 to Louis Clermont, which would indicate the year of birth of our Joseph as about 1770.[34]

But Gass states in his journal that Joseph Collin "was a young man who formerly belonged to the North West Company." Captain Lewis lists him as a member of the expedition as of May 26, 1804. It is possible that Collin went only as far as the Arikara. Ordway says (page 149) "we left one of our frenchmen with Tabbo [Antoine Tabeau] and took his Soon (Tabeau's son) in his place."

When the party returned from the Pacific they again met this man among the Arikara on August 21, 1806, and "as he

[32] In addition to data given in Introduction, information may be found in: Edwin L. Sabin, *Kit Carson Days,* Press of the Pioneers, N.Y., 1935; Quantrille D. McClung, *Carson-Bent-Boggs Genealogy,* Denver Public Library, Denver, 1962, pp. 4, 12, 61; Alice B. Maloney, "Alexander Carson, Wilhamet Freeman," *Ore. Hist. Qrtly.,* March 1938, p. 16.   [33] See footnote no. 23.   [34] See footnote no. 23.

wished to return [to St. Louis] the Captains consented" and he was taken along. (*Gass,* Aug. 22, 1806.)

There is no record of wages paid him, so he was probably paid in cash by Captain Lewis, either at the Arikara or at the Mandans.

51. ENGAGE "ROKEY" (ROSS; ROCQUE).

Sgt. Ordway in his journal (page 392) calls him "Ross," which suggests that "Rokey" is a nickname. There were also many Rocques active in the fur trade at this same time, so perhaps Rocque is the proper form of the name.[35]

After the split of the parties in the spring of 1805 at the Mandans, "Rokey" obviously remained on the upper Missouri. When the Lewis and Clark party returned to the Arikara on August 22, 1806, they found "Rokey" there. They state: "He was one of our engagees as high as the Mandans. This man had spent all his wages and requested to return with us" to St. Louis. Ordway, same date, says: "Ross joined us in order to go down with us."

There was a Charles Ross who was an Oregon pioneer in the employ of the Hudson's Bay Company.

ALONG WITH THE EXPEDITION PARTY WERE:
SCANNON, Captain Lewis' Newfoundland type dog. This animal was much admired by the natives for his sagacity and they frequently offered to trade for him — which Lewis always refused to do. He had paid $20.00 for him.

FOUR HORSES. These were taken from St. Charles by the hunters to go along the river banks while the boats were being worked upstream. Three horses were lost enroute and the last one was stolen by the Teton Sioux on September 24, 1804. They were valuable to the expedition for they enabled the hunters, in addition to bringing in game, to explore inland from the Missouri. The information thus obtained

---

[35] See footnote no. 23.

was added to the captains' written description of the creeks and country of the lower Missouri.

Alphabetical Listing of Members
(Numbers after the names refer to listings in the above roster)

Barter, Joseph	(39)	Lewis, Meriwether	(1)
Boley, John	(31)	McNeal, Hugh	(18)
Bratton, William E.	(9)	Malboeuf, Etienne	(42)
Carson, Alexander	(48)	Newman, John	(19)
Caugee, Charles	(47)	Ordway, John	(6)
Clark, William	(2)	Pinaut, Peter	(43)
Collin, Joseph	(50)	Potts, John	(20)
Collins, John	(10)	Primeau, Paul	(44)
Colter, John	(11)	Pryor, Nathaniel H.	(7)
Cruzatte, Pierre	(37)	Reed, Moses B.	(21)
Dame, John	(32)	Rivet, Francois	(45)
DeChamps, Jean B.	(38)	Robertson, John G.	(34)
Drouillard, George	(8)	Roi, Peter	(46)
Fields, Joseph	(12)	Rokey (Ross; Rocque)	(51)
Fields, Reuben	(13)	Shannon, George	(22)
Floyd, Charles	(4)	Shields, John	(23)
Frazier, Robert	(33)	Thompson, John B.	(24)
Gass, Patrick	(5)	Tuttle, Ebenezer	(35)
Gibson, George	(14)	Warfington, Richard	(30)
Goodrich, Silas	(15)	Weiser, Peter M.	(29)
Hall, Hugh	(16)	Werner, William	(25)
Hebért, Charles	(49)	White, Isaac	(36)
Howard, Thomas P.	(17)	Whitehouse, Joseph	(26)
LaLiberte (Barter)	(39)	Willard, Alexander H.	(27)
Labiche, Francois	(40)	Windsor, Richard	(28)
LaJeunnesse, Jean B.	(41)	York, Ben	(3)

Members who Joined after the Expedition was on the Way

Charbonneau, Baptiste	(see page 148)
Charbonneau, Toussaint	(see page 147)
Degie, Phillipe	(see page 114)
Dorion, Pierre, Sr.	(see page 83)
Gravelines, Joseph	(see page 112)
La Page, Jean Baptiste	(see page 147)
Sacagawea	(see page 148)

So here we have a roster of fifty-one men who are recorded at one place or another in the various journals as being members of the party. It seems to be the most accurate roster that can be determined.

A few names appear on tentative lists, that do not appear later on the expedition. They may be among those temporary men at Camp Woods for a time, but as Patrick Gass states: "Several men who voluntered for this expedition, relinquished the honor and privilege when the time came to start – in common phrase, they backed out."

In view of the number of men who returned in the spring of 1805, we need extra men above the forty-five stated, to fill the roster. I have attempted to show this situation in the "Diary" which follows.

A Personnel Diary
of the
Lewis and Clark Expedition

THE DEPARTURE OF LEWIS AND CLARK FROM ST. CHARLES, MISSOURI, MAY 21, 1804
From a painting by Charles A. Morgenthaler, Courtesy of St. Charles Savings and Loan Assn.

Introduction to the Diary

I have compiled this composite "Diary" from the Biddle condensation of the Lewis and Clark journals, *The Original Journals of Lewis and Clark,* and the journals of Gass, Ordway, Floyd and Whitehouse. These, with *The Field Notes of William Clark,* are all the journals known at this time. In this compilation, I have selected those entries which concern the men, their health and welfare, with only enough material to set the locale and scene of each day's activities. I have tried to preserve the language of the journalists, but have had to use words of my own in order to connect the statements made by the various journalists. As all the descriptions of geography, ethnology, zoology, botany, mineralogy, meteorology and astronomy are omitted in this compilation, the result becomes a relation principally of the men, and therefore runs the risk of reading like a glorious hunting expedition. When one considers that the command practically lived off the land for more than two and a half years, then he realizes the great numbers of game animals required to feed and clothe the men. In some cases trivial matter is retained only because the name of the member is mentioned.

In no sense is this "Diary" intended as a substitute for, nor a one volume condensation of, any of the journals. The real purpose of the expedition was not to extoll its members, but to explore and describe a new frontier. This purpose can only be found by a study of the original journals.

As the men are rather lost in the maze of descriptive matter found there, the aim of this condensation is to bring them back into sight. It reveals their personalities and characters, and for that reason may be needed. As such, this condensation differs from Bernard DeVoto's excellent one volume edition of *The Journals of Lewis and Clark,* Boston, 1953, which retains the spelling and punctuation of the original journals.

While some men receive more notice than others, yet it is a picture of them all, and one can sense the skills and qualifications of the men who overcame the various problems – and who made this particular expedition so successful. The reader becomes aware of the excellent planning of the commanders; their care to keep the men in good health under the most trying conditions; of their foibles and strength; their good times, hard times and sickness. Always apparent is the concern of the whole party to make the objects of the expedition a success. That this was accomplished at a considerable risk of life is evident by the continual detailing of a few men who were sent ahead, or remained behind, the main party, to secure food for the command's sustenance.

Where one journal may state "sent out 5 hunters," from another I have obtained the names of the men, and have inserted their names when found, into the text. In those entries where no names are given, it is because no journal records them. In several cases I have found that the various journals do not always agree on the events of a given day. It is to be remembered that frequently these journals were written days after the event had occurred. I have had to select that which seemed to be the accurate description. I have also incorporated into the text, for the convenience of the reader, modern names of rivers, and the full names of traders – with a brief identification taken from other sources.

In view of this "Diary" being a composite of several writers, I have not felt it necessary to retain their spelling and punctuation. In those cases where I have added material not found in the journal of a member, I have enclosed such matter in [brackets] and have given a citation to its source.

Let us return to St. Charles and begin the "Diary" on the day the expedition left that village.

I

St. Charles to the River Platte

MAY 21, 1804. All the fore-part of the day we were arranging our party and preparing the different articles necessary here at St. Charles. We set out at half past three in the afternoon, under three cheers from the gentlemen on the bank, and proceeded on to the head of an island. We left four of our Frenchmen in St. Charles to finish their business. George Drouillard and Alexander Willard set out by land to bring our four horses along.

MAY 22. We delayed an hour for the return of the Frenchmen whom we had left at St. Charles. Reuben and Joseph Fields were sent ahead to the settlement of Daniel Boone to purchase some corn and butter. At 6 a.m. we proceeded on, and later camped at the mouth of a small creek. Soon after we came to, some Indians arrived with four deer as a present. We gave them two quarts of whiskey.

MAY 23. We set out early and later passed an American settlement where we took in Reuben and Joseph Fields who had been sent yesterday to purchase some corn and butter. Many people came to see us. We proceeded on, and stopped at a large cave called "The Tavern." Capt. Lewis, who had been walking along the river, ascended the cliffs over-hanging the waters of the river. He slipped and fell down the rocks for some two hundred feet. Fortunately for his life, he caught himself at twenty feet, and with his knife, he dug in and saved himself. It was a very narrow escape.

MAY 24. We set out early and passed a very bad part of the river called "The Devil's Raceground." We hove to near the head of a sand-bar. The swiftness of the current wheeled the keel-boat; broke the tow-rope, and was near to over-setting the boat. All hands jumped out, and by the means of swimmers, we got a rope fast to the stern. We were near lost as the boat wheeled a third time before we got her to shore. At this place George Drouillard and Alexander Willard, the two men we had left at St. Charles to bring on the horses, joined us.

MAY 25. We set out early as usual, and enroute we met Mr. Regis Loisel, a St. Louis merchant, on his way down from Cedar Island. He gave us much information in regard to the Indians up river. We passed St. Johns, [La Charette] a poor village – the last white settlement on the Missouri River. The people gave us milk and butter.

MAY 26.   George Drouillard and John Shields were sent ahead by land with the horses to hunt. The Commanding Officers direct the [five] messes to be as follows:

Sgt. Charles Floyd	Sgt. Nathaniel Pryor
Pvt. Hugh McNeal	Pvt. George Shannon
Pvt. Patrick Gass	Pvt. George Gibson
Pvt. Reuben Fields	Pvt. John Shields
Pvt. John B. Thompson	Pvt. John Collins
Pvt. John Newman	Pvt. Joseph Whitehouse
Pvt. Richard Windsor	Pvt. Peter Weiser
Pvt. Francois Rivet	Pvt. Peter Cruzatte
Pvt. Joseph Fields	Pvt. Francois Labiche
Sgt. John Ordway	Patron, Baptiste Deschamps
Pvt. William Bratton	Engagé, Etienne Malboeuf
Pvt. John Colter	Engagé, Paul Primaut
Pvt. Moses B. Reed	Engagé, Charles Hebert
Pvt. Alexander H. Willard	Engagé, Baptiste La Jeunnesse
Pvt. William Werner	Engagé, Peter Pinaut
Pvt. Silas Goodrich	Engagé, Peter Roi
Pvt. John Potts	Engagé, Joseph Collin
Pvt. Hugh Hall	

Corpl. Richard Warfington
Pvt. Robert Frazier
Pvt. John Boley
Pvt. John Dame
Pvt. Ebenezer Tuttle
Pvt. Isaac White

[Though not mentioned with the forty-one men in the above orders, the following ten members had to eat with some mess:

Capt. Meriwether Lewis
Capt. William Clark
Servant, York
Interpreter, George Drouillard
Pvt. John Robertson
Pvt. Thomas P. Howard
Pvt. Joseph Barter
Engagé, Alexander Carson
Engagé, Charles Caugee
Engagé, ——— Ross, "Rokey"]

George Drouillard and John Shields are detailed to hunt with the horses.

DETACHMENT ORDERS:

Thomas P. Howard and the men who are assigned to the two bow and stern oars of the keel-boat are exempted from furnishing additional men to the pirogues in the event of a casualty.

George Drouillard, Corpl. Warfington and Patron Deschamps are exempt from guard duty. The last two named are to attend their pirogue at all times. Drouillard is to perform duties on shore such as scouting and hunting.

Sgt. John Ordway will issue provisions and make up the details for guard and other duty.

Labiche and Cruzatte will man the larboard [of the keel-boat] alternating, the one not engaged at the oar will attend as the bow-man.

MAY 27. As we were pushing off this morning, two canoes loaded with fur and peltries came to. They were from the Omaha nation, some 730 miles up the Missouri. Later, at 10 a.m., four rafts loaded with peltries also came to. They were from the Pawnees and the Grand Osage, but had no information of importance. George Shannon killed a deer today.

MAY 28. Reuben Fields killed a deer. Several of the men are out hunting. The eight Frenchmen on the large red pirogue under Patron Deschamps have been careless and many of the stores are wet and damaged. The pirogue had to be unloaded and the baggage dried. Joseph Whitehouse discovered a cave which he partly explored. The party are drying stores. The captains made observations until 4 p.m.

MAY 29. One of our hunters, Joseph Whitehouse, not having returned, a pirogue was ordered to lay over to wait for him. This evening the Frenchmen in the waiting pirogue fired their guns in order to attract Whitehouse, so the men on the keel-boat fired several guns for the same purpose. This enabled Whitehouse to find the pirogue.

MAY 30. We set out at 6 a.m. after a heavy shower. We passed several islands and creeks and then camped on Grindstone Creek.

MAY 31. It rained the greater part of the night and blew with great force which obliged us to lay by until 5 p.m. Capt. Lewis went out to the woods and found many curious plants and shrubs. Reuben Fields killed a deer.

JUNE 1, 1804. We set out early on a fair morning. We came to the point at the junction of the Osage River, and cut down some trees so that Capt. Lewis could make a celestial observation. This took him until midnight.

JUNE 2. George Drouillard and John Shields, who had been set ashore on May 26th with the horses to hunt, caught up with us today – much worse for wear. They had been out in the rain; had to raft or swim many creeks, and had no food except that which they could kill. They gave a flattering account of the Missouri country. Whitehouse and the Frenchmen in the pirogue also caught up with our two other boats.

JUNE 3. Capt. Lewis took observations this morning and evening. Between times he walked on shore. Capt. Clark has a cold and sore throat.

JUNE 4. We passed Cedar Island. While Sgt. Ordway was at the helm, the keel-boat was run under a hanging sycamore tree and the mast was broken. The captains explored a hill said to contain lead ore, this was on the information of Cruzatte and Labiche who are familiar with the territory by previous experience in it.

JUNE 5. Today we met a raft of two canoes tied together with two Frenchmen aboard. They had wintered on the Kansas River and had caught a large quantity of beaver. York swam to a sand-bar in the river to obtain cress and tongue-grass to be served as greens at the captain's dinner.

JUNE 6. Our party found timber to mend the broken mast. Capt. Clark is still ill with a headache and sore throat.

JUNE 7. Capt. Lewis took four or five men and went ashore to explore some salt licks which the French engagées had told him about. They hoped they might find some buffalo there, but none were seen. This evening George Drouillard and the hunters brought in a she bear and her two cubs which he had killed.

JUNE 8. Capt. Clark and Sgt. Floyd went out to explore the lower La Mine River for lead-mine sites which the engagees had reported. George Drouillard killed five deer by noon. We went on with the barge and later met with two canoes loaded with fur which had come from the Ottoe Nation. We encamped on the north side of the Missouri River.

JUNE 9. We had a narrow escape near a creek [Richland] with the boat. In passing around a snag, we nearly stove in when the stern struck a log under the water. The boat swung around on the snag – with her broad side exposed to the drifting timber. By the active exertions of the men, we got the boat off without injuring her. George Gibson was nearly lost in this adventure. Capt. Clark wrote: "I can say with confidence that our party is not inferior to any that [ever] was in these waters. . ." We encountered three more traders enroute down-stream from the Omahas. They were out of powder and provisions. We were able to furnish them some.

JUNE 10. Capt. Lewis killed a large buck today. We had a great difficulty in swimming the horses – which the hunters had with them – to the island where we had camped, and then getting them aboard the boat. We expect to cross them over to the other side of the river. With the abundant game about, the men's spirits are high, and there is much singing and dancing, etc.

JUNE 11. George Drouillard killed two bears. We now have abundant meat so some of it was cured for later use. We landed the horses on the banks of the river with some difficulty as it was blowing very hard today.

JUNE 12. At 1 o'clock p.m. we encountered two rafts – one loaded with furs and peltries – the other with buffalo grease and tallow. Our captains purchased three hundred pounds of the grease which we use to repel insects. Mosquitoes are abundant, so we were furnished nets to sleep under. On board this raft was Pierre Dorion, Sr., a trapper some twenty years among the Sioux. His party talked with us all afternoon. The captains induced Mr. Dorion to accompany us up to the Sioux nation as he is a friend of those people. He can speak several languages, so he was engaged as an interpreter.[1]

JUNE 13. John Robertson was dismissed and sent back with Dorion's crew to St. Louis. [It appears that Peter Pinaut was dismissed also, for he is not mentioned hereafter.] George Drouillard brought in another bear.

JUNE 14. While passing through a narrow pass between an island and the main river, the men had trouble with moving sand-bars. The current was swift and the river banks were undercut, and they were caving down into the river. The boat wheeled so rapidly that the men were almost swept off their feet. The active exertions of the men prevented the boat from turning and being capsized. Again Capt. Clark had cause to appreciate his men: "We

---

[1] "Old" Dorion lived in Cahokia in 1780. Later he lived among the Yankton Sioux, where Pierre Dorion, Jr., was born – son of a Sioux woman. Both of the Dorions were used by Lewis and Clark. Pierre, Jr., served the Astorians under Wilson Hunt, but was killed in 1814 by an Indian on the Boise River, Idaho.
Washington Irving in *Astoria*, 1897 edition, v. I, p. 196 writes:

Old Dorion was one of those French-creoles, descendents of ancient Canadian stock, who abound on the western frontier, and amalgamate or co-habit with the savages. He had sojourned among various tribes, and perhaps left progeny among them all; but his regular, or habitual wife, was a Sioux squaw. By her he had a hopeful brood of half-breed sons, of whom, Pierre Jr., was one. The domestic affairs of old Dorion were conducted in the true Indian plan. Father and son would occasionaly get drunk together, and then the cabin was the scene of a ruffian brawl and fighting, in the course of which the old Frenchman was apt to get soundly belabored by his mongrel offspring. Once one of his sons had him on the ground and was about to scalp him. "Hold! my son, you are too brave, too honorable to scalp your father." This appeal touched the French side of the half-breed's heart so he suffered the old man to wear his scalp unharmed.

saved her by some extraordinary exertions of our party who are ever ready to encounter the fatigues for the promotion of the enterprise." Drouillard, while hunting, found a small lake where many deer were feeding. He heard in this pond a snake making gobbling noises like a turkey. When he fired his gun, the noise was increased. [This happened on present Wakenda Creek, Carrol County, Missouri.]

JUNE 15.   The wind was from the S.E., so the party crowded sail and we made sixteen miles. We nooned at a former Indian settlement. The hunters came in with four bears and three deer. So we celebrated with a dram of whisky – and then rowed on.

JUNE 16.   Our flotilla pressed on upstream, and after a short distance we arrived at the river-bank camp of our hunting party. Here more game to feed our hard-working rowers was obtained. After a hard day of rowing, our party camped in a bad place where the mosquitoes and ticks were numerous.

JUNE 17.   Some of the men with Sgt. Pryor looked for ash timber to make oars. They got enough to make twenty oars. Drouillard and another hunter came in with more game, and also a young horse they had found in the prairie. Our party is afflicted with boils, and several have dysentery, which Capt. Clark attributes to the muddy water of the river. The boats were moved against the river by several methods. With a fair wind, the sails were used. With insufficient wind, the oars were used, and in narrow places with shallow water, poles were employed. Soldiers on both sides of the keel-boat, facing the stern, placed their poles in the bed of the stream and the first in line walked aft, pushing on the pole; the next in line followed in order, while those who had completed their maneuver, returned to the bow to fall in line again. Where the current was too swift and the river too deep for the poles, cordelling was resorted to. The rope was passed to men pulling from the shore, and the steersmen kept the rudder set so as to keep the craft from being pulled towards shore. All this was hard work, and the French engagés complained for the want of food – saying they were accustomed to five or six meals a day. The captains roughly rebuked them for this presumption, for the other men seemed to manage well.

JUNE 18.   Several of the men are ill with dysentery, ulcers and boils. The other men are finishing oars and are making ropes for cordelling. John Colter brought in a very large, fat beaver.

JUNE 19.   John Shields and John Collins were sent with the horses to hunt. The mosquitoes are so bad that mosquito bars were distributed to all the men to sleep under.

JUNE 20. Some of the Frenchmen in the large red pirogue could not make headway against the strong current, so they had to jump into the river and push their boat along. The heat and humidity cause the men to sweat profusely as they labor at the oars. Our flank hunters have been absent for the past two nights. York nearly lost an eye by a man throwing sand into it.

JUNE 21. Drouillard and Sgt. Ordway went out hunting today. Peter Cruzatte from the bow, studied the swift water flowing on each side of an island. We got the keel-boat through after much difficulty by using the tow-rope and anchors. A cabin window on the keel-boat was broken, and we lost some oars which had become entangled in the willow trees.

JUNE 22. Sgt. John Ordway killed a goose. Capt. Lewis walked in the prairie for several miles. John Shields and John Collins, who had been hunting since the 19th of June, were found in a camp, awaiting the arrival of our boats. George Drouillard killed a bear weighing near five hundred pounds.

JUNE 23. We set out at 7 o'clock but the wind blew so hard we had difficulty in getting along. Capt. Lewis had the arms examined, for the Kansas Indians in these parts demand a tribute from the boats passing up. Capt. Clark walked on ashore some six miles. Later he got mired in the mud, but killed a deer and made a fire, expecting the boats to come up. Drouillard took the horses, found him, and brought him back to the boats at dark. Capt. Clark could not get aboard as the wind blew strong, so he had to stay ashore all night.

JUNE 24. Capt. Clark came aboard this morning with a fat bear and two deer. Drouillard killed two deer and Reuben Fields one. John Collins killed three deer. Capt. Lewis and Sgt. Floyd brought in a deer, and also a turkey. The men are in high spirits. They are busy curing the surplus meat by drying it in the air without the use of salt.

JUNE 25. A thick fog detained us this morning. Our hunting party on shore did not join us this evening.

JUNE 26. We set out early and passed the Big Blue River. We proceeded on, and came to the mouth of the Kansas River where we saw a great number of parroquets this evening. The white pirogue had to be unloaded so that repairs could be made. We stayed at this camp for two days to recruit ourselves, and to make repairs, dress skins, sun the woolen things, and dry powder. We pitched the tents and made bowers in front of them. Drouillard killed eight deer. John Collins and Hugh Hall had to be punished for taking whiskey out of the barrel. It had been put ashore while the boat was unloaded, and this was too much temptation for them.

JUNE 27. We remained in camp while the captains made observations. The men are occupied drying our stores and dressing skins, etc.

JUNE 28. We sent out eight or ten hunters in different directions, while others repaired the pirogue and cleaned out the keel-boat. Reuben and Joseph Fields killed a young wolf and brought in another alive with the hopes of taming it. During the night it chewed the rope and escaped. Buffalo are sighted.

JUNE 29. A court-martial was held, and Collins received one hundred lashes on his bare-back for being drunk while on sentinel. Nathaniel Pryor presided, and John Colter, John Newman, Patrick Gass and John B. Thompson served as members of the court. John Potts acted as judge advocate. Hugh Hall received fifty lashes for drawing whiskey while Collins was on guard. The party was paraded while the sentence was executed at 3:30 p.m.

JUNE 30. We left this camp and set out today. The land party inspected the fertile land surrounding the Little Platte River. The weather is very hot which enfeebles the rowers. There is an abundance of game about, skipping in every direction. The mast of the keel-boat was broken again.

JULY 1, 1804. During the night we were challenged by either a man or a beast which caused an alarm and we prepared for action. We could not discover the cause of the alarm. Grapes, pecans and raspberries are found, which adds to our diet. Capt. Clark spent some time in perfecting his maps and correlating them with the maps of Evans and MacKay we have on board.

JULY 2. The current is strong today so the oarsmen have difficulty in making headway. They exert themselves extremely well. We encountered a quantity of drift-wood, and from a suitable piece, we made a temporary mast for the keel-boat. Drouillard reports that the lands he passed through yesterday and today are very fine. The hunting party did not return tonight.

JULY 3. We halted at a deserted trading post where our men found a stray, gray horse which had been lost for some time. Enroute, we had a strong current which we could barely stem.

JULY 4. We ushered in this holiday with a shot from the bow gun. Joseph Fields was bitten by a snake on his foot, which was quickly doctored by Capt. Lewis with bark and powder. The men dined on corn this day. Capt. Lewis walked on shore and discovered a high mound. Capt. Clark made an enumeration of the party. He lists the names of the engagés in his fashion. [They seem to be: Baptiste Deschamps, Joseph La Bartee (Barter), La

Jeunnesse, Paul Primeau, Charles Hebért, E. Cann (Alex. Carson), Peter Roi, Charles Caugee, Francois Rivet, Peter Cruzatte, William Labiche and Etienne Malbeouf. He does not list Peter Pinaut nor Ross ("Rokey"), and of course not John Robertson. He adds Pierre Dorion, making a total of forty-nine in the party as I construe the list. Note that Francois Labiche now becomes *William* Labiche.] [2] The day closed with the discharge of the bow gun and an extra gill of whiskey for the men.

JULY 5.   Today we passed the bend in the river [upon which is located present St. Joseph, Missouri]. The boat turned twice on the quicksand, and once on drift wood, but no damage was done.

JULY 6.   Robert Frazier is sick with sun-stroke. Our hunters out with the horses, did not return to the boats tonight. The day was hot – the sweat poured from the men in streams. Capt. Lewis thinks the Missouri River water is the cause.

JULY 7.   The rapid water encountered today caused the men to cordelle the boats. Sgt. Ordway went ashore with the horse party. He crossed a stream which the captains named for him. [Not so named today. It was north of St. Joseph]. Capt. Lewis and Sgt. Ordway shot at a wolf which they thought was mad. Robert Frazier is still sick. Capt. Lewis bled him and gave a dose of niter which has relieved him much. Sgt. Ordway was out all night.

JULY 8.   We came to the Nodaway River. Frazier is much better. Sgt. Ordway was waiting at the creek. Reuben Fields, Silas Goodrich and three other men are sick today with violent headaches, and several men have boils. The captains appointed a cook for each mess and put John Collins in Sgt. Pryor's mess; William Werner in Sgt. Ordway's mess, and John B. Thompson in Sgt. Floyd's mess. These "Supertendants of Provision" are held responsible for a judicious consumption of the provisions they receive; they are to cook the same for the several messes in a manner as most wholesome and calculated to give the greatest proportion of nutriment. They are also held responsible for all the cooking utensils. They are exempt from guard duty, pitching tents, collecting fire-wood and poles for drying meat. The Frenchmen have their own mess.

JULY 9.   Robert Frazier has recovered from the sun-stroke. William Bratton was sent back to blaze a tree to let the land party know our boats are ahead. The bow-gun was also fired to give our position. We pass the old camp-sites of French hunters on the river. [Some were possibly made by

---

[2] Osgood, 69.

Labiche and Cruzatte in former years.] The four men in the land party found a recent campfire which had just been put out. The captains thought this might have been made by a Sioux war party. We put everything in readiness for defense.

JULY 10. Today we found wild rice and strawberries. The hunters continue to bring in deer. We found a great number of goslings along the river banks. Capt. Lewis killed two of them. We joined with the land party today.

JULY 11. We sent Drouillard and Joseph Fields out to hunt. Capt. Clark went ashore to explore, and he found a horse. He rejoined our boat party opposite the mouth of the Big Nemaha River. Drouillard killed six deer and Joseph Fields got one.

JULY 12. We rested today to wash clothes, inspect the guns and ammunition while the captains made observations. The hunters came in with four deer. Alexander Willard, who was found asleep while on his post last night, was tried by court-martial today. He was sentenced one hundred lashes, to be given on four different evenings. Capt. Clark and five men, in a pirogue, ascended the Big Nemaha River about five miles, when they found on the level plains, several artificial mounds or graves. On the adjoining hills they found others of a larger size. Our hunters saw elk and buffalo.

JULY 13. We set out at sunrise. Capt. Clark walked on shore and killed two goslings, nearly grown. We camped on a large sand-bar.

JULY 14. We had a hard storm early in the morning which lasted about an hour and a half. This caused the men to have to leap into the river to hold the boats in the wind. Even so, we shipped about two barrels-full of water. George Gibson had less trouble with the pirogues. Reuben Fields, who had charge of the horses, did not join us last night, but he came in today. Capt. Clark and Drouillard shot at some elk on shore, but the distance was too great. However, George Shannon swam after them, for the wounded elk had trotted into the river.

JULY 15. Drouillard and Sgt. Floyd went ashore. Sgt. Ordway and Capt. Clark went ashore on the south side and explored the prairie all day. This evening the boats overtook them, and also the horse party under Reuben Fields and Silas Goodrich came in. Joseph Fields had killed a deer. [The party is in the vicinity of the Little Nemaha River in Nebraska.] Two of our men are unwell – one has a felon on his finger.

JULY 16. The river is very twisting now, and the keel-boat ran onto a sawyer. The river continues to fall in volume of water.

JULY 17. We delay to hunt and make observations. We have to correct the chronometer which ran down on the 15th. Capt. Lewis and Drouillard explored the country and saw the headwaters of the Nishnabotna River. Drouillard brought in three deer this evening. Reuben Fields one. Several of the party have tumors of different kinds which are difficult to cure.

JULY 18. The Missouri is falling fast. We found a dog and he appears nearly starved to death. He must have been left by a party of hunters or Indians. We gave him some meat, but he would not come near us. We think this is a sign of Indians. Capt. Clark had a breakfast of roasted deer-ribs and coffee, then went ashore.

JULY 19. We observed some iron ore in the banks of the river. The rolling sands in the river are now more frequent and dangerous than any we have seen before. We found a great quantity of choke-berries which we put in the whiskey barrel. William Bratton found some sweet-flag plants opposite the place where we camped [near Nebraska City, Iowa]. We saw two catfish which had a hold on each other and they could not get apart. One of the Frenchmen killed the two with one shot.

JULY 20. George Drouillard is sick today. William Bratton swam the river to get his clothes and gun left last night while he was gathering the sweet flag. Capt. Clark and Reuben Fields explored the L'eau qui pleure Creek for several miles and then crossed the plains to the river with hopes of finding elk. They were out all day and only killed a large yellow wolf. Capt. Lewis tried without success to kill two swans. Sgt. Pryor and Joseph Fields, with the horses, brought in two deer. The party consumed the last of the butter yesterday, so we named one of the islands "Butter Island." Other names given, such as "Baker's Oven," "No preserves" and "Biscuit," helped keep the men in good spirits with these good natured jokes. Capt. Clark says "that the party has been much healthier on this voyage than any other parties in the same situation." Boils have been troublesome to them all, and our party has suffered from them for the past month which broke out under the arms, on the legs and in parts most exposed to action. After a few days, they disappear without assistance, except for a poultice of the bark of elm, or of India Meal.

JULY 21. With a good breeze to help, our party reached the mouth of the Platte River. Capt. Lewis and Capt. Clark with six men ascended the River Platte in a pirogue for about a mile. Peter Cruzatte, our French bowman, who had previously spent two winters on the Platte, reports that it cannot be navigated by boats or pirogues. The captains made tests to determine the velocity of the Missouri River. Drouillard's party with the horses, brought in four deer.

July 22.   Our party went on ten miles beyond the Platte to a wooded island where we camped for a few days to make celestial observations and refresh the men. We have selected a position where we can be comfortable and have the benefit of shade. From here we hope to send dispatches back to the Government. We pitched our tents and made bowers for shade, with the expectation of holding a council with the Ottoe Indians of the lower Platte. The hunters killed five deer and caught two beaver.

2

The Platte to Vermillion River

JULY 23. We commenced drying our provisions, dressing skins and made new oars for the boats. The captains prepared dispatches and made maps of the country we have passed. George Drouillard and Peter Cruzatte were sent to the Ottoes or Pawnee nation with a present of tobacco and an invitation to their chiefs to visit us. A flag was hoisted over our camp to show the new United States possession of these lands.

JULY 24. We named our camp, "White Catfish Camp" because Silas Goodrich caught one of these large fish. Great quantities of ripe grapes are found here. Our men are making oars and the captains are preparing papers and maps to send back. [They were not sent back to St. Louis at this time.]

JULY 25. Drouillard and Cruzatte returned, having found no Indians. At this season they are on the plains hunting buffalo. John Collins killed two deer and Joseph Fields killed one turkey today.

JULY 26. The wind blew hard and raised such clouds of sand that Capt. Clark could not complete his map in the tent, so he tried the boat, but that rolled in such a manner that he could do nothing there, so he was compelled to go into the woods and combat the mosquitoes. He had opened the tumor on the left breast of one of the men and it discharged a half a pint of matter. Five beaver were caught near camp, the flesh of which was shared by the party.

JULY 27. We reloaded the boats, completed the oars, and crossed the horses to the s.w. side of the river where the traveling is better. At 1 o'clock p.m., we proceeded on under a gentle breeze. Capt. Clark and Reuben Fields walked on shore all afternoon, and did not reach camp until after dark. [That evening they camped at the present site of Omaha, Nebraska.] George Shannon killed a deer. Joseph Whitehouse cut his knee very bad. Captain Clark killed a deer. The mosquitoes are very bad here.

JULY 28. Today George Drouillard and his party brought a Missouri Indian in to camp. This Indian reports that he lives with the Ottoe Indians about four miles from the river, but that his tribe is now on the plains hunting buffalo.

JULY 29. We sent Joseph Barter (La Liberté) and the Indian to their camp to invite them to meet us at the next high point of land. Our men caught three catfish, very large and fat. Alexander Willard, in attempting to cross a creek on a log, lost his gun, but Reuben Fields dove and brought it up. Two men are sick and several have boils. The Missouri River is very crooked at this place. We passed and named a creek after John Potts. Joseph Fields shot a badger — the first seen by our party. The skin was saved to send back.

JULY 30.   We went to a clear open prairie [near present Fort Calhoun] and formed a camp to wait for the return of Joseph Barter and the Indians to form a treaty with them. A flag was raised over our camp. Captains Lewis and Clark walked in the high prairie and were enchanted with the view they saw. We caught several catfish and a beaver. Turkeys, geese and ducks were also obtained. Everything is in prime order, and the men are in high spirits, even though several have bad boils. Joseph and Reuben Fields did not return this evening from their hunt. Drouillard brought in a deer. [They called this place "Council Bluffs" which is some fifteen miles from present Council Bluffs, Iowa.] Capt. Clark is engaged in making a drawing of the courses of the rivers. Sgt. Floyd is very unwell — a bad cold, etc. Drouillard caught a beaver alive.

JULY 31.   Three hunters went out this morning to inspect the traps set last night. Drouillard killed a very fat buck. Joseph and Reuben Fields returned without the horses, but with a small beaver. A party of three, with one of the Fields brothers, was sent out to find the horses. Sgt. Floyd has been very sick for several days but is now feeling some better. He says he has recovered his health again. Joseph Barter has not returned with the Indian party, but it may be that they are so scattered that it takes time to get them ready to come. We wait for them.

AUGUST 1, 1804.   We sent Drouillard and two men to look for the horses and one man back to where Joseph Barter was sent to find the Indians. This man returned and informed us that no person had been there since we left them on the 28th of July. The horses were found twelve miles off. John Shields brought in a deer, and George Shannon brought in the skin, tallow and some of the meat of a fat buck he had killed. Capt. Clark was thirty-four years old today, so the men had a celebration of a dinner of fat venison, elk fleece and a beaver tail, with a dessert of cherries, plums, raspberries, currants and grapes of superior quality. The Indians have not yet arrived, but a very ornate peace-pipe has been prepared for their reception.

AUGUST 2.   Drouillard and John Colter returned with the horses loaded with elk. Our hunters, Collins, Willard, Cruzatte, Reuben Fields and Gibson, brought in three large and fat bucks today. At sunset, six chiefs and seven warriors, along with a French interpreter, Mr. Fairfong, arrived amid the firing of their guns. Mr. Fairfong has lived with these Indians for some time, and has a family with them. They were given presents of tobacco, roasted meat, pork, and meal. They in turn, presented us with water melons. The bow gun was fired in honor of the occasion. We learned that our man, Joseph Barter, had set out from their camp a day before them. We are in hopes that he may have become lost and will soon return [but they never saw him again]. With these Indians about, every man is on guard and is ready for anything.

AUGUST 3.   Captains Lewis and Clark held a council with the Indians. Speeches were made and we told them of the change in government. We gave them medals, along with presents of tobacco, breech cloths, garters and paint. The three Ottoe and three Missouri chiefs present expressed great satisfaction with our speech, and appeared glad that they were freed from their former powers. They made sensible speeches and drank with us. The air gun was fired which astonished them greatly. They shook hands and departed after giving some of our men small presents. We had to reproach Drouillard for his attitude today. [Perhaps he was sulky because other interpreters, such as Mr. Fairfong and Cruzatte, were used.] We set off at about 3 o'clock p.m., and went five miles and camped on an island amongst troublesome mosquitoes.

AUGUST 4.   We set out early and passed a difficult area where the river banks were caving in, and therefore trees were falling into the river. Above this we passed the remains of an old trading post where Peter Cruzatte, two years ago, had traded with the Omaha Indians. Moses B. Reed went back to our council camp to look for his knife. He has not returned this evening.

AUGUST 5.   Capt. Lewis took a celestial observation. Capt. Clark went ashore, killed a turkey, and returned at dusk. We passed a bend or peninsula which was only 370 yards across, but we had to row twelve miles to reach the opposite side. We fear that Moses B. Reed has deserted.

AUGUST 6.   We set out early and proceeded on. Reed has not come up yet, neither has Joseph Barter. Upon examining Reed's knapsack, we found that he had taken his clothes and all his powder and balls – without any just cause for deserting us.

AUGUST 7.   We dispatched Drouillard, Reuben Fields, William Bratton and William Labiche back after the deserter, Moses B. Reed, with orders to put him to death if he did not give up peacefully. Also they are to go to the Ottoe village and inquire for Barter and bring him up to the Omaha village. They are also to advise the Ottoes that we will attempt to make peace between them and the Omaha and Sioux. Capt. Clark and John Collins walked ashore along the bottoms. Collins killed an elk. Capt. Lewis killed a pelican on an island covered with thousands of them.

AUGUST 8.   Today we passed the River de Sioux where Mr. Dorion tells us he has been on its headwaters. John Dame killed a pelican.

AUGUST 9.   We had a good breeze today and sailed fourteen miles. Capt. Clark with Sgt. Floyd, went ashore and killed a turkey. We camped above a beaver dam this evening.

AUGUST 10.   Last night we caught some fish and a beaver. We camped on an island four miles below the bluff on which Blackbird, the Omaha chief, is buried.

AUGUST 11.   We landed at the bluff where Blackbird was buried four years ago. Captains Lewis and Clark with ten men, visited the grave which is about twelve feet in diameter. He is said to be buried astride his horse. We placed a white flag, bound with red, white and blue, on a pole over the grave. His grave is still supplied with foodstuffs, for the Indians revere his memory with superstitious awe.

AUGUST 12.   We sent a man across the bend of the river where it loops back on itself, and he made it 974 yards across. The distance around the bend by water is 18¾ miles. Peter Weiser is appointed cook of Sgt. Floyd's mess. Beaver are plentiful around here. The mosquitoes are very bad. The captains are still hopeful of sending back dispatches, and are busily engaged in preparing them. Capt. Clark broke his favorite decanter.

AUGUST 13.   We formed a camp on a sand-bar on the south side of the river. We "detatched Sgt. Oderway, Peter Crusatt, George Shannon, Werner & Carrn [Carson] to the Omaha village with a flag and some tobacco to invite that nation to see and talk with us tomorrow." [1] Sgt. Ordway found a deserted village and stuck up a pole as a signal for Drouillard, who was to meet him there. Nothing but graves about — a result of the small-pox that ravaged some four hundred of these people.

AUGUST 14.   The party which was sent out yesterday returned today at noon. They could not find any Indians. The party sent in search of the deserters have not returned. We provided ourselves with a new mast for the keel-boat. Game is scarce here. Capt. Clark and a party of ten men, including Sgt. Floyd, made a small brush drag which was hauled up Omaha Creek to catch fish.

---

[1] Thwaites, v. I, p. 109.

AUGUST 15.   We caught 318 fish of different kinds: pike, bass, red-horse, small cat, and a kind of perch. Capt. Lewis sent Mr. Dorion and three men to examine a fire which sent up a huge smoke not far from our camp. The party returned and informed us that the fire arose from some trees which had been left burning by a small party of Sioux who had passed by that place several days ago. Our party are all in good health and spirits and are fiddling and dancing, except for Sgt. Floyd, who was seized with a complaint somewhat like a violent chorlick [sic]. He was sick all night.

AUGUST 16.   Capt. Lewis and twelve men went to the creek, and with a brush net, caught about seven hundred fish of the same kinds caught yesterday. The new mast was hoisted and put in place. Sgt. Ordway was up all night on duty.

AUGUST 17.   A fine morning as we await the Indians. At 6 p.m., Labiche returned and informed us that the search party, under Drouillard, was behind with the deserter, Moses B. Reed, and the three principal chiefs of the nation. The Indians had caught Joseph Barter, but he had deceived them and had got away again. Two beaver were caught today. We set the prairies on fire as this is the usual signal made by the traders to bring the Indian parties to them.

AUGUST 18.   The party of Indians and an interpreter, Mr. Fairfong, a Frenchman, arrived for council, and were given presents and food. The court-martial proceeded for Moses B. Reed. He confessed to desertion and stealing a government rifle, shot-pouch, powder and balls. He was sentenced to run the gauntlet four times through the party. The three principal chiefs petitioned for pardon for this man, for they said they never beat any person, even a child. After we had explained the customs of our country, the Indians were satisfied, and were witness to the punishment. We talked with the chiefs regarding peace among the tribes. This being Capt. Lewis's thirtieth birthday, the evening was closed with an extra gill of whiskey for the men, and a dance was held which lasted until 11 o'clock p.m.

AUGUST 19.   Captains Lewis and Clark each made a speech about peace. They gave one chief a medal, and made others chiefs, and gave all of them presents. Capt. Lewis invited the head chief to visit the President in Washington. Sgt. Floyd was taken suddenly ill this morning with a colick. We attempted in vain to relieve him. We could get nothing to stay on his stomach a moment. Every man is very attentive to him – York particularly. Our Indian guests were shown the magnet, and the air gun was fired which surprised them. However, they are troublesome by begging whiskey and little articles, and were not satisfied with the presents already given them.

Capt. Clark rebuked them very roughly for having in object only goods and not peace. After some firmness on both sides, we gave them a dram and broke up the council.

AUGUST 20.   Sgt. Floyd is weaker. We gave Mr. Fairfong a few presents and his Indians a cannister of whiskey. We set out on a gentle breeze, and the Indians departed for their village. John Shields went along the shore with the horses. Sgt. Floyd has no pulse and nothing will stay on his stomach or bowels. Capt. Clark sat up with him most of all last night. We stopped to prepare a warm bath, hoping it would brace him, but he died before we could get him to it. He died at 2 p.m., aged twenty-two years, with a good deal of composure. He said to Capt. Clark: "I am going away, I want you to write me a letter." We buried him on a bluff, one and a half miles from a small river to which we gave his name. Capt. Lewis read the funeral service, and he was buried under a cedar post with his name thereon, with the honors of war, and much lamented. This man at all times gave proof of his firmness and determined resolution to do service to his country and honor to himself. Sick as he was, he kept up his journal until the day before yesterday. After paying all the honor we could to our deceased brother, we camped at the mouth of Floyd's River to perpetuate the memory of the first [and only] member who has fallen on this important expedition.[2]

AUGUST 21.   We set out early under a hard breeze. The white pirogue could hardly sail for want of ballast. George Shannon went out to hunt and got lost. We sent a man to look for him. They joined us late in the evening. John Shields and another man who are with the horses, did not join us today. Mr. Dorion reports that the Great Sioux River is navigable upwards of two hundred miles, and near its headwaters there is a place where pipestone is found where the Indians make their peace-pipes. This is a sacred ground among the Indians, and even tribes at war may meet here without hostility. We gave to Sgt. Pryor the things that belonged to Sgt. Floyd, for he is his nearest relative, except his shot-pouch and tomahawk which we will send back to his parents in Kentucky.

AUGUST 22.   We set out early. At three miles we landed at a bluff where John Shields and another man who had gone with the horses, were waiting with two deer. Capt. Lewis examined the bluff which contained alum, copperas, cobalt and pyrites. In testing the quality of these minerals, Capt. Lewis nearly poisoned himself from the fumes and taste of the cobalt and pyrites which contained arsenic. These minerals floating on the surface of

---

[2] In 1857, after erosion had endangered the original burial site, Floyd's grave and monument were transferred to Sioux City, Iowa.

the Missouri may be the cause of the stomach disorders with which the party has been much afflicted since we left the Sioux River. Henceforth, we were ordered to dip our drinking water at some depth in order to avoid the scum on the surface. Capt. Lewis took a dose of salts to work off the effects of the arsenic. We permitted the men to name their man as a candidate for a new sergeant to replace the late Sgt. Floyd. Patrick Gass, Alexander Willard and George Gibson were nominated. Patrick Gass received nineteen votes, the highest number cast. Last night in Capt. Clark's sleep the name of Rolojo came to him, and as he is hard pressed to think up names to give the numerous streams we pass, he gave that name to a creek we passed today. Drouillard caught a beaver. Reuben Fields and George Shannon have been out hunting and did not return this evening.

AUGUST 23. Drouillard and Joseph Fields went hunting. Capt. Clark killed a fine buck. Joseph Fields returned and informed us that he had killed a bull buffalo. Capt. Lewis, Sgt. Ordway and ten other men were sent to butcher it, and brought the meat back to the boat. This was our first buffalo. John Collins killed a deer. We salted two barrels of the buffalo meat and jerked the venison. John Shields shot an elk standing on a sand-bar.

AUGUST 24. We passed some blue clay bluffs which appear to have been lately on fire, and are now too hot for a man to bear his hand in the earth at any depth. We found buffalo-berries which are deliciously flavored and made delightful tarts. Capt. Clark, York and a Frenchman, walked on shore where they killed two bucks and a fawn which we put in the boat before a rain set in. The two captains walked on shore again, and got very wet, while they shot two elk and visited a high hill, believed by the Indians to be a place of devils and evil spirits.

3

The Vermillion to Teton River

AUGUST 25. This morning Capt. Lewis, Capt. Clark, Drouillard, Sgt. Ordway, John Shields, Joseph Fields, John Colter, William Bratton, —— Carr [Carson], Francois Labiche, Cpl. Richard Warfington, Robert Frazier, York and the dog, Scannon, set out to visit the "Mountain of Evil Spirits." The Indians had told us there were little men eighteen inches tall, with big heads and armed with sharp arrows, at this place. Capt. Lewis became very tired and dropped out. When we descended at evening, York was nearly exhausted by the heat, thirst and fatigue. Capt. Clark said this is because York is too fat and unaccustomed to walk so fast. We set fire to the prairie at two places to let the Sioux know we are on the river. The boat party under Sgt. Pryor also fired the prairie near them. As it began to rain, the mountain party camped out all night. Meanwhile, Reuben Fields brought in five deer and George Shannon killed an elk. Last night, Joseph Whitehouse and party caught nine catfish which would weigh a total of three hundred pounds, so it was a big day for game taken.

AUGUST 26. The land party rejoined the boats at 9 o'clock a.m. We jerked the meat killed yesterday, and prepared the elk skins to make rope. We set out, leaving Drouillard and Shannon to hunt our lost horses – with directions to follow us, keeping on the high land. The captains appointed Patrick Gass a sergeant, vice, Charles Floyd, deceased. He is to take charge of Floyd's former mess. This appointment is confirmed by the commanding officers as the result of the high opinion they have formed of the capacity, diligence and integrity of Sergeant Gass. Great quantities of grapes and three kinds of plums are found. All have an excellent flavor, particularly the yellow kind.

AUGUST 27. Twelve fine catfish were caught last night. This morning Drouillard called from shore, and a pirogue was sent over for him. He had not found the horses, nor Shannon. John Shields and Joseph Fields were sent out to find Shannon and the horses. While we were at the mouth of James River, an Indian boy swam to the boat. He was of the Omaha nation. He told us there was a Sioux camp near. Two other Indians joined us when we landed, and Sgt. Pryor and Mr. Dorion went with the last two Indians to their camp to invite them to visit us. The Indian boy stayed with us all night.

AUGUST 28. We went up the river for six miles where the Indian boy left us. He returned to the Sioux. Captains Lewis and Clark are much indisposed. They think it might be caused by some hominy they ate. The large red pirogue ran a snag through her bottom and was near sinking. We formed a camp on a beautiful plain. The pirogue was unloaded and some of the baggage was found to be damaged. The captains are still thinking of sending one of the pirogues back to St. Louis. The Fields brothers, who were sent to look for Shannon and the horses, joined us and informed us that they could not overtake him. Shannon, not being a first-rate hunter, made us determined to send John Colter in pursuit of him with some provisions. We raised a flag pole over our camp, expecting the Indians.

AUGUST 29. In the afternoon, Sgt. Pryor and Old Dorion, with his son, Pierre Jr., who happened to be trading with the Sioux, arrived and brought with them sixty Indians of the Sioux nation. They appear to be friendly and camped on the opposite shore. Sgt. Pryor and young Dorion carried over to them some hominy, kettles, tobacco, etc. Sgt. Pryor anxiously reported that the women in the Sioux village are mostly old and homely. Drouillard killed a deer, and we caught many large catfish. The pirogue was repaired, and she was reloaded. The men are making a tow-line out of the green elk hides. When Sgt. Pryor first found the Sioux camp they presented him and his party with a fat dog, already cooked, of which they heartily partook and found well flavored. Capt. Clark is engaged in writing a speech, as the Indians are to meet with us tomorrow. The young warriors had killed two elk and six deer enroute, which they use to feed themselves.

AUGUST 30. We prepared some presents and medals which we intend to give to the Indians. We sent Old Dorion over in a pirogue for the chiefs and warriors to bring them to our council. At 12 o'clock we met, and Capt. Lewis delivered a speech in which he explained the change in government, enjoined them to make peace, and invited them to send a chief to our President in Washington to receive his good counsel. We smoked the pipe-of-peace and gave them presents of clothes, tobacco, a flag, medals, cocked-hats and uniforms. The chiefs retired to divide their presents, while Captains Lewis and Clark went to dinner and to consult about other matters. Old Dorion was displeased that he was not invited to have dinner with them, and the captains were sorry that they had overlooked inviting him. The air gun was fired, and it was explained that this gun was our great medicine, and that the gun could do great harm. After a few firings, the Indians ran to the trees to see the holes the shots had made, and they shouted aloud at the execution this gun could do. At night a circle was formed about the camp fires. The chiefs looked on with great dignity while the warriors danced until late at night. Shannon and Colter have not yet returned.

AUGUST 31. The Indians remained with us all day. They want Old Dorion and his son to stay with them so that he could accompany their chief to Washington. The chiefs returned a speech with an eloquent account of their dire poverty, etc. They said they would make peace with the Pawnee and Omaha, and said one of them would visit our President next spring. They also wished the captains would give them something for their squaws. The captains told them we were not traders, but had only come to make the road open for the traders who would follow, and who would supply their wants at better terms than they had ever had before. We learned much of their habits and customs, which we collect for our Government. The captains gave them more tobacco and corn to take to their lodges. We commissioned Old Dorion to make peace with all the chief nations in the neighborhood. We gave him a flag and some clothes. He received this with pleasure and promised to do all that was necessary. The chiefs sent their young men home, while they stayed to wait for Mr. Dorion. We gave Dorion a bottle of whiskey, and he and his son – with the chiefs – crossed to the other side of the river to camp.

SEPTEMBER 1, 1804. As Dorion had left the kettle we had given him, we found it and sent it over to him. We then set out on our journey and came to a beaver house. Drouillard killed a buck elk. It is hardly necessary to mention the fish – we take them at any place.

SEPTEMBER 2. We have Drouillard, Reuben Fields and Collins out hunting today. They got three elk. Capt. Clark took the dimensions of an ancient fortification we found on a river bank. Newman and Howard killed an elk. We found a great abundance of grapes. Shannon and Colter have not returned yet. We jerked the meat of the elk and dried the skins as a cover for over the pirogues. We see a strange animal, new to science, which we call "Wild goats." [Later, in 1815, they were technically named: antelope.]

SEPTEMBER 3. We set out at sunrise. The plains are covered with buffalo and several wild goats were seen. They are wild and fleet. Capt. Clark collected the seeds of three varieties of the plum which he intends to send back to his brother, Jonathan.

SEPTEMBER 4. We set out early. Drouillard killed a turkey. The wind blew from the south, so we hoisted sail and ran very fast for a short time. We broke the mast again. The sand flew from the sand-bars very thick as we passed by them.

SEPTEMBER 5.   We took a cedar tree on board to make a mast. The Fields brothers and Drouillard are out hunting. They obtained two elk and a deer. John Newman and another man were sent out on the other side of the river to hunt. They got a fawn and a deer. We sent Shields and Gibson to the Ponca village. Gibson killed a buffalo in the town, as the people were away hunting. Shields killed a deer near the village. We called an island "No Preserve Island" as we are out of that provision. At 4 o'clock we camped. We made, and put in place, the new cedar mast.

SEPTEMBER 6.   We had a hard storm this morning, which, plus the sand-bars, obliged us to use the tow-line. Reuben Fields killed two deer. John Colter arrived – he had not found George Shannon nor the horses. He had killed a buffalo, an elk, three deer, a wolf, five turkeys, a goose and a beaver. The keel-boat got fast on a sand-bar and the men had to get into the river to get her off. Today we had rain and cold weather, so we were issued a gill of whiskey.

SEPTEMBER 7.   Shields killed a strange animal we call a barking squirrel [prairie dog]. We halted and the captains went out with ten men. By pouring water into the animals' burrow, they drowned out and took one of the animals alive. The men took all the vessels and kettles that would hold water in order to drive the animals from their holes. Though they worked at this business until night, they caught only one. Silas Goodrich caught a very large catfish. We found John Colter in a camp. He had made a scaffold for drying meat, and had supposed we were ahead of him, and had proceeded on for several days before he had discovered his error.

SEPTEMBER 8.   We sailed all day before a good wind. Drouillard joined us today with the horses. He had gone out last evening. He had also killed an elk, a deer and had caught two large beaver and a prairie dog. Capt. Clark walked along the north shore all day. Sgt. Gass went with Colter to where the latter had killed a buffalo, and had left his hat there to scare off the wolves. They found the wolves had devoured the carcass and had carried off his hat. In the afternoon we saw several buffalo swimming the river. Capt. Lewis walked ashore and came across a trading house which had been built in 1796 by Jean Baptiste Truteau. He killed a buffalo. Capt. Clark joined us after dark.

SEPTEMBER 9.   We set out at sunrise. Capt. Clark walked ashore in hopes of obtaining an antelope and a black-tailed deer. We need specimens of these new animals to send back to Washington. Drouillard killed a buck and two fawns and put them into the pirogues. Reuben Fields and York each killed a buffalo. Therefore we dined on fine meat tonight.

SEPTEMBER 10. After we had sailed all morning, we came to some black-sulphur bluffs on the south side. On top of the bluffs we found the skeleton of a fossil fish forty-five feet long. We collected the bones to be sent to Washington. John Newman went on the hills and killed a deer. We see many buffalo. Sgt. Pryor walked along the shore today and saw a large salt spring. Cpl. Warfington walked this afternoon and killed two buffalo. John Newman got a deer. We made twenty miles today.

SEPTEMBER 11. George Shannon, who had left us with the horses on August 26th, and believing us to be ahead, and had pushed on as long as he could, joined us today. He had used all of the few bullets he had with him, and in a plentiful game country, nearly starved to death. He was twelve days without provisions, subsisting on grapes and one rabbit. One of his horses gave out and was left before the bullets gave out. He was on the point of killing the horse when he discovered us coming upstream. We saw three large spotted foxes, a black-tailed deer and a porcupine. Capt. Clark, Sgt. Ordway, Sgt. Pryor and George Gibson walked ashore. Gibson got an elk. Ordway saw sixteen bull buffalo, and he went around and crept near them as they were feeding. As he was waiting to get one sideways, one of the bulls discovered him. Ordway was obliged to shoot at his head – not a good spot to kill a buffalo – but the bull turned and ran off. As it was raining hard, Ordway's gun got wet as he loaded, so he beat a retreat over rough hills and gullies and got out of danger. Reuben Fields went out with our one remaining horse.

SEPTEMBER 12. Drouillard caught four beaver in his traps last night. Capt. Clark, Sgt. Gass and John Newman went to hunt today and have not yet returned. The boat men under Sgt. Ordway had difficulty with the swift, shallow water and sand-bars. Capt. Clark and party saw several villages of prairie dogs – a number of grouse and three foxes. They also saw a bluff of mixed slate and coal.

SEPTEMBER 13. Drouillard caught three remarkably large beaver. Sgt. Ordway, Sgt. Pryor and Shannon went along the shore to obtain some plums. Shannon killed a porcupine which the party ate for supper. The numerous sand-bars in the river make it difficult to find the proper channel.

SEPTEMBER 14. Ordway, Pryor and Shannon who had stayed out all last night, rejoined us today. Capt. Clark and Alex Willard walked ashore to look for a volcano reported in this area. Reuben Fields, who had taken our horses on the 12th, met us today. John Shields killed a hare weighing six and one-quarter pounds. We stuffed the antelope and white rabbit to send back to Washington. It is cloudy, drizzly and disagreeable today. All the hands were in the water several times in order to drag the boats over the sand-bars. The captains write up detailed descriptions of the white goat and hare for their scientific reports, for these animals are of a different description than any seen in the States.

SEPTEMBER 15. We set out early and passed the mouth of a creek where Shannon had lived on grapes while waiting for the boat of a trader, Mr. Clintens [Charles Courtin?], whom we believe is in this area. Shannon had supposed we had gone on and left him. We named the creek "Shannon Creek" [present Ball Creek]. Captains Lewis and Clark halted at the mouth of the White River and went up it a short distance. It is a handsome river in a handsome country. Sgt. Gass and Reuben Fields went to examine the same river some twelve miles higher up. Capt. Clark killed a hare, a deer and an elk. Many wolves are howling about, and the evening is cold.

SEPTEMBER 16. Whitehouse and another man went hunting. Sgt. Gass and Reuben Fields returned from their exploration of the White River. Having found that our party had passed on, they proceeded up the Missouri and found us encamped, drying provisions and stores. We had to lighten the keel-boat, for we found, because of the low water and sand-bars, that we could not proceed with the present loading. We have been planning, as instructed, to send a pirogue back to St. Louis, but our captains now concluded to detain her, and her crew of soldiers under Cpl. Warfington, until spring. We put some of the load of the keel-boat into the red pirogue. The hunting party under Capt. Lewis, obtained buffalo, elk, antelope and a magpie. We use the buffalo skins to cover the pirogues. It now being very cold, Capt. Clark gave a flannel shirt to each man, and powder to those who had expended theirs. John Collins, who had been with the horse, joined us. Baptiste Dechamps killed a buffalo and Peter Roi killed a deer.

SEPTEMBER 17. Capt. Lewis with a party of six men went hunting all day and to observe the habits of the antelope and view the country. He wanted to obtain a female antelope, for we already have a specimen of a male. John Colter killed one of these strange goats, and also a black-tailed deer – new to us for they are not found in other parts of our country. The hunters brought in eight fallow deer and five common ones. Capt. Lewis killed a rattlesnake in a village of prairie dogs. We finished drying our provisions, some of which were wet and spoiled. Drouillard caught a beaver. Gibson killed a deer – its tail was eighteen inches long, and also different from any yet seen by our party. A new magpie with a greenish-purple and blackish color – with a very long tail, was also taken. We saw coyotes, skunks and the shy, but very fleet, wild goats [antelope].

SEPTEMBER 18. We set off early today. Capt. Clark, Drouillard and Joseph Fields killed eleven deer. We camped early to jerk the venison before dark. Joseph Fields did not return tonight. Drouillard killed a prairie wolf which was of a different description than any in the States. Its bones and skin were saved to send home.

SEPTEMBER 19. Capt. Clark, York and eleven men walked on shore to inspect the Sioux Pass of the Three Rivers and Calumet ground – an important Indian trail. Capt. Clark killed a fat buffalo, and York killed an elk. The hunters got four deer and the boat crew killed two buffalo swimming the river. Joseph Fields, who was with the horse, killed a black-tailed deer and hung it on the bank where the boat crew found it and took it on board. Capt. Lewis and Drouillard got two black-tailed deer. As Capt. Clark arrived at dark where the party was encamped, he named the place "Night Creek." We are at the beginning of the Great Bend of the Missouri River.

SEPTEMBER 20. Drouillard and Shields took the horse and crossed the neck of land. It is twelve miles across to the river again, and thirty miles around by water. Capt. Clark walked on shore to inspect the bend, while Capt. Lewis and Reuben Fields went hunting. We passed a long range of bluffs of a dark color which melts like sugar. From these and many others like them, the Missouri gets its muddy color. Both the captains and Reuben Fields joined us at our evening camp. They had obtained a male and female wild goat and a long-tailed deer. We saved the skins and bones to send back to the States next spring. John Newman and John Thompson picked up some salt. At night the river bank began to fall in very fast. The sergeant on guard gave the alarm to raise all hands. We changed camp during the night to another place one mile further up the river. We had not arrived at the opposite shore before the bank over our old camp fell into the river. Capt. Clark estimates we have come 1283 miles so far on our voyage.

SEPTEMBER 21. Capt. Lewis shot some plovers for his dinner. We passed around the Great Bend some thirty miles. At the nearest place, it is only one and one-fourth miles across the neck. The catfish are small and not in such plenty here as below.

SEPTEMBER 22. One of our Frenchmen has been in pain for the past ten or twelve days with an abscess on his right thigh. We pass a fort built of cedar by Mr. Registre Loisel. It is about 48 x 32 feet in size. The hunters came in and complained of their moccasins being burnt by the salts on the hills. Drouillard and Shields who had been sent over the neck of land, joined us today. John Colter went on with the horse. Capt. Clark walked on shore and killed a large doe.

SEPTEMBER 23.   We set out early. Reuben Fields went to hunt and returned later in the day with a wild goat. Capt. Clark walked on shore
and observed great herds of buffalo, and a great fire on the plains to the
south. This is taken to mean that Indians have discovered us. We name a
creek "Reuben" because he was the first of our party to reach it. In the
evening three boys of the Teton Sioux nation swam across the river and
informed us that two parties of Sioux were camped on the next river. We
treated them kindly and sent them back with an invitation to a conference
in the morning.

SEPTEMBER 24.   We found the camp of John Colter who had killed four
elk. We prepared some clothes and a few medals for the chiefs we expect to
meet at the next river. Colter ran to the bank and reported that some Indians had taken his horse, bridle and some salt from him. We saw five
Indians who demanded to come aboard. We told them that we were friends
and wished to remain so, but that we were not afraid of any Indians. We
told them that some of their men had stolen a horse sent by their Great
Father, and that we would not speak to them any more until the horse was
returned to us. We proceeded on to the Teton River. Capt. Clark went
on shore and smoked with a chief who had come to see us here. He said he
knew nothing of the horse, etc. Capt. Clark informed him that we would
hold a council tomorrow. Peter Cruzatte could only speak Omaha, so we
were only partly understood by these Sioux. Old Dorion, who could speak
this language is not with us anymore, for we had left him below. Everyone
remained on board all night – on the alert for any trouble.

4

Teton River to Fort Mandan

SEPTEMBER 25. We raised a flag pole over our camp and put up an awning and a sand-bar in readiness for the Indians. At 10 o'clock they came — about fifty in number. We gave them food and tobacco. They have some captive Omaha squaws, so Cruzatte could talk to them, and they in return, translated into Sioux. The captains in this manner delivered a speech, gave medals and presents of knives, clothes, a cocked-hat, and other small articles. We paraded our party and invited the chiefs on board the boat. There we showed them many curiosities and gave them a half wine glass of whiskey. They took up an empty bottle and soon began to be troublesome. One of them, "The Partisan," pretended to be drunk and reeled about the boat. With some difficulty, Capt. Clark took the other chiefs ashore and tried to reconcile them, but as he landed, three warriors seized the cable. The chief who affected drunkenness was exceedingly insolent both in words and gestures, saying we could not depart. He said that they were poor and would keep our pirogue, and that they had soldiers as well as we. Capt. Clark, in moderation, told them we had a long way to go — and would go — and that we were not squaws, but soldiers. The chief's insults became so personal, and his intentions so evident to do us injury, that Capt. Clark at last drew his sword, and at this motion, Capt. Lewis ordered the men in the boat under arms. The large swivel gun was loaded with buck-shot. The five men who were with Capt. Clark had previously taken up their guns with full determination to defend him if necessary. The Grand Chief, "Black Buffalo," then took hold of the cable and sent the young warriors off, and the lesser chiefs went to the Indian party about twenty yards back. All of them had their bows strung and guns cocked. Capt. Clark felt warm and spoke in positive terms to them all, but principally to the First Chief. Capt. Clark offered him his hand, but the chief refused it — but let the rope go and went to his party. Capt. Clark pushed the pirogue off and had not gone far when the First Chief and three principal men walked into the water and requested to come on board. They were taken in and we proceeded about a mile and anchored near a small island which Clark named "Bad Humored Island." The four Indians stayed with us all night.

SEPTEMBER 26. We set out early but soon came to to let the squaws and boys see the boat as the chiefs had requested. Great numbers of men, women and children were on the banks watching us. They are fond of dress and show, and appeared spritely, but generally ill looking. After landing, Capt. Lewis and five men, including Whitehouse, went on shore with the chief who appeared to want to make up and be friendly. After Capt. Lewis had been on shore about three hours, Capt. Clark became uneasy for fear of deception, and sent a sergeant to see him. Capt. Lewis reported all was well and that the Indians wanted us to remain one more night so that they could show their good disposition towards us – so we determined to remain. After Capt. Lewis returned to the boat, Capt. Clark went on shore. He was received on an elegant buffalo robe and was carried to the village by six warriors and was not permitted to touch the ground until he was put down in the grand council house on a white, dressed robe. Under this shelter, about seventy men sat in a circle and the pipe-of-peace was smoked. A large fire was near in which food was cooking. Soon after they sat Capt. Clark down, the warriors went for Capt. Lewis and they brought him back in the same manner. An old man arose and spoke in approval of what we had done, and informed us of their situation, requesting us to take pity on them. We told him the Great Father wanted his children to live in peace and that he would want them to give up the Omaha prisoners and make peace with that nation. After much talk, the Great Chief then rose and with great state he spoke to the same purpose. With great solemnity he took up the pipe-of-peace, lit it, and presented the stem to us to smoke. He took some of the most delicate parts of the dog which had been prepared for the feast, and made an offering to the flag to acknowledge transfer of the country. We smoked for an hour until dark when all was cleared away. A large fire was made in the center and about ten musicians beat on tambourines. Men and women came on highly decorated and proceeded to dance the War Dance. They did this with great cheerfulness until about midnight, when we informed the chiefs that they must be tired. Accompanied by four chiefs, we returned to the boat, and they stayed with us all night. They promise to deliver the prisoners to Mr. Dorion. All of our men are on board, anchored about one hundred paces from shore. Everyone is in high spirits this evening [Nothing is mentioned about the recovery of the horse].

September 27. The bank was lined with Sioux. We gave the two principal chiefs a blanket and a peck of corn each. Capt. Lewis accompanied the chiefs to their lodges. Capt. Clark wrote a letter to Mr. Dorion and prepared some commissions and a medal, and sent them to Capt. Lewis. At 2 o'clock Capt. Lewis returned with four chiefs and a brave man which they call a sort of police. After a half an hour, Capt. Clark, Sgt. Gass and others took them on shore and they left us with reluctance, but we are still alert for any treachery. They offered the captains a young woman for companionship, which was refused. At dark the dance was begun as usual, performed as last night. About 11 p.m., we returned to the boats with two chiefs, but by bad steering, the pirogue struck the keel-boat's cable with such force as to break it near the anchor. The chiefs became frightened and alarmed, and the Indians came down in great haste, armed for action. They found the incident harmless, but about twenty of them camped on shore all night. As we had lost our anchor, we were obliged to lay to under a bank much exposed to the hostile intentions of these Tetons whom we had every reason to believe intended to stop our boats and rob us. Peter Cruzatte came in at night and informed us that the Omaha prisoners told him that the Tetons intended to stop us. Under Sgt. Ordway, a guard was kept all night, but we showed no sign of our knowledge of these evil intentions.

SEPTEMBER 28.   We made many diligent attempts to find our anchor without success, for the sand had covered it up. We were determined to proceed, and after breakfast we, with great difficulty, got all the chiefs but the First Chief, out of the boat. When we were about setting out, the Indian soldiers took possession of the cable. Black Buffalo, who was still aboard, was informed of this. He went to Capt. Lewis, who was at the bow, and told him the warriors wanted tobacco. Capt. Lewis was nearing giving orders to cut the rope and fire on them. He said to the chief; "You told us you are a great man and have influence; now show your influence by taking the rope from these men." This appealed to his pride and had the desired effect. We gave a twist of tobacco to the First Chief who gave it to his men. The chief took the cable from them and gave it to us. We proceeded under a favorable breeze. We took in the Number Three Chief who was waiting two miles above. He told us that the Number Two Chief, the one who had pretended drunkenness, was a double-spoken man. Soon afterward, we saw a man riding full speed up the bank. We brought him aboard, and later sent him back with a talk for his nation, i.e. – if they were for peace, they were to stay at home – and if they were for war, or determined to stop us – then we were ready to defend ourselves. We substituted large stones for an anchor, and stopped at a small island in the middle of the river. Capt. Clark feels unwell from all the tension and lack of sleep. Under the circumstances, everyone stayed aboard the boats.

SEPTEMBER 29.   We set out early. At 9 a.m., we observed the Number Two Chief and three men and two squaws on shore. They wanted to come on board, but we refused to let any more sail with us. They offered us the squaws but we told them that we would not speak to another Teton except the one on board – and he could go ashore anytime he pleased. We proceeded on until evening, the Indians still following – when our chief requested to be put ashore – which we did. We later camped on the south side of the river.

SEPTEMBER 30. We had not proceeded far when we discovered at a distance a great number of men, women and children descending the banks towards the river, above which the chief told us there was another band of Sioux of about four hundred souls. About 10 a.m., we anchored opposite the camps of this band. We told them that we took them by the hand as friends. As a token of this we would send to each chief a twist of tobacco, and some to the principal men. We also said we had been badly treated by the band below, and would not land again, as we had not time to delay. They wanted us to eat with them, but we declined, and proceeded under a double-reefed sail. The chief on board tossed to those who ran along the shore small pieces of tobacco and told them to open their ears to our councils. About 4 p.m., we went to shore to take on some fire-wood. When we put off, the stern got fast. The boat swam around in the stream, and as the wind was high, she got in the trough of the waves and rocked very much before we got her straightened out. The chief on board was very much afraid and ran and hid himself. He said our boat was bad medicine and would not go further with us. Our captains gave him a blanket, knife, some tobacco and put him on shore. We told him to keep his men away from us. We camped on a sand-bar, everyone on guard.

OCTOBER 1, 1804. We passed the Cheyenne River. The Missouri is filled with sand-bars and we were obliged to haul the keel-boat over one. We saw a man whom we discovered to be a Frenchman. He was recognized by one of our engagés. We brought him over to the boat in one of the pirogues. We then came to a trading post where Mr. Jean Vallé and two men kept a few goods to trade with the Sioux. Mr. Vallé gave us information of the Cheyenne Indians and the interior country.

OCTOBER 2. Mr. Vallé came on board, and could speak English. He said we would not be troubled by any more Sioux. He came a short distance with us, and then returned to his post. We proceeded on. In the afternoon we discovered some Indians on the hills, and one of them came down to the river. He told us he wanted us to come ashore. We told him we had spoken to his chief – and proceeded on. We expected to be attacked around the next bend – and were ready for them. Nothing happened, so we went on. We camped on a sand bar, one half mile from shore. There was no hunting today for the Indians are troublesome, so we are forced to keep the company together and be on the alert.

OCTOBER 3. We set out early. At noon we examined our stores. Several bags had been cut into by mice and some corn was scattered. Some of the cloths and paper were cut also. At 1 o'clock an Indian came with a turkey on his back, and four others joined him. We had no intercourse with them. We saw gulls and white brant flying to the southward in large flocks. We camped on the south side of the river.

OCTOBER 4. As there was no outlet in the channel before us, we had to drop back three miles to get into the proper channel. We saw several Indians on the bank and they yelled and skipped a ball before us. One swam to us and begged for powder. We gave him a small piece of tobacco and told him we were not traders but were a government party strong enough to defend ourselves. Capt. Lewis and three men walked along a large island in the center of which is an old village of the Arikara. It appears to have been deserted for about five years. We camped on a sand-bar at the upper end of this island.

OCTOBER 5. We had frost this morning. Later we saw a herd of wild goats swimming the river. One of our hunters ran up the shore and killed four of them. Capt. Clark walked on an island and killed a buck and a wolf. We found the fresh meat very good and sweet, for we had had no other fresh meat on hand. We camped on a mud-bar and refreshed the men with whiskey.

OCTOBER 6. We nooned at a deserted Arikara village of eighty round lodges covered with earth. We found squashes growing in the village. John Shields killed an elk. Capt. Lewis and one soldier hunted along the handsome bottoms. The two captains and two more men knocked for a bow pack.[1]

OCTOBER 7. Heavy frost last night. Capt. Clark walked up the river. He saw the tracks of a very large white bear. We saw two Teton Indians. They asked for, and we gave them meat to eat. We passed an island and Capt. Clark, Sgt. Ordway and three men hunted on it. One of them killed a badger and a large doe. The island is covered with rye-grass and there were hundreds of sharp-tailed grouse feeding on it. The hunters came on board. Our camp was made on the north side of the river.

OCTOBER 8. We passed the Grand River. Our hunters discovered an Arikara village on an island above. We passed this village in the presence of a great number of spectators, and camped above it at the foot of some high

---

[1] The interpretation I deduce from this sentence from Ordway's journal, page 148, and of which Quaife states that the last word is not clear in the manuscript, is that it refers to pulling the keel-boat over a sand bar. The captains write: ". . . the river became shallow, and after searching for a long time for the main channel, we at last dragged the boat over one of them, rather than go back three miles for the deepest channel." (Coues, *Lewis and Clark*, v. 1, p. 155.) If this interpretation is correct, the sentence may be edited to read: The two captains and two more men sounded for a bow path.

land. Mr. Joseph Gravelines, a French interpreter, joined us. Capt. Lewis, Mr. Gravelines and three of our men went to the village. They took some tobacco and visited the Chiefs. Capt. Clark formed a guard on shore around the boats and anchor. Robert Frazier was selected to be one of the permanent members of our party, being transferred from among those who were enlisted for only the Missouri portion of our expedition. He joined Sgt. Gass' mess. Capt. Lewis returned late. Mr. Joseph Gravelines and Mr. Pierre Antoine Tabeau, a trader from St. Louis, accompanied him.

OCTOBER 9. We delayed here all day among these friendly Indians. They use the bull-boat; a frame of boughs made in the shape of a bowl, which is covered with a single buffalo hide. These boats can carry from three to six men, and can ride the highest waves. This nation had never seen a black man before and were much astonished with York. They call him "The Big Medicine." By way of amusement, he told them that he had once been a wild animal, but was caught and tamed by his master, and to convince them (for he is a remarkably stout, strong negro), he showed them feats of strength, which, added to his looks, made him more terrible than we wished him to be. He told them that children were very good to eat. It was a cold, blustery day, but some of the men went to the village.

OCTOBER 10. We asked Mr. Gravelines and Mr. Tabeau to invite the chiefs to a conference. At 1 o'clock, the chiefs assembled at our camp under an awning. We delivered a speech similar to that given to the tribes below and gave them flags, medals, cloth, paints, etc. After the council, we shot the air gun which astonished them. We observed two of the Sioux in our council whom we had seen below. We were told they came to intercede with the Arikara to stop us. These Indians are not fond of liquor of any kind, and were surprised that our Great White Father would present them with a liquor that would make them foolish. Sgts. Ordway and Gass visited the village. They raise corn, beans, pumpkins, squash, watermelons and a kind of tobacco. Sgt. Gass observes that this tobacco answers for smoking, but not for chewing. We left one of our Frenchmen [Joseph Collin ?] with Mr. Tabeau and took Tabeau's son in his place. They gave us corn, beans, dried pumpkins and squash. Some of their women are very handsome and clean. We set our corn-mill up and showed them how it operated.

OCTOBER 11. At 11 o'clock a.m. we met again in council. The chiefs thanked us for what we had given them, and promised to follow our advice. They asked that we make peace with the Mandan nation above. The chief told us the road was open for us and no one would dare shut it. We took the Grand Chief and his nephew on board and set out for the upper village.

Enroute, we picked up another chief. This second village gave us corn and beans – the last a well flavored bean which they rob from the nests of mice. We gave them a steel mill which pleased them. Although an axe was stolen from our cooks, all else is tranquility.

OCTOBER 12. We proceeded to the first village where ceremonies as before were repeated. They wanted us to take one of their chiefs up to the Mandan nation to make peace. The chief and his people gave us about seven bushels of corn, some tobacco, seeds, leggins and a robe. We continued on to another village where ten bushels of corn, summer squash and beans were given us. We gave them sugar, salt and a sun-glass each. One of them went with us to the Mandans. They have an unusual custom of showing appreciation. They think they cannot show sufficient acknowledgment without offering their guests their handsome squaws. They are displeased if the squaws are not received. The squaws are very insistent about it and followed us to our camp. Our men found no difficulty in procuring companions for the night. York participated in these favors, for the maidens desired to preserve among them some living memorial of this wonderful stranger. An Arikara invited him to his lodge and presented his wife to him, and retired outside the lodge. One of York's comrades came looking for him, but the gallant husband would permit no interruption until a reasonable time had elapsed. Our men traded small articles for buffalo robes. We set off with fiddles playing and horns sounding. John Newman and Moses Reed are confined to camp for uttering expressions of a highly criminal and mutinous nature, to the obvious subversion of discipline and loyalty on the part of other members of the expedition.

OCTOBER 13. We proceeded on. At noon we halted and a court-martial was held for two hours. Nine of the men served on the jury: Sgt. Ordway, Sgt. Gass, John Shields, Joseph Collins, William Werner, William Bratton, George Shannon and Silas Goodrich. John Newman was sentenced to receive seventy-five lashes on the bare back and to be henceforth discarded from the permanent party engaged in the Northwest discovery. He is relieved from guard duty, but instead shall be exposed to such drudgery as we think proper. We sent out hunters and they returned with one deer. We found more grapes here than any we had yet seen.

OCTOBER 14. We set out in the rain which continued all day. We inflicted the punishment on John Newman. This caused the chief who was with us to cry until the reason was explained to him. The chief observed that such things were necessary, but that he punished such disloyalty by death, for his nation never whipped anyone, even their children.

OCTOBER 15.   We passed another Arikara village. Several of the natives visited us and gave us meat. We gave them fish-hooks, beads, etc. Their women are very fond of caressing our men, and are much pleased with York. He had fun terrifying the children who constantly follow him.

OCTOBER 16.   Capt. Lewis, the Arikara chief and one of our men walked ashore in the evening. Our hunters got three antelope. The Indians sang and were merry all night.

OCTOBER 17.   The wind was against us, so we were obliged to use the tow-line. Capt. Clark walked on shore with the Indian chief and Mr. Gravelines. He killed three deer and an elk and our hunters killed four deer. We built a scaffold to keep the deer meat from the wolves. The boat party picked it up later and dressed it.

OCTOBER 18.   After proceeding three miles we came to the mouth of the Cannon Ball River. Here we met two Frenchmen, Phillipe Degie and ———— Grenier [also spelled: Greinyea], who are in the employ of Mr. Gravelines. They had been robbed by the Mandans of their traps, furs and other articles, and were descending the river in a canoe. They turned back and followed us with the expectation of obtaining redress.

OCTOBER 19.   We sailed with a good southeast wind. Capt. Clark walked on shore and observed great numbers of buffalo. Sgt. Gass was one of the hunting party out today. They killed eight deer, the skins of which were all given to the men of our party.

OCTOBER 20.   We had a favorable wind for sailing. Capt. Clark killed three deer and the hunters ten. They also wounded a grizzly bear.

OCTOBER 21.   At daylight it began to snow, but we set out early. We procured a buffalo and an otter today.

OCTOBER 22.   Capt. Clark, who before had complained of a pain in his neck, was suddenly attacked with rheumatism so bad that he could hardly move. Capt. Lewis put a hot stone wrapped in flannel on his neck which provided some relief. We passed a war party of fourteen Sioux. We have every reason to believe that they intend to steal horses from the Mandans. Several beaver are caught every night.

OCTOBER 23.   We pass five deserted Mandan villages. One was the village where Degie and Grenier (who are with us) were robbed. Three hunters were out today but they took nothing.

OCTOBER 24.   We came to an island where we were visited by the Grand Chief of the Mandan Indians. They met our Arikara chief with great cordiality and smoked together. They had some handsome women with them. Capt. Lewis visited their camps. Not much game is found around their villages.

OCTOBER 25. We passed an old Mandan village. Like Capt. Clark, Reuben Fields is afflicted with rheumatism in his neck. Moses Reed has it in his hips, and Peter Cruzatte in his legs. We ran aground several times today and passed a very bad point of rocks, after which we camped on a sand point. Other than those mentioned, all of the party are well.

OCTOBER 26. After stopping at a Mandan village where we took on two chiefs and their baggage, we proceeded on. At this village we saw Mr. Hugh McCraken, a free trader employed by the North West Company of Canada. He came here nine days ago to trade for horses and buffalo robes. Another man came with him from their post at Fort Assiniboine in Canada. We landed about a half mile below the first Mandan town. Soon after, many men, women and children flocked down to see us. They were much pleased with the corn-mill which we set up on the boat. They were surprised at the ease with which it reduced the corn to flour. Capt. Lewis walked to the town with the principal chiefs and interpreters.

5

Among the Mandans

OCTOBER 27. We set out early and later stopped at a chief's lodge. Capt. Clark smoked with him, but could not eat because of the rheumatism in his neck. This displeased the Indians somewhat. Here he met Mr. René Jessaume, a free trader working out from the North West Company's posts on the Assiniboine River.[1] His wife was a Mandan woman. Capt. Clark employed him to interpret for us, and he went along with us. We proceeded on to a central point opposite the Knife River and formed a camp, and raised a flag staff. Capt. Lewis and Jessaume walked down to the second village of Mandans. We sent three carrots of tobacco to the chiefs and invited them to council with us tomorrow. We are 1610 miles from the River du Bois, where we first embarked on this expedition.

OCTOBER 28. Many of the Minnitaree nation from further up the Missouri, as well as the Mandans, came to see us, but the high wind today prevented us from holding a council. They wished to see the keel-boat, because it was strange and mysterious to them, they viewed as great medicine – as they also did York. The Grand Chief of the Mandans, "Black Cat," with Capt. Lewis, Capt. Clark and an interpreter, walked up the river about a mile and a half to view conditions there as a fort for ourselves. We found the situation good, but timber there is scarce. Drouillard caught two beaver above our camp last night. The Mandan women sent us presents of corn, hominy and garden stuffs. The captains presented to the chief's wife an earthenware glazed jar, and she received it with great pleasure. Our men are very cheerful this evening.

OCTOBER 29. We met in council under an awning with the sails from the boat stretched around to keep out as much wind as possible. In our speech, we mentioned friendship and trade, and the offer of peace from the Arikara. They all smoked the peace pipe with the Arikara chief. We told them that some of our party would be discharged here, and also spoke of the robbery they had committed on the two Frenchmen from below. They are to answer us tomorrow. We gave them presents of suits of clothes. The air gun was

---

[1] René Jessaume (Jesseaume – Jusseaume – etc.) had been an independent trader of the North West Company among the Mandans and Gros Ventre for some fifteen years. In 1795 he had built a fort located between the Mandan and Gros Ventre villages. Nasatir, *Before Lewis and Clark,* 93, 95, 331.

fired and we gave them a steel corn-mill which was very pleasing to them. The prairie got on fire with such speed and violence that a man and a woman were burned to death. A small half-breed boy was saved by crawling under a fresh buffalo skin. The fire passed our camp at 8 p.m., and was truly tremendous.

OCTOBER 30.   Capt. Clark took eight men in the small pirogue and went up the river about seven miles to see if a place could be found for our winter quarters. He then determined to drop down the river to another site where there was wood and game. On the return to camp, Capt. Clark gave the men a dram. The men danced for the Indians this evening, which pleased them very much.

OCTOBER 31.   Capt. Clark was invited to visit Black Cat, the Mandan chief. He walked down and was seated with great ceremony by the side of the chief. The latter concurred in the benefits of peace, etc., but wanted more presents. Two of the traps stolen from the Frenchmen were laid before Capt. Clark. In the evening the chief, dressed in his new uniform and cocked-hat, visited our camp. Our men danced until 10 p.m., which is common with them when not rowing all day. Mr. Hugh McCraken, the British trader, returned to his post which is about 150 miles from here. He took a letter from our captains expressing cordial relations and good will to all persons at their posts.

NOVEMBER 1, 1804.   We were visited by the Mandan chiefs who were concerned as to where we would locate this winter, for they knew, as we did, that we would have to be supplied with food during the long winter. Capt. Clark and all the party went down to the place we have selected to winter. Capt. Lewis, Sgt. Ordway and others called at the village above to get corn. These Mandans live very well and have plenty of corn, beans, squash, meat, etc. The promised corn was not ready, but they told us we could have it tomorrow, so we dropped down the river some nine miles to a bottom covered with timber where we went into camp on the north side of the Missouri River.

NOVEMBER 2.   We pitched our tents, cut trees, and began to build our winter quarters. All the men worked diligently. The Arikara chief who had come with us, desired to return to his home. He set out with a chief of the Mandans. We sent presents with them. Capt. Lewis, Sgt. Gass and some of the men went back up to the village where eleven bushels of corn were delivered. One of our French hands ["Rokey"], was discharged, and has gone down the river.

NOVEMBER 3. We dispatched six hunters down the river to hunt. We discharged the nine French hands. [Baptiste Deschamps, Baptiste Lajuennesse, Etienne Malboeuf, Joseph Collin, Paul Primeau, Francois Rivet, Peter Roi, Charles Caugee and Charles Hebért would be the nine if I am correct that Peter Pinaut left the party on June 13, at the time John Robertson was discharged. Pierre Cruzatte and Francois Labiche were of the permanent party and were not discharged.]

Two or three volunteered to remain with us during the winter. Two Frenchmen, who together with two others, have established a small hut and resided within the vicinity of Fort Mandan under our protection. [These could be Dechamps, Malboeuf, Carson and Rivet.] The others are building a pirogue to return to St. Louis. [They apparently changed their minds and remained, although two of these did go down the river to trap until November 14, 1804, when they returned to Fort Mandan.]

Mr. René Jessaume, his wife and child, moved to our camp. Six men went in a pirogue down the river some twenty or thirty miles to the good hunting grounds in order to obtain meat for our party. We caught two beaver near camp. Jean Baptiste La Page, a French-Canadian trapper who lives here among the Mandans, was engaged to join our party in the place of John Newman. He had trapped the upper Missouri, so we thought this experience would be of much value to us. Some of the squaws came from the village bringing meat. The men are busy building cabins.

NOVEMBER 4. A Frenchman, Toussaint Charbonneau, a Mandan trader who also speaks the Minnitaree language, came to visit us. He wants to be hired as an interpreter, and informed us two of his wives were Shoshoni Indians. We engaged him – and one of his wives, Sacagawea, is to go along to interpret the Shoshoni or Snake languages. We continue our labors on the fort. The timber we use is very large and heavy – and is mostly cottonwood with elm and some ash of inferior size. We got one line of our cabins raised, and got the eave-beams raised on all. These eaves were large timbers, and it took all the men with much hard lifting, to put the sixteen-foot beams in place.

NOVEMBER 5. All hands are working to raise the other line of cabins and splitting puncheons to lay the loft, which we intend to cover with earth in order to make the cabins warm and comfortable. We dug a vault [trench? – privy?] one hundred yards about the huts in order to keep the place healthy. Late at night we were awakened by the sergeant on guard to see the beautiful Northern Lights. Capt. Clark has rheumatism very bad. Capt. Lewis was writing all day, preparing instructions for Mr. Gravelines who is going below to his post among the Arikara.

NOVEMBER 6.   Mr. Gravelines, Paul Primeau, La Jeunnesse, with two of our French boys [Roi and Degie ?] set out for the Arikara nation. We gave them directions to take an Arikara chief to Washington next spring. The geese are flying south, and the Missouri has frozen over an inch and a half thick. It was too cold to do much work on the fort.

NOVEMBER 7.   We continue to work on the cabins and chimneys. The captain's room was hewn down on the inside, and covered over with a tarpaulin and earth. Chief Shahaka came down to our camp and told us that buffalo were on the prairie. Capt. Lewis, Sgt. Gass and ten more men went out to hunt. They got eleven buffalo. The Indians on horseback got thirty or forty buffalo.

NOVEMBER 8.   René Jessaume, our Mandan interpreter, went up to the villages, and on his return, informed us that three Englishmen had arrived from the Hudson's Bay Company posts in Canada and would visit us to-morrow. Cottonwood timber is our hope for making shakes to roof our buildings. We had to give up the idea, however, for the wood is so twisted that it is impossible to split it. [Though not mentioned in their journals, the captains must have purchased, or borrowed, some horses from the Mandans about this time.]

NOVEMBER 9.   We are anxiously awaiting the return of our hunters, for we are in great want of fresh meat. Capt. Lewis walked to the hill back of our camp. We continue to build our cabins under many disadvantages.

NOVEMBER 10.   We finished raising the second line of cabins, and commenced hewing and guttering the puncheons for the purpose of covering them.

NOVEMBER 11.   Two of our men cut themselves with axes. Charbonneau's two wives came down to our camp. They brought four buffalo robes and gave them to the captains, who in turn gave them to the men. Sgt. Ordway got one.

NOVEMBER 12.   It is clear and cold today, so we continued building. We brought the load from the second pirogue into the store-room of the fort so that we could use her for hauling stones for making the chimneys. We are in want of meat, for the hunters have not yet returned. Three of our men are sick. Chief Shahaka and his squaw came down to our camp. She carried about one hundred pounds of meat, for which we gave presents. We also gave her an axe with which she was much pleased.

NOVEMBER 13.   We name our winter quarters "Fort Mandan." The ice in the river began to run, so we unloaded the keel-boat for fear that the ice would carry her off. We put the goods in our storage room though it is not yet quite completed. We were visited by Black Cat, the first chief of the Mandans along with a chief of the Assiniboines named, "The Crane," with seven of his head men. They live above the Mandans on the Missouri. They trade with the British fur companies, and are an ill disposed lot. Capt. Clark gave this last chief a gold cord and a carrot of tobacco for his men. The cord was given so that we would know him again. Whitehouse and five men went up to bring back the provisions we had obtained at the Mandan village.

NOVEMBER 14. We have a snowy morning. Drouillard and a Frenchman [Labiche ?] were sent down on horseback to meet the pirogue to see why the hunters are delayed so long. We are reduced to eating salt-pork. At dusk, two Frenchmen [Roi and Degie ?], arrived from trapping down the river. They had left us some days ago, and had caught twenty-two beaver. [So some did return.]

NOVEMBER 15. Drouillard and the Frenchman who were dispatched yesterday, returned from the hunters camp which is about thirty miles below. After an hour, we dispatched another Frenchman with orders to the hunters to proceed back without delay through the floating ice to the fort. We sent by him some tin to be put on the bow of the pirogue, and other parts exposed to the ice. We also sent along a tow-rope. All other hands are working on the cabins.

NOVEMBER 16. The trees about are covered with ice. The men moved into the rooms although they are not finished. They still need daubing with clay, etc. We had built a provision and smoke house 24 x 14 feet in size.

NOVEMBER 17. We are engaged in finishing our cabins to make them more comfortable. Several Indians visited us today, and one stayed all night. The Frenchman returned with a fat elk. Fat meat is most welcome, for most of the game is very poor and lean at this season.

NOVEMBER 18. Black Cat came to see us. He mentioned the friction between his tribe and the Assiniboines who get the major part of their supplies from the British traders, and therefore treat the Mandans badly. We told him to remain at peace, for the Mandans could in the future depend upon getting supplies from our traders coming up from the States, but it would require a little time to put this trade into operation.

NOVEMBER 19. We daubed our store and smoke house with clay. The hunters arrived from below bringing thirty-two deer, eleven elk and a buffalo. All this welcome supply was hung in our new smoke-house.

NOVEMBER 20. Our captains moved into their cabin. We work as usual making stone chimneys, etc. Charbonneau returned from the Gros Ventre Indians located up river, with four horses loaded with peltry, meat, etc. He brought another of his wives with him. This makes four now with us.

NOVEMBER 21. Sgt. Pryor and five men were sent in a pirogue up to the Mandan village for corn. We completed building the backs of the chimneys. Sgt. Pryor and party returned with about twelve bushels of corn. The Mandans had taken it out of the ground where they have it stored in holes about the village. Mr. Jessaume had been promised one hundred bushels, but only got thirty. We had some misunderstanding about one of the squaws who has been staying in the fort with one of the interpreter's wives. Her husband beat and stabbed her, and was about to kill her. The husband said that she had slept with Sgt. Ordway, and if he wanted her, he would give her to him. We directed Sgt. Ordway to give the man some presents, and further ordered that no man of this party have any intercourse with this woman under penalty of punishment. At this moment the Grand Chief, Black Cat, arrived and he lectured the husband. The husband and wife went off, apparently dissatisfied.

NOVEMBER 23. We are busy making a large rope of nine strands of elk skin for the purpose of drawing the keel-boat up onto the bank. We fixed up a rope works. John Shields is unwell with rheumatism.

NOVEMBER 24. Several of the men are sick with bad colds. We finished the rope, and cover our cabins with hewed puncheons. Our guard is reduced to a sergeant and three men, so we are making progress on the fort. The cabins are built in two rows of four rooms each, and are joined at a triangle at one end. When raised about seven feet high, a floor of puncheons or split planks are laid, and covered with grass and clay – over this, we have built a warm loft. The loft projects a foot over, and the roofs are made shed fashion – raising from the inner side of the triangle – making the outer wall about eighteen feet high. The part not enclosed by the buildings, we intend to close with a high picket fence. In the angle formed by the two rows of cabins, we have built two rooms, one for holding provisions and stores, the other for a smoke house.

NOVEMBER 25. Capt. Lewis, Charbonneau, Jessaume and six men set off this morning to go some twenty-four miles above to visit the Minnitaree in that neighborhood. The six men went in a pirogue, while Capt. Lewis and the interpreters went by horseback. Enroute, they met Francois-Antoine Larocque, a North West Company trader. In a very friendly manner, Capt. Lewis invited Mr. Larocque to visit with us at the fort. Capt. Lewis was surprised to find that his intended host, "Horned Weasel," "was not at home," so he and his party were obliged to find lodging elsewhere. These natives are accustomed to look upon every white man as an inferior being. One chief admitted that he admired the air gun, as it could discharge forty shots at one load, but he dreaded the magic of its owners. He said, "Had I these white warriors on the upper plains, my young men on horseback would soon do for them as they would do for so many wolves. There are only two sensible men among them, the worker of iron and the mender of guns." [2]

The balance of the party is completing the huts. Capt. Clark entertained two chiefs today. One is a Minnitaree – and the first of that nation to visit with us since we have been here. Our interpreters, being with Capt. Lewis, prevented Capt. Clark from being perfectly understood. He gave them presents and paid them particular attention – which pleased them very much. As it happened, Capt. Lewis was visiting their village at the time.

We have completed our huts just in time for the weather turned bitterly cold.

NOVEMBER 26. The wind shifted to the north-west and blew very hard with a keen, cold air, which confined us, and prevented us from working. Capt. Lewis and his party are still visiting the upper villages.

NOVEMBER 27. The river is crowded with floating ice. Capt. Lewis and his party returned from the Minnitaree villages with two chiefs of that nation. They are also called Gros Ventres or "Big Bellies." They were alarmed at the tales the Mandans had told them – of how we intended to join the Sioux and cut them off during the winter. Some circumstances we admit gave force to these tales – our building a big fort – the interpreters and their wives moving in with us at the fort, etc. Some of these tales had been given them by the North West Co's. traders, such as Mr. Baptiste La France, who has taken it upon himself to speak unfavorably about us.[3] These chiefs said they were glad they had come to see us and hear our straight talk.

Mr. Larocque asked Charbonneau to come and help him interpret among the Minnitarees. Charbonneau replied, that being engaged with us Americans, he could not do so without the captain's permission. Capt. Lewis told Mr. Larocque that he was willing for Charbonneau to help him, provided he would not be caused to say anything to the natives which might prejudice them against us or the United States.

We had a dance this evening. Francois Rivet "danced on his head," that

---

[2] L. R. Masson, *Les Bourgeois de la Compagnie du Nord-ouest,* Quebec, 1889-90, v. I, p. 330.

[3] Jean Baptiste La France had accompanied Jessaumé to the Mandan nation in 1793-4, and also in 1797. Nasatir, *op. cit.,* 105, 502.

is, he danced upside down on his hands. The chiefs were delighted at our fun, and have a better impression of us.

NOVEMBER 28. There was some jealousy between George Gibson and George Drouillard last evening. Perhaps the cause of the misunderstanding is because Sgt. Ordway says that Gibson is one of our interpreters.

NOVEMBER 29. We set about unrigging the keel-boat, and by accident one of the sergeants [Pryor?], dislocated his shoulder. We took out the mast and everything on the boat, and let her lay on the river's edge.

NOVEMBER 30. A Mandan Indian informed us that a few days ago eight of his men were out hunting and were attacked by a party of Sioux, who killed one of their men, and wounded two more – and also carried off nine of their horses. Our captains thought it wise to offer the Mandans assistance if they were disposed to fight the Sioux. Capt. Clark, Charbonneau, Sgt. Ordway and twenty-two men volunteered, and immediately set out with the intention of pursuing the Sioux. They went up to the first village, but the Mandan warriors did not seem disposed to turn out. They suggested that the weather was too cold; the Sioux too far gone, etc., and put off the expedition until spring. Therefore, Capt. Clark and the party returned to the fort. The Mandans appeared pleased that we would help them. They used us very friendly, and had the party eat in every lodge they went in. Our officers gave every man a drink of Taffee Rum – which we stood in need of.

DECEMBER 1st, 1804. Charbonneau left with Mr. Larocque and Mr. Baptiste Turenne for the Minnitaree village. We commenced bringing in the pickets and prepared a very high picket fence to enclose the opening between the two rows of huts.

In the evening we were visited by Mr. George Henderson, a trader from the Hudson's Bay Company. He brought tobacco, beads and other merchandise to trade for furs, and a few guns to trade with the Mandans for horses. We have assured them they are free to trade in our country.

DECEMBER 2. The Indians reported buffalo were on the plains. Capt. Lewis and fifteen men turned out to hunt.

DECEMBER 3. The men are busy putting up pickets at the Fort.

DECEMBER 4. We discover that our interpreter, René Jessaume, is an assuming, arrogant and discontented man.

DECEMBER 5. We laid a platform over the store room and smoke house as a place for the sentinel to walk.

DECEMBER 6. It was too cold today to work. In the night the river froze over an inch and a half thick. Capt. Clark set out with a hunting party. They camped out overnight.

DECEMBER 7. Capt. Clark and party returned with eight buffalo. Capt. Lewis went hunting with a party of eleven men. They killed eleven buffalo. The weather was so cold and the wolves so numerous that they saved only five of them.

DECEMBER 8. The captains alternate with hunting parties. Capt. Clark, Sgt. Ordway and a party of fifteen went out today. Several of the men were badly frost-bit. York's feet and private parts were frosted a little. Two of the men were hurt by slipping on the ice. Two men remained with the meat and camped out all night. It is twelve degrees below zero today and the geese are flying south – too high to get any of them.

DECEMBER 9. Capt. Lewis, Sgt. Gass and eleven men – with four horses (three hired and one bought) went out to bring in the meat killed yesterday – and to hunt more. Charbonneau and Jessaume went to the Mandan village. Capt. Lewis and party stayed overnight at the hunting camp some five miles from the fort. They used the hides from the buffalo for shelter from the cold.

DECEMBER 10. After a breakfast on marrow bones, Capt. Lewis, Sgt. Gass, and three others returned to the fort. The five men left behind camped there. On Capt. Lewis' return, they met one of our men who was going down with the horses to bring in meat. At evening, two of the hunters came in with the horses loaded. The men who were frost-bitten are recovering.

DECEMBER 11. We sent some men and three horses to bring back meat and to tell all the hunters to return to the fort as soon as possible. Black Cat, the Grand Chief of the Mandans, paid us a visit.

DECEMBER 12. Capt. Clark lined his gloves, and had a cap made from the skin of a lynx. Many antelope are near the Fort, but the captains feel that the men's constitutions should be hardened gradually before going out in this severe climate. We are making three small sleds to haul meat on. Our rooms are very close and warm, so we can keep ourselves comfortable in this sub-zero weather. The sentinel, who stood in the open weather, had to be relieved every hour all this day. It is thirty-eight degrees below zero.

DECEMBER 13. We have two sleds ready. Two men went out and killed two buffalo. One man came back, and five men went out with him – taking a sled, and brought in the two buffalo. Two of the men of Sgt. Ordway's mess went up to the first village and brought back some corn and beans in exchange for paint and a few rings. Mr. Hugh Heney of the North West Company, came down from the Minnitaree village to visit us. He was co-operative and intelligent, and gave us information of the country which lies between the Mississippi and the Missouri, and of the tribes which inhabit the land.[4] Joseph Fields killed a buffalo cow and calf a mile from our fort.

DECEMBER 14.   Capt. Clark and fourteen men went out hunting and they took the three sleds with them. In the evening, five of the men returned. Capt. Clark and the other nine men camped out overnight.

DECEMBER 15.   Capt. Clark and his party returned to the fort today. Sgt. Ordway with one or two of the party, went to the village. The buffalo have left the river.

DECEMBER 16.   Sgt. Gass and some of the men visited the Mandan village. Three traders, George Henderson, Francois A. Larocque and George Bunch, from the North West Company, came to the fort and brought a letter to the captains.[5] They stayed all night with us. The object of their visit was to ascertain our motives for visiting this country, and to gain information with respect to the change of government over this land. Our captains told them that one of their interpreters, Mr. Baptiste La France, had been making unfavorable remarks to the Indians about our party. They were warned of the consequences if they did not put a stop to all such ill-founded expressions. Mr. Larocque was told that the captains had heard that he intended to give flags and medals to the Indians. He was forbidden to do so, as this act would be objectionable to our Government.[6]

DECEMBER 17.   It is forty-five degrees below zero today, so we all remained in garrison. Sgt. Gass fitted up one of the sleds for the trader, Mr. George Bunch, to return to his post with.

DECEMBER 18.   Eight of our men went out to hunt, but saw nothing but antelope. Mr. Heney and Mr. Larocque set off this morning despite the

---

[4] Hugh Heney (Henney - Enné – etc.), a former Montreal innkeeper, had led a trading expedition from St. Louis to the Mandans in 1800. In 1801 he was in partnership with Regis Loisel, being outfitted by Chouteau and Clamorgan of St. Louis. In 1804 he joined the North West Company. Nasatir, *op. cit.,* 114.

[5] Larocque was the leader of a group of traders who came down from Fort Assiniboine. The following spring he tried to join the Lewis and Clark party to the upper Missouri, but was turned down by the captains. After they had departed, Larocque took a small party and explored the Yellowstone River in the summer of 1805. His journal of this trip is found in *Publications of the Canadian Archives,* Ottawa, 1910, no. 3, 17.   [6] Masson, vol. I, pp. 304, 307.

frigid weather. We sent René Jessaume to Black Cat to know why he took Charbonneau's horse. The reason was that Mr. La France, the North West Company trader, had told the chief that Charbonneau owed him a horse. The sentinel pacing the roof of our fort had to be changed each half hour because of the intense cold.

DECEMBER 19. We went about setting up the pickets. Capt. Clark is working on his maps and papers – adding information received from the traders.

DECEMBER 20. We are busy extending the picket fence down to the river.

DECEMBER 21. We are bringing in pickets and setting them about the fort. The Indian who was stopped from killing his wife on Nov. 22nd, came in and brought his two wives, and showed great anxiety to make up with Sgt. Ordway. A woman brought a child with an abcess on the lower part of its back and offered as much corn as she could carry for medicine. Capt. Lewis cheerfully administered to the child.

DECEMBER 22. A great number of squaws, and men dressed like squaws, came with corn, beans and moccasins to trade. They took any trifling thing in exchange – old shirts, buttons, knives, awls and other merchandise pleasing to their eye.

DECEMBER 23. We are putting pickets around our fort. A chief brought his wife and son loaded with corn. She made us a favorite Mandan dish – a mixture of pumpkins, beans, corn and choke-berries all boiled together in a kettle. It was by no means unpalatable. The chiefs are fond of sleeping in the fort. We find them troublesome to have about as they are curious about everything.

DECEMBER 24. We finished the pickets around the fort, and erected a blacksmith's shop. In the evening the captains distributed some flour, pepper, dried apples, etc., to our party so we could celebrate Christmas in a proper and social manner.

DECEMBER 25. We ushered in the day with a discharge of the swivel gun, one round of small arms by all the party, and then another from the swivel. Capt. Clark presented a glass of brandy to each of the men. We hoisted the American flag, and each man had another glass of brandy. We prepared one of the rooms for dancing – which was kept up until 8 p.m., all without the company of the female sex, except the three squaws of the interpreters, who only looked on. The captains had requested the natives to stay away on this, our great medicine day.

DECEMBER 26.   Mr. William Morrison, a trader from the North West Company, came down from the Gros Ventres to get Charbonneau to assist him in trading.[7] Seven of our men went up to the Mandan village.

DECEMBER 27.   We laid a floor in the interpreter's room, and finished the blacksmith's shop. The Indians are surprised at the bellows and the method of making articles of iron. John Shields is our head blacksmith.

DECEMBER 28.   Nothing remarkable today. We have the usual Indian visitors.

DECEMBER 29.   We finished the floor in the interpreter's room. The natives brought axes and kettles for the blacksmith to repair, and gave corn, beans and squashes in trade. One Indian visitor stole a drawing knife, but we took it back again. Generally these people are honest.

DECEMBER 30.   The Mandans continue to trade food stuffs for blacksmiths work. One deer was killed and one of the men shot a wolf.

DECEMBER 31.   The Indians came to have their utensils repaired for which they bring corn to trade. Three of our men went for timber to make dugout canoes. We live in peace and tranquility.

---

[7] William Morrison was a voyager of the North West Co., and had accompanied Larocque from Fort Assiniboine in Canada. They left there on November 11, and arrived at the Mandans on November 25, 1804.

6

At Fort Mandan

JANUARY 1, 1805. Two guns were discharged from the swivel to usher in the New Year, and each man of the party fired a round of small arms. A glass of old ardent spirits was given to the men. About 10 a.m., one of the interpreters, Sgt. Ordway and about half of the party went, at the Mandans request, to the first village to dance. We took fiddles, tambourines, Jew's harps and a sounden horn. Francois Rivet danced up-side-down, and everyone danced around him. The Mandans gave us food and buffalo robes, and were very much pleased to see our dance. Somewhat later, Capt. Clark with three men came up. This evening, he and some of the men went back to the fort. The balance stayed all night with the Mandans.

JANUARY 2. Capt. Lewis, Sgt. Gass and a greater part of the party went to the second village to frolic in the same manner as the party did yesterday. The Indians used them very friendly. A number of the Indians and squaws came to the fort. They brought us some corn to pay the blacksmiths to repair their axes, bridles, etc. Most of the men returned in the evening. We discover that the Mandans feed their horses cottonwood tree branches to sustain them through the winter.

JANUARY 3. Eight hunters went out for game, but obtained only one old bull buffalo. One of the men killed a beautiful white hare.

JANUARY 4. Nine of the hunters went out, and three of them stayed out all night – the rest came back. Capt. Clark is rather unwell.

JANUARY 5. Capt. Clark is employed drawing a map of the country from the information he has obtained from the chiefs and traders. At the first village, the natives have been having a "Buffalo Dance" for the past three nights. During this dance they offer their wives for intercourse. We sent one of our men to this dance and he was given four girls. This dance is to cause the buffalo to come near the river so that they can kill them.

JANUARY 6. William Bratton caught a fox in a steel trap at the place where the fox had gnawed a hole through the pickets. Chief Shahaka, or "Big White," as he is also known, dined with us and gave Capt. Clark a sketch of the country as far as the High [Rocky] Mountains. He also described the country on the south side of the Missouri River.

JANUARY 7.   Three men returned from down the river where they had been hunting. Capt. Clark continued to add to his map, material from his own observations and that given by the traders and Indians. From this information he learns that the Great Falls of the Missouri are estimated to be about five hundred miles directly west of us.

JANUARY 8.   We sent Sgt. Ordway to observe the "Medicine Dance" now being performed at the Mandan villages.

JANUARY 9.   Capt. Clark, with three or four men, accompanied by a chief and a party of Indians, went off to hunt. They obtained some buffalo, but we are uneasy for one of our men who became separated during the chase and has not yet returned. A young Indian, thirteen years old, came to the fort with his feet frozen. Capt. Lewis doctored him by putting his feet in cold water. His feet are coming to. Three men are out hunting and they intend to stay several days.

JANUARY 10.   Five men got ready to hunt and look for the man who stayed out all night, but before they started. the man came in. He had made a fire and was fairly comfortable last night. John Newman, with an ardent wish to atone for the mutinous expressions he had made in an unguarded moment, is exerting himself to be useful. He has exposed himself too much, and has his feet and hands frozen.[1]

JANUARY 11.   We sent out three men to join the three men at the hunting camp below our fort. Charbonneau's oldest wife is sick. Two of the hunters came in. They had killed three elk.

JANUARY 12.   Joseph and Reuben Fields took a sled and went down to the hunting camp for meat.

JANUARY 13.   Charbonneau and one of the men who had gone with him to the Minnitarees returned with their faces much frost-bitten. He informs us that the agents of the Hudson's Bay Company had been endeavoring to make unfavorable impressions regarding us, and that the North West Company intended to build a fort at the Minnitaree village.

JANUARY 14.   Sgt. Pryor and five men went out hunting and will stay several days. George Shannon came in this afternoon and told us that Joseph Whitehouse had his feet frost-bitten and could not come in without a horse. Shannon and John Collins had killed a buffalo, a wolf, two porcupines and a white hare. Several men have the venereal – caught from the Mandan women.

---

[1] Last two sentences adapted from the letter Lewis wrote to Henry Dearborn, Washington, Jan. 15, 1807, appearing in Jackson, 365.

JANUARY 15. We were visited by four of the most distinguished chiefs of the Minnitarees. We showed them marked attention, as we knew that they had been taught to entertain prejudices against us. These we succeeded in removing. Whitehouse was brought in and given care. His case is not too serious. Shannon was sent with the horses down to the hunters camp. To-night we had a total eclipse of the moon which helped the captains determine the longitude of this place.

JANUARY 16. We had a conference between the Mandans and the Minnitarees. There has been a misunderstanding regarding us which we tried to clarify. The Minnitaree chief told us he was planning a war against the Shoshoni tribe to the west. We convinced him that this would displease our President, etc. [It appears he made war anyway.] He gave us a simple chart of the upper Missouri River. Four of our men who had been hunting returned, one was badly frosted. Several squaws, loaded with corn, came for blacksmith's work.

JANUARY 17. It is blizzardly and cold, so not much happened.

JANUARY 18. Mr. Larocque and Mr. Mackenzie of the N.W. Company, and several Gros Ventres came to see us. This afternoon two of our hunters returned with four deer, four wolves and a badger. They told us that Sgt. Pryor's party had killed three elk, four deer, and two porcupines.

JANUARY 19. We sent two men with three horses and the sleds down on the river ice to the hunting camp. It is thirty miles distant from the fort. Mr. Larocque and Mr. Mackenzie returned to their post. Jessaume's squaw left him and returned to her village.

JANUARY 20. Some misunderstanding took place between Jessaume and Charbonneau on account of their squaws. Sacagawea is pregnant and sick. York had been ordered to give her some stewed fruit and tea at different times – which was the cause of the misunderstanding. The natives bring us considerable corn in exchange for blacksmith's work. Capt. Clark, hearing that Mr. Larocque's horses were in danger of being stolen up at his post, offered to take care of them along with our own. White Wolf, a Minnitaree chief, came down to the fort to get his gun mended. Though these Indians were suspicious of us at first, they are now very fond of us, for our smith is always employed making different things for the Indians.

The hunters returned to the fort, the horses loaded with deer and elk meat. Sgt. Gass and one of the men went to the village where they were treated very well.

JANUARY 21. Two of our men went up to the Gros Ventres village to trade some wolf skins with the North West traders for some tobacco. They got three feet of tobacco for each wolf skin. Our men use much tobacco.

JANUARY 22. The cold having moderated, all hands attempted to cut the keel-boat and pirogues out of the ice. We were obliged to desist because the water gushed out between the layers of ice – so we could not use the axes.

JANUARY 23. Two of our men are making sleds for the natives. For this they give us corn and beans.

JANUARY 24. Five of our men are employed in cutting timbers to make charcoal for the forge. The hunters who have been out, returned very successful.

JANUARY 25. Our men are generally employed in cutting and splitting fire-wood and setting up a charcoal pit. Others, under Sgt. Gass, are cutting away the ice from around the boats. They find this tedious work.

JANUARY 26. One of our men has come down with pleurisy. Capt. Lewis bled him and applied remedies common to that disorder. The party continue making charcoal and cutting the ice from the boats. John Shields, our head blacksmith, makes war axes and ordinary axes for the natives. These are exchanged for corn, which is fortunate for us, as we could not bring enough provisions with us to sustain our large party over the winter.

JANUARY 27. Some of our men are employed in cutting hay from the prairie to cover the coke-kiln. We were forced to take off the toes of that young Indian boy who was so badly frost-bitten on January 9th. Charbonneau returned, bringing three of Mr. Larocque's horses. The latter wished to have them kept with ours so they would not be stolen by the Assiniboines.

JANUARY 28. The man with pleurisy is getting well. René Jessaume was unwell this evening. All hands are employed in cutting the ice from around the keel-boat. We used large pries in an attempt to shake her loose, but we found that considerable more ice cutting is necessary.

JANUARY 29. We gave Jessaume a dose of salts. We heated stones with the view of warming the water in the keel-boat, and by that means to separate her from the ice. We were defeated – for the stones fly all to pieces in the fire when we heat them.

JANUARY 30. Sgt. Gass and a party of men went up the river to find a different kind of stone, but we found that these burst in the same manner – so the keel-boat and pirogues remain fast in the ice. We are obliged to give up that plan.

Mr. Larocque arrived at 2 p.m., to get his compass fixed. The glass is broken and the needle will not point due north. He wanted to see how his horses were and also would like to accompany us on our western journey this spring. This last proposal our captains thought best to decline. Capt. Lewis repaired his compass very well – which took him most of the day.

JANUARY 31.   René Jessaume is some better. Drouillard was taken with the pleurisy last evening. Capt. Lewis bled him and gave him some sage tea. This morning he is much better. Five of the men went hunting and took two horses with them.

FEBRUARY 1, 1805.   Our five hunters came back today, but had killed nothing. One of Jessaume's squaws has taken sick. Mr. Larocque left us today. One man went out and killed a deer.

FEBRUARY 2.   Our interpreter, George Drouillard, is still unwell. Sgt. Ordway burned his hat accidentally. A hunter went a short distance from the fort and killed a deer – and packed it in.

FEBRUARY 3.   John Shields, now having a new supply of charcoal, resumed his blacksmith operations. Our boats are in an alarming condition – firmly enclosed in the ice, and covered with snow. The ice about them lies in several strata of unequal thickness, and are separated with streams of water. When we cut through one thickness, the water gushes up so high that it is impossible to cut away at the lower strata. As a last resort we are preparing some iron spikes, attached to poles, to pry the boats up. We have already prepared a large rope of elk skins, and a windlass for pulling it.

FEBRUARY 4.   Capt. Clark and René Jessaume and sixteen men with the sleds, are out hunting. The game is scarce, and our provisions of meat is nearly exhausted. We must have plenty, for our present needs as well as to prepare more for use on our voyage this coming spring. John Shields killed two deer, both very lean. One of them had shed its horns.

FEBRUARY 5.   We were visited by many natives who brought corn for blacksmith's work. We were running out of iron, so the blacksmith uses an old iron stove which we had used, and had burnt out while we were ascending the Missouri, as a source. He makes iron scrapers and battle axes for them. A piece about four inches square will trade for seven or eight gallons of corn. The blacksmiths, Shields, Willard and Bratton, are our greatest resource for procuring corn. This work brings more than our few trade articles will buy, and we need to conserve these few for use on our long journey ahead.

FEBRUARY 6.   John Shields killed three antelope. The men bring them in.

FEBRUARY 7.   The captains ordered a lock be put on the gate of our fort, for one of the interpreter's wives has been unbarring it during the night. We order that no person be admitted from sun-set to sun-rise.

FEBRUARY 8.   Black Cat, chief of the Mandans, visited us today. This man possesses more integrity, firmness and intelligence than any other we have met. Capt. Lewis thinks he can be made a useful agent in furthering the views of our Government. He dined with us and stated he had not tasted meat for several days, his people suffer very much for lack of it. We gave his squaw a looking-glass and some needles, and his son some fish-hooks in exchange for the moccasins they had given us. We hear that Capt. Clark's hunting party have killed ten elk and eighteen deer. They had built a pen to secure the meat from the wolves.

FEBRUARY 9.   Mr. Charles Mackenzie visits with us.[2] This evening, Thomas Howard, whom Capt. Lewis had given permission to visit the Mandan village, returned after the gate was locked. Rather than call the guard to have it opened, he scaled the works. An Indian, who had been looking on, followed his example. Howard was committed to the guard. As he is an old soldier, this bad example heightens the offense.

FEBRUARY 10.   Mr. Mackenzie left us. Charbonneau returned with one of our Frenchmen and informed us that he had left below three horses and two men with the meat, but the horses could not cross the ice, not being shod.

FEBRUARY 11.   Six men were sent down the river with two sleds to bring up the meat. The horses were brought back by land so they could be shod. Sacagawea, Charbonneau's wife, was delivered of a fine boy. René Jessaume informed Capt. Lewis that the natives administered a small portion of the rattle of the rattlesnake in such cases, which hastened the birth of a child. This being the first birth of Sacagawea, and the labor tedious – the pain was violent. Capt. Lewis, having a rattle near by, broke two rings in small pieces, which with some water, was given to her. In ten minutes time, she brought forth, although Capt. Lewis was not sure that the rattle was the remedy. The hunting party had killed much game, and had put the meat up on scaffolds to keep it safe from the wolves.

---

[2] Mackenzie, who apparently had little respect for Canadians who joined the Americans, says: "A mulatto (Drouillard), who spoke bad French and worse English, served as interpreter to the captains, so that a single word to be understood by the party required to pass from the natives to the woman (Sacagawea), from the woman to the husband (Charbonneau), from the husband to the mulatto, and from the mulatto to the captains." Masson, I, p. 336-37.

FEBRUARY 12.   Capt. Clark, Sgt. Gass and party arrived at the fort. John Shields is busy shoeing the horses. Drouillard arrived with the rest of the horses. While on the hunt, Joseph Fields had one ear frost-bitten.

FEBRUARY 13.   Two men were sent eighteen miles down the river to butcher an elk taken yesterday. They arrived late in the evening at the fort.

FEBRUARY 14.   Drouillard, Robert Frazier, Silas Goodrich and John Newman were sent with the shod horses and two sleds down for the meat which Capt. Clark's party had killed. Twenty-two miles below they were rushed by 106 Sioux who robbed them of their two horses – so they returned. At midnight, Capt. Lewis called for twenty volunteers – who immediately turned out. The Mandan chiefs were advised, and a few of their warriors are to set out with Capt. Lewis and his men.

FEBRUARY 15.   At sunrise, Capt. Lewis, Sgt. Ordway, Sgt. Gass and a party of twenty-four set out in the pursuit of the Sioux. One of the chiefs returned, and informed Capt. Clark that the Sioux had burned part of the meat. They had found one of the scaffolds, but not the other.

FEBRUARY 16.   Thomas P. Howard returned from below with his feet frosted. Capt. Lewis and party are still trailing the Sioux.

FEBRUARY 17.   Capt. Lewis' party concluded not to follow the Sioux any more, but to return to hunting. In this they were successful. Mr. Mackenzie visited the fort. One of the horses the Sioux had stolen belonged to him. One of the Mandan chiefs brought some dried buffalo meat and some tallow to the fort.

FEBRUARY 18.   Mr. Mackenzie left today. Our stock of meat is exhausted, so that we confine ourselves to corn and beans. Capt. Clark is making a descriptive list of the rivers which flow into the Missouri above the fort.

FEBRUARY 19.   Capt. Lewis, Sgt. Ordway, Sgt. Gass and party started to return to the fort. They fleeced the meat and ate the marrow from the bones. One horse draws a sled, the other, heavily loaded with meat, is led by the party of fifteen men on the river ice. They killed a deer on the way back. At the fort, our smiths, Shields, Bratton and Willard, are engaged in making and repairing axes in exchange for corn.

FEBRUARY 20.   Most of the hunting party returned to the fort. Others, under Sgt. Ordway, are left behind to hunt and bring in elk.

FEBRUARY 21.   Sgt. Ordway's party got in before sunset with all the meat and skins. The men are much fatigued by the cold and heavy, 2400-pound load. We had some rain this evening – the first since last November. It cleared in the afternoon so we put our clothes out to sun.

FEBRUARY 22. Two of our hunters arrived from below. We cleared the snow from around the keel-boat and pirogues.

FEBRUARY 23. All of the party are engaged in cutting the ice from around the boats. By evening, by hard cutting and use of pries, we got one pirogue loose and pulled it out and turned it over on its side. We loosened the ice from around the other pirogue. The father of the Indian boy whose foot had been so badly frozen, and which we had now cured, came today and carried him home on a sleigh.

FEBRUARY 24. We freed the other pirogue and worked at cutting out the keel-boat. The caulking had come out in places and the keel-boat was leaking. We found the leak and fixed it.

FEBRUARY 25. We drew the pirogues up on the bank. The keel-boat was too heavy for our elk skin rope which constantly broke. We had prepared rollers and skids. Night came on, and we had to leave her on the skids.

FEBRUARY 26. We got timber, doubled the ropes, and raised the keel-boat. We got the windlass working, and after much difficulty, got the boat safe on the bank. This operation attracted a great number of Indians who watched us. Some of the chiefs requested permission to stay all night with us — which was granted.

FEBRUARY 27. We prepare our tools to build more canoes to use on our western journey, as we intend to send the keel-boat back to St. Louis. Capt. Clark commences drawing a duplicate map of the Missouri country. The men are fixing skids on the keel-boat to save her from injury, and are moving the pirogues to the shady, north side of the fort to keep the sun from cracking them. Four men are assigned to build canoes. We need four, and intend to use these, along with the pirogues, for the western voyage.

FEBRUARY 28. Mr. Heney of the N.W. Company, sent us by two men, letters and also the root of a plant they use to cure the bite of mad dogs, snakes, etc. We sent out, under Sgt. Gass, sixteen men to find timber to make the four canoes. They inform us that they found trees some distance up the Missouri which they hoped would anwer for boats. They made camp there. Mr. Joseph Gravelines, Peter Roi and another Frenchman, Mr. Croix, with two Indians, arrived from the Arikara with letters from Mr. Pierre Antoine Tabeau. He sends us information of the tribes to the south.

MARCH 1, 1805. The whole party are engaged in making ropes and canoes, making charcoal, and making battle axes to trade for corn. The party making canoes are at work at their camp. Some of their men came down to the fort to get supplies and have their axes sharpened. They then returned to their camp. Capt. Clark is busy making a copy of his maps.

MARCH 2.   Everyone is busy preparing for our departure. Mr. Larocque visits us and informs us of the English fur companies. The blacksmiths are busy making articles for the Mandans and keeping our tools in order. The Missouri began to break up in places.

MARCH 3.   The men are busy packing and making other preparations.

MARCH 4.   An engagé from the North West Company came for a horse. He requested in the name of his trader, some silk of three colors – which we furnished him.

MARCH 5.   We sent back with Mr. Croix and an Indian a letter to Mr. Tabeau at the Arikara nation. The men are making charcoal, etc.

MARCH 6.   Several of the Gros Ventre Indians stayed with us over night. Some Mandans came this morning with corn. The water now runs over the ice which makes it difficult to cross the river.

MARCH 7.   Some of the men from the boat camp came to the fort last night. They took provisions and returned today. A chief brought a sick child. Capt. Lewis gave him some of Dr. Benjamin Rush's pills.

MARCH 8.   We were visited by two Indians who gave us an account of the country and people near the Rocky Mountains. The Mandans continue to bring corn, tallow and dried meat in exchange for blacksmiths work.

MARCH 9.   Capt. Clark walked up about five miles to the boat-builders' camp to see the party. On the way he met "Le Borgne," the head chief of the Minnitaree, along with four Indians who were on their way to visit our fort for the first time. Capt. Clark inspected the canoes and found them well along. He then went to the upper Mandan village and smoked a pipe with the chief there. Upon his return to the fort, he found La Borgne about to return home. Capt. Lewis gave him a medal, arm bands, a flag, shirt, scarlet cloth, etc., with which he was much pleased. This chief had lost one eye, hence his nickname, "Le Borgne" or, "one-eyed." He said he had heard that we had a black man among us, and wished to know if this were true. We sent for York. Le Borgne examined him closely; rubbed his skin and spit on his finger to see if the color would come off. Only when York showed his short, kinky hair, was Le Borgne convinced that he was not a painted white man.

MARCH 10.   We were visited by a chief of the Moccasin tribe who stayed all night. He gave us accounts of his nation. His people live on the upper Knife River and are related to the Mandans.

MARCH 11.   We determined to have two additional canoes made to transport our provisions. We have every reason to believe that Charbonneau has been corrupted by the North West Company. We gave him the night to reflect and decide if he intends to go with us or not under the terms we have agreed on.

MARCH 12.   Two of our men went up to the traders at the Gros Ventres to get some tobacco. Charbonneau decided he will not go with us if he has to work, stand guard – or if miffed at any man, he wishes to return if he pleases. Also he wants the disposal of as much provisions as he chooses to carry. These terms are inadmissable to us, so we suffer him to be off the engagement.

MARCH 13.   Mr. Mackenzie, the N.W. Co. trader, arrived to see our captains. Our blacksmiths have not had a moments leisure, for so many Indians are anxious for battle axes. They produce an abundance of corn in exchange.

MARCH 14.   The day being warm and clear, we have all our Indian articles set out to dry before packing for our departure. Mr. Charbonneau has pitched a lodge outside our fort and has moved out. Mr. Joseph Gravelines has joined us in his place. The balance of the party are building boats and shelling corn.

MARCH 15.   We put out the parched corn, clothing, etc., to sun and dry.

MARCH 16.   One Indian is much displeased because Joseph Whitehouse struck his hand with a spoon while eating. Mr. Joseph Garreau, an Arikara trader, showed us the way the Arikara Indians make their large beads. This method is a secret confined to a few Mandans and Arikara. Two men are employed in hauling corn to the fort.

MARCH 17.   Mr. Charbonneau sent us an apology for his recent improper conduct, and agreed to go with us and perform the same duties as the rest of the corps; therefore we took him again in our service. William Werner has lost his tomahawk – he expects that the Indians stole it.

MARCH 18.   Two men came down from the boat camp for provisions, and two men went up to the Gros Ventres village. Capt. Clark and two men are packing up the Indian goods in eight divisions so as to preserve a portion of each in the event of accident. Charbonneau enlisted with us as an interpreter this evening. Capt. Clark is unwell.

MARCH 19.   Shahaka and Little Crow, Mandan chiefs, and a man, wife and sick child, visit with us. Capt. Clark gave some medicine to the child. Sgt. Gass came down to the fort to report that the canoes are finished and he needs more help to draw them the mile-and-a-half to the river.

MARCH 20. Capt. Clark and six men went up to help draw the canoes to the river. Capt. Clark later visited Black Cat and smoked with the chief and several old men to keep up our good diplomatic relations.

MARCH 21. The canoes were hauled to the river and all the men, except those who were left to watch them, returned to the fort. Capt. Clark on his way down, collected some pumice stones, plants and other curiosities.

MARCH 22. We were visited by the second chief of the Minnitarees. We gave him a medal and some presents. Mr. Mackenzie and Mr. Larocque also came to see us. Mr. Mackenzie writes: "We became intimate with the Americans, who on all occasions seemed happy to see us. . . Capt. Lewis could speak fluently and learnedly on all subjects, but his inveterate disposition against the British stained, at least in our eyes, all his eloquence. Capt. Clark was equally well informed, but his conversation was always pleasant, for he seemed to dislike giving offence unnecessarily." [3] They stayed with us all night, and saw the men dance, which is the common amusement of the men. Francois Rivet took home his pirogue. [Took back his pirogue from among ours? As we shall see, he did not depart for the Arikara at this time. This statement would indicate that he had spent most of the winter at Fort Mandan.]

---

[3] Masson, *op. cit.*, I, p. 336.

FORT MANDAN

From a painting, based on historical research, made for this work by Charles G. Clarke.

7

Fort Mandan to Yellowstone River

MARCH 23. Our visitors of yesterday departed. A brother of Le Borgne, with some other Indians, came to the fort. He gave us a vocabulary of his nation.

MARCH 24. We are busy preparing for our journey. Six men went up to bring the canoes down to the fort, but they returned about noon without them as they are not calked nor ready. Two men made cages for the magpies and prairie-hens which are to be sent down the river to Washington.

MARCH 25. Two men are making a steering oar for the keel-boat. Others are shelling corn. The river rose nine inches, and the ice began breaking away so as to endanger our canoes. Swans and geese are flying to the north-east.

MARCH 26. Several men are sent up for the canoes. About 2 p.m., they returned with four of them, but before they had landed, the ice started out. Therefore, we had to speedily draw them in to shore so that they might not suffer any injury. The ice stopped running, and jammed up several times, but stopped completely before night.

MARCH 27. We brought all of the canoes to the fort and went to calking them – and getting everything ready for our voyage.

MARCH 28. Our canoes are tinned over and are now ready. We intend to set out as soon as the river is sufficiently clear of ice to permit us to pass.

MARCH 29. The ice came down in great quantities. We have few Indian visitors today as they are busy catching the floating buffalo stranded on the blocks of ice in the river.

MARCH 30. All of our goods were exposed to the sun and the keel-boat was calked and made ready to descend the Missouri. The plains have been set afire on both sides of the river for the benefit of the horses, and to bring buffalo to the Indians. Our party is generally healthy except for a few men who have venereal complaints.

MARCH 31. The ice does not run as thick as it did yesterday. All of the party are in high spirits. But few nights pass without a dance.

APRIL 1, 1805. We put the keel-boat and pirogues into the water and began packing and loading the cases to be sent to St. Louis.

APRIL 2.   We are writing and preparing dispatches all day. Capt. Clark concluded to send his rough journal in its original state to President Jefferson for his perusal. He has written it every night from May 13th, 1804, and will finish it tomorrow, April 3rd, 1805. This has left him little time to write to his family and friends. Mr. Mackenzie and Mr. Larocque visit us today. Mr. Mackenzie wishes us to pay for his horse which was stolen when our men were robbed by the Tetons. We shall pay this man.

APRIL 3.   The articles which were to be sent back to the States were boxed and are ready to go on board. John Newman asked forgiveness and begged to be permitted to continue with the overland party. Though he stood acquitted in the captains' minds, Capt. Lewis deemed it impolitic to relax the sentence, so he will be returned to St. Louis.

APRIL 4.   We packed a stuffed male and female antelope, a weasel, three squirrels, the skeleton of a prairie wolf and other animals. Also a number of articles of Indian dress, a buffalo robe – highly ornamented, bows and arrows, Indian tobacco seed, Mandan corn, boxes of plants, another of insects, three cages of burrowing squirrels, a prairie hen and four magpies – all alive. Mr. Larocque and Mr. Mackenzie left us for the last time.

APRIL 5.   We sorted our loading and divided a proportion of each sort for each boat. We loaded the two pirogues and got ready to start on our journey.

APRIL 6.   The Mandans continue to come to the fort. They informed us of the arrival of a party of Arikara on the other side of the river. We sent our interpreter and two Frenchmen to inquire the reason for their coming. Our captains decided to wait until they know the meaning of this visit.

APRIL 7.   Our men returned with an Arikara chief and three of his people. He brought a letter from Mr. Tabeau which mentioned the wish of their Grand Chief to visit the President, and requesting permission for himself and four men to join our boat when it descends. The captains consent to this as it will then be manned by fifteen hands and be able to defend itself against the Teton Sioux. [Sgt. Gass says there were thirteen men in the returning party.]

The Arikara Chief, Kah-hah We-to (Raven Brave), requested that one of his men who was lame, might descend in the boat. This we agree to. We have but little doubt that the returning party will be fired on by the Sioux, but they have pledged themselves to us that they will not yield while there is a man of them living.

We dismissed the keel-boat and crew, with orders to return without loss of time to St. Louis. A small canoe with two Frenchmen accompanies the keel-boat. These men had ascended the Missouri with us last year as engagés. The keel-boat crew consisted of six soldiers and two Frenchmen. Two Frenchmen and a lame Arikara also take passage down in her as far as the Arikara villages, at which place they expect Mr. Tabeau to embark with his party, who in that case will make an addition of two, perhaps four, men to the crew of the keel-boat. We gave Richard Warfington, our corporal, the charge of the keel-boat and crew, and confided to his care our maps and dispatches to the Government, letters to our private friends, and a number of articles to the President of the United States.

One of the Frenchmen, Mr. Joseph Gravelines, an honest, discreet man and an excellent boatman, is employed to conduct the keel-boat as its pilot. Mr. Gravelines speaks the Arikara language, and he has also been employed to conduct a few of the Arikara chiefs to the seat of government in Washington.

[Due to the frequent departures and arrivals of unnamed Frenchmen during the past winter – and the confusing text of the journals, it is impossible to be certain just which Frenchmen accompanied the keel-boat on its return. It would appear that the return party was:

1. Corporal Richard Warfington
2. Pilot Joseph Gravelines, a Frenchman
3. Private John Boley
4. Private John Dame
5. Private John Newman.
6. Private Moses B. Reed
7. Private Ebenezer Tuttle
8. Private Isaac White
9. A lame Arikara Indian
10. Patron Baptiste DeChamps (the other Frenchman?)
11. Engagé Jean Baptiste LaJuennesse
12. Engagé Paul (Charles) Primeau
13. Engagé Etienne Malboeuf

And in a canoe of their own, accompanying the keel-boat:

14. Engagé Francois Rivet
15. Trapper, Phillipe Degie

The above is the basic evidence for my assumption that the original party set out with fifty-one men. John Robertson and Peter Pinaut had early on the trip been sent back. Sergeant Charles Floyd had died, Joseph Barter had deserted and Robert Frazier had been transfered to the permanent party. Ross, alias "Rokey," Alexander Carson and Peter Roi, seem to be the Frenchmen who returned to the Arikara when the Frenchmen were discharged on November 2, 1804. Another Frenchman, Grenier (Grienyea), though never a member of the party, was at Fort Mandan at different times during the winter, and did come up with the expedition from the Arikara villages. He may be one of the Frenchmen mentioned, along with Joseph Collin, as going back and forth between Fort Mandan and the Arikara. It also appears that Grenier, Ross ("Rokey"), and Francois Rivet returned to the Mandans in 1806, for they seem to be the Frenchmen found there by the Lewis and Clark expedition when the permanent party returned from the Pacific. These three, with Phillip Degie, had stayed with the Arikara at least part of the winter of 1805-1806]

[While no journals seem to have been kept by Cpl. Warfington nor any members of his return party, we do know a few details of their voyage. After leaving Fort Mandan, they stopped at the Arikara village and took aboard an Arikara chief and his party. Mr. Joseph Gravelines conducted the chief to St. Louis and then on to Washington, where the chief died. Some of the Frenchmen remained with the Arikara such as Francois Rivet, Phillipe Degie, "Rokey" and possibly Joseph Collin.

Capt. Lewis later reported that "John Newman was extremely serviceable as a hunter on the voyage to St. Louis, and that the boat, on several occasions, owed her safety in a great measure, to his personal exertions, being a man of uncommon activity and bodily strength." [1]

The party reached St. Louis on May 20, 1805, and turned the Indians, the reports, letters and crates of natural history objects over to Charles Gratiot, who was acting agent during the absence of Capt. Amos Stoddard. As the terms of enlistment for the soldiers entitled them to discharge upon termination of the voyage, some of them returned to civilian life. Others, such as Richard Warfington, re-enlisted with their former units. They all had been discharged as of June 1, 1805, having performed their assignment with fidelity.]

[At the same moment that the keel-boat departed from Fort Mandan, Capt. Clark embarked with the permanent party in two pirogues and six dug-out canoes and proceeded up the Missouri. As Captain Lewis had had no exercise for several weeks, he determined to walk some eight miles on shore. He joined the boats later at the lower Mandan Village. The party now consisted of:

---

[1] Thwaites, vol. 7, p. 357.

1. Captain Meriwether Lewis
2. Captain William Clark
3. Sergeant John Ordway
4. Sergeant Nathaniel Pryor
5. Sergeant Patrick Gass
6. Private William Bratton
7. Private John Colter
8. Private John Collins
9. Private Peter Cruzatte
10. Private Robert Frazier
11. Private Joseph Fields
12. Private Reuben Fields
13. Private George Gibson
14. Private Silas Goodrich
15. Private Hugh Hall
16. Private Thomas Proctor Howard
17. Private Francois Labiche
18. Private Hugh McNeal
19. Private John Potts
20. Private George Shannon
21. Private John Shields
22. Private John B. Thompson
23. Private William Werner
24. Private Alexander H. Willard
25. Private Richard Windsor
26. Private Joseph Whitehouse
27. Private Peter Weiser
28. Interpreter George Drouillard

29. PRIVATE JEAN BAPTISTE LA PAGE.

La Page had been up the Missouri as far as the Little Missouri River prior to enlisting in the party on November 3, 1804, when he was recruited in place of John Newman. On March 3, 1807, he received extra pay of $116.33. The captains described him as "entitled to no particular merit."

30. INTERPRETER, TOUSSAINT CHARBONNEAU
    (CHARBONO; SHARBONO; etc.)

Charbonneau was born in Canada of French parents about the year 1758. He was enlisted as an interpreter and engagé on March 18, 1805. He had previously been employed by the North West Company as a trader. He was verbose and excitable. At one time he had lived among the Minnitaree where in 1794 he is reported to have won Sacagawea in a gambling game from Red Arrow, her Indian captor. Other than as an interpreter for the party, he was not of much value. After the party's return from the Pacific to the Mandans again, he, his wife and son, remained with the Mandans. He was with Major Long's expedition to the Rocky Mountains. He came down to St. Louis in 1811 with his three children who were turned over to Governor William Clark to educate, and then he returned to the Mandans. In 1839 he came back to St. Louis, aged eighty, having served the United States Government as an interpreter from 1819 to 1838.

31. SACAGAWEA (SACAJAWEA; SAKAKAWEA, etc.)

Sacagawea was a Shoshoni girl born about 1788. She was a sister of Cameawait, a chief of a Shoshoni band in 1805. She had been captured by the Minnitaree when about 12 years old, and later became one of the wives of Charbonneau. She was a valuable guide in the far, upper Missouri country, and was as brave a soldier as any of them. She was virtuous, modest and unexcitable. She gave birth to a son, Jean Baptiste, on February 11, 1805, while at Fort Mandan, and carried the infant to the Pacific and return to the Mandans. Capt. Clark called her "Janey." One account,[2] states that she died on December 20, 1812, with which Clark seems to concur,[3] while another,[4] says she lived until April 9, 1884, when she died at the Wind River Indian Agency. I use the spelling of her name as adopted by the United States government.

32. JEAN BAPTISTE CHARBONNEAU (POMP).

Jean Baptiste Charbonneau was born February 11, 1805, in Fort Mandan, the son of Toussaint Charbonneau and Sacagawea. He was nicknamed "Pomp" – meaning a leader or head man – a title often given the first-born of a Shoshoni mother.

About 1810, according to the promise given to Capt. Clark by his parents, he was brought down to St. Louis to be reared and educated by Clark. About 1821, Jean Baptiste apparently entered the service of the Missouri Fur Company. In October, 1823, Prince Paul, Duke of Württemberg – highly impressed with the outstanding young man – took him to Germany for an education in Europe. In late 1829, they returned to Missouri.

Jean Baptiste went to the mountains, probably with Drips and Fontenelle, in the spring of 1830. Then followed many years in various capacities as a fur trapper-trader with several outfits. Later he was an interpreter for Frémont, Emory, Abert and several others.

---

[2] *Luttig's Journal of a Fur Trapping Expedition 1812-13*. Edited by Stella M. Drumm, Missouri Historical Soc., St. Louis, 1920, pp. 106, 132; Russell Reid, *Sakakawea;* and Helen Crawford, *Sakakawea.*

[3] Clark's list of members 1825-28, reprinted in Jackson, 638.

[4] Grace R. Hebard, *Sacajawea, Guide of the Lewis and Clark Expedition*, 208.

He is said to have worn his hair long, was the best man on foot on the plains and mountains and an active and useful man. Several writers who met him note his fine character, pleasant manners and particularly fine education. He could converse in English, French, German, Spanish as well as several Indian languages.

In 1846, Jean Baptiste Charbonneau went to California as a guide for the Mormon Battalion commanded by Philip St. George Cooke. Then he served as alcalde at the San Luis Rey district of San Diego. When gold was discovered in northern California, Jean Baptiste went up there to seek his fortune. With his old friend, Jim Beckwourth, he mined on the Middle Fork of the American River and at other places in Placer County for several years – always respected by the community. In 1866 he decided to go to the newly discovered mines in Montana. Enroute, he died of pneumonia about the first of May, 1866, at Inskip's Ranch, located in the Jordan Valley of south-east Oregon. He was aged sixty-one. Near the ranch are three old graves, one of them presumed to be the grave of Jean Baptiste Charbonneau.[5]

33. YORK. Capt. Clark's servant.

34. SCANNON. Capt. Lewis' Newfoundland dog.]

APRIL 8, 1805. We set out early. Capt. Lewis walked on shore and visited Black Cat. One of the canoes filled with water and its loading got wet. Capt. Clark went back to lend assistance. We lost a half bag of biscuit and about thirty pounds of gun powder. The powder was spread out to dry with the hope of restoring the greater part of it. At the noon camp, an Indian came up with a woman who was extremely solicitous of accompanying one of the men [Ordway?] of the party. This the captains refused to permit. The Indian man, being acquainted with the upper Missouri, was allowed to accompany us.

APRIL 9. We set out early and passed a hunting party of the Gros Ventres. The Indian man who joined us yesterday, now informed us he would not continue with us, and accordingly returned to his village. Capt. Clark walked on shore today. When we halted for dinner, Sacagawea went out with a sharp stick which she used to penetrate the holes of gophers. She collected and brought us a quantity of wild artichokes, which the animals gather and hoard in large quantities.

APRIL 10. At 1 p.m. we overtook three Frenchmen who had left the fort a few days before us in order to make the first attempt on this river of trap-

---

[5] Hafen, *Mountain Men*, vol. I, p. 205; also, Hebard, *Sacajawea*, pp. 111-48.

ping beaver. They mean to accompany us up to the Yellowstone River for protection. [These could be Grenier, Jessaume and the previously mentioned, Mr. Croix. However, this is pure speculation on my part, and is only offered as a clue. It would seem that if they were any of the former members of the party, one of the journalists would have mentioned it.]

APRIL 11.   Capt. Clark walked on shore with Drouillard to hunt, and at breakfast, they brought a deer and two beaver, which was most acceptable, as we have had no fresh meat for several days. We halted at 2 p.m., and had dinner on venison, beaver tails and the biscuit which had got wet on the 8th. The powder which was wet at that time appears to be almost restored. A beaver was caught by one of the Frenchmen. We have now only four: Cruzatte, Labiche, La Page and Charbonneau. The latter is usually at the helm of the large red pirogue. The day was warm and some of the men worked almost naked except for a breech-cloth.

APRIL 12.   Drouillard shot a large beaver swimming in the river. We arrived at the mouth of the Little Missouri River where we halted while the captains made observations. La Page tells us that this river is not navigable. We have ten hunters out. They killed a deer, a white eagle and found some wild onions. Capt. Clark killed a white rabbit which is now changing its color to grey. We remained here for the rest of the day to air our baggage. Several of the men have been cutting into the bags of corn and parched meal.

APRIL 13.   We hoisted the sails in the white pirogue and sailed under a favorable wind until afternoon. About 2 p.m., a sudden squall struck and turned the pirogue so much on its side, as to alarm Charbonneau who was steering. In his excitement, he threw the pirogue into the wind, which nearly upset her. Drouillard took the helm, and the sails were taken in. This accident nearly cost us dearly, for all our instruments, papers, medicine and most valuable merchandise were aboard. We had thought that the largest pirogue was the most steady and safe boat we had, hence the loading. Our party caught eight beaver, and the three Frenchmen, seven, last evening. As there appeared to be many beaver here, the three extra Frenchmen who were accompanying us, concluded to remain here and not continue further with us. Capt. Clark walked ashore to inspect the country.

APRIL 14.   Several of our men are out hunting – one killed a muskrat. Capt. Lewis killed an elk. Capt. Clark killed a buffalo – as did Robert Frazier. We passed a stream this afternoon which we named for Charbonneau, as he had been here before. Baptiste La Page has been on the headwaters of the Mouse River – one of the very few white men ever to visit those parts.

APRIL 15.   Capt. Clark was near shooting a grizzly bear, one of our first encounters with this dreadful beast. The river is nearly as wide here as it is at its mouth. Capt. Lewis went ashore after Capt. Clark had returned to the boat. It is a rule with us that one of the captains shall be with the vessels at all times.

APRIL 16.   Capt. Clark walked ashore this morning and killed an antelope. There are abundant beaver about and a very large one was caught last night.

APRIL 17.   We saw a great many buffalo and elk on the plains which are now becoming green. Capt. Lewis went out and in a few minutes killed a buffalo. John Potts also killed one. Some of the men caught two beaver and several small catfish. Capt. Clark walked ashore this morning. Three beaver were caught. The men prefer the flesh of this animal, the tail and liver particularly. The elk and buffalo are so lean that we do not use much of them except the marrow bones.

APRIL 18.   We caught one beaver in two traps – it having a foot in each. The traps belonged to different men, so a contest ensued which might have terminated in a serious encounter had not the captains' timely arrival prevented it. The party had to use the tow-lines today. A high wind came up in the afternoon. It was with great difficulty that the canoes could be kept from filling with water. Capt. Clark, Charbonneau, Sacagawea and infant, walked ashore. Two men went up the river to set their beaver traps. They met a bear, and being without arms, thought it best to return. One man killed a goose, and Scannon, Capt. Lewis' dog, brought it in to the boat.

APRIL 19.   The wind blew hard, so we were obliged to lay by all day. The game is becoming more plentiful and is much more tame here than below. Some of the men caught a quantity of small catfish while we laid over. Sgt. Gass explored the countryside while we were waiting.

APRIL 20.   The wind was less severe than yesterday, so we set out before 7 a.m. Capt. Lewis walked on shore while Capt. Clark stayed with the boats. Soon after we started out, the bank caved in and nearly swamped one of the canoes. The high wind and blowing sand prevented much progress. The hunters obtained three elk, four geese and two deer. The elk and deer are poor at this season. The men's good health and appetite make up for the deficiency, and they eat heartily of them. Drouillard shot a beaver.

APRIL 21.   Capt. Clark walked on shore and shot four deer and a buffalo. One of the party climbed a tree which had a goose nest in it, and obtained four eggs. John Potts shot an elk which, with four others, was floating on a drift. One other was obtained by Drouillard. We passed the mouth of the White Earth [Muddy] River and camped near it.

APRIL 22.   The wind was hard ahead so we proceeded with difficulty — even with the assistance of tow-lines. The party halted while the captains went to the White Earth River to explore it.

APRIL 23.   A violent wind came up at 9 a.m., and it was with much effort that the canoes could be brought to a place of tolerable safety. Some of the canoes shipped water. Several parcels of lading were wet, which were opened and aired. We remained until 5 p.m., when the wind abated. We reloaded and went on. Capt. Clark killed three black-tailed deer and a buffalo calf.

APRIL 24.   The wind blew hard all day and we were unable to move. One of the men caught six wolf puppies and brought them in. The party are much afflicted with sore eyes occasioned by the clouds of dust driven from the sand-bars. In short, we are compelled to eat, drink and breathe dust.

APRIL 25.   The water froze on the oars as the men rowed. Due to the head wind, we are not making much progress. Capt. Lewis, Drouillard, Sgt. Ordway, Joseph Fields and one other man decided to go overland to the mouth of the Yellowstone River to make observations and determine its position. Enroute, the whole face of the country was covered with herds of buffalo, elk and antelope. They are so gentle that we pass near them, and sometimes they approach us to determine who we are. The overland party encamped on the bank of the Yellowstone, two miles south of its confluence with the Missouri.

APRIL 26.   This morning Capt. Lewis dispatched Joseph Fields to examine the Yellowstone up as high as he could, and return the same evening. Drouillard and another man are directed to bring in the game we had killed last evening. Capt. Lewis and Sgt. Ordway went down the Yellowstone to make a view of its confluence with the Missouri. Some timber was found there. At noon we heard the discharge of guns which announced the arrival of the boat party under Capt. Clark. After making the observations, we joined them. Scannon caught an antelope in the river. Sgt. Gass climbed a point to view the country. Our party are in good health and are much pleased at having arrived at this long wished for spot. A dram was issued to each person which soon produced the fiddles, songs and dancing — and much hilarity. Joseph Fields returned and reported that the Yellowstone was crooked and meandering for eight miles up. [He possibly was the first white man to ascend the Yellowstone this high.]

APRIL 27.   After taking the azimuth of the sun, we set out. At 11 a.m., the wind arose and the sand blew off the points in such clouds as to almost cover us on the opposite bank. We saw great numbers of antelope, elk, swans and other game, but killed nothing but what we could make use of. Capt. Lewis walked on shore and could not get back to the boats until night.

8

The Yellowstone to the Musselshell

APRIL 28. One of the men caught a large beaver last night. The wind blew gently, so we sailed part of the day. Capt. Clark and Charbonneau walked on shore. We saw many bear today.

APRIL 29. Capt. Lewis and a hunter were on shore when they met two grizzly bears. Both fired and one bear turned on Capt. Lewis and pursued him seventy or eighty yards. A third shot from the hunter brought the grizzly down. We saw numerous mountain sheep. In the evening we camped at the entrance of Martha's [Big Muddy] River.

APRIL 30. Capt. Clark, Charbonneau and Sacagawea walked on shore the greater part of the day. Sacagawea found a plant with fruit like a currant. Capt. Lewis walked ashore this evening and killed a buck elk.

MAY 1, 1805. We sailed until noon when the wind became high. The canoes became separated and were unable to rejoin us because of the high waves. John Shields is sick today with rheumatism. George Shannon killed an avocet – a sort of plover. Joseph Whitehouse and another man were in a canoe on the opposite shore and because of the high wind, were obliged to lay out all last night without blankets.

MAY 2. At daylight it began to snow, and did not stop until 10 a.m. Joseph Fields in passing near an old Indian camp, found several yards of scarlet cloth suspended on a bough as a sacrifice to the diety of the Assiniboines. Capt. Clark and Drouillard shot four beaver. Not being trapped before, the beaver are tame and show themselves in the daylight.

MAY 3. Capt. Clark walked ashore and killed an elk. We came to a large creek which we named the "2000 Mile Creek," because we have come this far. We sent Reuben Fields to examine it [Red Water Creek]. It is very cold today. Capt. Clark ascended Porcupine [Poplar] Creek several miles. The rudder irons broke on the large red pirogue.

MAY 4. We were detained until 9 a.m. to repair the rudder irons. Joseph Fields is very sick with dysentery and a high fever. Capt. Lewis gave him a dose of Glauber's salts which operated very well. In the evening his fever abated, and Capt. Lewis gave him thirty drops of laudanum.

MAY 5. Soon after setting out, the rudder irons of the small white pirogue were broken by running over a sawyer. She was refitted in a few moments with some thongs of raw-hide and nails. As usual, there are multitudes of animals about. Capt. Clark, during his walk, found a den of young wolves, and he and Drouillard killed the largest grizzly bear this evening we have yet seen. Scannon caught a young antelope. Joseph Fields is worse today.

MAY 6. Joseph Fields continues unwell. We find that the curiosity of our party is pretty well satisfied in respect to the grizzly bear. Their formidable appearance, added to the tenacity with which they die, has staggered the resolution of many of our men. We make observations at every opportunity in this land new to the white race.

MAY 7. About noon a bad wind came up, and our boats being under sail, one of the canoes turned over. Fortunately we were near the shore. Capt. Clark and one man walked ashore and killed two buffalo near where we camped. Our party took three buffalo, one elk and eight beaver today.

MAY 8. We nooned on the Milk River which Capt. Lewis explored and took observations – as he does nearly every day. Here we found wild licorice and the "white apple" whose edible roots we found tasteless, but no doubt are nutritious food. The game is so plentiful we can send out any time and obtain whatever we wish. Capt. Clark walked ashore with Charbonneau and Sacagawea. Sgt. Pryor killed a deer.

MAY 9. Capt. Clark killed two deer and two buffalo. We passed and explored the Big Dry River. Capt. Lewis killed a buffalo, which for a change, was fat. We set Charbonneau to prepare what he calls "Boudin Blanc," a sort of sausage using the intestines of the buffalo. We camped on a small creek which we called "Werner's" after one of our men – William Werner.

MAY 10. An Indian dog came to us today, which induced us to believe that we are near the hunting grounds of the Assiniboine – a vicious, ill disposed people. It was necessary to be on guard, and we inspected our arms, which we found in good order. We sent several hunters to scour the country, but they returned this evening, having seen no smoke, tents nor recent tracks of Indians. Boils and abscesses are very common among the party, and sore eyes continue with all of us. For the abscesses we use an emollient poultice, and apply a solution of sulfate of zinc and sugar of lead in water to the eyes.

MAY 11. About 5 p.m., William Bratton, who is afflicted with boils and a sore hand, came running to the boat with loud cries and every symptom of terror and distress. After we had taken him aboard, he told us he had shot a brown bear, which immediately turned on him and was in close pursuit of him. Capt. Lewis and seven men went immediately in search – found the bear – and shot him. We have many hairbreath escapes from the falling banks of the river.

MAY 12. We find pine and cedar trees growing here. Capt. Lewis walked on shore for exercise, and to examine the country. He usually goes alone, armed with a rifle and espontoon. The bottom lands are getting narrower. A high wind came up about noon, and we were obliged to lay by. The men hunted.

MAY 13. We had some high wind and squalls of rain this morning. Some of the men went hunting. At 2 p.m., the weather turned pleasant and we set off. Some of the hunters had not returned. We went nine miles and the hunters joined us at camp. George Gibson had wounded a very large bear while hunting. The river becomes more clear, and we anticipate a change of country shortly.

MAY 14. Our men are hunting bears. This evening Charbonneau was at the helm of the white pirogue instead of Drouillard, who was ashore with the captains. Charbonneau cannot swim, and is perhaps the most timid waterman in the world. In this pirogue were embarked our papers, instruments, books, medicine and the greater part of our Indian goods. The pirogue was under sail when a sudden squall of wind hit her, and Charbonneau, instead of putting her before the wind, luffed her into it – and she went to one side. Cruzatte gave orders repeatedly to take hold of the rudder, and at last Cruzatte himself saved her. Capt. Lewis was in the act of attempting to swim to the pirogue, but realized the danger. Sacagawea with equal fortitude and resolution, caught and preserved most of the light articles which were washed overboard. We gave the men a drink of grog to console them and cheer their spirits.

MAY 15. We remained here all day to spread the articles to dry which got wet yesterday. As the weather is damp, the goods benefited little by the exposure. Our hunters procured buffalo, deer and beaver.

MAY 16. This was a fine day, and by 4 p.m. we had all our articles dry and on board again. Our loss was not as great as we had first thought – the medicine suffered the greatest injury. One of our party wounded a large panther. Sgt. Ordway killed an antelope. A grizzly bear tore a coat which Labiche had left on the plains. Though late, we proceeded on.

MAY 17. We have a clear, pleasant morning. The banks were firm which favored the use of the tow-line. We find this the safest and most expeditious mode of traveling, except the sails and a steady, favorable wind. Capt. Lewis, Sgt. Ordway and several others killed a small, female grizzly bear.

Capt. Clark walked on shore in the evening and narrowly escaped from being bitten by a rattlesnake. In camp at night we were roused by the sergeant of the guard. A large tree which branched over the captain's tent had taken fire. We had the tent removed and a few moments later a large proportion of the tree crashed down on the place where the tent had just stood. The wind blew hard and spread the fire, which endangered the party considerably.

MAY 18.   We used the tow-line the greater part of the day, and proceeded on tolerably well. We named a creek for Peter Weiser [now Fourchette Creek]. Capt. Clark, during his walk, killed four deer.

MAY 19.   We had some fog this morning, and used the tow-line most of the day. The men are much afflicted with sore eyes and abscesses. Scannon got bit in the leg by a beaver. Capt. Clark killed three deer. Our hunters got three deer and three beaver today.

MAY 20.   At 11 a.m. we arrived at the mouth of the Musselshell River. We halted to make observations, and sent some hunters in every direction to explore the country. About five miles above the mouth, a handsome creek discharges itself into the Musselshell which we name "Sacagawea's Creek" [now Crooked Creek], after Charbonneau's wife. John Shields found a bold spring issuing from the hills about four miles up the Missouri. Capt. Clark walked today and killed three deer. The hunters killed several elk and deer and took the skins to make leggings of. Some of our men stayed out all night on the plains.

MAY 21.   The weather being fine, we used the tow rope. The men who stayed out overnight, returned. They had to swim the Musselshell to get across. Capt. Clark walked today and killed two elk. The hunters killed several deer and a buffalo cow. We had camped on a bar, but were so annoyed by clouds of dust and sand that we could neither eat nor sleep. We moved our camp to the foot of an adjoining hill which was sheltered somewhat from the wind.

MAY 22.   We have caught few fish since we left the Mandans. Those we have caught are white catfish, running from two to five pounds. We encamped early to render the fat of a bear we had taken. Capt. Lewis walked before noon and killed a deer. After our noon meal, Capt. Clark ascended a butte to view the country. The land is rolling but produces little than the prickly pear cactus. One of our hunters stayed out all night.

9

The Musselshell to Maria's River

MAY 23.   The hunter who stayed out all night rejoined us. He had killed four deer, one elk and a beaver. The river is beginning to rise and the current becomes more rapid.

MAY 24.   The ice in our vessels froze last night one-eighth of an inch thick. We have been passing for some days what our Frenchmen name the Black Hills. After starting with the tow-line, a fine breeze came on at 9 a.m. and we sailed for the rest of the day. We sent a man ten miles out to explore the country towards the distant mountains. He returned this evening. The air is so clear that distance is deceiving. Six men in two canoes waited and got the best meat of the buffalo that Capt. Clark had killed. They did not come up this evening.

MAY 25.   The men who left yesterday to bring in the meat, rejoined us this morning, so we all left at 8 a.m. We employed the tow-line mainly today. We saw some big-horn sheep, and Drouillard was sent to kill one. Capt. Clark and William Bratton also got one each. Buffalo are now scarce and we fear that our harvest of white puddings is at end. George Gibson, in trying to climb a cliff, dislocated his shoulder, but we got it in place again.

MAY 26.   We used the tow-line, only resorting to the oars when we had to pass the mouths of rivers – thus taking advantage of the banks for pulling. We came to a creek which we named "Windsor's Creek" [now Cow Creek] after our man, Richard Windsor. Capt. Lewis first caught sight of a distant view of the Rocky Mountains – the object of our hopes, and the rewards of our ambitions. We came to a rapids, which by doubling the crews, and using both the ropes and poles, we ascended with great difficulty. Capt. Lewis walked among the hills and killed a fat buffalo which we are in want of.

MAY 27.   The wind blew hard, so we used the tow-lines most of the day. The country is bare and desolate. We camped near two dead-topped cottonwood trees for the benefit of the fire wood found there.

MAY 28.   We had rain and thunder today. We used the tow-line mostly and came across some floating poles and a football and other articles which indicate Indians are probably above us. Capt. Clark walked on shore and saw many big-horned sheep. He killed some deer. We name a creek, "Thompson's," after a valuable man of our party – John B. Thompson.

MAY 29.   Last night we were alarmed by a large buffalo bull which swam over from the opposite side and clambered over the white pirogue in attempting to land. He then ran full speed towards where the men were asleep, missing their heads by inches. He then took a direction towards the captain's tent. Scannon chased him off. The camp was in an uproar, but no one was hurt. In crossing the pirogue, the buffalo trod on York's rifle and bent it, and shattered the stock of a blunderbuss. It seems to us that the white pirogue is attended by some evil genii, for so many mishaps befall her.[1] We passed a large river which Capt. Clark, who ascended it, felt proper to name the "Judith River," in honor of Miss Julia Hancock of Virginia [who later became his wife]. We found the remains of Indian sites of recent date, perhaps twelve or fifteen days old. Sacagawea examined the moccasins found, and stated that they were not of the Shoshoni nation, but probably of the Minnitaree or Blackfoot tribe.

MAY 30.   It is cold and rainy today. We had great labor in towing the boats. Our lines made of elk skin were worn, and broke several times, but fortunately without injury to the boats. The banks are wet and slippery, so the men can hardly walk. Capt. Lewis said that the men's labor is incredibly painful and great, yet the faithful fellows bear it without murmur.

MAY 31.   We proceeded in the two pirogues, leaving the six canoes to bring on the meat of the buffalo killed last night. The shore conditions of yesterday continue today, and fatigue the men excessively. One fourth of the time they are in the cold water up to their armpits. They cannot wear their moccasins because of the mud, and sometimes have to walk over yards of sharp rocks. At noon, the captains gave the men a dram which they received with cheerfulness, and was well deserved. Capt. Lewis walked ashore in this wild, eroded country, and killed two big-horn sheep, and a fat buffalo.

JUNE 1, 1805.   We set out early and proceeded as usual by the tow-line. One of the party killed a big-horn sheep which had fine horns. We stopped at 2 p.m. to dine and air our goods. The country is more level now, and coal seams appear in the bluffs.

JUNE 2.   We towed the boats and went on much better than for the past two days, as the banks are well calculated for towing. As game is abundant, we begin to make a collection of hides for the purpose of making a leather

---

[1] While the white pirogue does seem to have more than her share of troubles, yet it was the only boat of the three that originally started out, that made the return trip to St. Louis with the main party.

boat. The hunters brought in six elk, two buffalo, two mule deer and a bear – the last nearly causing the death of Drouillard and Charbonneau. We came to a large river which Capt. Lewis named "Maria's River," where we camped.

JUNE 3.   We moved our camp over to the point between the two rivers. Both are equally large so we had to determine which of these rivers is the true Missouri. To choose the wrong stream might lose us the whole season, and would probably dishearten the party and defeat the expedition altogether. To this end, an investigation of both streams was the first thing to be done. We dispatched two canoes with three men each up these two rivers with instructions to discover the bearing of these rivers by ascending the rising grounds. The parties are to return by evening. The men seem to feel that the north fork [the Maria's] is the real Missouri, but the captains reserve the opinion that the south fork is the correct one. We are astonished that the Mandan Indians had not given us more precise information. The party in camp is busy dressing skins for clothing. Many of them can scarcely walk because of mangled and bruised feet. The canoe parties returned in the evening with their reports. Sgt. Pryor had ascended the north fork and had taken distances. Sgt. Gass with Joseph Whitehouse had ascended the south fork. The Fields brothers had walked up the north fork some seven miles. Their reports were not convincing of the fundamental points, so the captains concluded to ascend both rivers far enough to observe the main direction the rivers took so that they could satisfy themselves on the one which would be most expedient to take for the journey to the Pacific. They gave orders for Sgt. Pryor, Drouillard, Shields, Windsor, Cruzatte and La Page to hold themselves in readiness to accompany Capt. Lewis in the morning. Capt. Clark selected Joseph and Reuben Fields, Sgt. Gass, Shannon and York to accompany him.

JUNE 4 AND 5.   At the same hour this morning, Capt. Lewis' and Capt. Clark's parties set out to explore the two rivers. Capt. Lewis investigated the north fork and stayed out all night. On the morning of the 5th they saw two deer feeding, and Drouillard was sent to kill one for breakfast. This excellent hunter soon exceeded his orders by killing them both.

Capt. Clark and his party explored the south fork. At camp that evening two grizzly bears nearly caught Joseph Fields. He could not fire his gun as it was wet. The rest of the party yelled and fired guns which alarmed the bears, and they took off. Capt. Clark and party returned to the main camp.

JUNE 6.   Capt. Lewis now became convinced that the Maria's took its course too much to the north to be the true Missouri, and he decided to return tomorrow. He sent Pryor and Windsor to proceed up the river to a commanding hill to take bearings. They returned at noon and reported that the river ran north-westerly. The canoes which the party were using were overloaded with the five elk skins we had taken on, so most of the party decided to return by land.

JUNE 7. It rained during the night. At daylight all but the boat men descended by land. In passing along the face of a bluff, Capt. Lewis slipped, and but for a fortunate recovery by means of his espontoon, would have been precipitated into the river down a craggy precipice of about ninety feet. He reached a place where he could stand and heard Windsor's voice behind him saying "Good God, Captain, what shall I do?" Capt. Lewis turned and found that Windsor had lost his foothold and had slipped down to the very edge of the precipice, where he lay on his belly, with his right arm and leg over the precipice. Capt. Lewis told him to take his knife and dig a hole to recover his right foot. Windsor did this, and then raised himself on his knees. He crawled in this manner to a safe place. The rest of the party waded the river to avoid this dangerous place. The party camped in an old Indian lodge made of sticks, after a wet, nasty and adventurous day.

Maria's River to the
Great Falls of the Missouri

JUNE 8. Capt. Lewis' party descended the north fork and he became convinced that this was not the main stream, nor the one advisable to ascend, so he gave it the name of Maria's River, in honor of his cousin, Miss Maria Wood. His party reached the main camp in the afternoon, much to the relief of us who feared for their safety, for they had been out two days longer than the appointed time, and it was feared they had met with some accident. Meanwhile the men at the base camp were busy hunting, airing the stores and dressing skins. Capt. Clark plotted the courses of the two rivers as far as they had been explored. The maps we have brought with us, such as Arrowsmith's of 1795, with corrections to 1802, cause us to suspect their veracity.

JUNE 9. We determined to deposit at this place the large red pirogue and all the heavy baggage which we could possibly do without – along with some provisions, salt, blacksmith's tools, powder and lead. We do this to lighten our vessels, and at the same time, add to them the crew of the seven hands who heretofore have been employed in navigating the red pirogue. We sent a party of seven men to dig a hole to bury the goods. Peter Cruzatte, being acquainted with the method of making a cache, was left the supervision of constructing it. Cruzatte is an old Missouri navigator, and from his integrity, knowledge and skill as a waterman, has acquired the confidence of every individual of the party. Cruzatte declared it is of his opinion that the north fork is the true Missouri – and could be no other. Finding the men so determined in this belief, and wishing that if the captains were in error to detect it and rectify it as soon as possible, it was agreed among the captains that Capt. Lewis would take a small party by land up the south fork until they found the Great Falls by which means we would know the true Missouri. As Capt. Clark is the best waterman, he is to depart with the canoes the day after tomorrow. Some of our arms and the air-gun needed repairs, and as we intend to cache the blacksmith's bellows and tools here, we set about making the repairs. Capt. Lewis made several observations to fix this important location. In the evening Cruzatte gave us some music on the violin and the men danced, sang, and were extremely cheerful.

JUNE 10.   We dried all of our merchandise and John Shields renewed the main spring of the air gun. We have been much indebted to the ingenuity of Shields on many occasions. Without having served any regular apprenticeship at any trade, he makes his own tools, and works extremely well in either wood or metal, and has been most serviceable to us. He is a good hunter and an excellent waterman. We conceal at different places some ammunition, powder and lead, axes and all superfluous baggage of every description – totaling about one thousand pounds, including most of the beaver traps. We made the large pirogue fast in the middle of an island, and covered her with brush. Capt. Lewis is unwell with dysentery but ordered Drouillard, Joseph Fields, George Gibson and Silas Goodrich to be ready to leave in the morning with him by land. Sacagawea is very sick this evening. Capt. Clark bled her. The canoes are calked and ready for travel.

JUNE 11.   Capt. Lewis set out with his party for the south snowy mountain. They got as far as the Tansy [Teton] River, when Capt. Lewis was attacked with violent pains. He made a brew of choke-cherry twigs which relieved his pain; his fever abated, and in the morning, was quite recovered. Meanwhile, Silas Goodrich, who is remarkably fond of fishing, had caught several dozen fish. They killed some elk and hung them along side the river for Capt. Clark's party coming up with the canoes.

JUNE 12.   Capt. Lewis' party bore away from the river a mile or two to avoid the ravines. About 10 a.m. they came to the river to slake their thirst. They killed two grizzly bears at the first shot. Leaving a note for Capt. Clark, they took to the higher land again.

Meantime, Capt. Clark and the canoe party proceeded upstream. Sacagawea is very sick and is placed in the covered part of the white pirogue – which is cool. One of the men has a felon rising on his hand. Another has a toothache, which has taken cold in his jaw. The rapid water gives us some trouble in forwarding the boats.

JUNE 13.   Capt. Lewis and his party walked along the higher ground and passed most beautiful valleys of large extent. Joseph Fields was sent to his right, and Drouillard and Gibson to his left to hunt. Later all were to join at the river to take dinner. Soon Goodrich called that he could hear the sound of falling water. The roar increased as the party advanced. At noon they reached the Falls of the Missouri. Capt. Lewis sat on the top of some rocks opposite the center of the falls to gaze on this sublimely grand spectacle which, from the commencement of time, has been concealed from the view of civilized man. He determined to send Joseph Fields down in the morning to inform Capt. Clark and his party of this important discovery, and to settle in their minds all doubts as to the real Missouri. The hunters arrived, loaded with excellent buffalo meat. Others had been killed, so we encamped to dry the meat. Goodrich has caught a half dozen very fine trout. Our fare was really sumptuous this evening.

Meanwhile, the party under Capt. Clark was working its way upstream. Sacagawea is still sick. Whitehouse is also very sick, and some of the men are still troubled with swellings.

JUNE 14.   Capt. Lewis dispatched Joseph Fields with a letter to Capt. Clark, and ordered Fields to keep near the river so that he might form an idea at which point it would be best to begin a portage. One man with Lewis prepared a scaffold and collected wood to dry the meat. Others were sent to bring in the rest of the meat. Capt. Lewis walked to the upper end of the falls. He found a succession of them. He was charged by a grizzly bear and had to run into the river to escape. He then walked on until he arrived at the Sun River. After several other adventures with animals, he returned to camp after dark.

Joseph Fields reached Capt. Clark's party at 4 p.m. Sacagawea and some of the men are still sick. The rapid water makes progress with the boats slow.

JUNE 15.   Drouillard and the others are bringing in meat and are drying it. Capt. Lewis and Goodrich are fishing. Joseph Fields returned this morning with the news that Capt. Clark's party had arrived at the foot of a rapid about five miles below, and would wait for Capt. Lewis to come there. The boat party had to be in the water from morning until night, working with much difficulty in getting the boats upstream. Added to this, the rattlesnakes were numerous and require great caution to avoid being bitten. Sacagawea is much worse – will not take any medicine – and now Charbonneau wants to go home! We name a creek after John Shields [now, Highwood Creek].

JUNE 16.   Joseph Fields set out early for Capt. Clark's camp. At noon the hunters arrived and they and Capt. Lewis set out for the lower camp. Here he found Sacagawea extremely ill. This gives us all concern for the poor woman has, in addition, an infant in her arms. She is the only dependence we have for acquiring horses from the Shoshoni Indians, which we will need for crossing the mountains between the Missouri and Columbia rivers. We estimate the portage around the five falls of the Missouri to be eighteen miles. Capt. Clark sent two men along the south side of the river to examine the country. We unloaded the four canoes, and by means of ropes, we hauled them over the rapids. We found a strong sulphur spring, the virtues of which Capt. Lewis resolved to try on Sacagawea. Six men were sent to look for timber to make wheels in order to convey our canoes and baggage. We determined to leave the white pirogue at this place and to make a further deposit of our stores. Capt. Lewis gave Sacagawea barks and opium, which produced a stronger pulse, and caused her to drink the sulphur water altogether. Capt. Lewis determined to remain at this camp and make celestial observations and restore the sick woman. The men also drank freely of the sulphur water. [See illustration at page 167.]

June 17.   Some of the men are taking the canoes up a little river [Belt Creek] some 1¾ miles. Six men under Sgt. Gass are making small, low wagons to haul the canoes and baggage over the portage. Capt. Clark and five men went to survey the portage road beyond the falls to where they can reach the river again. Two hunters went to get elk skins to cover the iron frame boat. We had trouble with the canoes in the rapids – one turned upside down and nearly drowned the two men who were in her. We got the canoes up safe and turned them on their sides to dry. Sacagawea is much better today. She is free from pain, clear of fever, her pulse regular, and eats heartily. There is rational hope for her recovery.

June 18.   We drew the white pirogue on shore into a thick bunch of willows, fastened her securely, drove out the plugs in her bottom, and covered her with bushes and driftwood to hide and shelter her from the sun. We now selected a place for a cache, and set three men to complete it. All others, except those making wagons, were overhauling, airing and repacking our Indian goods, ammunition, provisions and stores. Capt. Lewis knocked down the frame of his iron boat, and found all complete except one screw, which the ingenuity of John Shields can replace, a resource which we have very frequent occasion for. The hunters returned with ten deer – but no elk. Capt. Lewis prefers the elk skins for covering the frame boat. The wagons were completed this evening. Sacagawea is improving fast and walked for the first time since coming to this camp. Capt. Lewis continues the same regimen of medicine, and added one dose of oil of vitriol this noon. Lots of gooseberries grow about. This evening Alexander Willard, while going for a load of meat, was attacked by a grizzly bear and was very near being caught. He ran near camp. Capt. Clark and three men pursued the bear for fear he would change and attack John Colter who was near. Before they got close, the bear had chased Colter into the river. As we approached, the bear retreated, and we went to the aid of Colter in the water. Capt. Clark discovered a giant spring today.

JUNE 19.   Drouillard, Reuben Fields and Shannon were sent up the north side of the river to the Medicine [Sun] River to endeavor to kill some elk. The cache was completed today. Sacagawea was so much better than she ate heartily of the raw, white (tuber) apples, together with a considerable quantity of dried fish. Her fever returned. Capt. Lewis rebuked Charbonneau for allowing her to eat such food, for he had previously told him what she should eat. Capt. Lewis then gave her a dose of diluted vitriol, and later thirty drops of laudanum, which gave her a tolerable night's rest. The men are making packages of the baggage and renewed the wax on the powder-cannister tops. We greased the iron frame to prevent rust. In the evening the men repaired their moccasins and prepared themselves for the portage. Capt. Clark is plotting the portage route, and is making sketches. A high wind came up suddenly and blew away some of his notes and sketches.

JUNE 20.   While waiting for Capt. Clark and his party to return, Capt. Lewis sent out four hunters to obtain meat, the object being to lay in a supply to subsist the party while they are engaged in the portage. Sacagawea is quite free from pain and is walking about and fishing. Two hunters returned and informed us that they had killed eleven buffalo. All hands were sent to bring the meat back to camp. About half of it was brought back, and three men were left to stay all night with the balance. Capt. Clark and party returned this evening, having staked out the portage route. He had directed that sticks be set up on the prairie to mark the way of the portage. There are several ravines that have to be avoided. Not having seen any Indians, nor knowing if in fact they could be depended upon for friendship or hostility, we have conceived that our party is already small, and have concluded therefore not to dispatch a canoe with part of our men back to St. Louis, as we had intended to do when we made our plans this spring. The captains had never hinted to any of the party that they had such a scheme in contemplation. The men all appear to have made up their minds to succeed in this expedition, or perish in the attempt. Joseph Fields called attention to the noises which sounded like a cannon being fired some distance away. We are at a great loss to account for this phenomenon. We recollect hearing the

Minnitarees say that these Rocky Mountains make a great noise. It is possible that they have named the Medicine River thus because of the rumbling sounds heard nearby – for everything unaccountable to them is called "medicine."

SACAGAWEA AT THE SULPHUR SPRINGS, JUNE 16, 1805
From a painting by Olaf C. Selzer. Courtesy of Thomas Gilcrease Institute, Tulsa, Oklahoma.

LEWIS AND CLARK AT THE GREAT FALLS OF THE MISSOURI
From a painting by Olaf C. Seltzer, Courtesy of Thomas Gilcrease Institute, Tulsa, Oklahoma.

II

Portaging around the Great Falls

JUNE 21. The greater part of the men are employed in transporting a part of the baggage to the top of the plain about three miles distant on the portage road. One of the canoes was placed on the wheels and dragged on. Capt. Lewis, Sgt. Gass, Joseph Fields and John Shields are enroute to the upper part of the portage with the frame of the iron boat, with tools and baggage, to construct a leather cover for the boat. Three men are shaving elk skins for this purpose. Other men are drying meat for use on the return from the portage.

JUNE 22. Captains Lewis and Clark set out with their parties for White Bear Island at the end of the portage. Sgt. Ordway, Charbonneau, Sacagawea and baby, Silas Goodrich and York remain at camp to take care of the goods still left. The mast from the pirogue, now used for the axle-trees and tongues of the wagons, broke and had to be replaced. Each man took as much of the baggage as he could carry on his back. They proceeded to the upper river encampment much fatigued. The prickly pears are extremely troublesome as the thorns penetrate the moccasins into the men's feet. York killed a fat buffalo.

JUNE 23. Capt. Lewis, Sgt. Gass, Joseph Fields and John Shields selected a camp under some shady willows where they start working on the cover for the iron boat. Gass and Shields were sent out to look for timber necessary for the boat, while Capt. Lewis and Joseph Fields descended the river in a canoe to the mouth of the Medicine River to look for the elk hunters sent there on the 19th. After ascending the Medicine River about five miles, they found George Shannon. He had killed many buffalo and deer, but no elk. He could give no further account of Drouillard or Reuben Fields. Meanwhile, Drouillard and Fields were looking for Shannon. The thorns and dry, cracked points of earth make the men lame. Capt. Clark and his party returned to the lower camp and were able to shorten the portage road considerably by cutting off some of the angles, yet Clark now estimates the portage as 18¼ miles. They got in camp early enough to send two more canoes from what we call "Portage Creek" to the top of the plains. The men are making and mending moccasins with double soles, because of the cactus.

JUNE 24. Capt. Lewis dispatched Joseph Fields up the Medicine River to look for Drouillard and Reuben Fields. Capt. Lewis and Shannon took the canoe to put Lewis on the other side of the Missouri, then Shannon went back to meet Joseph Fields and bring in the dried meat to the White Bear Island camp. Reuben Fields came to camp and told us that Drouillard was still out at their hunting camp guarding the meat they had dried. The iron frame boat is set up and is 36 feet long, 4½ feet wide at the beam, and 26 inches deep. The frame had been built at Harper's Ferry in Virginia at Capt. Lewis' orders.

Sacagawea is completely recovered. Sgt. Gass and John Shields had difficulty in procuring good timber. Robert Frazier is sewing the hides together for the boat. Capt. Clark had the remaining canoes drawn from the river and divided the baggage into three parcels, some of which was carried on the backs of the men, and some on wheels, to the portage road. Hoisting a sail, and with four men in harness, the canoes were moved along to the upper camp. At every halt the poor fellows tumble down and are so much fatigued that many of them drop asleep in an instant. In short, their fatigues are incredible; some are limping from the soreness of their feet, others faint and are unable to stand in this heat and altitude. Yet no one complains, and all go on with dogged cheerfulness.

JUNE 25.   The main party returned to the lower camp. Sgt. Gass and Shields were sent to the White Bear Island to look for timber. Robert Frazier is sent in a canoe to Drouillard's camp to bring in meat. Joseph Fields was sent up the Missouri to hunt elk, but soon had an encounter with three grizzlies, during which, he cut his hand and knee, but had a fortunate escape. Gass and Shields found a little bark and timber, and brought back two elk. Elk skins are best for covering the frame boat, for they are more strong and durable than buffalo skins, and do not shrink so much in drying. Drouillard and Frazier arrived at evening with one hundred pounds of tallow.

The main party arrived at the lower camp to bring up the one remaining canoe and baggage to the higher ground. Some of the men danced on the green to the violin music of Cruzatte. Charbonneau was made cook for the party. Sgt. Pryor is sick.

JUNE 26.   Sgt. Gass and Shields are sent back to look for timber. Drouillard and Joseph Fields killed seven buffalo. Frazier helped sew skins on the boat. Capt. Lewis made a suet dumpling for each of his men. Capt. Clark's party brought in two canoes and some baggage, containing parched meal, pork, powder, lead, axes, tools, biscuit and portable soup. They had again hoisted sails on the canoes to assist with the dragging. Whitehouse, while considerably heated and fatigued, drank a heavy draught of cold water and was immediately taken ill. His pulse was full, so Capt. Lewis used his penknife to bleed him which succeeded in restoring him to health. While at the lower camp, Capt. Clark had a cache prepared to receive Capt. Lewis' desk, specimens of plants, books, etc. The swivel gun was hidden under some rocks. Sgt. Pryor was given a dose of salts. Charbonneau rendered enough tallow to fill three bags.

JUNE 27. At the upper camp, Whitehouse and Frazier are sewing skins, and Gass and Shields are fitting horizontal bars of wood to the iron boat. Drouillard and Joseph Fields returned from their hunt, having killed seven elk and three bears. Scannon, the dog, is in constant alarm with the bears.

Capt. Clark at the lower camp, completed a copy of his maps of the Missouri from the Mandans to this place. It is intended to leave this copy here with the cached goods in order to guard against the accidental loss of the original. Sgt. Pryor is somewhat better. The party returned from the upper camp as Sgt. Ordway and three others took a canoe and went down the river to view the falls. Capt. Clark gave the men a drink of grog as they prepared their harness for the baggage pulling tomorrow. A violent storm came up and wet the men and baggage.

JUNE 28. There are seven men at the upper camp: Capt. Lewis, Sgt. Gass, Joseph Fields, Drouillard, Whitehouse, Frazier and Shields – all occupied in making the boat.

At the lower camp, Capt. Clark's party completed the cache, and some ammunition, provisions, books and a map of the Missouri from its entrance into the Mississippi, to this place, were put in it. After closing the cache, we broke up the camp and took all the remaining baggage to the high plain above the river. We spent the night on the road.

JUNE 29. Capt. Lewis determined to visit the large fountain or giant spring that was discovered by Capt. Clark on the 18th. He set out with Drouillard in a violent wind and rain storm which thoroughly drenched them. The other men continue to work on the iron boat.

Capt. Clark at the lower camp, decided to ascend the river to remake the sketches he had lost in the wind at the time of his first discovery. With him went York, Charbonneau, Sacagawea and Baptiste, the baby. The storm approaching, they sought shelter in a ravine with shelving rocks under which they took cover. A sudden cloud-burst quickly filled the ravine with a torrent of water. Shoving Sacagawea and the baby before him, Capt. Clark and Charbonneau climbed up the steep bluff just in time to escape from being washed away. This ravine was just above the great cataract of the Missouri where, had they been swept into it, they must have inevitably perished. York was hunting buffalo at the time, so was not in the ravine, but he was alarmed for their safety. Charbonneau lost his gun, shot-pouch, horn and tomahawk. The baby's cradle and clothes were swept away. Clark was afraid that Sacagawea would have a relapse from her recent illness. Capt. Clark lost his large compass and an elegant fusee, a tomahawk and an umbrella. The compass is a severe loss, for we have no other large one.

The canoe party during the excessive heat which had preceded the storm had removed their clothes and were practically naked when the storm overtook them. The large hailstones bruised and knocked them about, and cut the scalps of their heads. They were compelled to camp out on the road over night again. The men at the upper camp were in good order under the willow trees, but were concerned for the men on the road. But it all came out well, and Capt. Lewis used some of the hailstones to make a bowl of punch.

JUNE 30.   Capt. Clark sent two men to hunt buffalo, and two others were sent to the ravine to search for the articles lost yesterday. One man remained to cook, but the balance returned to the baggage left on the portage road to move it along. The search party found the compass! Four men are making axle-trees, for the ones we have frequently break and have to be replaced.

Frazier and Whitehouse are sewing skins. Gass and Shields are shaving bark for wadding, and Joseph Fields is making cross-braces. Capt. Lewis and Drouillard rendered a considerable quantity of tallow. We are impatient to be off, as the season is getting late, and we have not yet crossed the Rocky Mountains. The skin cover for the boat is finished and was put into the water to toughen before sewing on the boat sections tomorrow. It has taken twenty-eight elk and four buffalo skins to cover her.

JULY 1, 1805.   Frazier and Whitehouse are sewing the cover on the iron frame. Shields and Joseph Fields are collecting light wood, and are making a pit to make pitch. Sgt. Gass is making way-strips, and Capt. Lewis and Drouillard are rendering tallow. All this is for the iron boat. By evening, the skins were all attached to the boat sections, and were returned to the water. All is in readiness to commence putting the sections of the boat together tomorrow, except for the way-strips.

At 3 p.m., Capt. Clark and his party arrived and have brought in most all the baggage. We had a dram and a much deserved rest. William Bratton has swollen legs, so he is assigned to pitch making tomorrow.

JULY 2.   Sgts. Pryor and Gass are working on the way-strips. Shields and Bratton are working on the tar-kiln, while Capt. Lewis and other hands are putting the sections of the boat together. The remaining men were sent back to the six-mile stake to bring the remaining tallow and baggage in. At 2 p.m. they returned with the last of the baggage, pleased that the laborious task of the portage is over. Capt. Lewis made celestial observations, and then he, Clark and twelve men went over to the island to hunt bear. Drouillard shot one. The balance of the party is working on the boat, and putting their firearms in order.

JULY 3. Nearly all the party are employed on the boat, which is now almost completed. We have not been able to obtain pitch from our kiln, which causes some embarrassment. Some hunters were sent ahead to kill buffalo so that we can make pemmican. We were told that we would leave the buffalo country shortly after passing the falls. If so, we will miss the white puddings that Charbonneau makes. Capt. Lewis fears the boat will be a blunder and useless, for the lack of pitch to seal the seams which had to be sewn together with a coarse needle. The boat looks good and is very light in proportion to its size. The river looks so gentle above the falls that all the men are anxious to be moving onward. Sgt. Gass having been engaged until now on the boat, has not yet seen the Great Falls. He, McNeal and three others were permitted to go down the river to view them, and also the giant springs. The others are working on the canoes and repairing moccasins. A good pair will not last more than two days in this country. The Gass party returned from the falls, bringing the tongues and brains from the buffalo they had killed.

JULY 4. We turned the iron boat over and built small fires under her to dry the skin, and applied pitch and tallow to the seams. We hear those noises towards the north-west when the weather is calm. Capt. Clark completed a map of the Missouri from Fort Mandan to this place, which we intend to deposit here. We have not seen any Indians, let alone the Shoshoni on whom we depend for horses. We all believe we are about to enter upon the most difficult and perilous part of our journey, yet no one repines, and all appear ready to meet any difficulties which might await us. Our work being completed, we had a drink of spirits – the last of our stock – save a little reserved for sickness. The fiddle was played by Cruzatte, and the men danced until 9 p.m. Festive jokes and songs prevailed, and the men were merry until late at night. Thus we celebrated the 4th of July in a civil and jovial manner.

JULY 5. We exposed the keel to the sun and pounded charcoal, beeswax and tallow into the gaping stitches. A large herd of buffalo came near camp and Capt. Clark and the hunters got three of them. Three other men visited the falls today – the last of the party who have not yet seen them. In the evening they returned and reported many buffalo about the falls. We sent some hunters there to bring back some meat.

JULY 6. Heavy showers kept the hides on the boat wet and we could not complete her calking. The red and yellow currants are now ripe, though rather acid as yet. Capt. Clark caught some small fish this evening. Four hunters were sent down the river to get buffalo – they did not return this evening. Some of the men are dressing skins to make clothes.

JULY 7. We have no tents now for they were put into the cache, so we are obliged to use the boat-sails to keep off the wet weather. The men's leather clothing soon rots by being constantly exposed to water, and they are busy preparing new skins. The iron boat is finished except for greasing and drying. The buffalo are leaving this place to go to the plains below. Joseph Whitehouse is busy making clothes for the men. York is sick and was given a dose of tartar emetic. He is better this evening. One of our party is making sacks of wolf skins in which to carry and keep the astronomical instruments.

JULY 8. Capt. Clark set out to replace the maps and measurements previously made of the river and falls, and a large party went along to kill buffalo. The day being fair and warm, about noon we applied the charcoal-tallow-beeswax composition to the boat. It gives her the appearance of being one solid piece of covering – particularly after the second coat. We call her the "Experiment." Joseph Whitehouse remained in camp making clothes.

JULY 9. The boat was put in the water and she swam perfectly well. The seats were fixed and the oars fitted. We loaded the boats, but a storm came up, and the boats had to be unloaded. The composition separated from the skins and left the seams exposed, so the iron boat leaked very much. As we cannot repair her without pitch, and that article is not to be procured here, we are forced, reluctantly, to abandon her. We therefore need two more canoes to transport our baggage. Capt. Clark and the ten best workmen went upstream to where there are trees large enough to construct canoes. The iron boat was taken apart and the party prepared to transport our goods in the present six canoes. The men sharpened their axes this evening on a small grindstone we had brought from Harper's Ferry, so that we could make an early start in the morning. We made a cache in which we will leave a few papers at this place.

JULY 10. Capt. Clark and ten men left overland for the canoe building camp. Sgt. Ordway with four canoes and eight men, including Whitehouse and Bratton, take up a load of baggage to Clark's camp. It is more than twice the distance by water as it is by land. The men are to return for the balance of the goods. Capt. Lewis and Sgt. Gass and five other men dismantled the iron boat and dug a cache in which to deposit her. They buried the wagon wheels in the pit that had been dug for the pitch kiln. Sgt. Ordway's canoe party got to within three miles of Clark's camp, but a violent storm prevented them from getting any closer. The canoe builders under Clark and Pryor found two large cottonwood trees – which though windshaken – must do, for no better can be found.

JULY 11.   One of Ordway's canoes joined Capt. Clark this morning, but the others, having on board valuable articles which might be injured by water, went more cautiously, and did not reach his camp until evening. The men with Capt. Lewis were occupied in hunting, but without much success. The men are much afflicted with painful felons. William Bratton is unable to work by the complaint on his hand. The canoes did not return to Capt. Lewis' camp. Capt. Clark's men are busy making canoes. Sgt. Pryor was sent with three men to bring in the buffalo meat that had been killed by the hunters. Sgt. Ordway started back to Lewis' camp with three canoes and three men for the remainder of the baggage, but a wind came up which forced them to camp for the night enroute. Whitehouse killed a rattlesnake.

JULY 12.   Sgt. Gass and three men were sent overland to Capt. Clark's camp to assist with the canoes. Bratton came down for a couple of axes and then returned to the canoe camp. Gass' party arrived at 10 a.m. and started working on the canoes, hunting, drying meat, etc. Sgt. Pryor dislocated his shoulder carrying meat, but it was replaced immediately. It is painful, but is not apt to cause injury. We take more otter now that the water is clear, for we can shoot them. The mosquitoes and black gnats are very troublesome. Ordway and Whitehouse's party with the canoes arrived at noon. The men had put the frame of the iron boat in the cache.

JULY 13.   The rest of the baggage was embarked in the six small canoes and each was manned by two men. We now bid adieu to the White Bear camp. La Page is sick, so Charbonneau was sent in his place in the canoe. Capt. Lewis, La Page and Sacagawea walked overland to the canoe camp and arrived at 9 a.m. The six canoes under Ordway made their way up the river despite strong winds. They had to unload and drain the canoes which prevented them from reaching camp. We eat very much meat; it requires four deer, an elk and a deer, or one buffalo to supply us for twenty-four hours. We reserve our flour and parched meal for later when game might not be so plentiful. The hunters killed three buffalo which were made into pemmican – dried and pounded meat, mixed with fat. The canoes are finished except for putting in some knees. We have to use our nets to protect us from the mosquitoes.

JULY 14. Sgt. Ordway, Whitehouse and the others arrived about noon with the canoes. The new canoes were put into the water this evening. One is thirty-three feet, and the other is twenty-five feet long. Both are three feet wide and only need seats and oars to be complete. The older canoes were unloaded so that the baggage could be dried. We are ready to leave tomorrow.

12

The Great Falls to the Three Forks

JULY 15. We arose very early and loaded the canoes. We now have eight canoes and all are heavily laden despite the goods we have cached. We do have a considerable amount of dried meat and tallow, but the men add bulky articles of little value or use to them. At 10 a.m. we were under way. Capt. Lewis, John Potts and La Page walked ashore all day. We went into camp at a place where Drouillard had wounded a deer in the river. Scannon retrieved it. The river has a gentle current but is very crooked – and is full of beaver. We came about twenty-six miles and camped on the north side.

JULY 16. Sgt. Ordway went back for an axe he had forgotten last night. The party proceeded on with the canoes. Drouillard killed a buffalo on which the party had breakfast. Capt. Lewis walked ashore with John Potts, La Page and Drouillard. They walked all day and Capt. Lewis forgot to bring his mosquito bar – for which he suffered considerably from the mosquitoes this evening. The canoe party made twenty-three miles.

JULY 17. We set out early and joined Capt. Lewis and party at the foot of the Half Breed Falls. Capt. Lewis had the box containing the instruments carried by land so that he could make some observations. The canoes had to pass some rapids which caused some difficulty, but no injury. We double-manned the canoes and used the tow-line. The navigation is now very laborsome as the river is deep and the banks over-hang the water. The mountains come close to the river on each side.

JULY 18. We set out early and passed the entrance of a considerable river which we name the "Dearborn" after our Secretary of War. As we are anxious to meet the Snake Indians, we thought it wise for one of the captains to take a small party by land some distance to discover them, as they might be alarmed by the discharge of our guns as we hunt. Accordingly, Capt. Clark, John Potts, Joseph Fields and York set out after breakfast. The boat party proceeded tolerably well, using the oars, setting poles and tow-lines at times. We passed a creek which we named after Sgt. Ordway [now Prickly Pear Creek]. We saw several bands of big-horn sheep on the cliffs, but they were out of reach of our guns. Capt. Clark followed an Indian trail all day.

JULY 19. The canoe party encountered a strong current with high rocks close on each side. We call the place "The Gates of the Mountains." We see many beaver – but no buffalo. Capt. Clark saw some pine trees which had the bark peeled off. Sacagawea informs us that the Indians do this to obtain sap and the soft part of the wood to use as food. Clark's party had to pass a mountain of sharp flint and prickly pears – both injurious to the feet. He camped after walking about thirty miles. He passed a beautiful creek which he named after Sgt. Pryor. Capt. Lewis and Drouillard walked ashore and killed an antelope.

JULY 20.   By using the tow-rope, we were able to overcome the swift current. The country begins to open out. We passed a large creek which we named "Potts Creek," after John Potts. We saw a large smoke up the valley which we learn is made by the Indians as a warning that enemies are near. We found an elk and a note which Capt. Clark had left, mentioning that he would await us beyond the mountains just above us. The whole country is so infested with the prickly-pear that we can scarcely find room to lie down in to camp.

JULY 21.   The canoe party under Capt. Lewis made slow and laborious progress. Scannon caught some swans. We passed a creek which we named after our Sgt. Nathaniel Pryor [now, Mitchell's Creek]. Capt. Clark and party joined us today. He told us that he had been on the headwaters of this creek on the 19th and had named it "Pryor's" then. Capt. Clark had killed a buck, and Joseph Fields got a buck and a doe. The party is much fatigued.

JULY 22.   The canoe party threaded a course through numerous islands. On a large one Capt. Lewis gathered about a half bushel of wild onions. While we were taking breakfast the men also gathered these onions. Capt. Lewis shot an otter but it sank to the bottom. The water is so clear that he dove in and retrieved it. As the canoes had taken different routes through the islands, it was some time before we all gathered at dinner time. Sgt. Ordway went back a mile for a thermometer which Capt. Lewis had left. Sacagawea recognizes this country as the land she had lived in as a girl, and that this is the river on which her relatives live. This information cheers the party. Though Capt. Clark's feet are blemished and sore, he is determined to scout the land. Finding him so anxious, Capt. Lewis resolved to remain with the canoes. He ordered Robert Frazier, Joseph and Reuben Fields and Charbonneau to be in readiness to accompany him in the morning. Drouillard missed our camp and continued up the river.

JULY 23.   Capt. Clark and party set out for the Three Forks of the Missouri. About 10 a.m. we came up with Drouillard who had missed us last night. He had killed five deer which we took on board. We passed a large cluster of islands and a creek which we named "Whitehouse Creek" [now either Confederate or Duck Creek]. We halted early to dry some articles which had become wet. Gigs were fastened to the ends of the setting poles which helped our progress. Capt. Clark followed an old Indian trail and is much in advance of us. He arrived at the Three Forks of the Missouri. Leaving a note for the canoe party below, he went up the north fork [Jefferson] as it seemed to bear more to the west. He ascended it about thirty-five miles and encamped, much fatigued and his feet blistered and wounded by the cactus thorns. Charbonneau gave out – his ankles failed him – so was unable to proceed farther.

JULY 24.   The boat party set out at sunrise and passed a bluff of crimson earth which Sacagawea tells us her people use for paint. We see mountains all about us which makes us fear that we will have more falls to portage, notwithstanding the assurances of Sacagawea that the river continues unobstructed as it is.

Capt. Clark on his land exploration saw a horse but could not get near it. He saw much Indian sign but it was not of recent date.

JULY 25.   The boat party set out early. The water is still strong and has some riffles. We killed a pair of young geese, but they are small game to subsist a party as large as ours. The men are forbidden to waste ammunition on them for it delays our progress. We passed a number of mammoth springs, and a stream we named after Sgt. Patrick Gass [now Hot or Warm Springs Creek]. Capt. Clark and his party looked for Indians on the upper Jefferson.

JULY 26.   We passed the entrance of a creek which we named "Howard's Creek" [now Green or 16-Mile Creek]. We found the note left by Capt. Clark. He had left Charbonneau and Joseph Fields at the camp while he, Reuben Fields and Robert Frazier went on to the top of a mountain where they had an extensive view of the valley. They saw no Indians. They descended by way of an Indian trail and rejoined Charbonneau and Joseph Fields. In passing an island on the Jefferson River, Charbonneau was nearly swept away by the current – and he cannot swim. Capt. Clark rescued him. Immense numbers of beaver and otter are seen here. Capt. Clark crossed over to, and descended, the middle fork [the Madison]. Our hunters killed four deer.

JULY 27.   The river is rapid, and the men begin to weaken from the exertion of rowing. We arrived at the Three Forks of the Missouri and camped for breakfast. Capt. Lewis climbed a hill and made a map of the meanderings of the streams. The canoe party went up the middle [Madison] fork for a mile and camped to give the men a much needed rest. We unloaded the canoes and securely covered the baggage on shore. It is important that we select the correct fork to ascend. Each fork seems to carry the same amount of water, so to call any one of them the "Missouri" would be giving a preference not warranted. The hunters returned at evening with six deer, three otter and a muskrat.

At 3 p.m. Capt. Clark arrived very sick with a high fever. He took five of Dr. Rush's pills. We intend to stay here for several days, so the men put their deer skins in the water to prepare them for dressing tomorrow. We are concerned that we do not find the Shoshoni Indians, for the success of our expedition is doubtful if we do not find some Indians with horses. We take consolation in the thought that if the Indians can live here and acquire food to subsist – so can we. It was near here that Sacagawea was captured by the Minnitaree about five years ago.

13

Three Forks to the Beaver's Head

JULY 28. Capt. Clark is somewhat better this morning since the pills have operated. We sent two men up to the southeast fork to examine that river. The captains concur in the impropriety of naming any of the forks the Missouri. Therefore they named the north-west fork – which they mean to ascend – the "Jefferson"; the middle-fork the "Madison," and the southeast fork, the "Gallatin." A small bower was erected for the comfort of Capt. Clark, as the leather lodge, when exposed to the sun, is very hot. The party are engaged in dressing skins, making moccasins, leggings and otherwise making themselves comfortable. Whitehouse is employed in making the main part of the clothing for the party. The hunters killed eight deer and two elk. Sacagawea shows no emotion or joy at being again in her native land. If she has enough to eat and a few trinkets to wear, we believe she would be contented anywhere. We took the altitude and made other observations.

JULY 29. The hunters brought in four fat bucks – the venison is now fat and fine. The men are all leather dressers and tailors, and are busy making garments. Capt. Clark is better, but still languid. Capt. Lewis prevailed upon him to take some barks, which he did. Both are busy making celestial observations.

JULY 30. Having completed the observations, and Capt. Clark being better, we reloaded the canoes and set out – ascending the Jefferson River. Capt. Lewis, Charbonneau, Sacagawea and two invalids, walked on shore. At 1 p.m., Capt. Clark and the canoes overtook them. After dinner, the two invalids and Charbonneau and Sacagawea boarded the canoes. Capt. Lewis continued to walk until evening, thinking the boats were below him. He fired his gun and shouted, but was not heard – so he camped out all night.

JULY 31. Capt. Lewis waited at his camp, wondering if the canoes were below or above him. Soon Charbonneau appeared and informed Lewis that the canoes were below. The boats had been detained by the twistings and rapidity of the river. After they all had breakfast, Capt. Lewis resumed his walk. At evening, Drouillard discovered a brown bear, but it escaped. We killed nothing today and are out of fresh meat. When we have plenty of it, it is impossible to make the men take care of it, nor use it with the least frugality. We expect that only necessity will teach us this art. Many of the men are lame and have boils. One man had his arm dislocated, but it was replaced and is well again. Sgt. Gass slipped and fell on the "gunwall" of the canoe. It gives him much pain to work the canoe. Charbonneau has a lame ankle, but likes to walk with Capt. Lewis.

AUGUST 1, 1805.   Capt. Lewis, Sgt. Gass, Drouillard and Charbonneau set out by land, hoping to find Indians. This being Capt. Clark's birthday, some flour was given to the party as a special celebration. Whitehouse left his tomahawk-pipe back at last night's camp. Capt. Lewis and party walked about eleven miles but he is indisposed by dysentery because he had taken a dose of Glauber's salts. He felt better when they reached the river – and killed two elk. They cooked these for themselves and for the men of the canoe party. The Fields brothers were sent out to hunt by Capt. Clark, and they killed five deer which provided the party with provisions again. We named a creek after Reuben Fields [North Boulder Creek]. We then came to another creek which we named "Frazier Creek" after our Robert Frazier [South Boulder Creek].

AUGUST 2.   Capt. Lewis and party resumed their march. The mountain tops around us are covered with snow, but the valleys are so hot that it nearly suffocates us. The goose and service berries are of excellent flavor. Sgt. Gass lost Capt. Lewis' tomahawk in the brush and was unable to find it. Capt. Lewis is well again. Capt. Clark walked along the river. We pass numerous beaver dams.

AUGUST 3.   Capt. Lewis walked ashore and left a note for Capt. Clark. About 11 a.m. Drouillard killed a doe, and they halted for breakfast. Afterwards, they walked about twenty-three miles and encamped for the evening.

Capt. Clark's party with the canoes set out early, while he walked ashore. The river is rapid and shallow, and in many places the men were obliged to drag the canoes over the gravel and spend much time in the water. Reuben Fields killed a large panther, 7½ feet from tip of tail to nose.

AUGUST 4.   Capt. Lewis and party are still walking ahead exploring the branches of the river. They descended the river and left a note for Capt. Clark to advise him to take the middle fork should he arrive there before Capt. Lewis returned. He has seen no signs of Indians in the course of his route. Charbonneau complains of his leg which detains Capt. Lewis considerably.

Capt. Clark set out at sunrise and sent two hunters ahead. At 8 a.m. he arrived at Capt. Lewis' camp of the 2nd, and found the note. The men have to drag the canoes over the shoals, being unable to use the tow-line because of the brush along the river banks.

AUGUST 5. Charbonneau and Sgt. Gass were sent back to make camp on the middle fork, seven miles distant, while Capt. Lewis and Drouillard continue upstream to explore the most direct river to the west. They returned a round-about way during which Drouillard missed his step and had a dangerous fall. They struck an old Indian road, but saw no recent tracks. They then directed their course to where Gass and Charbonneau had been told to make camp.

Capt. Clark and party set out at sunrise. The Fields brothers were sent ahead to hunt. They killed two deer on which the party made breakfast. The river is now rapid and the progress slow and painful. We came to the forks where Captain Lewis had left the note, but later found that a beaver had cut the green pole and had carried away both the note and the pole. So accordingly we took the wrong [Big Hole] branch for about a mile. The men are so fatigued that they wish such navigation would end, and that it were possible to go by land hereafter.

AUGUST 6. Capt. Lewis and party set out to return downstream to the forks. Drouillard was sent to hunt, and Sgt. Gass was to follow the river in case Capt. Clark's party were found. Capt. Lewis and Charbonneau went direct to the forks and the others were to meet him there. After going about five miles he heard the whooping of Clark's party to his right, so Lewis changed his route towards them. There they met, and discovered why Clark had taken the wrong stream. He had previously met Drouillard descending the stream to the forks. One of the canoes had just overset, and we lost some medicines and other articles. Whitehouse had been thrown out of the canoe, and was nearly crushed to death by the canoe passing over him. Much of our stores are wet, so we camped at the forks on a gravely bar to dry our goods. George Shannon had been sent out to hunt, but is lost again. Even Drouillard could not find him. We fired our guns, but Shannon did not return this evening. However, as we have reversed our course without Shannon's knowledge, he is not to blame.

AUGUST 7. We dispatched Reuben Fields to search for Shannon. Our stores are so reduced, we found that we could proceed with one less canoe. We therefore drew one of them into a high thicket and secured her in the event the river should rise. The air gun was out of order but was repaired by Shields, and now is regulated and shoots as well as ever. The baggage now being dry, the party under Capt. Clark proceded up the Beaverhead Fork. Capt. Lewis and Sgt. Gass remained at the forks to obtain some observations, then rejoined the canoe party at the evening camp. Drouillard brought in a deer. We have not heard from Shannon.

AUGUST 8. As one canoe had been left behind, we have more men for hunting. We therefore dispatched four men to hunt. The seven canoes were set off at sunrise. At noon Reuben Fields arrived, but had no news of Shannon. The boil on Capt. Clark's ankle has discharged, but is still painful. Sacagawea recognized a point on a high plain which she said was the summer retreat of her people. She calls the point the "Beaver's Head." Capt. Lewis resolved to go in search of the Indians.

AUGUST 9. We set out early. Capt. Lewis walked on shore to a point where he expected the canoes to arrive at 8 a.m. — the usual hour for breakfast. While we were here, Shannon arrived. He had lived well on game but was a good deal worried with his march. After breakfast, Capt. Lewis, Drouillard, John Shields and Hugh McNeal started out to find Indians, or a portage to the Columbia River. Game is scarce here.

AUGUST 10. Capt. Lewis and his party followed an Indian road towards the mountains which took them into a valley where the river divided itself again. Here the Indian road also forked. Drouillard was sent to explore one, while Shields took the other to determine the most traveled one. Meanwhile, Capt. Lewis wrote a note to Capt. Clark, recommending that he wait at the forks. He put this note on a *dry* willow pole. His party decided to take the western road, as it was the most used and led in the direction they wished to travel [Prairie Creek].

Capt. Clark set off at sunrise with the canoes, but the river was very crooked and shallow, so we were obliged to drag the boats over many riffles. Only one deer was killed today, but we found another that had been killed by Joseph Fields three days before, which he had hung up near the river. We passed the large outcrop of rock called the "Beaver's Head." [1]

---

[1] Some fifty miles farther up the river, near its forks with Prairie Creek, is a bluff which Lewis had named "Rattlesnake Cliffs" because of the number of snakes he found there. As its form more resembles a beaver than does the one which Sacagawea called "The Beaverhead," this has resulted in some confusion. Locally, the cliffs are now known as the "Beaverhead" while the proper one is called the "Point of Rocks." It was in this area that John Potts was later killed by the Blackfeet.

CLARK, CHARBONNEAU, AND SACAGAWEA MEET THE SHOSHONI, AUGUST 17, 1805
From a painting by Charles M. Russell. Courtesy of Thomas Gilcrease Institute, Tulsa, Oklahoma.

14

Beaver's Head to the Great Divide

AUGUST 11. Capt. Lewis' party set out early on the Indian road, but the track soon disappeared. He therefore set out towards a narrow pass on the creek with the hopes of recovering the trail. He sent Drouillard to the right and Shields to the left with orders to search for the road, and if successful, to signal by placing their hat on the muzzle of their gun. Capt. Lewis and McNeal kept on, and after going about five miles discovered an Indian on horseback coming towards them. They were overjoyed at the sight of this stranger. When we had come within a mile, the Indian halted, and Capt. Lewis did also. He unloosened the blanket from his pack and threw it up in the air by holding two corners, he then spread it on the ground as a signal of friendship. This signal did not seem to have the desired effect on the Indian, for he watched Drouillard and Shields on either flank of Capt. Lewis with suspicion. Capt. Lewis took some presents and walked towards the Indian, calling "tab-ba-bone," which in Shoshoni means "white man." [1] Drouillard saw the predicament, but Shields kept coming on, so when Capt. Lewis was about one hundred paces away, the Indian put the whip to his horse and vanished. We now set out on the track of the horse, hoping by that means it would lead to an Indian camp. We decided that if we followed too closely, the Indians might move off, so we made a camp on an elevated position where we took breakfast. Capt. Lewis prepared a small assortment of trinkets consisting of moccasin awls, beads, paint and a looking glass which was attached to a pole and planted near the fire with the thought that should the Indians return to our camp, they might discover by this token that we were friendly. A rain came up which made the track hard to follow, but we went some five miles where we saw signs of many horses. We camped on a small creek and planted a flag.

Capt. Clark with the canoes found the stream shallow and rapid, which caused the men to be in the water much of the day. The hunters killed three deer and an antelope.

AUGUST 12. Drouillard was sent as soon as it was light to try to discover

[1] Bakeless, *Lewis and Clark, Partners in Discovery*, 235, reveals that "tab-ba-bone" actually means "stranger, alien, outsider." The Shoshoni at that time had no word for "white-man," and this was the closest word that Sacagawea could come up with – unfortunate as it turned out to be. Therefore any stranger was looked upon as an enemy to the Shoshoni rider and accounts for his distrust of Lewis' intentions.

the route the Indian had taken. He followed it to the mountain where it ascended, then he returned to camp. Capt. Lewis determined to follow the base of the mountain with the expectation of finding an Indian road which would lead over the mountains. Drouillard was sent to the right, and Shields to the left to look for fresh tracks. After going four miles we found some recent bowers where the Indians had been gathering roots. We fell in with a large Indian road which we followed in and out of the ravines and streams. Drouillard shot at a large animal which might have been a wolverine, but it got away. Four miles further brought us to the distant fountain of the mighty Missouri – in search of which we have spent so many toilsome days and restless nights. Two miles below, Hugh McNeal had stood astride the little riverlet and had thanked his God that he had lived to have a foot on each side of the heretofore deemed endless Missouri. We proceeded on up the dividing ridge from which we saw immense ranges of high mountains lying to the west. We descended the mountain [by Lemhi Pass] to a creek of cold, clear water [the Lemhi], whose waters find their way to the Columbia. Here we camped for the night.

Captain Clark had to urge his boatmen on. They are sore from being constantly in the water – but still they labor on.

AUGUST 13.   Capt. Lewis and his little party followed the Indian road in a westerly direction. At about four miles we saw two women, a man and some dogs on an eminence immediately before us. They viewed us with attention, and two of them sat down to await our arrival. The rest of our party halted while Capt. Lewis walked slowly towards them, making signs of friendship, but the Indians disappeared. We followed the back track which led us along the road we had been traveling. We had not gone but a mile when we came upon three females. One ran off, but the two others saw we were too near them for escape, and they hung their heads as if reconciled to die. Capt. Lewis raised the elderly woman, repeated the word tab-ba-bone, and unbared his arm to show her his skin. The women were instantly reconciled, and he gave them some beads, moccasin awls, paint and pewter looking-glasses. Drouillard was directed to tell the woman to call the younger woman lest she alarm the camp. The old woman did so, and the fugitive girl returned. Capt. Lewis also gave her some presents, and painted their tawny faces with vermillion which is emblematic of peace. We informed them by signs that we wished to meet their chiefs. They ran off and we set out on the road along the river. We went two miles and were met by about sixty warriors mounted on excellent horses, who came on at nearly full speed. When they arrived, Capt. Lewis advanced, leaving his gun with our party about fifty paces behind. The women showed the advanced group the presents we had given them. The warriors then advanced and embraced

Capt. Lewis very affectionately. Both parties then came forward, and we were besmeared with their grease. We smoked the pipe, and the principal chief, Ca-me-ah-wait, addressed the warriors. We then moved on to their encampment on the river, four miles from where we had first met them. We explained the objects of our journey, and all the men and women looked at us – the first white people they had ever seen. It was now late, and as we had not tasted food since the evening before, they gave us some cakes made of service and choke berries. Cameahwait informed us that this stream, the Lemhi, discharged itself into another [the Salmon] but the latter was confined between inaccessible mountains and canyons and was impossible of travel. They have a great number of horses and we are hopeful of obtaining enough to transport our stores. The Indians danced nearly all night.

Meanwhile, Capt. Clark and his party set out, having dispatched some hunters ahead. The stream became more rapid and shallow. They passed a creek which they named after Hugh McNeal [Blacktailed Deer Creek, near Dillon, Montana]. They killed only one deer, but caught a number of fine trout.

August 14.   In order to give time for our canoes to reach the forks of the Beaverhead River, Capt. Lewis decided to remain here and collect all the information he could. The Indians having no food in camp, Drouillard and Shields borrowed some horses to hunt. About the same time the young warriors set out for the same purpose, but they all returned without success. Having secured the goodwill of Cameahwait, Capt. Lewis informed them through Drouillard's sign language, of his main party on the other side of the divide and asked if his warriors would take about thirty horses to transport our goods. Capt. Lewis promised them that they would be well rewarded for their trouble. Cameahwait made a long harangue to his warriors, then told Capt. Lewis that they would accompany him in the morning.

Captain Clark's party made about fourteen miles by water, though in a straight line the distance was only some six miles. The Fields brothers supplied them with five deer and an antelope. In a fit of temper, Charbonneau struck Sacagawea, for which Capt. Clark gave him a strong reprimand.

August 15.   Capt. Lewis awoke early and hungry. We found we had two pounds of flour left. McNeal was directed to divide this into two parts. He made one half into a berry pudding – the other half to save until evening. We gave some to the chief. The Indians do not seem anxious to move, and it developed that some of them thought we were in league with their enemies the Pahkies [Blackfeet].[2] Capt. Lewis appealed to the honor of Cameah-

2 Hodge, Frederick W., editor, *Handbook of American Indians North of Mexico*, Washington, 1912, v. 2, fn. 570.

wait which touched on his bravery. After a harangue, six or eight warriors joined him. At noon we set out, and had not gone far when ten or twelve more joined us, and before long it seemed as if the whole village, including some women, were with us. About sunset we reached a place which we called "Shoshoni Cove." Drouillard had been sent ahead to kill some meat but was unsuccessful, so Capt. Lewis divided the remaining flour which was stirred into a little boiling water.

Capt. Clark and party set out after breakfast with the canoes. The water was cold and the men were much exposed to it. They named a creek "Willard Creek" [now Grasshopper] after Alexander Willard. Capt. Clark and Sacagawea were near bitten by rattlesnakes. We killed a buck – the only game taken today. Capt. Clark paused to make celestial observations, then the party came on fifteen miles.

August 16.   Capt. Lewis sent Drouillard and Shields ahead to hunt as neither the Indians nor ourselves had anything to eat. A deer was killed and when the Indians heard of it, they rushed to the kill and were soon devouring the internal parts raw. McNeal skinned the deer, and reserved a quarter for us – the balance was given to the chief to be divided among his people. A second deer was killed by Drouillard, and the Indians enacted the same scene. At breakfast time, Drouillard joined us with a third deer. This was shared with the Indians, who were now filled with good humor. Shields killed an antelope as we neared the place where we expected to meet Capt. Clark's party. We made a halt. Capt. Lewis put his cocked-hat on Cameahwait who in turn placed Indian trinkets on Capt. Lewis. With Lewis' tanned skin, long hair and leather clothes, he looked like a complete Indian. We rode on two more miles, and were mortified that the canoe party was not there. The Indians were suspicious, and feared an ambush, which required every act of diplomacy on our part to allay their fears and keep them with us. Drouillard is to be sent with a note to Capt. Clark in the morning, for we are confident that there was not a moment to spare. Capt. Lewis slept fitfully, concerned over the delay of the canoe party and the fickleness of the Indians. We had explained to them that we had a woman of their nation with the party, and also a black man. The Indians were curious and seemed as anxious to see this monster as they were for our merchandise.

Capt. Clark and his party struggled against the rapids and narrow bottoms. Sacagawea gathered service berries while others caught some trout enroute. One deer was killed. Moving the canoes was hard and slow, and the men were fatigued and exhausted.

15

Crossing the Great Divide

AUGUST 17. This morning Drouillard and an Indian were sent down to the river while John Shields was sent to hunt. McNeal cooked the remainder of the deer on which we breakfasted with the chief. An Indian came to camp and reported that white men were coming. The Indians were as overjoyed as Capt. Lewis was. Shortly afterwards, Capt. Clark, Charbonneau and Sacagawea arrived. She proved to be the sister of Cameahwait, and their meeting was really affecting – particularly with another woman, "otter woman," who had been taken captive at the same time she had been, but who had escaped and rejoined her people. At noon the canoes arrived and we had the satisfaction of being all together again; and the prospect of being able to obtain horses so that we could prosecute our journey by land. We unloaded the canoes and arranged the baggage on shore. At evening we called the Indians together and through the medium of Labiche, Charbonneau and Sacagawea, we communicated the object that had brought us into their country. We made them sensible of their dependence on our government for merchandise, defence and peace. We told them we wanted to go as far as the western ocean as a means to find a more direct route to bring merchandise to them. We told them we needed horses to accomplish this, but would pay them in return. They appeared well pleased. We gave medals to the chiefs and also clothes and presents, and some hominy, which was the first they had ever eaten. York and the sagacity of Scannon were objects of their admiration. The hunters killed four deer and an antelope which we shared with the Indians.

Our captains now concerted measures for our future operations. It was agreed that Capt. Clark would take Sgt. Pryor, Sgt. Gass, Collins, Colter, Cruzatte, Shannon and probably Gibson, Shields and Joseph Fields, with the necessary tools for making canoes on the other side of the divide. Also, Charbonneau and Sacagawea and the Indians are to go with him to hasten the return of the Indians there with horses for Capt. Lewis. Meanwhile, Capt. Lewis was to bring the rest of the party and baggage to Shoshoni Cove. The spirits of the men are now much elated. We concluded to leave our canoes at this place, for we may need them when we return home later.

AUGUST 18. We bartered for four horses to outfit Capt. Clark and his men, and the whole Indian party except two men and two women, set out with him for the Shoshoni camp. We have reached the extreme navigable point of the Missouri. We had the stores and baggage aired, and began making packages of proper size for transportation by horse back. We put raw hide in the water for later making of thongs and gear for packing. Drouillard killed a deer, and one man caught a beaver. Today Capt. Lewis is thirty-one years old, and he resolved hereafter to live for mankind instead of for himself.

AUGUST 19.   At daylight three hunters went out. Some of the men are in want of moccasins and leggings, so are dressing skins. Others are making packsaddles, repacking baggage, etc. We made a seine of willow branches and caught a number of fine trout. The hunters returned with two deer. These Indians have a custom of bartering their infant daughters for future marriage. Sacagawea had thus been disposed of before her capture, and her proposed husband is living here with this band. He was more than double her age, and has two other wives. He claimed her, but as she had had a child by Charbonneau, now he did not want her. Our men are instructed to give these Indians no cause for jealousy by having connections with their women without the knowledge of their husbands. Cameahwait is a man of influence, good sense and of reserved manners, and appears to possess much sincerity. He wears his hair cut close all over his head, in mourning for his deceased relatives. These Shoshoni are now on the eve of their departure for the Missouri to hunt buffalo.

Captain Clark continued his route and was met by an Indian with two mules. This Indian had the politeness to offer one for Capt. Clark to ride, for which a waistcoat was given him for his civility. They value their mules three or four times to that of horses.

AUGUST 20.   The men are hunting and packing. We selected a spot, unseen by the Indians, to make a cache for the articles we intend to leave here, such as specimens of plants, minerals, seeds, etc. Having no nails or boards, we substituted thongs of raw hide to make packsaddles. We did use some of the planks from the packing cases, and some of the oars, for frames. We put the goods in the leather bags we had made. In this way we made twenty packsaddles. The Indian women have been making and repairing moccasins for the men. Drouillard recovered a trap that he had set last night, two miles below the place he had set it. Silas Goodrich caught several dozens of fine trout.

Capt. Clark and his party reached the new camp of the Shoshoni over the divide, and they halted for rest. He was given a salmon and some cakes of dried berries. He requested a guide to accompany him down the river. An elderly man was pointed out who consented to undertake the task. The chief drew a map of the country on the ground. He placed a number of heaps of sand on each side of his sketch of the [Salmon] river to represent vast mountains of rock through which that river passed. He described the river as being confined in a narrow channel through steep cliffs –filled with sharp, pointed rocks and foam. He said that none of his nation had ever been down this river beyond these mountains. The old man confirmed the statements just made, but informed us that *his* nation, the Nez Perces, resided at a twenty-one-days march from here, and that they traded with white people for articles from the sea, cloth, metal, etc. He told us that to get to his relations we would be obliged to climb over steep and rocky mountains for seven days where game was scarce. He also described other routes which appear to be across deserts towards the Gulf of California. Capt. Clark determined to explore this river to see if the accounts were true, and if so, to take the other mountain route, for he reasoned that if women and children could pass it, then our party could. Capt. Clark went on, leaving Charbonneau and Sacagawea to return to Capt. Lewis' camp with the Indians and horses. He left Cruzatte to purchase a horse and then overtake him. An old Indian continued with him.

AUGUST 21.   This morning is cold and the ink freezes in Capt. Lewis and Sgt. Ordway's pens. Drouillard was sent to hunt before the Indians arrived. By evening, all the packages, saddles and bags were ready for the march. We deposited some articles in the cache. The hunters returned unsuccessful, so the party was issued pork and corn.

Capt. Clark resumed his exploration and met some Indians who gave him boiled and dried salmon. They take them in weirs and with gigs. He sent John Collins and an Indian in search of Cruzatte who had not yet joined us. An Indian presented us with Drouillard's tomahawk which had been lost or stolen at the Indian camp. Capt. Clark was joined this evening by Collins and Cruzatte who brought five fresh salmon given them by Indians. He is much pleased with the intelligent, friendly old guide. In justice to Capt. Lewis, who was the first white man to see this [Salmon] river at the time when he was looking for Indians, we named it, "Lewis' River."

AUGUST 22.   A couple of men finished covering the cache which we could not do last night in the dark. Drouillard returned with a fawn and some Indian plunder. While hunting, he had come across some Indians. While talking with them, they took his gun and fled on their horses. After trying to recover his gun, he decided to bring their baggage to camp. It mostly consists of roots, of which Capt. Lewis had samples prepared to make notes of. Whitehouse is employed making leather shirts and overalls.

At 11 a.m., Charbonneau, Sacagawea, Cameahwait and about fifty men, women and children arrived at Lewis' camp. The Indians camped near us. Having no meat, Capt. Lewis prepared beans and corn for them to eat. We gave Cameahwait some dried squashes which we had boiled. He said it was the best thing he had ever tasted – except sugar – a small lump of which his sister, Sacagawea, had given him. In the evening the men built a brush drag, and in two hours they caught 528 very good fish – mostly trout. We gave most of the fish to the Indians. Capt. Lewis purchased five good horses. The Indians are very orderly and do not disturb our articles they see lying about. They borrow knives, kettles, etc., from our men, but always return them.

Capt. Clark with his guide, examined the north fork of the Salmon, encountering many Indians who were taking salmon from the streams. The country is very rocky and steep, and the river is rapid with stones scattered throughout. The Indian account was not exaggerated.

AUGUST 23.   The Indians appear to depend on us for food, so we sent two hunters out on horseback to hunt at a greater distance. Our stock of corn and flour is too low to indulge them with more. We laid up the canoes in a pond, and after taking out the plugs, we weighted them down with stones. We hope by this means to guard them against the effects of high water and the fires which are kindled in the plains by the natives. The Indians went on a hunt and got two mule deer and two common deer. At 3 p.m. the expected party of Indians arrived, but we learned that most of them were on their way to the buffalo country. This causes us some anxiety, for they had promised to assist us over the mountains. Capt. Lewis traded for one horse, but the natives are not inclined to part with any more.

Capt. Clark's party proceeded with difficulty in the exceedingly rough country. He followed an Indian track at times and ascended a mountain from which he had a view of the mountains to the west. He was now satisfied of the impracticability of this route, either by land or water, and so informed the old Indian guide. This guide, whom we call "Tobey," drew maps in the sand and by his evident familiarity with the country, Capt. Clark was convinced that the trail to the north which the guide had indicated, is more practical. Sgt. Pryor is unwell. We decided to rejoin Capt. Lewis and party.

AUGUST 24.   Capt. Lewis traded for three horses and a mule in exchange for a battle axe, a knife, a handkerchief and a little paint. The Indians told us they have no more horses to trade. We now have nine horses and a mule, and with two hired, make twelve. We had given Charbonneau some articles so that he could trade for a horse for Sacagawea to ride. The Indian squaws loaned us their horses, so we have twenty in all. We loaded the horses and

set out at noon. An Indian offered Capt. Lewis a horse to ride. Peter
Weiser is very ill with colic. Capt. Lewis gave him peppermint and laudanum, which relieved him. Sgt. Ordway had remained with him while he
was sick. Weiser was mounted on Lewis' horse, and the captain walked.
Silas Goodrich, our fisherman, caught several fine trout. We camped near
the Cove, making only five miles because of Weiser's illness.

Capt. Clark and party retraced their former track. He dispatched John
Colter on horseback to Capt. Lewis to notify him of the impossibility of
proceeding by way of the Salmon River, and advised him to purchase a
horse for each man if possible for the mountain trail. Capt. Clark slipped
and bruised his leg severely on a rock.

AUGUST 25.   Capt. Lewis' party loaded the horses and set out at sunrise.
We went about seven miles and halted. The hunters brought in three deer
which was divided among the Indians. Charbonneau mentioned that Sacagawea had told him that they expected to meet all the Indians tomorrow on
their way to the Missouri. Capt. Lewis was alarmed by this information,
for he learned that Cameahwait had requested his men to meet him to go to
the hunting grounds, consequently leaving us and our baggage on the mountains. Capt. Lewis therefore called the three chiefs together, smoked the
pipe, and asked them if they were men of their word. Cameahwait confessed
that he had done wrong, but his people were hungry, and this fact had influenced him. He promised to keep his word and assist us. We moved on to
the Cove where the creek enters the mountains. Frazier fired his musket at
some ducks, and the bullet rebounded from the water and passed within a
few feet of Capt. Lewis.

Capt. Clark and party worked their way upstream, subsisting on salmon
and berries, and on a beaver which Shannon had killed. Richard Windsor is
sick, which delayed their march somewhat.

AUGUST 26.   Capt. Lewis' party collected the horses and set out at sunrise.
We soon arrived at the extreme source of the Missouri, and the men drank
of the water and consoled themselves at having at length arrived at this
long wished for point. We crossed the divide at Lemhi Pass and drank the
water of a stream flowing to the Pacific. We halted at a spring to dine and
graze our horses, there being fine grass where the spring moistens the soil –
all else being dry and parched by the sun. We gave a pint of corn to each
Indian who has been helping us transport our baggage, and the same to our
men. One of the Indian women paused to give birth to a child, but within
the hour she arrived in camp with her newborn babe, apparently as well as
ever. We came to the Indian encampment where we found John Colter who
had just arrived with a letter from Capt. Clark. Upon reading the letter,

Capt. Lewis advised Cameahwait that we wished to purchase twenty more horses. We asked for a guide, but were informed that the old man with Capt. Clark was better informed of the country than any other man. Matters being arranged, Capt. Lewis ordered the fiddles to be played and our men danced for the amusement of the Indians so that we could obtain more horses.

Capt. Clark sent three men ahead to hunt. As his horses were missing, the old guide and four men went to look for them. This delayed us until 9 a.m., when we then proceeded up to the forks. We had nothing to eat but a few salmon.

16

Down the Lolo Trail

AUGUST 27. Capt. Clark had eight men out hunting, but they had no success. We had to subsist on salmon which we bought from the natives. Capt. Lewis, after paying off the women who had helped us over the pass, began to trade for horses. Charbonneau bought a horse for a red cloak. Our hunters come in with four deer and nine fine salmon. Capt. Lewis obtained eight horses in exchange for merchandise.

AUGUST 28. Capt. Clark dispatched Sgt. Gass to Capt. Lewis' camp and he returned this evening with the news that Capt. Lewis had obtained twenty-three horses, which with Capt. Clark's two, total twenty-five. Meanwhile the men made up three packsaddles, and bought some fish roe – which when dried and pounded, makes a good soup. Capt. Clark and party set out to join Capt. Lewis.

AUGUST 29. Capt. Clark and party joined us this morning and we continued to bargain for horses. In the end we obtained twenty-nine, but some have sore backs. Sgt. Gass and another man did not come back with Capt. Clark, but remained below to make packsaddles. Our hunters supply us with two or three deer every day.

AUGUST 30. Having made our purchases, we loaded our horses and prepared to start. We have thirty horses. We took leave of the Shoshoni, who set out for the Missouri, and we at the same time, with Tobey and his four sons – and another Indian, began the descent of the Lemhi River. Though Sacagawea departed from her people, she showed no emotion, and seems perfectly happy to remain with the white people [She probably never saw her people again]. The hunters brought in three deer, so we did not feel the want of provisions. We camped at the place where we found Sgt. Gass and his companion, for there is good grass here.

AUGUST 31. We resumed our journey, and in three hours halted to let our horses graze near Salmon River. We then went on by Tower [Boyle's] Creek where we left Capt. Clark's path on his tour of seventy miles, and began a new route. We camped at night near some old Indian lodges.

SEPTEMBER 1, 1805. We proceeded on over high, rugged hills in a north direction. We gigged some salmon and killed a deer. All the Indians left us except old Toby and one son. A great abundance of service and choke berries are growing here. York's feet became so sore he had to ride. Some of the men were sent to buy salmon from the Indians and they returned with 25 pounds.

SEPTEMBER 2.   We went up Fish Creek and had to cut our way through the thickets of brush. The party is too busy with the horses to do any hunting. We made a hungry camp this evening, and it rained, making an uncomfortable night. One of the horses became lame and we had to unload him.

SEPTEMBER 3.   We sent two men back two miles for the load of the horse which was crippled yesterday. We are crossing the mountains [Bitterroot Range] which are high and steep. The last of our thermometers was broken by accident. We also ate the last of our salmon and pork. Some of the men threatened to kill one of the colts, they are that hungry.

SEPTEMBER 4.   There was snow on the ground this morning. We ascended the mountain and kept on the dividing ridge for a few miles [Lost Trail Pass] until we came to a creek which appeared to run in the direction we wished to go. Our hunters killed a deer which we made good use of. We went down the creek five miles to its forks [Ross' Hole] where we met a party of about thirty-three lodges or some four hundred people and at least five hundred horses of the Flathead nation. They received us with much friendship. We camped with them, smoked the pipe and made speeches. We are the first white men they have ever seen on their waters.

SEPTEMBER 5.   We tried to tell these people who we were and where we wished to go, but their language is very strange, so we proceeded to the more intelligible language of giving presents. We purchased twelve horses, and swapped seven of our lame ones. They helped us as much as they were able.

SEPTEMBER 6.   We purchased two more horses and made a vocabulary of their language. We could now lighten our loads as we now have forty horses and three colts. We set out at 2 p.m., as the Indians went off in the opposite direction to meet the Shoshoni at the Three Forks of the Missouri. We came down and made camp in a small bottom. We secured our horses well for fear of them leaving us, or being stolen. We named the stream we are on "Clark's River" [the Bitterroot River of Idaho].

SEPTEMBER 7.   We continued north along the river, and at six miles we came to the [Nez Perce] fork from the left, after which the [Bitterroot] valley widens. One of our hunters stayed out all last night – having lost his horse. He overtook us today. Our hunters, who are now supplied with horses, brought in two deer – a subject of much joy and congratulation to us.

SEPTEMBER 8. We set out early and proceeded twenty-three miles through the open valley. Two of our hunters came in with a deer and an elk. Drouillard killed a deer and one of the captains got a prairie fowl. We found two mares and a colt. We ventured to let our recent purchase of horses loose tonight.

SEPTEMBER 9. We proceeded down the river. The surrounding valley is five to six miles wide. Drouillard arrived with two deer. This river has no salmon in it which leads us to believe that there must be a considerable waterfall somewhere below. Old Tobey could not inform us where this river discharges itself into the Columbia. He knew of the [Hellgate] branch that leads towards the Missouri. We continued down the west side of the river and camped on a large creek that falls in from the west. We determined to rest here and make observations, so we call this creek "Traveler's Rest Creek" [Lolo Creek]. From here we will take the trail that our old guide knows through the mountains.

SEPTEMBER 10. All the hunters were sent out, and the rest of the party are repairing their clothes. Two men were sent down seven miles to the junction of this river [Bitterroot] with the [Hellgate] branch. Towards evening, Colter returned with three Indians he had met up on (Lolo) creek. Our Nez Perce guide could not speak with them, but by the sign language we found they were Flatheads. One was persuaded to remain with us to guide us to his people who reside on the Columbia. Our hunters got four deer, a beaver and three grouse.

SEPTEMBER 11. Our horses had strayed and this delayed our start this morning. We set out at 3 p.m. and turned to the west up Lolo Creek, accompanied by the Flathead Indian, but he became restless and set out alone. We went seven miles and camped at some old Indian lodges. We had sent four of our best hunters to precede us.

SEPTEMBER 12. We proceeded up Lolo Creek and came to a bath-house or sweat house covered with earth. We found some game here. We had to cross over a steep mountain before we came to the creek again. Some of the party did not get into camp until 10 p.m. The men and horses are much fatigued.

SEPTEMBER 13. Capt. Lewis and one of the Indian guides lost their horses during the night. He and four men were detained to look for them. The rest of us went on, and at two miles we came to several hot springs [Lolo Hot Springs]. Several roads lead to these springs, and our guide took a wrong one, which took us out of the way some three miles. Capt. Lewis came up without the horses, and we went up over a mountain, and made a camp where we had good feed for the horses.

SEPTEMBER 14. We set out early and crossed a high mountain where it was snowing and then crossed Glade Creek. There is no game up here, so we were compelled to kill a colt for the men to eat. We also had some of the portable soup – which the men did not like. We had brought it from the States.

SEPTEMBER 15. During the day we ascended a high mountain. Some places were so steep that the horses fell down backwards and rolled down the rocks some twenty or thirty feet, but none was killed. The horse which carried Capt. Lewis' desk and small trunk turned over, and rolled down forty yards before he lodged against a tree. This broke the desk, but the horse was but little hurt. When we arrived at the top of the mountain, we could find no water, so we used snow to cook the remainder of the colt, and made some soup. Our horses begin to fail, and two are so worn out and poor that we are obliged to leave them behind.

SEPTEMBER 16. When we awoke we were covered with snow. We mended our moccasins and some of the men wrapped their feet with rags. Towards evening we descended the mountain over a rocky, rough road and camped in a cove. All being tired and hungry, we killed another colt and ate half of it.

SEPTEMBER 17. Our horses were so scattered in the timber that we were detained until 10 a.m. before they were collected. We killed a few pheasants but they were insufficient for our sustenance, so we killed another colt. It was agreed that Capt. Clark should go ahead with six hunters to kill something for our support.

SEPTEMBER 18. Capt. Clark and six hunters set out. Alexander Willard lost a horse which detained us. We sent him back for it, but he returned at 4 p.m. alone. We finished the last of the colt and supped on a scant proportion of portable soup and bear's oil.

SEPTEMBER 19. Capt. Clark and his hunters found a horse on a small plain on which they breakfasted, and hung the balance of the meat in a tree for the party in the rear. He came to a creek which he named "Collins Creek," for Collins – one of the hunters with him. The men are growing weak and are losing flesh; several are afflicted with dysentery, and eruptions of the skin are very common among us. We discover the appearance of level country about forty miles ahead, which brings much joy to the corps. Frazier's horse fell from the road and rolled a hundred yards into the creek. We expected that the horse was killed, but when the load was removed, the horse arose, and within twenty minutes was reloaded and was off again.

SEPTEMBER 20. Capt. Lewis and party were detained for the collection of his stray horses. After going on two miles we found the horse meat and a note Capt. Clark had left. In it he advised us he was going on to the level country where he expected to find game. La Page's horse is missing, so he was sent back to search for it. At 3 p.m. he returned without the horse. His load was of considerable value; consisting of merchandise and all of Capt. Lewis' winter clothing. Therefore two of the best woodsmen were sent back to search, while we proceeded on.

Capt. Clark went on, and at noon reached a plain where he found many Indian lodges. He came across three Indian boys to whom he gave ribbons, and sent them to their village. Soon after, an Indian came, with great caution, to meet us. He conducted us to a large lodge. We learned by signs that this was the lodge of his great chief who then was absent on a war hunt. The women gave us buffalo meat, berries, dried salmon and roots. After such a long abstinence, this was a sumptuous feast. We gave them some presents and moved on two miles with a chief to his village. We were treated kindly, so we camped with them. The hunters discovered some signs of game, but could kill nothing.

September 21.   The free use of food made Capt. Clark sick. He sent out the hunters while he collected information as to the route from the Indians. These Indians call themselves Chopunnish, or "Pierced noses" [Nez Perce]. The chief drew a map of the river which led to the Columbia. Capt. Clark purchased as much dried salmon, roots and berries as he could with the few articles we happened to have in our pockets. He sent Reuben Fields with an Indian back to Capt. Lewis, while the rest of us went to the camp of Twisted Hair, a head Nez Perce chief. After going twelve miles, we arrived at his camp. At 11 p.m. Capt. Clark gave Twisted Hair a medal and smoked with him until 1 a.m. Twisted Hair is about forty-five years old, and is cheerful and sincere.

Capt. Lewis and party struggled down the mountains to a small plain where there was tolerable grass for the horses and encamped.

September 22.   Capt. Lewis had ordered the horses hobbled last night, but one of the men neglected the duty, so the horses strayed, and we were delayed until 11:30 a.m. before we could renew our march. We soon met Reuben Fields whom Capt. Clark had sent. He brought dried salmon and roots, so we halted for refreshment for there was enough food to satisfy our hunger. He had also killed a crow. At 5 p.m. we arrived at the first Indian lodges. The men searching for the lost horses came in. They had found the horses, but think they had been stolen last night.

Meanwhile, Capt. Clark met the chief on the river, and they both set out for Lewis' camp. He sent out the hunters, leaving one man to watch the baggage. Enroute back, Clark and the chief met John Shields with three deer. Capt. Clark exchanged horses with Shields, but the horse threw Capt. Clark three times, and his hip was hurt. Nevertheless, we reached the village at sunset where we found Capt. Lewis and party encamped [Weippe Prairie]. We cautioned them of the consequences of overeating so soon after their fast. Capt. Lewis had lost three horses – one of which belonged to Tobey. The Indians had stolen from Reuben Fields a shot-pouch, a knife, wipers and a steel and compass. Having no interpreter, we communicated by sign language. Twisted Hair drew on a white elk skin a map of the rivers of this country.

September 23.   We traded with the Indians for roots, camas bread and dressed elk skins. We make shirts of the skins. The Indians were assembled and we told them where we had come from, and where we wanted to go. We gave them flags and medals and told them we had come to make peace between all tribes. This appeared to satisfy them very much. We gathered our horses and proceeded to the second village two miles distant. Capt. Lewis and two men are very sick this evening and Capt. Clark's hip is painful. The Indian women are busy gathering and drying camas roots which are good and nourishing – they taste like pumpkins.

September 24.   Our horses are scattered over the plains and are mixed in with the native's horses – of which they have many. John Colter was sent back to look for the horses which had been lost in the mountains. Here the weather is hot and oppressive. Seven of our men, including Sgt. Gass, are sick from eating heartily of the sweet roots and salmon. Capt. Clark gave them Dr. Rush's pills. We went to the [Clearwater] river, where the hunters joined us with four deer and two salmon. We hunted for trees large enough to build canoes, and then camped along the river [near present, Orofino, Idaho].

September 25.   Capt. Clark with the chief and a young man, went down the river to hunt suitable trees for canoes. At the junction of the middle and north forks of the [Clearwater] river we found fine timber. Capt. Lewis is very sick. Three men are hunting. Colter returned with a horse he had found.

September 26.   We moved down to a bottom opposite the forks of the river and made camp. The axes were distributed so that the men could start making canoes. The day is very hot and many of the men are sick. Capt. Clark administered salts, pills, jalap and tarter emetic as remedies. We purchase fresh salmon from the natives, and constructed a pen to keep our baggage in.

IN THE LOLO PASS
From a painting by Olaf C. Seltzer.
Courtesy of Thomas Gilcrease Institute, Tulsa, Oklahoma

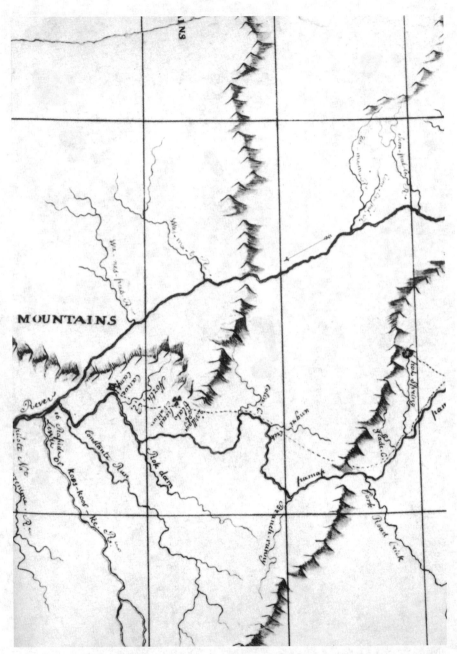

A section of Robert Frazier's (here spelled Frazer) map of 1807, showing the area from the Lewis River to the junction of the Snake and Columbia rivers. Note his misplacement of "Traveler's Rest" and Lolo "Hot Springs," far to the west of the Bitterroot River, on a branch of the Clearwater River. Courtesy of the Library of Congress.

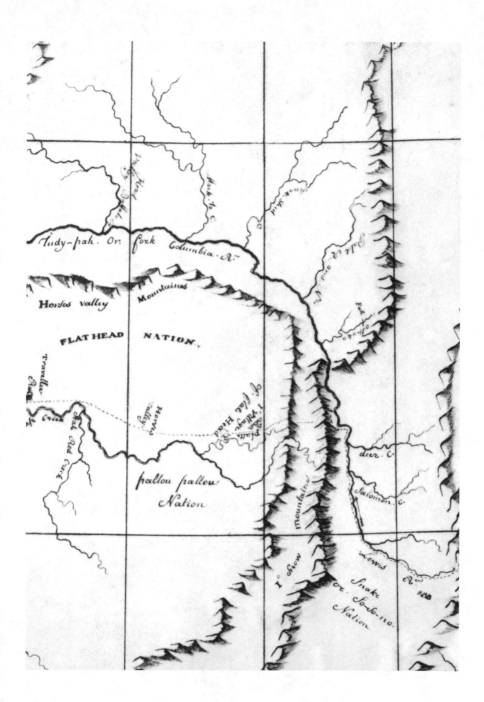

SEPTEMBER 27.   The well men are divided into five parties and were set about felling trees. John Colter came in with the horse and a cannister of shot which was left in the mountains. Also a deer. This is nourishing food for our invalids.

SEPTEMBER 28.   Some of the men are getting better, but Drouillard is still sick. The rest that are able, are working on the canoes and oars. Two men are out hunting. We fixed some gig poles to catch salmon. Game is very scarce here so we are obliged to live on fish and roots.

SEPTEMBER 29.   The two hunters, Drouillard and Colter, stayed out all night but returned at noon with three deer – a most welcome sight. To save hard cutting, we use the Indian method of burning out the canoes. Three-fourths of our men are sick.

SEPTEMBER 30.   Our hunters killed a deer. We get along slowly with the canoes.

OCTOBER 1, 1805.   We examined and dried all our goods. There is little game to kill so we live on a diet of dried fish. Capt. Lewis is getting better. We built fires on several of the canoes to burn them out and found that this works very well. We are visited by several Indians from the tribes below.

OCTOBER 2.   We sent Frazier and Goodrich up to the village with six horses and some merchandise to trade for salmon and camas bread. Our hunters returned with nothing but a prairie wolf – which we ate. The party is weak from lack of meat, so we killed a horse which we ate with as good an appetite as we did the finest beef back in the States.

OCTOBER 3.   Our men are employed on the boats. We are building five of them.

OCTOBER 4.   Frazier and Goodrich returned from the village with the fish and roots. Some of our Frenchmen [Labiche, Cruzatte, La Page] ate a fat dog. Capt. Lewis is recovered so as to be able to walk about a little.

OCTOBER 5.   The canoes are nearly finished, and it became necessary to dispose of our horses. We collected thirty-eight of them and they were branded with an iron we had brought from the States. They were delivered to three Indians – one the son of the chief. We cropped the fore manes of the horses so that we could recognize them again later. The old chief, Twisted Hair, has agreed to take good care of them until we return. To each of the Indians we gave a knife and some small articles. The hunters were unable to kill anything, so we are therefore obliged to eat dried fish and roots. These roots have very active properties, for after eating them in the evening, we are so swelled with gas as to be scarcely able to breathe for several hours. Tonight we launched two canoes which proved to be very good in the water.

OCTOBER 6. We had a cache made for our saddles, and during the night we buried them. We also left a cannister of powder and a bag of balls at the place where John Shields had made a canoe from a tree. All the canoes are finished and were put in the water. The captains, though sick, made observations.

OCTOBER 7. The canoes were loaded, the oars fixed, and every preparation was made for setting out. We have four large canoes and one small one, and found that our baggage was carried in them comfortably. The two chiefs who promised to accompany us were not to be found – and at the same time we missed Capt. Clark's pipe-tomahawk. We therefore went on without them. We passed ten rapids in descending. The captain's canoe struck a rock and sprang a leak. We, however, continued for nineteen miles, and then camped where we could fix the canoe. Tobey and his son, who came over the mountains with us, continue with our party.

OCTOBER 8. We set out at 9 a.m. and passed a large creek [Potlatch] to which we gave the name of "Colter's," after John Colter. After leaving this creek, and as we were passing the last of the fifteen rapids, one of the canoes which Sgt. Gass was steering, struck a rock and sank. Fortunately, the water was only waist deep, so our baggage was saved, though it was thoroughly wet. We were obliged to halt for the night and spread the baggage to dry. We found the two Nez Perce chiefs, Twisted Hair and Tetoharsky, here who had promised to go with us to help as pilots. After we had had a smoke, they willingly came aboard. We bought some salmon and two dogs from the Indians. John Thompson was hurt when the canoe upset.

OCTOBER 9. We found that the canoe could be repaired by the time the goods were dry, so we set Sgt. Pryor, Sgt. Gass, Joseph Fields and George Gibson to work on her. We set out to collect resin from the pine trees. By 1 p.m. the canoe was stronger than ever. One man was sent to trade for fish, rootbread and dogs. At dark, we found that our old guide, Tobey, and his son had left us, and were seen running back up the river several miles. We could not account for their leaving, unless it was that they were afraid of being cast away in the rapids. Tobey had received no pay, nor hinted of his intentions. Capt. Lewis is recovering rapidly. The Indians here are troublesome, and we have to put two sentinels around our baggage to prevent stealing. Labiche, Cruzatte and La Page prefer dog flesh to fish, and have traded for some from the Indians.

OCTOBER 10. We loaded our canoes and set off at 7 a.m. We passed several rapids and halted near the confluence of the [Snake and Clearwater] rivers. The Indians flock around us and we bought a few dogs from them to eat. They ridicule us for this and call us "dog-eaters." Sgt. Gass was unable to steer the canoe today as he has a fit of the ague. At 11 a.m. we came to a very bad rapid which was full of rocks. We had to take the boats down one at a time. One of them struck a rock and received a hole. We got her safe to shore, and then unloaded and repaired her. The Indians caught some of our oars which had been washed ashore. At 5 p.m. we came to the [Snake] river. A misunderstanding arose between the two Fields brothers and Charbonneau. We believe it was started over a jest.

The branding iron mark used on the horses
of the Expedition on October 5, 1805

17

Rapids of the Snake to Tidewater

OCTOBER 11. We set out early. At six miles we came to some Indian lodges and took breakfast. We purchased all the salmon we could, and seven dogs. Later, at another Indian camp, we purchased some roots and five more dogs. Most of our men have been accustomed to meat and do not relish fish. They prefer dog meat, which, when well cooked, tastes very well. We passed nine rapids – all of them great fishing places. Two Indians accompany us in a small canoe.

OCTOBER 12. After purchasing all the provisions these Indians could spare, we set out. We passed several rapids – some of them very bad. We came to one to view it before we attempted its descent. We found it was about two miles in length, with many turns necessary to avoid the rocks. Two of the Flatheads remained on board with us and acted as pilots. We determined to camp above. We find wood is very scarce which we need to cook our victuals.

OCTOBER 13. We took two of the canoes down the rapids at a time. The Indians went on before to pilot us. The men who could not swim were sent by land and carried the rifles, instruments, etc. We got safe below by noontime. We came to a large stream which we named "Drewyer's" [now Palouse] after George Drouillard, our interpreter.

OCTOBER 14. We embarked early. About 1 p.m. a canoe steered by Sgt. Ordway, hit a rock, and partly sank. A number of things floated out. With the assistance of the other canoes, all the men got safe to shore, but the baggage was wet, and some articles were lost, including bedding, shot pouches, loose powder, roots, etc. Fortunately the lead cannisters of powder were tied down, or we would have lost them when the canoe turned over. We halted on an island to dry the baggage. A small canoe, and three of the Indians in another one, were out of sight at the time of our misfortune, and did not join us. We have made it a point at all times not to take anything belonging to the Indians – even their wood. But in this emergency we are obliged to take some of their split wood for our fires, for no other can be found in any direction. One of the men killed eight ducks.

OCTOBER 15. We set out late as the captains were making observations and drawing sketches of the route we have passed. We sent out some hunters, but they could not get game of any kind. Labiche killed two geese and two ducks of large size. Our Indians who had piloted us, crossed over to the place where they thought it proper to delay us above a dangerous rapid. We camped at a place [Rattlesnake Flats] just above Fish-hook Rapids.

OCTOBER 16.   We set out early and all the canoes, except Sgt. Pryor's, ran the rapids. Pryor's ran on a rock, but by the assistance of the three other canoes, it was unloaded and pulled off the rock. There was no injury, other than wetting the greater part of the loading. Whitehouse was in the canoe with Pryor. We reloaded and proceeded on. Capt. Clark walked around the rapids. We halted on a point at the junction of the Snake and Columbia rivers. There were Indians here and we smoked with them. About two hundred came from their camp, singing and dancing as they came. We smoked with them also. We bought from them seven dogs, and they gave us several fresh salmon and some dried horse meat.

OCTOBER 17.   This morning the captains made lunar observations. The chief of the tribe came down and we purchased some dogs from his people. Capt. Clark and two men went up the Columbia River to the first fork to inspect that place. Hunters were sent out to shoot some prairie-cock – a large fowl found near the river. Capt. Lewis took a vocabulary of these Indians, and also of those Indians who live upstream on the [Yakima] river. Capt. Clark and his men returned at dark. The party is employed in dressing skins, mending clothes and putting their arms in order – the latter always being a matter of attention with us. Many of the natives have sore eyes, perhaps caused by the reflections from the water where they are continually fishing in an open country, hence the eyes have no rest. They are friendly and not beggarly – but they stole an axe from us last night.

OCTOBER 18.   Several heath hens lit near us and the men killed six of them. The captains are busy taking measurements of the rivers and making meridian altitudes. We purchased forty dogs today. The fish offered by the natives are spoiled and very bad. There are thousands of them washed up on the shores. We set off down the Columbia accompanied by the two chiefs. Our Flathead Indians left us as they are unwilling to go any further. The Great Chief drew us a map of the Columbia River above us and of the tribes that live on its waters.

OCTOBER 19.   Several of the chiefs visited us today. We gave them medals and strings of wampum. Peter Cruzatte played the fiddle which pleased and astonished them. Capt. Clark walked ashore with the two chiefs, and Charbonneau and Sacagawea. Upon ascending a cliff, he discovered to the west a high mountain covered with snow. We think it is Mt. St. Helens as laid down on Vancouver's map [It was Mt. Adams]. We saw many lodges, but the natives fled and hid. Capt. Clark searched one lodge, and upon entering, found thirty-three people, some of whom were crying and wringing their hands. He gave them his hand and distributed a few small presents, which pacified them. Drouillard and the Fields brothers also used every means to convince these people of our friendly intentions. It seems they were frightened because they had seen Capt. Clark kill a crane in the sky, and they therefore thought that we came from the sky. As soon as they saw Sacagawea, who was with Capt. Lewis, they all came out of hiding and assumed new life, as they knew no squaw ever accompanies a war party. We smoked with them, and then dropped down the stream. We landed, and were joined by many natives who brought us some fire wood — which was very acceptable, for none is to be found about. Cruzatte and George Gibson played the violins which delighted them greatly.

OCTOBER 20. We breakfasted on dog flesh and then set out. Some of the natives have white men's clothes which they have traded for from the coast tribes. On Memaloose Island we saw a place where the Indians deposit their dead. There was a frame of boards and old canoes sixty feet long and twelve feet wide. There were a great number of human bones covered with mats, fish nets, various kinds of trinkets, etc., heaped with them.

OCTOBER 21. Having no wood, we could not cook our breakfast. John Collins made some excellent beer from the camas root bread which had become wet and soured from our past accidents. We passed on down until we came to a large [Owyhee] rapid which we halted to examine. All who could not swim walked on shore. After passing this rapid we came to a small river which we named "La Page" [John Day River], after one of our Frenchmen. We came to some natives and purchased from them a little wood to cook our dog meat and fish. The natives all have pierced noses and do not receive us with the same cordiality as the natives above did. From the last rapid we saw Mount Hood.

OCTOBER 22. We pressed on, and came to a very considerable rapid where an immense body of water was compressed into a narrow channel two hundred yards wide. Two miles above this we had passed a [Des Chutes] river. At the [Celilo] falls we landed and walked down to find the best route for a portage. We took every article except the canoes across the portage where we formed a camp in a suitable position to protect our stores from theft. The Indians with their horses helped us carry the heavy articles. We sent two men to examine the river.

OCTOBER 23. We took the canoes over the portage with much difficulty. One got loose and was caught by the Indians below, whom we had to pay for its recovery. Our old chief heard the Indians below say that they intended to kill us. We have our arms in order. As these Indians will not sell us their good fish, we purchased eight dogs for the party to eat. We exchanged our small canoe and a hatchet and a few articles, for a large, new Indian canoe built for riding the waves. This place is full of fleas so we are obliged to strip naked in order to brush the pests off. The Indians left us earlier than usual, and our chiefs appeared very uneasy this evening with their fears and suspicions of an intended attack.

OCTOBER 24. The Indians approached our camp with caution. Our two old chiefs are determined to return home, as their nation is at war with the nations below, and they are afraid of being killed. We persuaded them to stay two nights longer with us with a view of making peace. Capt. Lewis and three men went to study the falls, while Capt. Clark set out with the land party. It being impossible to portage the canoes around the boiling rapids, we had to ride the canoes through them. We had confidence in our head waterman, Peter Cruzatte, which was well placed. The Indians who watched from the high banks were astonished. The men who could not swim went on shore carrying the goods, guns, ammunition and papers. We proceeded down the channel and landed at a village of twenty-one wooden houses. Here we found Capt. Lewis and a chief from below with a large party of men. Cruzatte played the violin, and the men danced, which pleased the Indians. We visited their wood houses, the first we had seen since leaving the Illinois. This presented a good opportunity to hold a council to make peace – which we are satisfied we accomplished. They furnished us with dogs, cranberries and some of their root bread.

OCTOBER 25. The captains walked down to see the place which the Indians say is the best place for passing through the channel. As there was no portage for the canoes, we decided to run the canoes through the long narrows. As usual, the men who could not swim, walked around, carrying the stores. Our best watermen took the canoes through. We stood by with ropes should there be any difficulty. The first three canoes passed through safe, while the fourth nearly filled with water, and the last one passed through shipping only a little water. We are grateful and pleased that we have passed the worst part of the river. We loaded the canoes and set out, but one of the canoes struck a rock and was in danger of being lost. We came to a village where we met our old chiefs and a party with whom we smoked and gave a medal. The old chiefs parted with us at this place. They had purchased a horse each, and intended to return to their villages on the

[Clearwater] river. Drouillard killed a deer and saw much sign of others. We formed a rock fort for defense should the Indians decide to attack us. They are in the habit of collecting a levy from all who pass this part of the Columbia.

OCTOBER 26.   We sent six men to hunt deer and collect rosin to patch the canoes which have become very leaky from being hauled over the rocks. We are drying our stores while the canoes were drawn out and turned over. Many of the articles are spoiled from repeated wetting. We were visited by some chiefs from above the falls who were out hunting at the time we passed over the falls. We gave them medals, paint, knives, etc., and acknowledged them as chiefs. Cruzatte played the violin as they sat around our fire, and York danced for them – which pleased them exceedingly. Our hunters returned with five deer. One of our guards gigged a salmon trout which we thought the most delicious fish we had ever tasted. We dried all our articles and repaired the canoes. The fleas bother us as we do not have a change of clothing. The party amused themselves by dancing at night. This lay-over enabled the captains to take observations and vocabularies of this nation.

OCTOBER 27.   We sent out the hunters this morning. They brought back four deer and a pheasant. These chiefs and party continue with us. We treat them well and feed and smoke with them. They were joined by seven others from below who wanted to take liberties with our goods, and after we declined being taken advantage of, they returned down the river in ill humor. Soon the chiefs decided to go home, and we put them across the river. These natives flatten their heads by compressing them between boards when infants.

OCTOBER 28.   Some Indians came down from the village above. One had a round hat, others a musket and a sword, and brass tea kettles of which they were very proud. We purchased five dogs, some dried berries and a white bread made of roots. We laid by because of the high wind, but this wind did not deter the natives at all, as their canoes are designed to ride the highest waves. Our hunters killed a deer.

OCTOBER 29.   We set out at daylight and went to a village five miles down. The people here are very friendly, and gave us filbert nuts, pounded fish and root bread. We gave the women pieces of ribbon which pleased them. We purchased twelve dogs of them, and then went to another village where we obtained four more dogs. We camped near another village where they gave us high-bush cranberries, roots, etc. They were pleased with the music of Cruzatte's violin. We had passed a river on the left which we called "Labiche's River" [Hood River], after our fine waterman.

OCTOBER 30.   After a light breakfast on venison, we set out. Capt. Clark and two men went on an old Indian path to view the Cascades which we found were impossible to pass without a portage. They returned at dark. Meanwhile, Capt. Lewis and five men went to the village and found the people there friendly. He got some berries and nuts, but could get no information as to traders who visit them. It rained all day. One of the hunters killed a deer. We named a stream the "Cruzatte" [Wind River] after Peter Cruzatte.

OCTOBER 31.   Capt. Clark, Joseph Fields and Cruzatte went down the river to view the Cascades. Cruzatte was sent back to examine the rapids near the shore, while Capt. Clark and Joseph Fields continued on for ten miles, after which the current became uniform. They had reached tide water. They passed a large burial place which contained many bones, sea shells, brass kettles and wooden, carved images. These things we do not touch. Joseph Fields killed a sand-hill crane, then the party all returned to camp. During this time, Capt. Lewis and his party unloaded the canoes and took two of them down, one at a time, over very high rocks. We got only two over as it was hard work.

NOVEMBER 1, 1805.   We set all hands packing the baggage over the portage — 940 yards of bad rocks and slippery hill sides. Some of the canoes were injured and had to be repaired. We brought down the two other large canoes and the small one. Towards evening we had all of them safe below the rapids, and then we camped.

18

Tidewater to the Ocean

NOVEMBER 2. We took the baggage over a portage of a mile and a half. The canoes ran the rapids without much damage. We took breakfast and made a meridian altitude, and then set out. Labiche killed fourteen geese and a brant. John Collins killed one, and the Fields brothers got three.

NOVEMBER 3. We had heavy fog this morning which detained us until 10 a.m. Before we set out, Collins killed a large buck and Labiche killed three geese flying in the air. The captains explored the mouth of Seal [Washougal] River — a considerable stream. We see Mt. Hood to the south-east of us. We landed on the north side of an [Government] island and encamped. Capt. Lewis and some others went hunting. An Indian woman of the Snake nation came to visit us, but Sacagawea could not converse with her sufficiently well to be understood (for Sacagawea is a Shoshoni). Capt. Lewis and three men set out after night in search of swans, ducks and geese which appear in great numbers in a lake on this island. They got several on which we had a sumptuous supper. We shared this with our Indian visitors. They tell us in two sleeps we shall see the ocean and white people.

NOVEMBER 4. We set out at 8:30 a.m., having dispatched four men in the small canoe to hunt. Later we landed at a large village and were treated very kindly by the natives. They gave us a round root about the size of a hen's egg. They roast them and call them "wappato." Many Indians visit us and have more European trinkets than the natives above. Some Indians arrived and are armed with pistols, war axes and ready sprung bows and arrows. They are a sort of middlemen between the coast tribes and those above. They were assuming and disagreeable. However, we smoked with them and treated them with friendship. They stole a great coat from one of the interpreters which we later found stuffed under the root of a tree. They also stole the pipe-tomahawk of Capt. Clark — which we never found. We saw crab apples and raspberries. The hunters got two deer and some ducks.

NOVEMBER 5. The noise made by the swans, geese and ducks on the lake kept us awake last night. We set out at sunrise and the river began to widen out. We dined at an island and the hunters obtained many fowl. We made thirty-two miles today and then camped. Tonight is the first time since our arrival on the Columbia that we have been free of Indians.

NOVEMBER 6. It is a cold, wet morning. We set out early and passed the

Cowlitz River. We overtook some Indians in canoes with articles to sell. We purchased wappato roots, salmon-trout and two beaver skins. They spoke a few words of English and told us that they traded with a man named Mr. Haley. We camped on the south side of the river under a cliff of rocks.

NOVEMBER 7.   We set out early in a fog so thick that we could not see the other side of the river. We passed a village where we bought some fish, wappato roots, three dogs and two otter skins, for which we gave fish-hooks. After remaining an hour and a half, we set out, piloted by an Indian to the main channel of the river. We then passed down to another village where Capt. Clark purchased two beaver skins to make a robe, as the one he has is rotten and worthless. We proceeded on twelve miles and encamped near a fine spring under a high hill opposite Pillar Rock. Two Indians accompanied us from the last village and were sent off after we detected them stealing a knife. Our small canoe, which got separated this morning in the fog, joined us this evening. Great joy in camp! We are in view of the ocean which we have been so long anxious to see.

NOVEMBER 8.   We changed our wet clothes, so did not set off until 9 a.m. We went past several islands in the bay which here is five or six miles wide. We coasted along an inlet we call "Shallow Bay" [Gray's Bay]. We avoided an old Indian village for they are usually full of fleas. We took advantage of the returning tide to go to a point on the right, but the waves ran high, and several of the men became sea-sick. We camped on a point and raised our baggage on poles to keep it above the tide. We passed a disagreeable night – the rain never ceased.

NOVEMBER 9.   The tide did not come into our camp, but the canoes, exposed to the waves, were filled. With great attention we saved them until the tide left them dry. When the tide returned it brought large tree-trunks and tossed them in such a manner as to endanger our canoes. Our camp was under water, and every man was wet. Notwithstanding our disagreeable situation, we must spend another night here, for the waves are too high to proceed. The men are cheerful and anxious to see further into the ocean.

NOVEMBER 10.   The wind has lulled, so we loaded our canoes and went on until the wind came up again, when we landed in a small niche on the lee side of Point Ellice. We secured our canoes as best we could, and made a camp on a pile of drift logs.

NOVEMBER 11.   It rained and stormed all day. We built large fires to make ourselves as comfortable as possible, for we have no tents nor coverings except our blankets. We sent Joseph Fields and John Collins to hunt.

We purchased thirteen salmon-trout from the Indians. The hunters returned and reported that the hills are covered with fallen timber and underbrush so thick they could not go any distance. Some of the men caught fifteen fine fish.

NOVEMBER 12. A stormy day, but the wind lulled, and we moved our camp around the point a short distance to a cove. We sent the men out to hunt. Gibson, Bratton and Willard attempted to descend the bay in our small canoe, but could not proceed as the waves tossed them about at will. We dried our bedding and ourselves, and were tolerably comfortable.

NOVEMBER 13. Capt. Clark walked to the top of the first part of the mountain behind the cove to view the river. Sacagawea was displeased that she did not get to go, and made a fuss. We sent Colter, Willard and Shannon below in our Indian canoe which can ride the high waves, to see if they could find a good harbor, and also to learn if there are any white people there. They did not return this evening.

NOVEMBER 14. The wind blew hard and one canoe was broken by the waves dashing her against the rocks. About 11 a.m., five Indians came up through the immense waves and informed us that they had seen our three men, Colter, Willard and Shannon, some distance below. Soon afterwards, Colter arrived by land and informed us that he and the others had gone as far as they could, and did not find a harbor nor any signs of white people. He had found two camps of Indians below, and that these Indians now with us had taken his gig, basket and knife. We forcefully took them back, and ordered them off. At 3 p.m. Capt. Lewis, Drouillard, the Fields brothers and Frazier set out down the shore to see if any white people were below. They took an empty canoe and five men to set them on a gravelly beach which Colter informed us is at no great distance below. Capt. Lewis' object is to find a small bay as laid down by Vancouver. The canoe returned, half full of water which was dashed over her while passing the point, having landed Capt. Lewis and his party safely on the beach [Baker's Bay].

NOVEMBER 15. This morning was cold and fair which gave us an opportunity to dry our bedding and examine the baggage – the greater part of which is wet. We put our goods in order and examined the ammunition. Capt. Clark tried to examine the point in a canoe. This is the sixth day of rain and it has prevented us from hunting or finding a better situation. About 3 p.m. the wind lulled, and we loaded in great haste to set out, passing the point to the sand beach below. Shannon and five Indians met us there. He told us that he had met Capt. Lewis some distance below, and that Lewis had taken Willard with him, and had sent Colter up to meet us.

The natives with him are rogues; the night before they had stolen both Colter's and Willard's guns. Capt. Lewis arrived just in time, and the Indians were alarmed and delivered up the guns.

Capt. Clark told these Indians that if any of their nation stole anything from us that he would have them shot. They understood his meaning very well. As the tide rises here, we concluded to form a camp at the highest place. The evening is fair and the men are comfortable in the camps they have made from some old boards which they found in an abandoned village above us.

November 16. We sent out several hunters to kill fowl, deer and elk. One man is sick with a violent cold caught from lying in his wet clothes for the past several nights. Our hunters killed two deer, one crane and two ducks. York killed two geese and eight brant. The deer are large but poor.

November 17. At 10:30 a.m. Capt. Lewis returned, having traversed the [Baker's] Bay to Cape Disappointment and the sea coast to the north for some distance. Some natives arrived with roots to sell. We find it a bad practice to receive a present from these Indians for they are never satisfied, even if they received ten times the value in return. Our hunters brought in three deer, four brant and two ducks. They have discovered elk sign hereabouts.

November 18. Capt. Clark, York, Charbonneau, Sgt. Pryor, Sgt. Ordway, Joseph Fields, Reuben Fields, George Shannon, John Colter, William Bratton, Peter Weiser and William Labiche set out at daylight to go down the shore to see the ocean. Enroute they killed four brant, and Labiche killed forty-eight plovers – which we had for dinner. Near Cape Disappointment, Reuben Fields killed a vulture [a condor]. The men having seen the ocean, are cheerful and express a desire to camp up the river near the falls this winter.

In Capt. Lewis' camp, three men went out to hunt. We traded with some natives for dried salmon and roots. In the evening the hunters returned with a deer, two brant, a squirrel and a flounder. Capt. Lewis took down a vocabulary of the Chinook language.

November 19. Capt. Clark and his party proceeded on through thickets to a third point where they breakfasted on a deer which Joseph Fields had killed. He took observations in order to make a sketch of the mouth of the Columbia and its surrounding bays. The men found a pine tree on which Capt. Lewis had carved his name, and we added ours and the date. Capt. Clark named a point after his companion and particular friend, "Point Lewis" [North Head]. Several Indians visited Capt. Lewis. One of them had a very handsome, waterproof hat made of cedar, which was purchased for an old razor. The hunters got three deer.

November 20.   Joseph Fields and John Colter were sent to hunt elk, and Labiche to hunt brant for our breakfast. Labiche brought in eight large ducks. Afterwards we came to a river, made a raft, and Reuben Fields crossed over to get one of the canoes left at an Indian cabin. We all crossed over and made our way to Capt. Lewis' camp where we found all well. Meanwhile we met some Indians whom Capt. Clark had employed to bring in our canoe which had been left by the party. He gave them a large fish-hook for this service. One of the Indians had a robe made of two sea-otter skins. Capt. Lewis offered him many articles for the robe – all of which he refused. At length it was purchased for a belt of blue beads which Saca-gawea wore. The hunters had killed several deer and fowl of different kinds.

November 21.   Most of the Indians left us. We gave Sacagawea a coat made of blue cloth in exchange for the belt of beads she had loaned us. Several natives and squaws came this evening to gratify the passions of the men. They sport openly with our men and appear to have the approbation of their relatives in so doing.

November 22.   The sea runs high and the rain prevents us from leaving camp. We purchased some wappato roots which are nearly equal in flavor to the Irish potato. With our more strict indifference to the Indians, we find they are better behaved. Our hunters killed three bucks and some ducks.

November 23.   The men all marked their names on the trees about camp. The hunters killed four brant and three ducks today. Others are mending the canoe which was split in the storm yesterday. Our hunters got three deer and twenty-one fowl.

November 24.   We sent out six hunters while the captains made observa-tions on this fair day. We dried our wet bedding and articles. We took a vote of the men as to the location for our winter quarters. Some are for investigating the other side of the Columbia for a suitable site – while others prefer a camp upriver near the falls, or at least up the river where it is less rainy. Sacagawea is in favor of a place where there are plenty of wappato. The vote resulted: 5 for the falls, 12 for the Seal [Washougal] River, and 12 for across the Columbia. Therefore Capt. Lewis and another man will cross to the other side to see if good hunting is there, for we can-not depend on the natives for food. We prefer to be near the harbor in the event a ship will come this winter. The advantage of procuring goods from a vessel would off-set living on poor deer and elk higher up the river.

NOVEMBER 25.   We loaded the canoes and set out, keeping near the north shore as the waves were too high to cross over. After dark, we reached a spot near Pillar Rock, near our former camping place of November 7th.

NOVEMBER 26.   We proceeded up the river and crossed a short distance above the rock, then proceeded along the south side. We dropped down to see if a favorable place could be found. We encamped in a thick woods.

NOVEMBER 27.   At daylight three canoes with eleven Indians came with roots, mats and skins to sell. They asked such high prices that we were unable to purchase anything of them. As we were about to set out, we missed one of our axes which was found under an Indian robe. We came to a point which we named "Point William" after Capt. William Clark [Tongue Point]. Here we formed a camp on a neck of land which joins Point William to the mainland. One canoe split before we could get her out of the water.

NOVEMBER 28.   Most of the men went to the point to drive for deer, but got nothing. All our robes are wet and rotten, and we cannot procure others. We had a disagreeable day.

NOVEMBER 29.   Capt. Lewis determined to go down the river in search of a site for winter quarters. He set out in the small canoe accompanied by Drouillard, Reuben Fields, George Shannon, John Collins and Labiche, and went down to the [Young's] bay. Other hunters were sent out and they obtained four deer, seven ducks, two brant and an elk. We camped in an old Indian hunting lodge which afforded us shelter from the rain.

NOVEMBER 30.   Capt. Lewis sent out three men to examine the country to the southwest. They returned in two hours and reported that the wood was thick and obstructed by marshes and lakes. We now returned to Meriwether's Bay [Young's] where the Clatsop Indians had told us there was much game. The water was quite sweet so we concluded it must be supplied by a large creek. Capt. Clark sent five men in a canoe to hunt fowl, and two men to hunt elk. We dried our articles and all the men are dressing skins. Sacagawea gave Capt. Clark a piece of bread made of flour which she had carefully saved for her child. Some of the men are sick from using salt water with their pounded fish.

DECEMBER 1, 1805.   Capt. Lewis sent his men to hunt and examine the country. They all returned except Drouillard. They informed him the woods were so thick as to be almost impenetrable. We heard Drouillard shoot five times. We fervently hope he has fallen in with a herd of elk.

Capt. Clark sent out five men to hunt in the marshes. It has been twenty-four days since we arrived in sight of the Pacific Ocean. We think it has

LEWIS AND CLARK ON THE LOWER COLUMBIA RIVER

From a water color by Charles M. Russell. Courtesy of Amon Carter Museum, Fort Worth, Texas.

FORT CLATSOP

From a painting, based on historical research, made for this work by Charles G. Clarke.

been the reverse of pacific, for it has been stormy every day. The men are making shoes, leather clothes and dressing skins. We have heard nothing of Capt. Lewis.

DECEMBER 2.   Capt. Clark sent three men to hunt, and two others with York to fish. Joseph Fields came in with the marrow bones of an elk he had killed six miles distant. Six men, along with Joseph Fields, went back in a canoe for the meat. We see a great deal of sign, but this is the first elk we have killed on this side of the river. The men in the canoes did not return.

DECEMBER 3.   Sgt. Pryor and George Gibson who went to hunt yesterday, have not returned. Sacagawea boiled the shank bones of the elk and extracted a pint of grease and tallow. Sgt. Pryor and Gibson returned after dark and informed us they had killed an elk, which they had to leave. The canoe party returned with elk meat. Capt. Clark marked his name on a large pine tree: WILLIAM CLARK, DECEMBER 3rd, 1805, BY LAND FROM THE U. STATES IN 1804 & 5.

DECEMBER 4.   Sgt. Pryor and six men were sent for the elk that had been killed yesterday, with orders to take the loads to the river below in the next bend. We had intended to proceed to that place as soon as the tide goes out this evening, but the waves were so high as to prevent us so doing. We have no account of Capt Lewis. We fear that some accident has befallen his party.

DECEMBER 5.   Capt. Lewis returned with three men – the other two being left to guard six elk and five deer. They have found a good location to winter where there are sufficient elk. It rained hard which prevented our moving today.

DECEMBER 6.   We had wind and high waves today. We were obliged to move our camp to higher ground.

DECEMBER 7.   We have a fair morning. We loaded the boats and set out to the place which Capt. Lewis thought well situated for our winter quarters. We proceeded on and met Sgt. Pryor and his party returning to camp. It was impossible for them to land. We went around a point into a bay and here Sgt. Pryor's party joined us except for York. We delayed an hour and then York came up – we then proceeded around Meriwether's Bay [Young's Bay]. This we named for Captain Lewis who was no doubt the first white man to ever survey this bay. We ascended a river [the Netul – now Lewis and Clark's] to a high point of land with a thick growth of trees. It is certainly the most eligible situation for our purpose of any in the neighborhood. Here we intend to build a fort for our winter quarters.

19

At Fort Clatsop

DECEMBER 8. Capt. Clark took five men and set out to find the nearest route to the ocean to find a place to make salt, and to make a road so that the men out hunting might find their way should they get lost in fog or bad weather. They passed through bogs and open lands, and discovered a band of elk. They obtained one and made a shelter of the skin – and dined on the flesh, refreshed by a tolerable fire. Sgt. Gass with eleven men went in canoes to bring in the meat that the hunters had killed. They carried two large loads to the canoes and then proceded back to camp.

DECEMBER 9. Capt. Clark sent Drouillard and Shannon for the elk meat and with three others, set off for the ocean. They met some Indians who treated them well, and they camped with these Indians all night.

At Capt. Lewis' camp, Sgt. Ordway and eight men were sent after elk. They returned at evening and also found the canoe which the tide had carried out the other night. The other men are clearing a place to build the huts and fort.

DECEMBER 10. Capt. Clark shot some brant as they lit, which astonished the Indians. After breakfast he returned, accompanied by a young chief who had crossed the party over three creeks in his canoe. They returned in a heavy rain. Capt. Lewis and his party are busy felling trees to build with. In the evening we laid the foundation for our cabins.

DECEMBER 11. We are all employed in putting up our huts. Sgt. Pryor is unwell again from having his shoulder out of place. Joseph Fields is sick with tumors. Werner has a sprained knee, and Gibson is ill with dysentery.

DECEMBER 12. All hands are employed with cutting logs and raising our winter cabins. Two men are detached to split boards for the roofs. In the evening two canoes of Clatsops came to visit us. They bring wappato roots – a black root from a thistle – and a small sea-otter skin which we purchased for a few fish-hooks and some Indian tobacco. We finished raising one line of huts.

DECEMBER 13. The Indians left us after a breakfast of elk meat of which they are very fond. The captains bought some skins to make coats of. Drouillard and Shannon returned from hunting, having killed eighteen elk. They butchered all but two. We find the timber splits beautifully and so our roof problem is solved. We raised another line of huts and began the last line – forming three sides of a square. There are seven rooms 16 x 18 feet large. The other side we intend to picket and have gates at the corners so as to have a defensive fort.

DECEMBER 14.   We sent two men back with Drouillard and Shannon to guard the elk meat they had left in the woods. We finished a room to store our meat in. The sick are getting better, but York is sick with "cholick and griping."

DECEMBER 15.   We sent sixteen men in three canoes up the river to bring in the elk meat. All hands, including Capt. Clark, pack in the meat. Sgt. Ordway, John Colter, Joseph Collins, Joseph Whitehouse and Hugh McNeal were lost and stayed out all night in the rain. Sgt. Gass and two others remained to finish the quarters of the captains, while two others made puncheons for covering the huts.

DECEMBER 16.   The five men came in this morning from the meat camp where Capt. Clark and party had stayed out all night. They loaded the canoes with eleven elk, and twelve men were dispatched with two elk to meet us below. All the meat was brought to the fort on this stormy day, and was hung in the meat-house.

DECEMBER 17.   All hands are at work chinking the huts. Some are daubing and cutting out doors. The seven men left at the hunting camp to bring in the elk, arrived with two of them. We fleeced all the meat and hung it over a small smoke. The captains' old leather lodge is so rotten that the least strain tears holes in it.

DECEMBER 18.   We continue working on the huts. The men are but thinly dressed and have no shoes, but only moccasins without socks.

DECEMBER 19.   We dispatched Sgt. Pryor and eight men in two canoes across the bay for the boards of an abandoned Indian house. At evening the party returned with two loads of planks. The rest of the party is working on the buildings. Sgt. Ordway is unwell.

DECEMBER 20.   We have four huts covered, and the men are working on the others. Three Indians came with roots, berries and some mats to sell, but they asked such high prices that we did not buy anything. They prefer tobacco and blue beads first, and white beads and fish-hooks secondly.

DECEMBER 21.   Our Indian visitors were detected in stealing a horn spoon, so they were asked to leave our camp. We sent two men to the open plains near the ocean for Sacacome – an article which we, and they, use to mix with our tobacco. The rest of the men are working on the cabins.

DECEMBER 22.   The puncheon floors and bunks are finished. Drouillard set out up Netul Creek, on which our fort is located, to set his traps for beaver. Sgt. Ordway, Gibson and York are sick. Some of our meat is spoiling from the damp, warm weather, despite a constant smoke we keep under it.

DECEMBER 23.   The captains moved into their cabin, though it is still unfinished. Two canoes of Clatsop Indians arrived with mats and bags made of reeds and rushes. We purchased them as well as a panther skin. We gave them some soft and mouldy salmon which they prize very highly. We sent a little pounded fish to Chief Cuscalar who is sick at his village and could not come to see us.

DECEMBER 24.   All hands are employed in finishing the huts and the greater part of the men moved into them. Chief Cuscalar, the young chief from the ocean village, came with his brother and two young squaws. They laid before the captains a mat and a parcel of roots. Later, he demanded two files for his presents, but we had no files to spare – which displeased him a little. They then offered a woman to us which we declined – which also displeased him. Joseph Fields finished a wide slab which he had hewed level for the captains to use as a writing table. Our store of meat is entirely spoiled, but we are obliged to make use of it. We have nothing else but a little pounded fish which we purchased at the Great Falls of the Columbia.

DECEMBER 25.   This morning we were awakened by the discharge of fire arms, shouts of "Merry Christmas" and other songs under the captains' windows. The men returned to their rooms and were cheerful all morning. After breakfast we divided half of our remaining twelve carrots of tobacco among the men who smoked, and to the others we made a present of a handkerchief. All the party are snugly fixed in their huts which have temporary fireplaces in them. Capt. Clark received a Christmas present of a shirt, drawers and socks from Capt. Lewis, a pair of moccasins from Joseph Whitehouse, and a small Indian basket from Silas Goodrich, Sacagawea gave him two dozen white weasel tails and some black roots she had obtained from the Indians. [Capt. Lewis did not keep a diary on this day, so there is no record of what he received, but he and the men probably received similar gifts as Capt. Clark.] We would have spent the day in feasting, but we had no whiskey, and our dinner consisted of poor elk and a few roots – with no salt to season that. But we are in good health, which we esteem more than all the ardent spirits in the world.

DECEMBER 26.   The wind blew, and our huts were filled with smoke, as we have no chimneys as yet. Joseph Fields finished a table and two chairs for the captains. We dry our powder and goods, and try to remove the fleas from our bedding. We start to build the chimneys.

DECEMBER 27. The men completed the chimneys and bunks. We sent Reuben Fields and John Collins to hunt, and Drouillard, Shannon and Labiche are to set out tomorrow to hunt. Joseph Fields, William Bratton and George Gibson are to make salt from sea water near Point Adams. Alexander Willard and Peter Weiser are to assist them in carrying the five kettles, etc., to the ocean. All the others are to make pickets and gates for our fort. The natives traded us some roots and dried berries. These are timely and grateful to our stomachs.

DECEMBER 28. We sent our men as assigned yesterday — the others are putting up pickets. Cruzatte is sick with a violent cold. York is still sick from the strains of lifting logs and packing meat. We are told a whale is stranded on the shore, and the natives are collecting fat from it. Reuben Fields and John Collins are sent out to hunt.

DECEMBER 29. York is better. Capt. Lewis is in readiness to go and collect some whale oil. It rains all the time and the winds are high. A young chief came with wappato and skins to trade. We gave him a medal and a piece of red ribbon to tie around his conical hat. We purchased about a bushel and a half of roots which we are grateful to have. Whenever these natives visit with us they leave a great quantity of fleas behind.

DECEMBER 30. Drouillard, Shannon and Labiche returned and informed us that they had killed four elk. A party of six men were immediately sent for the meat. They returned at dusk. We had s sumptuous supper of elk tongues and marrow bones which were truly gratifying. Our fort is completed and we name it "Fort Clatsop" in honor of the native tribe who are our neighbors. However, we let the Indians know that we will shut the gates at sunset, at which time they must leave the fort. These Indians are very forward and disagreeable, and they left our huts with reluctance. We have had the best day yet — only three showers of rain. There are lots of slugs about. We posted a sentinel to be constantly on duty, as becomes our military status and safety.

DECEMBER 31. The Indians put out of our quarters have formed a camp near us. More of them arrive and bring roots, mats and dressed elk skins. We purchased some roots, two mats and a small pouch of tobacco of their make. We gave fish-hooks in exchange, of which they are very fond. The sight of the sentinel makes these people better behaved, and they left before sunset without being asked to do so. We built a sentinel box to protect our guard against the rain. One of the Indians brought a musket for Shields to repair. He gave a peck of wappato in exchange. We were visited by a half-breed about twenty-five years of age who has red hair and freckles. His father was an English sailor, and this young man has "Jack Ramsay" tattooed on his arm. He did not speak English and had all the habits of the Indians.

JANUARY 1, 1806.   Our party fired a volley of small arms to usher in the New Year. This is the only mark of respect we have to offer on this celebrated day. Our repast, though better than that of Christmas, consisted principally in anticipation of that which we would have next year, when we hope to be with our friends and families. At present we are content with boiled elk, wappato roots and pure water. We are uneasy that Willard and Weiser, who were dispatched with the salt makers, and who were to immediately return, have not yet done so. We sent two men out hunting.

Our fort being completed, our commanding officers direct that the guard shall consist of one sergeant and three privates, and that the same shall be changed at sunrise. The post of the new guard shall be in the room of the sergeant respectfully commanding the same. It shall be the duty of the sentinel to announce the arrival of Indians to the sergeant of the guard, who shall immediately report the same to the commanding officers. The garrison is charged to treat the natives in a friendly manner, nor are they at any time to abuse or strike them, unless such abuse be first given by the natives. The sergeant of the guard, assisted by Charbonneau, may evict any native who insists on remaining in the rooms or fort – unless they have been invited to remain. It shall be the duty of the guard to keep the key of the meat-house and visit the canoes to see that they are safely secured. All must mount guard but the interpreters and cooks. All are to return tools after use, and in no case are any to be kept out all night. Only John Shields is excepted from the rules regarding tools.

The hunters killed two elk about three miles from the fort.

JANUARY 2.   We sent out a party of twelve men and they brought in the two elk. Willard and Weiser have not returned, nor have the party of hunters who set out on the 28th last. Our fort is infested with fleas, nor do we expect to divest ourselves of them while we are here. Drouillard caught an otter.

JANUARY 3.   We were visited by our neighbor, Chief Comowool, and six Clatsops. They brought roots, berries and three dogs, and some fresh blubber. Our original aversion to dog meat has long since been overcome. Reuben Fields, John Potts and John Collins – the hunters who had been sent out on the 28th, returned from a hunt to the eastward, but only got enough to sustain themselves. This teaches us the necessity of keeping out several parties of hunters in order to supply us against any emergency. We sent Sgt. Gass and George Shannon to the salt makers who are somewhere on Clatsop Beach [present Seaside, Oregon] to inquire of Willard and Weiser who have not yet returned.

JANUARY 4.   Chief Comowool left this morning highly pleased with an old pair of satin breeches we gave him. The hunters set out in all directions. Our store of wappato is exhausted. Sgt. Gass and Shannon are still at the seacoast.

JANUARY 5.   At 5 p.m. Willard and Weiser returned. They had not been lost, but informed us that it was not until the 5th day, before they could find a suitable place to make salt. They brought some of the blubber from the whale that was stranded near the salt works. We found that it tasted something like beaver or dog, only somewhat more coarse. They also told us that Joseph Fields, William Bratton and George Gibson had erected a comfortable camp and had a good store of meat, and made three to four quarts of salt a day. They brought back about a gallon. We found it strong and white and a great treat, for we have not had any salt since December 20th. Capt. Clark seems indifferent about it, and he also does not care for dog meat. He can get along without either. John Collins came back from an unsuccessful hunt. Capt. Clark determined to set out with two canoes and twelve men in quest of the whale. He prepared a small assortment to trade for some whale meat and blubber.

JANUARY 6.   Capt. Clark, Charbonneau and Sacagawea and the party set out down the river into Meriwether's Bay. Sacagawea observed that she had traveled a long way with us to see the Great Waters, and now that a monstrous fish was to be seen, she thought it very hard not to be permitted to see either, for she had not yet been to the ocean. Therefore we indulged her to go.

Those at the fort overhauled the merchandise and dried it before the fires. The humidity is excessive, and we have not been able to keep anything dry. Our merchandise is reduced to a mere handful, and our success on our return across the country depends on it. Therefore we must regret the reduced state of this fund of supplies.

Meanwhile, Capt. Clark and party after arriving in the bay, found the waves so high that they put into a small creek, left the canoes, and went overland. We killed an elk and finally made the shore. We made fires of driftwood and spent the night. It is clear, with a full moon – the first we have seen in months. Sgt. Gass and George Shannon reached the salt makers' camp.

JANUARY 7. Drouillard found a beaver and an otter in his traps. The beaver was large and fat, and we dined sumptuously on it. Also it was a prize, for being a full grown male, it had the glands which are used for scent and bait to trap others. It being a fine day, we dried our lodge tent and put it away under shelter.

In Capt. Clark's party we all ate of the elk except about eight pounds which was carried away by the tide. We came to shore and traveled south for three miles when we came to a large river. Capt. Clark hired a native to put us across in a canoe, for which service he gave two fish hooks. We went on two miles where we found the salt makers, and among them Sgt. Gass, Shannon, Joseph Fields, Bratton and Gibson. They have a neat camp, convenient to wood and water. They are also situated near the houses of the Clatsops and Tillamooks who are very kind to them. Capt. Clark hired a native to guide us to the whale. Sgt. Gass and Werner were left to make salt, while Bratton went with us. We went two and one-half miles over slippery stones to a high hill [Tillamook Head]. The guide said we had to cross the hill, so we went on a very bad trail to the top. Here we met fourteen Indians loaded with blubber. We left the top of the precipice and camped on a small creek, all much fatigued.

JANUARY 8. Capt. Lewis sent Drouillard and Collins to hunt as meat is scarce in camp. The guard duty being hard for those who remain in camp since the departure of Capt. Clark's party, the cooks now have to stand guard. Sgt. Gass and Shannon have not returned. Because of the clouds, Capt. Lewis has not been able to make observations at this place.

Capt. Clark and party on the mountain beheld a grand prospect of ocean and shore. After taking courses and computing the distances, we went down a steep descent to the beach. We proceeded on some two miles to where the whale was stranded. It was already stripped of its meat and we found only the skeleton of the monster. It measures 105 feet long. We returned to the village where the Tillamooks were boiling the blubber, and we traded our goods for some three hundred pounds of it and four gallons of oil – which we prize highly. While smoking with the Indians there was an outcry, and the guide informed us that someone had been killed. On examination, we found that Hugh McNeal was absent. Sgt. Pryor and four men were dispatched, and they met McNeal on a creek. McNeal had been friendly with a native man, but now a native informed him that the man intended to assassinate him for the sake of the few articles on his person. The squaw had given the alarm. The Indian ran off before McNeal knew what had occasioned the alarm. We returned to the salt makers' camp where we found that Joseph Fields, Gibson and Shannon were out hunting. We stayed all night. Joseph Fields brought in an elk.

JANUARY 9.   The men at Fort Clatsop were engaged in dressing skins for clothing and moccasins. They heard the report of guns and expect Drouillard and Collins have fallen in with a herd of elk. The Indians tell us that the ships which visit the Columbia are either English or American ships, for they speak the same language as we. The natives have learned a few words – most of it blackguard phrases. [They did not tell us that the Boston ship, the *"Lydia,"* Capt. Samuel Hill commanding, was at sea at this time in this area.] [1] These ships trade old guns, clothes, copper and brass kettles and many other articles with them for otter, beaver and other skins.

JANUARY 10.   At Capt. Lewis' camp, some Indians arrived, and an exchange of presents was made. Drouillard and Collins returned, having killed only two elk. One of these had laid out overnight, so was of course spoiled. They returned to hunt as meat is scarce with us.

Capt. Clark and most of the party returned at 10 p.m., he having left some men to assist the salt makers, and bring in the elk which Gibson and Shannon had killed – and to send two others to hunt. Sgt. Gass and Shannon were found with the salt makers and were ordered to return. Robert Frazier had lost his big knife and was sent back to search for it, with directions to join the other men who were packing meat, then all are to return together to the fort.

JANUARY 11.   We sent a party under Sgt. Ordway to bring in the elk which was killed on the 9th. Drouillard and Collins returned without having killed anything. This morning the sergeant of the guard reported the absence of our large Indian canoe. We found that those who came in last night were negligent in securing her, and the tide had taken her off. We sent a party down to the bay in search of her, but they returned unsuccessful. If we do not find this canoe it will be a loss, for she is so light that four men can carry her for a mile or more without resting. She will carry four men, and ten to twelve hundred pounds of lading.

JANUARY 12.   This morning we sent Drouillard and one man to hunt. They returned in the evening – Drouillard having killed seven elk. We could scarcely subsist if it were not for the exertions of this excellent hunter. Our other hunters also exert themselves, but do not have the tracking knowledge that Drouillard has – yet if there is any game to be had of any kind, we are certain of our hunters procuring it.

JANUARY 13.   Capt. Lewis took all the men who could be spared to bring in the elk Drouillard had killed, and they found it in good order. This eve-

---

[1] Thwaites, v. 3, p. 327 note.

ning we finished the last of our candles – but we had brought molds and wicks, and we can make more of elk's tallow. We learn the trading ships usually arrive at the mouth of the Columbia in April and remain until October. They usually lay at anchor in a bay on the north side of the Columbia where there is wood and water, and there the natives trade with them.

JANUARY 14. Six men are employed in jerking the elk meat. The large canoe got way, but we found it. We drew three of the canoes up out of the reach of the tide. The other we keep secured by a long cord, ready for any emergency. We sent two men to the salt works.

JANUARY 15. Capt. Lewis had a large coat made from the skin of a panther he has obtained from the Indians. It rained so hard all day that the hunting parties could not go out. The captains are working on a full report of the population and customs of the Indians in this part of the country.

JANUARY 16. This evening we finished curing the meat. We have plenty at present and a little salt. Our huts are dry and comfortable. We have decided to remain here until the 1st of April, and everyone seems content with his situation and fare. It is true that we could travel now as far as the Falls of the Columbia, but the Indians inform us that the snows are deep in the basin above, and it would be madness for us to proceed, as there is no game nor fuel to be found there at this time of year.

JANUARY 17. This morning we were visited by Comowool and seven of our nearest neighbors, the Clatsops. They left later in the evening. They had brought some roots and berries for which they asked such high prices which our poor stock in trade would not permit us giving. John Colter was sent to hunt and he shortly returned with a deer. Venison is a rarity with us for we have not had any for several weeks. Drouillard also went out with one man. He intends to hunt elk and trap beaver.

JANUARY 18. The men are engaged in dressing skins with which to clothe ourselves on our homeward journey. It is another wet day.

JANUARY 19. We sent out two parties of hunters. Collins and Willard were sent down the bay towards Point Adams, while Labiche and Shannon were sent up the Netul [now Lewis & Clark River]. We were visited by some Clatsops who brought some sea-otter skins. We purchased one, giving in return the remainder of our blue beads. We also purchased a small quantity of whale oil and a hat, for brass arm bands and some fish-hooks. These hats are made by the natives, and are light and waterproof.

JANUARY 20. We consume an alarming amount of meat. The skill of our hunters is of some consolation, for most of the party are very expert with the rifle, and if there is any game in our neighborhood of any description, our men can track and kill it.

JANUARY 21. Shannon and Labiche returned having killed three elk. Sgt. Gass and a party were dispatched to bring it in. The hunters returned to hunt. The Chinook women have had intercourse with our men, and one or two have been afflicted with venereal disease so as to render salivation necessary.

JANUARY 22. The party sent for the meat returned this evening. Reuben Fields remained with Shannon and Labiche to hunt. We have not heard from the hunters who were sent down the bay – nor from those sent to the prairies above.

JANUARY 23. We sent Howard and Werner to the salt makers for a supply. The men of the garrison are busily engaged in dressing skins for clothes. This is difficult for the want of animal brains, which, when mixed with urine, is used for tanning the hides. We have no soap, for the pine logs we burn do not have the necessary lye in the little ashes that remain.

JANUARY 24. Drouillard and La Page returned this morning with Chief Comowool and six Clatsops in a large canoe. They brought two deer and the flesh of three elk and one elk's skin, having given the flesh of one, and the skins of the others as the price of transportation to our camp. The Indians remained with us all day and cannot comprehend the air gun which was fired for their amusement.

JANUARY 25. Comowool and the Clatsops departed early this morning. At noon Colter arrived and reported that his comrade, Willard, had continued his hunt from Point Adams towards the salt makers. In the evening, Collins, one of the salt makers, returned and reported they had made about a bushel of salt. He also said that they had hunted about their camp for five days without success, and had been obliged to subsist on whale meat which they had bought from the Indians.

JANUARY 26. Werner and Howard who were sent for salt on the 23rd, have not returned. We fear they might be lost, as neither are very good woodsmen, and the constantly cloudy weather makes it difficult even for an expert woodsman to steer a course. We sent Collins back to the salt camp with a few trade articles in the event they are still unfortunate in hunting. We had some snow – the first freezing weather of any consequence this winter.

JANUARY 27.   In the evening Shannon came in and reported that he and party had killed ten elk. Labiche and Reuben Fields had remained to guard the elk. Tomorrow we will send a party to bring in the meat. Goodrich has recovered from the venereal disease he contracted from an amorous Chinook damsel. Capt. Lewis cured him, as he did Gibson last winter, by the use of mercury.

JANUARY 28.   Drouillard and La Page set out this morning to hunt. Sgt. Ordway and fourteen men went to bring in the elk. They returned at evening with only three. The snow had so altered the appearance of the country that the hunters could not find the meat. About noon Howard and Werner returned with a supply of salt. We found the wood of the wild crab apple tree excessively hard when seasoned, and is very good for making axe-handles. The bark of this tree is chewed by our men in the place of tobacco.

JANUARY 29.   Our fare is lean elk meat with a little salt. Though we used it sparingly, the blubber is now exhausted. On this food the men are well, but do not feel strong, and have a keen appetite. It froze hard last night, so we did little but get wood for our fires today.

JANUARY 30.   Still cloudy and cold. The green pine wood when split, burns well.

JANUARY 31.   We sent a party of eight men up the river to renew the search for the elk killed, and also to hunt. The river was so obstructed with ice, they were obliged to return. Joseph Fields arrived this evening from the salt camp and informed us he had been hunting with Gibson and Willard for the past five days to supply meat for the salt camp. He had been unsuccessful until yesterday, when he killed two elk about six miles from here, and eight miles from the salt works. He left Gibson and Willard to dry the meat. McNeal has the pox.

20

Living off the Land

FEBRUARY 1, 1806. Four men set out with Joseph Fields to take the elk to the salt camp. Sgt. Gass and a party of five went up the Netul River to search for the elk which had been killed some days ago. We examined all our ammunition which had been secured in the lead cannisters. We found the powder as perfectly dry as when it was first put in them, although all of it had been under water for hours in our various accidents. These cannisters contain four pounds of powder and eight pounds of lead. By this happy expedient which Capt. Lewis devised, we have dry powder, and lead for bullets – an abundant supply to last us to our return home. This is our only defense on a route of some four thousand miles through a country inhabited by savages.

FEBRUARY 2. Nothing occurred worthy of notice. We are all pleased that a dreary month has passed which bound us to Fort Clatsop. Some of the men are bringing in the elk meat.

FEBRUARY 3. About 3 p.m. Drouillard and La Page returned. Drouillard had killed seven elk on the point below us. We directed Sgt. Pryor and a party to go after the meat which can be nearly reached by canoe. They returned at 10 p.m. but could not get the meat as the tide was out. We fear that the Clatsops know where the meat is, and will rob us of it. At 4 p.m. Sgt. Gass returned with his party. They brought with them the flesh of four elk the party had found – it being part of the ten killed the other day. He left Reuben Fields, Shannon and Labiche to continue the hunt. Later in the evening the four men who had been sent to assist the salt makers in packing their meat, also returned and brought all the salt that had been made, consisting of only a bushel, despite the fact that the kettles had been kept boiling night and day. This salt making is tedious business. We calculate that we will need three bushels to last us from here to our deposits in the caches at the Falls of the Missouri.

FEBRUARY 4. Sgt. Pryor and five men set out again in quest of the elk Drouillard had killed. Drouillard and La Page also returned to hunt in the same quarter. The elk are in better condition there than those found in the woods. The captains made several observations and corrected the error in the sextant.

FEBRUARY 5. Late this evening one of our hunters fired and whooped opposite our fort. We sent Sgt. Gass and a party of men over. The tide being in, they took advantage of a little creek that makes in that direction, and on their way they found our large Indian canoe – so long lost and much lamented. The hunter was Reuben Fields who had killed six elk a little above us. He reported that yesterday he had heard Shannon and Labiche fire after he had separated from them, and also supposed they had also killed some elk.

FEBRUARY 6. We sent Sgt. Gass and Sgt. Ordway with Reuben Fields and a party of nine men to bring in the elk which Fields had killed. Late in the evening Sgt. Pryor returned with the flesh of two elk and a few skins – the Indians having taken the balance of the seven elk which Drouillard had killed the other day. The party stayed out all night.

FEBRUARY 7. This evening Sgt. Pryor and Peter Weiser returned with a part of the meat which Reuben Fields had killed. The others of the party under Sgt. Gass remained there in order to bring in the balance of the meat. The men dined in fine style – our supper consisted of marrow bones and some elk meat which had the suggestion of a little fat on it. Sgt. Gass' party is still out.

FEBRUARY 8. We sent Sgt. Ordway and two men back to Sgt. Gass to help bring in the remainder of the meat. In the evening they returned with the fleece of five. Later, Sgt. Pryor, Shannon and Labiche and party returned from the hunt up the Netul. They brought in four elk which Shannon and Labiche had killed.

FEBRUARY 9. Collins and Weiser set out on a hunt. In the evening Drouillard returned. He brought only a beaver – but saw a black bear – the first seen around here. We are told they hibernate until this season. The men are jerking and preserving the meat.

FEBRUARY 10. Drouillard visited his traps but caught nothing. Collins and Weiser returned unsuccessful. Willard arrived late from the salt works – he had cut his knee very badly with his tomahawk. He informed us that William Bratton is very unwell, and that George Gibson was so sick that he asked to be brought back to the fort. John Colter also returned this evening. We continue the operation of drying meat.

FEBRUARY 11. Sgt. Gass, Reuben Fields and John Thompson went to hunt up the Netul. We sent Sgt. Pryor and four men by canoe to bring George Gibson back. Colter and Weiser are to continue at the salt works with Joseph Fields. As Bratton is sick, we desired him to return if he thought proper; and in the event of his coming back, Peter Weiser was directed to remain at the salt works.

FEBRUARY 12.   We were visited by a Clatsop man who brought three dogs as remuneration for the six elk he and his nation had stolen from us on the 5th. The dogs became alarmed and ran off. We suffered the Indian to remain in the fort all night. Sgt. Gass and his party remained out on their hunt.

FEBRUARY 13.   The Clatsop man left this morning. Our meat drying operation is finished and we think we have enough to last a month. One of our men bought a sea-otter skin from an Indian.

FEBRUARY 14.   We are uneasy about Gibson and Bratton who are sick at the salt works. Sgt. Pryor and party have not returned from there. Drouillard caught a fine, fat beaver on which we feasted. Sgt. Gass and party are still out. Capt. Clark completed a map of the country from Fort Mandan to this place. Capt. Lewis has been busy collecting botanical and ornithological specimens; making vocabularies and notes on the fishes and animals of the country.

FEBRUARY 15.   Drouillard and Whitehouse set out this evening to hunt. We have heard Sgt. Gass' party fire several shots, but they have not returned as yet. About 1 p.m. William Bratton arrived from the salt works, and informed us that Sgt. Pryor and party were coming up with George Gibson who is so sick he cannot walk, and they are bringing him on a litter. Bratton is much reduced by illness. Sgt. Pryor and party arrived with Gibson after dark. We do not consider him in any danger, though he had a fever and is much reduced. We gave him doses of niter; made him drink freely of sage tea, put his feet in hot water, and gave him thirty-five drops of laudanum.

FEBRUARY 16.   We sent Shannon, Labiche and Frazier out to hunt. No tidings yet of Sgt. Gass and party. Bratton is very weak and complains of pain in the lower part of his back. Capt. Lewis gave him barks. Gibson's fever still continues. He was given a dose of Dr. Rush's pills, which in the past have proven efficacious. The niter has produced profuse perspiration, and the pills operated by evening. He had a good night's rest.

FEBRUARY 17.   Collins and Windsor were sent to hunt on the prairies. Shannon, Labiche and Frazier returned with the flesh and hide of an elk wounded by Sgt. Gass' party. This fresh meat is needed for our sick. We gave the bark treatment to Bratton and Gibson. At 2 p.m. Joseph Fields arrived from the salt works and reported they had almost three bushels of salt on hand. We think this, plus the salt we have, is enough to last us until we reach our caches on the Missouri. We directed a party of six to go out with the Fields brothers in the morning to bring in the salt and kettles. Shannon and Labiche caught one of the buzzards [California condor] which they wounded and took alive. We believe this is the largest bird in North America. Shannon also brought a gray eagle. At 4 p.m. Sgt. Gass and party arrived — they had killed eight elk. Drouillard and Whitehouse also returned this evening with one elk.

FEBRUARY 18.   The party under Sgt. Ordway left for the salt works, and another ten men under Sgt. Gass were sent for the elk on the Netul River. In the evening Sgt. Ordway returned, saying the waves were so high in the bay he could not proceed. Collins and Windsor returned with a deer. We were visited by some Indians of whom we purchased a sea-otter skin and two of their cedar hats. When they departed an axe was missing. White-house brought a robe to Capt. Clark which was made of the skins of three lynx.

FEBRUARY 19.   Sgt. Ordway and party of six set out again this morning by land for the salt works. In the evening, Sgt. Gass returned with the meat of eight elk and seven skins. Shannon and Labiche stayed out all night on their hunt. The elk skins were divided among the men to make baggage covers for use when we set out in the spring. Our sick are slowly recovering. Capt. Clark gave Bratton six of Scott's pills which had no effect. Sgt. Ordway and party faced the rain all the way to the ocean. They found an old Indian house in which they stayed all night.

FEBRUARY 20.   We permitted Collins to hunt this morning. He returned in the evening unsuccessful, but brought some cranberries for the sick. Gibson is recovering fast. Bratton has an obstinate cough and pain in his back and appears to be getting weaker. Hugh McNeal, from his inattention to his disorder, has become worse. Willard has a high fever and complains of a pain in his head, and want of appetite. We were visited by Tah-cum, a principal Chief of the Chinooks and twenty-five of his nation with hats to trade. We gave them food and tobacco, and to the chief a medal with which he was much gratified. In the evening we desired them to depart as is our custom, for we never permit such numbers to be in the fort all night. We must be on guard at all times and never place ourselves at the mercy of any savages. Sgt. Ordway arrived at the salt works at noon.

FEBRUARY 21.   Drouillard and Collins went hunting. Sgt. Ordway and party returned from the salt camp which is now evacuated, and all the party are now in the fort. We now have about twenty gallons of salt, twelve gallons of which we secured in two small kegs and laid by for our voyage. We gave Willard and Bratton each a dose of Scott's pills. Gibson continues the bark three times a day and is on the recovery.

FEBRUARY 22.   We were visited by two Clatsop women and two boys who brought some excellent hats. Two of these had been made to measure for the captains, and they fit very well. We bought all their hats and distributed them among the men. In the evening the Indians left, and Drouillard went with them in order to get the dogs which the Clatsops have agreed to give us in repayment for the six elk they had stolen from us. One of the canoes broke loose and was going down with the tide. Sgt. Pryor and a party went after it. Our sick: Gibson, Bratton, Ordway, Willard, La Page and McNeal, are recovering. We have not had so many sick at one time since we left the settlements of the Illinois. The general complaint seems to be colds and fevers, and something Capt. Lewis believes is the influenza.

FEBRUARY 23.   Sgt. Ordway is still sick. The men are now fully provided with leather clothes and moccasins – being better off in this respect than at any previous period of our journey.

FEBRUARY 24.   The weather has been so bad that the captains have not been able to make as many celestial observations as they wish. Willard is somewhat worse, but the others are better. The Indians left us this morning. We bought about a half bushel of the small fish the Indians caught about forty miles up the Columbia. They call them eulachon. They are very fat and we eat them, bones and all.

FEBRUARY 25.   The sick men are doing well. Shannon and Labiche returned unsuccessful. Drouillard returned with Comowool, the Clatsop chief and a party of women and children. Drouillard brought two dogs. As it rained and blew violently, we permitted the party to stay all night. They had brought some sturgeon and excellent fish. Also some small fish which are beginning to run in the Columbia.

FEBRUARY 26.   We dispatched Drouillard and two men in our Indian canoe up the Columbia to take sturgeon and eulachon. If unsuccessful, they can purchase them from the Indians for which purpose the captains gave them a few trade goods. We sent Shields, Joseph Fields and George Shannon up the Netul to hunt elk, and directed Reuben Fields and John Collins to hunt on the prairie. Thus we hope to replenish our stores which are reduced to a mere minimum.

FEBRUARY 27.   Reuben Fields returned this evening empty handed. He reports there are no elk towards Point Adams. Collins hunted on the Netul and returned with one. Willard continues very sick. Goodrich and McNeal, who have the pox, are improving, the others on the sick list are nearly well. La Page is still complaining of feeling unwell.

FEBRUARY 28.   Reuben Fields and John Collins set out early to hunt, and stayed out all night. John Shields, Joseph Fields and George Shannon returned late, having killed five elk. The captains ordered them to go out tomorrow and continue the hunt. Sgt. Gass is to take a party of twelve men and bring in the elk. Peter Cruzatte traded his cloak for a dog.

MARCH 1, 1806.   Sgt. Gass and his party of four hunters and eight men set out today to bring in the elk meat. They returned late in the evening with the flesh of three. John Thompson and three hunters were left to jerk the meat of the remaining two. Reuben Fields and John Collins who went hunting yesterday, returned unsuccessful.

MARCH 2.   The sick recover slowly on a diet of lean elk meat. Late this afternoon Drouillard and two men arrived with a most acceptable supply of fat sturgeon and about a thousand fresh eulachon, plus a bushel of wappato roots. We feasted on eulachon and wappato.

MARCH 3.   Two of our canoes have been injured by standing on shore at ebb tide. We had them drawn out of the water for repairs. Baptiste La Page is still sick. We gave him Scott's pills which did not operate. Everything jogs along in the same way with the party. We count the days until April 1st which binds us here at Fort Clatsop. The men are dressing skins, etc.

MARCH 4.   Our fare is better, as the fish and wappato are not yet all gone. The fish soon spoil unless they are pickled or smoked, but in our case, there is little danger of them being kept that long. It rains as usual.

MARCH 5.   We were visited by some parties of Clatsops who brought fish, skins and a hat for sale. We purchased their stock and they departed. In the evening the hunters returned from the [Young's] river. They report the elk have gone to the mountains. We made an assortment of trade articles and directed Sgt. Pryor to set off tomorrow with two men to ascend the Columbia to purchase more fish. We also directed two parties of hunters to renew the hunt, for if the elk have gone away, we might decide to ascend the Columbia slowly to find sustenance on the way.

MARCH 6.   This morning the fishing and hunting parties set out as per instructions given last evening. Bratton is now weaker than any other of the convalescents. We are out of tobacco. Out of the thirty-three persons comprising our party, there are but seven who do not use it. We use crab-apple bark as a substitute. Hugh Hall injured his foot and ankle by the fall of a large stick of timber. Fortunately the bones were not broken, and we expect he will be able to walk shortly. Sgt. Gass and the men are repairing the damaged canoes.

MARCH 7. Drouillard and Labiche returned at sunset, having killed an elk. Bratton is much worse, suffering great pain in his back. We gave him a flannel shirt, and rubbed him well with a linament prepared from alcohol, camphor, castile soap – with a little laudanum. He felt better in the evening. We repeated the linament and bathed his feet to restore the circulation.

MARCH 8. Bratton is much better. Collins returned and informed us that he had killed three elk on the edge of the prairie towards Point Adams. He saw a large herd of elk in that quarter. We sent Drouillard and Joseph Fields to hunt those elk. A party was sent with Labiche for the flesh of the elk he and Drouillard had killed on the Netul. John Shields, Reuben Fields and Robert Frazier returned from the hunt on Young's River unsuccessful. They lost their canoe. McNeal and Goodrich are recovered from their illness and Capt. Lewis directed them to desist from using mercury hereafter. Willard is yet complaining, and is low spirited.

MARCH 9. We sent ten men out under Sgt. Ordway at daylight to bring in the elk meat Collins had killed. They returned in the forenoon. We think that Bratton has rheumatism as he is still uncomfortable. Drouillard and Joseph Fields returned, without any elk. Sgt. Pryor and two men who were sent to obtain fish, have not yet returned. We set Shields at work to make some sacks of elk skin to contain various articles, including our maps and papers.

MARCH 10. About 1 p.m. it became fair, and we sent out two parties on each side of the Netul – one above, and one below. We also sent out a party to hunt beyond Young's River. The hunters, Shannon, Reuben Fields and Frazier who had been on the Netul, informed us they had measured a fir tree which was 39 feet in diameter and was about 300 feet high.

MARCH 11. Sgt. Pryor and his two men arrived this morning in a small canoe loaded with fish. Some dogs at the fishing camp had chewed off the cord of his canoe which had thus set it adrift. He borrowed a canoe of the Indians and made his return, but enroute he found his own canoe and made her fast. Until we return, she will be secure until we recover it, and then will return the borrowed one to the Indians. We sent Sgt. Gass to search for the canoe which was left by Reuben Fields, Shields and Frazier on the 8th. Sgt. Gass returned without finding her. Drouillard, Frazier and Joseph Fields had set out at daylight to hunt.

MARCH 12.   We sent out a party under Sgt. Ordway to search for the lost canoe, but they returned without it. On taking inventory, we find the party is provided with 358 pairs of moccasins. Besides, we have a good stock of dressed elk skins. We sent one hunter out on this side of the Netul, but he did not return this evening. Reuben Fields and John B. Thompson went to hunt towards Point Adams.

MARCH 13.   This morning Drouillard, Frazier and Joseph Fields returned, having killed two elk and a deer. We sent Drouillard down to the Clatsop villages to purchase, if possible, a couple of canoes. Sgt. Pryor, Collins and one man made a search for the lost canoe, but were unsuccessful. Collins killed two elk. We sent Sgt. Ordway and a party of six for the flesh of the elk killed beyond the bay. They returned with it in the evening. Reuben Fields and Thompson have not returned. We had a fair day, so the captains took equal altitudes.

MARCH 14.   We sent a party of seven under Sgt. Gass after the elk Collins had killed. They returned with them about noon. Collins, Joseph Fields, Shannon and Labiche went in quest of the herd out of which Collins had killed two. Reuben Fields and Thompson returned unsuccessful. They are much fatigued, having only a goose and a raven to eat last night. Late in the evening, Drouillard arrived with a party of Clatsops who brought in an indifferent canoe and some roots and hats for sale. We bought the roots and hats, but the canoe was priced beyond our stock of merchandise. Capt. Lewis offered his laced uniform coat, but the Indians would not exchange.

MARCH 15.   This morning Shannon, Joseph Fields, Collins and Labiche returned having killed four elk. Labiche lost the fore-sight of his gun and shot many times, killing only the four. As the elk were lying at some distance apart, we sent two details of men out for them. Both parties returned at evening, bringing the flesh of three and the skins of four. We were visited by a chief and his wife, with six women of the tribe, which the old bawd had brought for market. This was the same party who had last November infested so many of our men with venereal disease, from which all are not yet free. We therefore gave the men a particular charge, which they promised to keep. Bratton is still weak. Drouillard and five men were sent up to the fishery to purchase a canoe if possible.

MARCH 16.   Drouillard and party did not return as expected. Our stock of merchandise is at a low state. Two handkerchiefs would now hold all the small articles we possess. The balance of the stock consists of six blue robes and one of scarlet; Capt. Clark's one artillerist's uniform coat and hat, five robes made of our large flag, and a few old clothes trimmed with ribbon. On this stock we have to depend for the purchase of horses and sustenance from the Indians — a scant dependence indeed for the distance yet before us. We sealed up some papers and letters and gave them to the Indians to deliver to Mr. Haley, the trader of the ship that visits this coast.

MARCH 17. The women still remain near us. They have set up a camp near our Fort and seem determined to lay close siege on us. The men have preserved their vow of celibacy made to the captains. We have had our canoes prepared for our departure, and shall set out as soon as the weather will permit. Drouillard returned this evening from the Cathlamets with our canoe which Sgt. Pryor had left there, and another which he purchased. For this he gave Capt. Lewis' laced uniform coat and nearly a half carrot of tobacco. We still need another canoe, and if the Clatsops will not sell at a price we can afford, we will have to take one of theirs in place of the six elk they stole from us this winter.

21

The Start for Home

MARCH 18. Drouillard was taken sick last night with a pain in his side like a pleurisy. Capt. Clark bled him. Several of the men are unwell. We directed Sgt. Pryor to prepare the two canoes which Drouillard had brought. They need to be calked and strengthened with knees. We were visited by Comowool and Delashelwilt. We furnished the latter with a list of our names, after which we sent him off with his female band. We have given such a list to several of the natives, as well as posted a copy in our quarters. The object is to inform the civilized world that our party had arrived overland from the United States. Our party is too few to leave any here to return by sea, particularly as we shall divide into three or four parties at some stages of our return journey in order to explore the important objects we have in view. This evening Drouillard took an otter in his traps and Joseph Fields killed an elk. Four of the men went over to the coast to take a canoe from the Clatsops, as our interpreter, Charbonneau had suggested. They brought it to the fort and concealed it, as Chief Comowool is here with us.

MARCH 19. A party was sent for the elk that Joseph Fields killed yesterday and they returned in a few hours. We gave Comowool a certificate of good conduct and also a list of our names. We had a hard shower of rain, intermixed with snow and hail, so could not complete the repairs on the canoes.

MARCH 20. Although we have not fared sumptuously the past winter and spring here at Fort Clatsop, we have lived as comfortably as could be expected. We have accomplished every end we had in view by staying at this place except that of meeting any of the traders who visit this coast. It would have been fortunate if some trader had arrived before our departure, for we would have been able to add to our stock of merchandise and therefore could have made a more comfortable homeward bound journey. We hope the men will be in better health traveling than they have been while stationary. Bratton and Willard remain weak. We found the guns of Drouillard and Sgt. Pryor were out of order. Fortunately we had taken the precaution to bring duplicate parts, and with the skill of John Shields, they were repaired. Now all are in good order.

MARCH 21. As we could not set out because of the weather, we sent Shields and Collins to hunt. They returned unsuccessful, so we have not more than one day's provisions on hand. We directed Drouillard and the two Fields brothers to set out tomorrow early to endeavor to provide us with some provisions in the bay beyond. Willard and Bratton do not seem to recover. Willard had a violent pain in his leg and thigh, while Bratton is now so reduced that we are uneasy about his recovery. Some natives visited us and we bought a few fish from them.

MARCH 22. Drouillard and the Fields brothers left early this morning as per orders. We sent seven hunters in different directions to hunt. We were visited by some Indians of whom we bought some dried fish and a dog for our sick men. We presented to Comowool our Fort Clatsop and its furniture, for he has been more kind to us than any other Indian in the vicinity. In the evening they bade us farewell and we did not see them again. All the hunters returned unsuccessful except John Colter, who did not return. We determined to depart tomorrow in any event.

MARCH 23. At 9 a.m. Colter arrived, having killed an elk, but at such distance that we could not send for it. We distributed the baggage and directed the canoes to be loaded. At 1 p.m. we bid final adieu to Fort Clatsop. We had not gone more than a mile when we were met by Chief Delashelwilt and a party of twenty Chinooks. He brought a canoe for sale, but as we were already supplied, we did not purchase it. By 6 p.m. we had doubled Point William and arrived at a small creek [John Day] where we found our hunters. They had killed two elk one and one-half miles away. We encamped here for the night. We have five canoes; three large ones and two small ones.

MARCH 24. We sent fourteen men under Sgt. Ordway to bring in the elk. They soon returned. We breakfasted, and then departed at 9:30 a.m., except for Sgt. Gass' canoe, which was left aground by the tide. In two hours he and his crew were able to set off, and they overtook us at a village where we had halted. Willard and Bratton are still weak. The party proceeded on. Enroute among the Seal Islands we mistook our way, which was observed by an Indian, who put us into the correct channel. He claimed the canoe we had taken from the Clatsops as his property, and we compromised by giving him an elk skin with which he was perfectly satisfied. We encamped at an old Indian village on the south side of the Columbia.

MARCH 25. This morning was cold, and the wind and current were against us, so we made slow progress. We landed at noon [near Clifton, Oregon] where we were joined by some Clatsops. Later we crossed over to the north side, and late in the evening we reached a spot fit for a camp. Here we found Drouillard and the Fields brothers who had been separated from us since morning.

MARCH 26.   We met a chief of distinction, Wallalle, to whom we gave a medal and invested it with the usual ceremonies. He was grateful and gave us a large sturgeon. We were overtaken by two Indians who had two dogs to trade for tobacco, but we are not disposed to trade this, as we have only three carrots left. Our men appear to suffer from the want of it and are now reduced to substitute the bark of the wild crab apple, which they chew. Our hunters joined us here, having killed three eagles and a large goose. We walked on shore on Fanny's Island, which Capt. Clark named in honor of his sister, Frances. We camped on an island [Grimm's] in the evening.

MARCH 27.   We set out early, and were soon joined by some Indians with fish and roots for sale. At 10 a.m. we stopped at some houses of Indians where we found Drouillard and the Fields brothers. They had not returned to our camp last night. These people gave us as much food as we could eat of dried fish, wappato, sturgeon and other roots. We sent Drouillard and Gibson in two small canoes with six hunters ahead to Deer Island in order to kill game by the time we should come up. We made camp this evening at a spot where we had plenty of good wood.

MARCH 28.   We set out very early and at 9 a.m. arrived at an old village on Deer Island where we found our hunters, Drouillard and Gibson. They had killed seven deer and they brought back a remnant of the flesh, for the vultures and eagles had devoured four deer in the course of a few hours. The party killed, and brought in three other deer, a goose, some ducks and a eagle. Drouillard also killed a lynx. Joseph Fields informed us that the vultures had dragged a large buck some thirty yards [these vultures must be condors]. The Columbia is now very high, which makes it difficult to ascend.

MARCH 29.   At an early hour we proceeded along the side of Deer Island and halted for breakfast at its upper end. We were visited by Indians who spread wappato and fish, and then asked presents in return. We exchanged the skins of the deer killed yesterday for twelve dogs and three sea-otter skins. We camped in a small prairie on the north side. Our sick are getting better.

MARCH 30.   We got under way early and passed several fishing villages on Wappato Island. Later we were joined by a fleet of canoes who continued with us some miles for the purpose of looking at us. They are friendly, but had taken the precaution of bringing along their war implements. We camped a little before sunset in a beautiful prairie [near present Vancouver, Washington]. We went out hunting but the game here is very shy.

MARCH 31. We set out early and proceeded, meeting the usual Indians until we came to Quicksand [Sandy] River where we camped. We decided to remain here a day or two to make celestial observations and hunt. Drouillard who was sent to below Seal [Washougal] River, informed us that game was scarce in that quarter.

APRIL 1, 1806. The Indians who followed us yesterday camped near us last night. The captains asked them questions relative to their country. Sgt. Pryor was sent with two men to examine the Quicksand River. He ascended it some six miles and reported that, as the Indians had said, it rises near Mount Hood. This causes us to believe that there must be a larger river which drains this vast area. We have not seen such a river, and the Indians gave us no indication of any such stream. While we were making these inquiries, a number of canoes arrived. These new people told us that they lived up river at the Great Rapids and that there was a scarcity of provisions there and above on the plains, there is no game on which we can subsist. After much deliberation, we decided to remain here until we collect enough meat to last us until we reach the Flathead nation. Our hunters returned from the opposite side, having killed two deer and four elk. Sgt. Gass and party were sent to bring in the meat. The rest of the hunters are to hunt on this side.

APRIL 2. Sgt. Gass' party returned with the elk meat this morning. We sent two parties of nine men to the opposite side. Sgt. Gass is to go below the [Sandy] river, and four men are to go above. We also sent out three others to hunt on this side. Those who remained in camp are collecting wood and making a scaffold, and are cutting up the meat to dry it. Among our visitors were two young men who reside at the falls of a large river which discharges itself into the Columbia from the south side some miles below us. They drew us a map, and it appeared that this [Multnomah; Willamette] river comes in behind an island. We had passed this island on the opposite side both coming and going, and therefore did not see this river. Capt. Clark determined to return, and took seven men: John Potts, Joseph Whitehouse, Peter Cruzatte, John Thompson, Thomas Howard, Peter Weiser and York in one of the canoes, and set off at 11:30 a.m. In exchange for a looking-glass he hired one of the natives to pilot him, and took the man on board.

Capt. Lewis shot the air gun for the natives about camp which much astonished them. As he had only 10 men in camp – the others all being out hunting or with Capt. Clark, Capt. Lewis took the precaution to awe and command respect from these Indians.

Capt. Clark and party stopped at a village with the hope of purchasing wappato. The natives were sulky and refused to sell any. With a portfire match [a sort of slow burning artillery fuze] and his compass and a magnet, Capt. Clark made a demonstration. The match was placed in the fire which made it burn vehemently and changed the color of the fire. The magnet was used to turn the needle of the compass briskly. This apparent magic astonished and alarmed the Indians who then quickly lay before him some wappato, and begged him to take out the bad fire. At this moment the match burned out and the fire returned to normal – and he put away the compass and magnet. Capt. Clark then smoked with them and gave them articles in exchange for the wappato – and went on. The party entered the Multnomah and camped on the stream. They discovered a high mountain south of Mount Hood which they had not seen before, and named it Mount Jefferson.

APRIL 3. A considerable number of Indians crowded about Capt. Lewis' camp. They all confirm the report of scarcity of food above. This morning Joseph Fields, Drouillard and himself, killed four elk. As the party was weak, and some thirty-seven Indians were about, Capt. Lewis thought it best to send a few men to the other side of the river and dry the meat there. Sgt. Pryor and two men returned with Joseph Fields for that purpose. His hunters were ordered to continue the hunt, while the others are employed drying meat.

At 6 p.m. Capt. Clark and his party returned from the Multnomah River. During the morning he had ascended that stream some miles [to near present Portland, Oregon] and then returned. He met an intelligent Indian who drew a sketch of the courses of the river and the island which guards it. Capt. Clark copied these in his notes. He purchased five dogs and returned to base.

APRIL 4. This morning we sent Sgt. Ordway in search of Sgt. Gass' party below the entrance of [Sandy] river. In the course of a few hours both parties returned. Sgt. Gass brought the flesh of a bear and some venison. Collins who had killed the bear, found the den of another in which there were three cubs. Sgt. Gass and Windsor returned with Collins to get the bear. The mother did not return, so they took the three cubs. About noon we dispatched Gibson, Shannon, Howard and Weiser in one of the canoes with orders to proceed up the Columbia six miles to a large bottom and hunt there until our arrival. Late in the evening Drouillard and Joseph Fields returned. They had killed two deer yesterday and saved the meat, which would be dry by noon tomorrow. We directed Drouillard and the two Fields brothers to ascend the river to join George Gibson and his party.

APRIL 5.   Drouillard and the Fields brothers went to join Gibson as directed yesterday. We sent Sgt. Ordway and a party to assist Sgt. Pryor in bringing in the meat of the four elk he had dried. At 1 p.m. they returned, but the meat had been so poorly dried that we feared it would not keep. We therefore directed that it be cut thinner and redried over a fire this evening — as we propose to set off in the morning. Sgt. Gass returned with Collins and Windsor, and brought the three cubs. We exchanged them with the Indians for wappato roots.

APRIL 6.   We had the dried meat secured in skin bags, and all the canoes loaded. We departed at 9 a.m. and went along the north shore to near the place where we had camped on November 3rd. We met with our hunters previously sent up. They had killed three elk this morning and wounded two others which they expect to get. We therefore determined to camp here in order to dry the meat. We sent out a search party and employed others in building scaffolds and collecting firewood. The search party returned in the evening with five elk. Drouillard and Shannon found the two wounded ones and killed them. Reuben Fields killed a bird of the quail type, while Frazier got a pheasant, and Joseph Fields killed a condor. Our supply of elk, in addition to the roots and dogs we can probably procure, will, by using economy, be sufficient to last us to the Flatheads. There we shall meet with our horses, and near that place there are deer to be procured. We direct that fires be kept under the meat all night.

APRIL 7.   Drouillard and the Fields brothers were sent ahead to hunt. The flesh of the remaining elk was brought in, and our dried meat was put in elkskin bags for an early departure. We had the men test the guns by shooting, and found that several had faulty sights. John Shields rectified them in the course of the day. Capt. Clark prevailed upon an old Indian to mark on the sand a sketch of the Multnomah River's upper reaches — and his map corresponded with the others we had been given. He also laid down the Clackamas River for us. Drouillard returned this evening stating that the game had been scared off above.

APRIL 8.   The wind blew so hard that we had to unload the canoes. Being obliged to remain here all day, we sent out Drouillard, Shannon, Collins and Colter to hunt. Capt. Lewis walked down the river to botanize. Shields cut out Capt. Clark's rifle and brought her to shoot very well.[1] Our party owes much to the ingenuity of this man, by whom our guns are repaired

---

[1] That is, he removed the accumulated lead from the bore of the rifle.

when they get out of order, which is very often. About 1 p.m., Collins, Shannon and Colter returned, and soon afterwards Drouillard came in – all with little success. The violent waves split one of our canoes before we could get her out of the water. Late at night the sentinel detected an old Indian trying to creep into our camp to steal. He was one of the six who lay encamped a couple of hundred yards below us. They all departed after our sentinel had discovered and alarmed them.

APRIL 9. We reloaded our canoes and set out at 7 a.m., and proceeded to pick up the Fields brothers. They had not killed any game. We did not stop, but continued to the village located on the north side about a mile below Beacon Rock. Here we halted and took breakfast. John Colter observed the tomahawk in one of the lodges which had been stolen from Capt. Clark on the 4th of November last. The natives attempted to wrest the tomahawk from Colter, but he retained it and thus retook our property. They denied stealing it, etc. With some difficulty we obtained five dogs and a few wappato. At 2 p.m. we set out and arrived at the first rapid. We found a good harbor and encamped. We saw deer sign, so sent Collins to hunt in the morning while the canoes were towed above the rapids. Gibson's crew were directed to delay for Collins and to collect rosin from the pine trees near our camp.

APRIL 10. We drew up our canoes by cords which was soon accomplished. Collins and Gibson not yet having come over, we directed Sgt. Pryor to remain with the cord to assist them in bringing their canoe up the rapid. Above, the current is so strong that it required five oars to make progress. We breakfasted at a village. Here they had a sheep-skin. The head and horns had been formed into a cap which was worn as a highly prized ornament. We obtained the cap for a knife, and gave two elk skins for the sheep skin.[2] At 10 a.m. we were joined by Sgt. Pryor, Gibson and Collins who had brought up their canoe and had killed three deer. We set out and continued on the north side of the river. As we had only one tow-rope, we could only take one canoe at a time. By evening we arrived at the portage where we landed, and conveyed our baggage to the top of a hill where we formed a camp. We had the canoes drawn on shore and secured. One small one got loose from Drouillard and the Fields brothers. The Indians in the lower village brought her up this evening, for which honesty we gave them a couple of knives.

---

[2] This cap and skin may be the same one which Lewis is wearing in the painting of him made by B. J. Saint-Memin soon after the return to St. Louis. A reproduction of this painting is found as the frontispiece of vol. 5, of the de-luxe, large-paper edition of Thwaites. The original is now in the McCullough Collection, New York.

APRIL 11. It rained all night, and our tents and skins which covered the men were wet. Our portage around the Cascades is 2800 yards long on a narrow, rough and slippery road. The duty of getting the canoes above the rapids was delegated to Capt. Clark, who took all but Bratton, who is so weak as to be unable to walk, and three others lamed by various accidents, and one other to cook for the party. A few men were absolutely necessary to guard our baggage from the thieving Indians who crowded our camp in considerable numbers. These people are the greatest scoundrels we have met with. One had the insolence to cast stones at our men as they were walking on the portage road.

By evening, Capt. Clark took four of the canoes above the rapids. They were much damaged by being driven against the rocks despite every precaution we took. The river appears to be some twenty-five feet higher than when we descended it last fall. On the return of our party in the evening from the head of the rapids, our men met several natives on the road. John Shields who has delayed to purchase a dog and was some distance behind, was accosted by two Indians who attempted to take the dog from him and pushed him out of the road. Shields, having no other weapon, pulled his knife, and the Indians fled through the woods. These Indians stole Scannon, Capt. Lewis' dog. Three men were sent in pursuit of the thieves, who discovered the party, and left the dog and fled. They also stole an axe, but John Thompson detected the act and wrested it from them. We informed them by signs that if they made any further attempts, or insulted our men, that we would put them to death. We are concerned for future travelers; no other consideration but our numbers protected us. We kept on constant guard, and our men are disposed to kill a few of them. This evening we sent Drouillard and the Fields brothers a few miles up the river to the entrance of Cruzatte's River [Wind River] to hunt until our arrival.

APRIL 12. Though it rained all of last night and this morning, we determined to haul the remaining canoe beyond the rapids. At one place the current sets with great velocity against a projecting rock, and in hauling the canoe around this point the current turned her side to the stream, and despite the utmost exertions, we were compelled to loose the cord, so both canoe and cord went adrift into the stream. After breakfast all hands were employed in taking the baggage over the portage. The men who had short rifles carried them to protect our baggage from robbery or injury. Sgt. Pryor and some other men were employed the greater part of the day in repairing and calking the canoes. We remained all night at the upper end of the portage.

APRIL 13. The loss of one of our canoes rendered it necessary to distribute her crew and cargo among the remaining canoes. This being done, we set

out at 8 a.m. We found the additional lading made our vessels hard to manage and unsafe in the event of high winds. Capt. Lewis with Sgt. Pryor and
Gibson went in two small canoes, to a friendly village where they were able
to purchase two additional canoes, four paddles and three dogs. He gave
them two buffalo robes, four elk skins and some deer skins in exchange. His
party crossed to the south side where later he found Capt. Clark's party with
the large canoes. They reported they had seen nothing of Drouillard and
the Fields brothers who had been sent ahead to hunt. We directed Sgt.
Ordway to take the canoes just purchased, for his mess and the loading
which we had carried in the lost canoe, and to have these canoes dried and
pitched with rosin. We sent Sgt. Pryor back up Cruzatte's [Wind] River
in search of the hunters with two men and an empty canoe to bring back
any meat they may have killed. John Shields returned after 6 p.m. with
two deer. Colter had been hunting with Shields.

APRIL 14.   This morning we were joined by Sgt. Pryor, his two men and
the three hunters – Drouillard, Reuben and Joseph Fields. They brought
four deer which Drouillard had killed yesterday. After breakfast we departed and kept along the north shore all day. At noon we halted at a
village where we purchased five dogs, some roots, filberts and dried berries.
Our men prefer fat dog meat to lean venison. After nooning, Capt. Clark
and Charbonneau walked on shore, and rejoined the party some six miles
upstream. We camped on a small run [near present White Salmon, Wash-
ington].

APRIL 15.   We delayed this morning to purchase some horses from the Indians, but they were unwilling to barter, so we gathered up our merchandise and at 8 a.m. we set out. The captains halted a few minutes at the
Sepulcher Rock to examine the deposits of dead at that place. We then proceeded along the north shore and arrived at another village where we tried
to purchase horses. All we could get were two dogs. We continued on until
evening when we camped on a [Mill] creek, where we had camped for two
days last fall. Drouillard and some others went to hunt and brought back a
deer.

APRIL 16.   Capt. Clark with Drouillard, Charbonneau, Sacagawea, Goodrich, Frazier, Cruzatte, McNeal and Weiser crossed to the north side in
order to trade with the natives for horses. He took the greater part of our
stores. Capt. Lewis remained in camp and sent out the hunters. Sgt. Gass
and Pryor, with another man, were detailed to make packsaddles. Capt.
Lewis collected specimens of the plants the natives here use for food. Reuben Fields returned in the evening with a large gray squirrel and two others
of a kind new to us. Joseph Fields brought in a black pheasant. There is no

wood on the river above us. Labiche returned this evening having killed two deer, which were brought in later by a party sent for them. One of Capt. Clark's men came over to inform Capt. Lewis that he had obtained no horses as yet, but had the promise of some at the village above the Long Narrows. Capt. Lewis sent the man back with some more trade articles for Capt. Clark. Upon receiving them, Capt. Clark and his party set out with the natives to their village, and remained all night.

APRIL 17.   Capt. Lewis sent out the hunters and additional men to make packsaddles. Joseph Fields brought in three eggs of the magpie. This evening Willard, Weiser, McNeal and Cruzatte returned from Capt. Clark, bringing a note informing us that he had not yet obtained any horses, but would go to another village, and would return tomorrow to the Skilloot village where we intend to meet tomorrow. Capt. Lewis dispatched George Shannon with a note to Capt. Clark advising him to double the price, so that five horses could be obtained. All of Capt. Lewis' hunters returned in the evening. John Shields killed a deer which he brought in with him. The twelve packsaddles were completed this evening. Some of our elk skins were soaked so that harness could be made from them.

Meanwhile, Capt. Clark and party took a position near the village and laid out the articles he had for trade. He obtained a sketch of the upper Columbia and Clark's rivers. The Indians sold him three horses. He also purchased three dogs and some onions to feed his party, and some roots for himself. Charbonneau purchased a mare for which he gave some ermine, elk's teeth, a belt and some other articles.

22

The Dalles to the Walla Walla

APRIL 18. Captain Lewis loaded his canoes and set off for the opposite side – transporting a few Indians who lived there. The party had to portage a short rapid and they drew up the canoes by the cord, assisted by setting poles. From here we proceeded to the basin below the Long Narrows and landed. After unloading the canoes and arranging camp, Capt. Lewis and Joseph Fields walked to the Skilloot village and joined Capt. Clark. He had procured four horses for which a high price had to be paid – at least double that we had given the Shoshoni. These were taken by Charbonneau and Frazier to Capt. Lewis' camp. At 3 p.m. Sgt. Ordway with three men arrived from the camp below with elk skins and a few articles including Capt. Clark's two coats, and four buffalo robes belonging to the men. Capt. Clark dressed the sores of the principal chief and left some medicine to cure his eyes. He also doctored the chief's wife by rubbing some camphor on her temples and back, and she felt restored. This presented a favorable opportunity to trade with the chief, and he sold us two horses. Capt. Lewis obtained a horse in exchange for a large kettle. We determined to make the portage to the head of the Long Narrows with our baggage and five small canoes. We could not take the two large ones any further, and therefore cut them up for fuel – much to the chagrin of the natives who would give us absolutely nothing for them, as they expected to get them free. In the evening the captains returned to the camp at the basin, and left Drouillard, Werner, Shannon and Goodrich with the merchandise at the upper village at the request of the natives, who promised to give us horses for it in the morning. Many natives resort here for trade, most of whom are troubled with sore eyes, and the older men are nearly all blind.

APRIL 19. This morning we had our small canoes drawn from the water, and all hands are employed in transporting our baggage on the backs of our four horses. We accomplished this labor by 3 p.m. and established our camp above the Skilloot village. We obtained four more horses today – trading two of our kettles. We now have only one small kettle to a mess of eight men. In the evening Capt. Clark set out with Sgt. Pryor, Shannon, Cruzatte and Labiche to the village at the Grand Falls in order to trade for horses. The people here are faithless in their contracts, for they frequently trade, and then later demand more, or revoke the exchange. They have pilfered several small articles from us this evening. We directed that the horses be hobbled and grazed at a little distance from our camp under the care of our men. Willard was negligent and suffered his horse to ramble off. It was not found when we ordered them up to be picketed. All except one are stallions and were restless all night.

APRIL 20.   This morning we were informed that the natives had stolen six tomahawks and a knife in the course of the night – and some spoons during the day. Capt. Lewis spoke to the chief on the subject – but the property was not restored. The horse which Capt. Lewis had purchased – and Willard had let get away, was gambled off by the Indian who had sold it, and it had been taken by a man of another nation. Capt. Lewis therefore took the goods back from the Indian. During the day two more indifferent horses were bought. We could not obtain any more, so we resolved to go tomorrow with those we had, and convey the balance of the baggage in two canoes. We therefore had a load made up for seven horses, reserving one for Bratton to ride, as he is unable to walk. We bartered two canoes, elk skins and an old piece of iron for beads. As they would not give anything for one canoe, we cut it up for fuel. We hobbled and picketed the horses within the limits of our camp and ordered the Indians away. We informed them that if they attempted to steal anything that we would beat them severely. They went off in a bad humor; we examined our arms and were on guard.

APRIL 21.   Notwithstanding all our precautions, one of our hobbled horses had broken his line and had gone off. We sent several men to search for him – but to return by 10 a.m. The Indians stole another tomahawk and the iron socket of a canoe pole. We gave the Indian who had taken the last article several severe blows and had the men kick him out of our camp. This is the first act of the kind on our entire expedition, but we had to do it. Capt. Lewis threatened to shoot any of them who stole, and told them that we were not afraid of them, and that we had it in our power to kill them all and set their houses afire, but it was our wish to treat them with kindness provided they let our property alone. The chiefs who were present hung their heads, but said nothing. At 9 a.m. Richard Windsor returned with the lost horse and the other searchers returned also. The Indian who promised to guide us to the Flathead nation produced two horses, one of which he politely permitted Capt. Lewis to pack. We left at 10 a.m., having nine horses packed – with another one which Bratton rode. At 1 p.m. we arrived at the village where we found Capt. Clark. He had been unable to purchase any more horses. We found the man who had won the horse, and he produced another in its stead rather than give back the large kettle and knife we had traded for the horse. We continued on, made the portage with Sgt. Gass, Reuben Fields, Colter and Potts in our canoes, and went into camp a little below the [Des Chutes] river. We bought some dogs and purchased another poor horse, and took the precaution of picketing and hobbling the horses near our camp.

APRIL 22.   Last night two of our horses broke loose, but they were recovered early. At 7 a.m. we set out, having previously sent our small canoe with Colter and Potts. Soon after we left, Charbonneau's horse threw his load, and taking fright at the saddle and robe which adhered, ran down to the village, where the saddle and robe were disengaged. An Indian hid the robe in his lodge. Capt. Lewis sent the guide and one man to assist Charbonneau to retake the horse, which he did. They found the packsaddle, but the Indian denied seeing the robe. Capt. Lewis sent Sacagawea on to ask Capt. Clark to halt, and sent some men back to assist us to make the Indians either return the robe or we would burn his house. Just as Capt. Lewis and party reached the village, Labiche met him with the robe which he had found in the lodge hidden behind some trappings. Capt. Lewis now rejoined Capt. Clark and party. The captains decided to divide the men afoot, and to march alternately with them each day – one captain in front, and the other at the rear. Thus we proceeded through open country for eight miles when we observed our canoes passing on the opposite shore. The wind being too high for them to cross over, they continued on. We halted to graze the horses and dined on some dogs we had purchased. Here we bought another horse. We went on four miles and camped near a village [near John Day's River]. Charbonneau purchased a horse this evening. Colter and Potts passed us in their canoe, but Sgt Gass and Reuben Fields joined us.

APRIL 23.   Charbonneau's two horses got away as he had not secured them to pickets as directed. We sent Reuben Fields and Labiche to assist Charbonneau in finding them. One was found at no great distance, but the other was given up as lost. At 8 a.m. Reuben Fields and Sgt. Gass preceded us in their canoe. During our delay for Labiche and Charbonneau, we made two packsaddles. We continued our march for twelve miles to a village near the rock rapid. The people here are friendly and sold us four dogs for pewter buttons we had made, and some old pieces of iron and brass. This evening Cruzatte played the violin and the men danced. The canoe parties camped near us.

APRIL 24.   We were up early and sent the men in search of the horses. All were found except McNeal's, which was brought back by a hired Indian about 1 p.m. Meanwhile, we made four packsaddles and purchased three horses, and hired three others of the Chopunnish man who accompanies us with his family and horses. Having enough horses for all to travel by land, we sold our canoes for six fathoms of white beads, and loaded up and departed at 2 p.m. Drouillard had to threaten to break up the canoes before the Indians would trade, as they had expected to get them for nothing. Many of our party complain of sore feet caused by the rough stones – having been so long on the soft sand at Fort Clatsop. Capt. Lewis' left ankle gives him much pain, but after bathing it in cold water he was relieved. We dined on two dogs and some root bread. We directed that our new horses be picketed, and the others be hobbled, and a strong guard kept.

APRIL 25.   We collected our horses and set out at 9 a.m., and proceeded on eleven miles to a village where we purchased five dogs and some wood – then took dinner. We tried to barter for more horses but were unsuccessful. Most of the Indians' horses have sore backs, but are otherwise generally in good order. We set out and went nine miles, where we found some willows which would answer for fuel, and made camp. Enroute, one of the horses we had hired of the Flathead guide, was taken from Hugh Hall, whom Capt. Clark had directed to ride. After making camp we traded for two horses which the captains intend to ride, as they have been walking in order to permit the sick to ride. We now have a sufficiency of horses to transport with ease all the baggage and the packs of the men. The natives surround us, and we had the fiddle played and some men danced to amuse them.

APRIL 26.   We set forward early and rode on twelve miles where we halted to have dinner on the remainder of the dogs and dried elk meat. The captains were obliged to go on foot again this afternoon to let some of the men ride whose feet are very sore.

APRIL 27.   Charbonneau's horse strayed again and we were detained until 9 a.m. before we could set out. Our dinner consisted of only dried elk, which is all we have. We were met by the chief of the Wallawallas and we went to his village where we were treated very kindly. Yellept, the chief, harangued his people in our favor for food, and they soon brought us ample, which was most welcome, for we have been on short rations for two days. These people told us of a good road to the [Clearwater] river, said to be level, with game and good water and grass – and eighty miles shorter. We concluded to take this road and to cross our horses over the Columbia River in the morning.

APRIL 28.   Yellept brought a very elegant white horse and presented him to Capt. Clark, signifying that he wished to have a kettle. Being informed we had already disposed with every kettle we could possibly spare, Capt. Clark gave him his sword, some balls and powder with which he was perfectly satisfied. It was necessary to lay in a stock of provisions, so we entrusted Frazier to purchase as many fat dogs as he could. He got ten. The chief loaned us some canoes by which means we swam our horses over the river and hobbled them there. Here was found a Shoshoni woman prisoner, so with Sacagawea to interpret, we conversed with the Wallawallas for several hours. Thus they understood us and the objects of our journey. They had many sick among them and we administered medical aid much to the gratification of these poor wretches. We gave them some eye-water which will render more beneficial service to them than any article we have in our power to bestow. Capt. Clark put in splints and bandaged the arm of a man who needed care – for the arm was broken and was hanging loose. We camped this night with these friendly people. We played the violin and danced for them. Nine-tenths of them had never seen a white man before, and they seem to have a sincere wish to know us, and be at peace.

APRIL 29.   Yellept furnished us with two canoes and we began to transport our baggage across, and to take a party of men over to collect our horses. By 11 a.m. we had all our party and baggage across to the south side of the Columbia. We were detained several hours in collecting the horses. Our guide now informed us it was too late to find a place to camp further on, so we remained on the [Wallula] river. The Indians have traded us two more horses in return for medical aid as dispensed by Capt. Clark who helped them all he could.

APRIL 30.   We have some difficulty in collecting our horses. We purchased two more and several dogs, and exchanged one of our poor horses with our Chopunnish associate for a very good one. We departed at 11 a.m. accompanied by our guide and the Chopunnish man and his family. We camped on the [Touchet] river where we had the pleasure of an abundance of wood again. Drouillard caught a beaver and an otter. We kept a part of the beaver and gave the balance to the Indians, as they do not eat dog. Reuben Fields overtook us with Capt. Lewis' horse, as we were obliged to start without finding him this morning. We now have twenty-three horses; some are young, but the greater part have sore backs. The Indians in general are cruel masters; they ride very hard, and their saddles are so poorly constructed as to wound and scarify the poor creatures' backs.

MAY 1, 1806.   We sent four hunters ahead and made an early start ourselves. At the distance of nine miles we overtook our hunters who had caught only one beaver. Our Indians differed as to the correct route, but we decided to follow the advice of our guide, and made twenty-three miles today. Our Chopunnish family left us today. Labiche killed a deer and we made camp. Soon afterwards, three Wallawallas arrived after a whole day's journey. They brought a steel trap which had been left behind at their village. We can honestly affirm that these Indians are the most hospitable, honest and sincere people we have met with on our journey.

23

The Walla Walla to
Lawyer's Canyon Creek

MAY 2. We sent two hunters ahead. We had much difficulty in collecting our horses, but by 8 a.m. had gathered all but the one we had obtained from the Chopunnish man who had left us yesterday. We had expected this horse would try to regain his companions, and had hobbled him closely, but he broke the thongs. Capt. Lewis engaged one of the Indians who had brought the trap last night to go with Joseph Fields to search for him. They returned about 1:30 p.m. with the horse which they had found seventeen miles back. We paid the Indian for his trouble and set forward. In the evening we camped on a [Pilot] creek. The three Indians continued with us. Our hunters caught a beaver and an otter. We set our traps here for there are many signs of beaver.

MAY 3. We set out at 7 a.m., and after going some distances we were met by Weahkoonut, a chief of the Chopunnish nation and ten of his men. Some of them had descended with us last fall. They had come a considerable distance to meet us. We camped in a small grove of cottonwoods which in some measure broke the violence of the wind which had blown all day, accompanied by snow and hail. Our guide and the three young Wallawallas left abruptly this morning, and we have seen nothing of them since. We divided the last of our dried meat as well as the balance of our dogs, and had a scant supper with nothing left for tomorrow.

MAY 4. We collected our horses and set out early. We arrived at a village where we purchased two lean dogs and some root-bread of which we made soup. One of our horses fell in the river with his pack consisting principally of ammunition, but fortunately neither horse nor load suffered any injury – the powder being sealed in cannisters. We crossed the [Snake] river, aided by three Indian canoes, and encamped. The chief, Tetoharsky, tells us that Tobey, our former Nez Perce guide, took two of our best horses away with him when he left us last fall.

MAY 5. We collected our horses and set off at 7 a.m. At four and one-half miles we arrived at the mouth of the [Clearwater] river and proceeded up it twelve miles when we arrived at a village at 1 p.m. Capt. Clark traded with an Indian a vial of eye-water for an elegant gray mare – the result of medical attention he had given last fall. This Indian, who had recovered, spread the fame of Capt. Clark as a doctor. We think this modest deception is pardonable, for they will not give us provisions without compensation, and our stock of trade articles is now reduced to a handful. We take care to give no medicine which can possibly injure them. We went to Collins' [Potlatch] Creek where we had sunk our first canoe last fall when we had descended the river. We camped on this creek at a little distance from the Chopunnish village. We had about fifty applicants for medical care, for which we asked dogs and horses in return.

MAY 6. This morning the husband of a sick woman whom Capt. Clark had treated last evening, brought a young horse which we killed and butchered for food. Capt. Clark was busy for several hours administering eye-water to a crowd of applicants. From this service we obtained a plentiful meal, much to the comfort of our party. Here we met with three men of the [Coeur d' Alene] nation who told Capt. Lewis of a large river which discharged itself into the Columbia to the north. Capt. Lewis named it "Clark's River" in honor of his worthy friend and fellow traveler, Capt. Clark. We set out, accompanied by a brother of Twisted Hair, the Chopunnish chief. Capt. Lewis directed Drouillard and John Colter to lead an unbroken horse which we intend to eat. A quarrel ensued between these men regarding the duty. Near evening the horse broke loose and made his escape, much to the chagrin of the party and the keenness of their appetite. This loss left us supperless in the rain.

MAY 7. We set out early, guided by the brother of Twisted Hair. We crossed the river, and here an Indian produced a cannister of powder which proved to be the same one which we had buried last fall. We rewarded him with a firesteel for his honesty. We camped near the place where we had built our canoes last October. We saw the tracks of deer, so we determined to remain here until noon tomorrow in order to hunt. The Indians inform us that the snow is deep in the mountains before us, and that we shall not be able to pass them until the next full moon – or about June 1st, or perhaps later. This is unwelcome news to men on horse meat and roots who have visions of buffalo to eat. We were accompanied by two Indians, one of whom can speak the Shoshoni language. We will therefore be able to converse with them through Sacagawea.

MAR 8. Most of the hunters turned out at daylight, but a few others remained in camp. We chide these for their indolence and inattention to orders. John Shields returned at 8 a.m. with a small deer on which we breakfasted, and at 11 a.m. all the hunters returned. Drouillard and Cruzatte each brought a deer. Collins had wounded another which Scannon, Lewis' dog, caught at a little distance from camp. Capt. Clark caught several trout with a trap. Twisted Hair's brother gave us a sketch of the principal water courses west of the Rocky Mountains. At 3 p.m. we departed for the lodge of Twisted Hair. We were received coolly by Twisted Hair which was unaccountable to us. The chiefs argued some twenty minutes, so to relieve our horses of their burdens, we went to the first water and made camp. We had been informed that the natives had discovered the deposit of our saddles and had taken them, and that our former herd of horses were now widely scattered. About an hour after we camped, Drouillard returned from hunting, so we sent him to Twisted Hair to make inquiries, and to invite him to smoke with us. It developed that there had been some misunderstanding between Twisted Hair and Broken Arm, another chief, but we would get our horses and saddles back.

MAY 9. We sent several hunters out early with instructions to meet us at the lodge of Twisted Hair. At 9 a.m. we set out and at six miles we arrived at his lodge. Twisted Hair set out with two young men, along with Alexander Willard, in search of our horses. Late in the evening they returned and brought about half of our saddles and some powder and lead that had been buried. At the same time the young men brought back twenty-one of our horses. The greater part were in fine order, but five had been ridden hard last winter and were quite injured. Three others had sore backs. We had them caught and hobbled. Chief Broken Arm lodged with Twisted Hair and have become good friends again.

MAY 10. It snowed this morning, but we collected our horses and set off. Drouillard turned off to hunt and did not return this evening. At 4 p.m. we arrived at a village and Broken Arm, its chief, showed us a place on the bank of a creek where we should camp. We stated our situation in regard to provisions, and the natives gave us some dried salmon and root bread. We told them our men were not used to living on roots for they made them sick. We proposed exchanging one of our poor horses for a young, fat one. The chief told us that they had an abundance of young horses, and that if we wished to eat them, we would be furnished with as many as we wanted. Accordingly, they soon produced two, one of which we killed – saving the other for later. This was the greatest act of hospitality we have witnessed from any nation. We smoked with our Indian friends and gave the chiefs medals. The chief had a large leather tent erected for the captains and invited them to make it their home for so long as we remain with them. As these people have been so liberal, we ordered our men not to crowd the natives' lodges in search for food, as hunger has compelled them to do at some lodges we have passed. We invited the principal men to the tent and spent the evening in explaining who we were, where we wanted to go, the objects of this journey and answering their inquiries. After this council, the Indians stayed with us all night. Our men played the fiddle and danced for them.

MAY 11.   The captains' tent was crowded with sleeping Indians, including all the principal chiefs of this nation. As some of them had been out hunting when we were here last fall, we had missed meeting them before. We explained our country; drew a map, and through our interpreters, made ourselves understood, though the translations had to pass through French, Minnitaree, Shoshoni and the Chopunnish languages. This was tedious, and took half a day, but they were highly pleased. We showed them the spy-glass, compass, watch, air-gun and other articles which proved novel to them. A young man presented us with a fine mare and colt. He said our words had opened his ears and had made his heart glad. Drouillard arrived at 3 p.m. with two deer. Many of the natives apply for medical aid which we give cheerfully as far as our skill and medicines will permit. Twisted Hair brought us six horses from our herd. They were in fine order.

MAY 12.   This morning a great number of Indians collected before Capt. Clark who is their favorite physician. He began to administer to at least fifty applicants. The chiefs held a council among themselves in regard to what we had told them yesterday. After haranguing the village, they came to us, and two of their men presented Capt. Lewis with a fine horse. It was agreed that Capt. Clark would attend the sick while Capt. Lewis would hear the answer of the chiefs. They said our words were good regarding peace among the tribes, and they would try to follow it. We gave a vial of eye-water to Broken Arm for the use of his people. We gave Twisted Hair a gun, a hundred balls and two pounds of powder as part payment for caring for our horses this past winter as we had promised. We also promised to give him the same quantity of powder and lead when we receive the balance of our horses. Three more were brought in, which leaves only six missing – as old Tobey and his son each took one of ours when they returned to their Shoshoni nation last fall.

We informed the Indians of our wish to form a camp at some proper place where we could fish, hunt and graze our horses until the snows on the mountains would permit us to pass. They recommended a place a few miles distant. As we will need guides to take us on the different routes we intend to take from Traveler's Rest [on the Bitterroot], and as Twisted Hair has several grown sons who are familiar with the different routes, we invited him to move his family and live with us while we remain here. He was grateful with this expression of confidence and promised to do so. Cutnose, the chief, gave Drouillard a horse, and several of our men swapped horses with the natives for better ones.

24

Camp Chopunnish
on the Upper Kooskooske

MAY 13.   Capt. Clark was busy with his patients. At 11 a.m. we collected our sixty horses and set out for the river escorted by a number of natives. We followed [Lawyer's] creek down to an extensive open bottom of the Kooskooske [Clearwater] River and halted at the place appointed to meet the canoe which was to take us across. As the canoe did not arrive until after sunset, we remained here all night.

MAY 14.   We dispatched Collins, Shannon and Labiche to hunt. At 10 a.m. we had our baggage and horses across the river. We reloaded after breakfast and went to the place selected for a permanent camp [near present Kamish, Idaho]. This is a very eligible spot near good hunting grounds and excellent pasture. Collins killed two bear, and Joseph Fields and Peter Weiser were sent with him to bring back the meat, which they did this evening. We gave the Indians some of the bear meat, which was a great treat to them. Labiche returned late and told us he had killed a bear and two cubs. He brought some large pheasants. George Shannon also returned with a few pheasants. Our seven stallions are so troublesome that we tried unsuccessfully to exchange them. Therefore, assisted by a native, Drouillard began to castrate them.

MAY 15.   Reuben Fields while searching for his horse, saw a large bear near camp, and several men went in pursuit. Labiche and Shannon went out to establish a hunting camp, and Gibson and Hall went with them to bring in the three bears Labiche had killed. Drouillard and Cruzatte went up the river to hunt. John Shields, Reuben Fields and Alex Willard hunted in the hills. In the evening they returned with a few pheasants. At 11 a.m. the men returned with the three bears Labiche had killed. Frazier, Joseph Fields and Weiser complain of violent pains in their heads, and Howard and York are afflicted with the colic which we attribute to the diet of roots. We had all our horses driven together near our camp so that they can get accustomed to each other. We intend to do this each day. Our party made more comfortable quarters of willow poles and grass, so they are secure from sun and rain. The captains sleep under an old sail, and have a bower to do their writing under.

MAY 16.   Drouillard's horse left his camp last night and was brought to us by an Indian. The sick men are better today. Sacagawea gathered a quantity of fennel roots which we found very agreeable. We also use onions which we find are an antidote for the wind-forming effects of the roots. Drouillard and Cruzatte returned with a deer. A little after dark Shannon and Labiche returned with a deer. Sgt. Pryor and Collins, who had set out this morning, have not yet come back. John Shields went hunting. We direct that our horses be driven up at noon each day. We ate two of our unruly stallions who did not survive after Drouillard's method of castration. The Indians' method was satisfactory.

MAY 17.   Sgt. Pryor and Collins returned from a bear hunt – each killing one. As these bears are very ferocious, we have directed that at least two hunters go together. We also ordered that the horses be equally ridden so that no one of them is injured by being constantly used on the hunt. We directed that the hunters be sent in different directions and not to return until they had killed some game.

MAY 18.   Twelve hunters turned out with their horses to go to different locations. John Potts and Joseph Whitehouse accompanied Collins to bring in the bear he had killed on the 16th. They returned this afternoon with it. Sacagawea is busy laying in a store of the fennel roots for use when we cross the mountains. The Indians erected a lodge and a wharf on the opposite side of the river to be in readiness for the salmon – the arrival of which they are as ardently waiting for as ourselves. Joseph Fields returned from the hunt very unwell. At a little before dark, Drouillard, Reuben Fields and La Page returned from their hunt unsuccessful. Capt. Clark doctored a few natives.

MAY 19.   We sent Charbonneau, Thompson, Potts, Hall and Weiser over to the village to purchase some roots to eat with our poor bear meat. The Fields brothers went to get the horse Capt. Lewis had ridden last fall, which was seen with a band of Indian horses, and is now very wild. About 11 a.m. Thompson returned with a party of Indians who wanted medical aid. Capt. Clark treated them for a variety of ailments, and they went away satisfied. At 5 p.m. Charbonneau and Potts returned with about six bushels of cowse roots and some bread made of the same root. The Fields brothers returned unsuccessful.

MAY 20.   Drouillard and the Fields brothers set out to hunt. Shannon and Colter came in without anything. At 2 p.m. Labiche came in with a large deer. He had left Collins and Cruzatte to continue the hunt. Labiche and La Page returned to them so as to get an early start tomorrow. Frazier returned from the village with some roots he had purchased. Rained all day.

MAY 21.   Shields and Gibson went to hunt towards the mountains. Collins came in and stayed about two hours. We sent five men to build a canoe for taking fish and crossing the river. The captains' tent is not sufficient to keep off the rain, so we had Sgt. Gass and others build a grass covered shelter for them to sleep under which will be rain-proof. We divided the trade articles among the party to trade for roots. Sgt. Ordway, Goodrich and Willard went to the village to procure roots. Willard returned, but Ordway and Goodrich stayed all night at the village. We ate the last of our meat, and have a horse ready to kill, as we seem unable to secure enough game. The men have been so accustomed to privations that the want of meat nor scanty funds excites the least anxiety among them.

MAY 22.   Windsor and McNeal went to the village. Sgt. Ordway and Goodrich returned with a good store of roots. Shannon and Colter went to the mountains to hunt. Sgt. Pryor went down the river to select a better place to camp, but finding nothing better, we resolved to stay here. We killed a fine colt for meat. Drouillard, the Fields brothers, Gibson and Shields arrived with five deer. They also brought two salmon they had purchased. Little "Pomp" [Baptiste], Sacagawea's child, is cutting teeth and is very ill. His jaw and neck are very much swollen. We gave him a dose of cream-of-tartar and applied a poultice of boiled onions as warm as he could bear it. Sgt. Pryor returned late in the evening. It being a fine day, we dried our baggage and roots.

MAY 23.   Sgt. Pryor wounded a deer near camp which was divided with some Indians who had helped recover it. Pomp is somewhat better, and we repeated the poultice to reduce the swelling. Shannon, Colter, Labiche, Cruzatte, La Page and Collins returned unsuccessful except for some birds. The captains made drawings and descriptions of these. Capt. Clark continues medical aid to all the Indians who apply. William Bratton has been nearly helpless these past three months. John Shields suggested that we try an Indian sweat-bath. Shields sank a circular hole four feet deep and three feet in diameter and built a large fire in it as a sweat-bath for Bratton. The fire was taken out, a seat placed inside, and the hole was covered with hoops of willow branches. Blankets were secured over the hoops on all sides. He was given a vessel of water to sprinkle on the hot walls and bottom to create steam. After twenty minutes, he was plunged twice in cold water, and then returned to the hole for three quarters of an hour longer. Afterwards he was taken out and covered with blankets so that he might cool off gradually. While in the hole he drank copiously of strong horse-mint tea. We continue to burn out the canoe. Most of the men went to the village and brought back a considerable supply of roots. The natives caught three salmon today.

MAY 24.   Four of our men, having made awls from the links of a chain from one of their old traps, traded these for a plentiful supply of roots. Pomp is still restless, though his fever has abated. We gave him a dose of cream-of-tartar, and a fresh poultice of onions. William Bratton feels much better and says he is free from pain. He is walking about today. Shields, Gibson, Drouillard, Cruzatte, Collins and the Fields brothers turned out to hunt.

MAY 25.   We were visited by the lame Indian chief whom we had treated previously. He had lost the use of his limbs, so we suggested a sweat-bath in the same manner as Bratton had taken. We showed him the horse-mint plant we had used for tea. Drouillard, Labiche and Cruzatte hunted towards the quawmash root grounds, while the Fields brothers hunted on the opposite side. Silas Goodrich visited the village and returned with a few roots. Gibson and Shields returned with only a sand-hill crane. Pomp is much better, so we gave him an enema. The lame chief and his party remained with us all night.

MAY 26.   Collins, Shannon and Colter set out to hunt. Pomp is much better. We gave the lame chief a few doses of cream-of-tartar, some flower of sulphur and some portable soup. The Fields brothers returned with some Indians from a village we had never seen or visited before. They had obtained there a large quantity of roots on moderate terms. We directed Sgt. Pryor with some men to visit that village tomorrow for more roots. In the afternoon the canoe was completed and put into the water. It will carry twelve men.

MAY 27.   Reuben Fields went in search of the horse the Indians had given us to kill, as we are out of meat. At 10 a.m. he returned with the horse and it was soon butchered. Our Indian guests told us to take any of their horse herd whenever we wished — a piece of liberality not expected from even our own countrymen. Sgt. Pryor and party set out for the new village. In the evening he, with Gibson and Shields, returned with a good store of roots and bread. The others, Charbonneau, La Page and York, remained at the village. We sent Sgt. Ordway, Frazier and Weiser to Lewis' [Snake] River for salmon. Drouillard, Cruzatte and Labiche returned with five deer. Pomp is much better, though we fear the swelling might leave an ugly scar below his ear. The Indians are anxious to have the lame chief sweated under our supervision and requested that we make a second attempt. The hole was enlarged so that the man's father could sustain him in the proper position while in the sweat-house. We could not make him sweat as copiously as we wished. Afterwards he complained of pain and we gave him thirty drops of laudanum, which composed him and he rested well.

MAY 28. Goodrich was sent to the village of Broken Arm. He returned in the evening with some root bread and some wild goat's hair which we desire to use for making saddle-pads. The Fields brothers went out to hunt. At noon, Charbonneau, La Page and York returned with four bags of dried roots. Collins, Colter and Shannon returned with eight deer. The lame chief is much better and can use his arms. He will stay with us to continue the sweat baths. Pomp is better and is free from fever. Sgt. Ordway, Frazier and Weiser, enroute to the [Snake] river camped near a village.

MAY 29. Once more we have a good store of meat and roots. Bratton is recovering very fast. Pomp is better, and the lame chief has the use of his arms and hands. He washed his face today which he has been unable to do for himself for the past twelve months. Our horses are so wild that we need half of the Indians to help catch them. They are dexterous at throwing a rope and taking the horse with a loop about the neck. As we cannot always depend on the natives, we had a strong compound built in order to take them at our pleasure.

With Sgt. Ordway's party, Frazier obtained two Spanish mill dollars in exchange for an old razor. We expect the Indians get these dollars from other Indians who live near the Spanish country to the south. Towards evening they arrived on the [Snake] river and were entertained at a native fishery.

MAY 30. La Page and Charbonneau went to trade for roots, while Sgt. Gass went to get goat's hair for saddle-pads. Shannon and Collins used the canoe to carry their proportion of merchandise to trade, but the current forced the canoe into some trees which sank the boat. John Potts, who cannot swim, had much difficulty in making the shore. They lost three blankets, a blanket-coat and a pittance of trade goods. In our bare state, this loss of clothing is serious, for there are only three men in the whole party who have more than a blanket apiece. We sent Sgt. Pryor and a party to raise the canoe, but the depth and strength of the current baffled every attempt. We gave the lame chief a sweat bath today after which he could move his legs and toes. In the evening Joseph Fields returned in search of a horse which had left him last night. He informed us that he and his brother had killed three deer at their camp.

Sgt. Ordway's party on the [Snake] river, purchased enough salmon and then proceeded to dry it before returning to our camp.

MAY 31. Goodrich and Willard visited the village and returned in the evening. Willard had bought a dressed bear skin. The Fields brothers also returned with three deer. The Indians brought us the last of our original stock of horses which we had branded and left with them last fall. We now have sixty-five horses in excellent order. The Snake Indians stole some of Sgt. Ordway's dried salmon in the night, but nevertheless they set out to return.

JUNE 1, 1806. Charbonneau and La Page returned from an unfortunate voyage in that they lost their merchandise in the river. Drouillard set out with a chief to recover two tomahawks stolen from us last fall. Colter and Willard went out hunting. We are anxious about Sgt. Ordway and his men, as we have not heard anything from them since they set out for the [Snake] river. We asked Drouillard to inquire of Twisted Hair, as he and his family have not camped with us. We fear we shall be at a loss to acquire a guide to the headwaters of the Missouri. We are out of trading goods, so we created a new fund by cutting off the buttons from our clothes and by preparing eye-water. We put the eye-water in phials and small tin boxes which had once contained phosphorous. The lame chief is better.

Sgt. Ordway and his men worked their way back towards the main camp.

JUNE 2. McNeal and York were furnished with the buttons which the captains had cut off from their coats, and were sent to trade for roots. They returned with three bushels — a most successful voyage. Collins, Shields, the Fields brothers and Shannon set out for a moose hunting trip. Through the influence of the chief, Drouillard was able to retake the stolen tomahawks. One was the property of our late Sgt. Floyd, and Capt. Clark was desirous of returning it to his parents. About noon, Sgt. Ordway, Frazier and Weiser returned from the [Snake] river with seventeen salmon and some roots. The distance was so great that the salmon were nearly spoiled. They had been twenty miles up the [Salmon] river — probably the first white men ever there. Capt. Lewis' Shoshoni stallion, which was one of those gelded, was shot, for he had no chance of recovery.

JUNE 3. Bratton is much stronger and can walk about with ease. The lame chief is recovering the use of his limbs. Pomp is nearly well. Colter, Joseph Fields and Willard returned with five deer and a bear. The Indians inform us it will still be twelve or fourteen days before we can cross the mountains. We do not entertain much hope of procuring salmon this early on our stream, and the Lewis [Snake] River is too distant for us.

JUNE 4. About noon the three chiefs left us, with no promise of any of their young men to go with us as guides. John Shields returned with two deer. Chief Broken Arm invited us to his village as he wanted to give us some roots before we set out over the mountains. We decided to remain and hunt here a few days longer.

JUNE 5. Collins and Bratton went to the village to trade for roots. They were successful. We gave the lame chief another sweat bath today and he appears to improve. Pomp is coming along slowly. This evening Reuben Fields, Shannon, Labiche and Collins returned with five deer and a brown bear.

JUNE 6. Capt. Clark visited Broken Arm and took Drouillard and three men. Broken Arm could promise no guides, but told us a party of Shoshoni had arrived who had heard our talk last fall and had come to make peace. He gave Capt. Clark a pipe to smoke with the Shoshoni. Meanwhile our party obtained a good supply of roots and bread – enough for our trip over the mountains.

At Capt. Lewis' camp, Twisted Hair had arrived, but as Drouillard was with Capt. Clark, conversation was difficult. Capt. Clark arrived at 5 p.m., along with some chiefs and Drouillard. The Indians remained all night. During the morning Frazier had arrived with more roots and bread.

JUNE 7. Two of the chiefs returned to their villages accompanied by Sgt. Gass, McNeal, Whitehouse and Goodrich, with the hope to procure some pack ropes in exchange for pieces of iron, gigs, old files and some bullets. They were also to get some bags to hold our roots. All returned except Whitehouse and Goodrich, who remained at the village. They obtained a few ropes – but no bags. A chief brought a horse to Frazier who had given him a pair of Canadian shoe packs [snow shoes]. Drouillard went hunting. We are engaged in preparing saddles and arranging loads of provisions for our departure. Frazier is very fond of conversing with the Indians and learning more of their language.

JUNE 8. Drouillard returned unsuccessful from his hunt. The lame chief has gained strength and can now stand. Bratton is not considered an invalid any more. He had a long, tedious illness which he bore with much fortitude and firmness. We exchanged two of our horses with sore backs for fine horses in good order. Our men run foot races with the Indians. One of them proved as fleet as Drouillard and Reuben Fields – our swiftest runners. Afterwards the men divided into two parties and played prison base by way of exercise before entering the mountains. In short, those who are not hunters are getting rather soft and slothful. After dark, Cruzatte played the violin, and the men danced for the amusement of ourselves and the Indians.

JUNE 9. We were visited by several Indians and we exchanged one of our poor horses for a better one. We ate the last of our meat and have lived on roots only today. We intend to move to better hunting grounds, so our party is much elated with the idea of getting on that much nearer towards their homes and country. We have everything in readiness for a move, and have been passing the time with foot races, pitching quoits, prison base and other activities.

JUNE 10.   We had our horses collected except one of Cruzatte's and one of Whitehouse's which were not found. After a search, Cruzatte's was obtained, and the Indians promised to find the other and bring it to the quawmash flats where we propose to camp for a few days. At 11 a.m. we set out, each man well mounted, and a light load on a second horse. Besides, we have extra horses in case of accident or want of provision. We therefore feel ourselves perfectly equipped for the mountains. We camped near the same place [Weippe Prairie] where we first met the Chopunnish last September 22nd. We sent out our hunters, and Collins killed a doe on which we supped.

JUNE 11.   All the hunters were out by daylight. Labiche killed a bear and Gibson got a fine buck. Whitehouse returned to our former camp in search of his horse. Shannon killed a buck. The hunters were sent out in the afternoon to hunt at some distance, and to stay there all night. The natives all left us and we remained in quietness by ourselves.

JUNE 12.   All the hunters except Gibson returned. Only Shields had any success and he brought in two deer. In the evening the hunters went out again. Whitehouse returned with his horse.

JUNE 13.   Reuben Fields and Willard went to the prairie in the mountains eight miles distant to hunt there until we arrive. The hunters: Gibson, Shannon, Collins, Joseph Fields, Drouillard and Labiche returned with a deer each. Shields had two — in all, eight deer. Labiche and Cruzatte killed a deer but they reported the buzzards had eaten it up after they had hung it in a tree. Colter killed a crane. We caused the venison to be cut thin and dried in the sun. The captains have compiled a list of the native tribes living west of the Rocky Mountains.

JUNE 14.   Our hunters set out early. Colter brought in a deer and eight duck eggs by 10 a.m. The other hunters, except Drouillard, returned early without having killed anything. We packed all our articles and made ready for a forced march to Traveler's Rest. We are apprehensive that the snow and want of food for the horses will prove embarrassing to us on our four days journey across the mountains. Everyone is anxious to be in motion to reach the United States.

JUNE 15.   Our sixty-five horses were scattered, and so we did not set off until 10 a.m. We went to the prairie where Reuben Fields and Alex Willard had been hunting. We found two deer hung up in a tree, and at two and one-half miles further we found our hunters. They had killed another deer. We halted, dined and grazed our horses. We then set out and later camped in a glade with plenty of grass which was near the place where we had stopped on September 20th, 1805. The rains made the road slippery and rendered our progress slow and difficult.

JUNE 16. We set out at 6 a.m. and proceeded up Lolo Fork [1] and went to a glade where we grazed our horses. Windsor broke his rifle near the muzzle. We went on through fallen timber and were soon in snow. We stopped at Hungry Creek. Capt. Lewis killed a pheasant.

JUNE 17. We set out early and ascended a very steep hill, and soon found ourselves enveloped in snow from twelve to fifteen feet deep. Drouillard, our principal woodsman and guide, was doubtful if we could go on without severe loss to our animals. We came to the resolution to return to lower levels where there is hunting and plenty of grass. We made a deposit of all our baggage which we did not immediately need, also the roots, except an allowance for a few days. We left our instruments, papers, etc., believing them safer here than to risk them on horseback down over the roads and creeks which we would have to pass. We returned to Hungry Creek. The party was quite dejected by this, our first retrograde march.

JUNE 18. We had difficulty in collecting our horses as they were scattered in the timbered mountain sides where they were searching for food. By 9 a.m. we had collected all but Drouillard's and two of Shields. We set out leaving Shields and La Page to collect the lost horses and follow us. We dispatched Drouillard and Shannon to the Chopunnish village to secure a guide and hasten the arrival of the Indians who promised to accompany us. We sent a rifle as a reward to any who would conduct us to Traveler's Rest on the [Bitterroot] river. John Potts cut his leg badly with a big knife as he was cutting out the trail. Capt. Lewis had to tie the veins to stop the blood. Colter's horse fell, and both of them rolled over each other down the rocks. He lost his blanket, but retained the rest of his gear. We returned to the glade where we dined on the 16th. The Fields brothers went hunting with instructions to join us tomorrow on Collin's Creek. Colter and Gibson fixed a gig in order to catch salmon-trout.

JUNE 19. Collins, Labiche and Cruzatte turned out to hunt. Colter and Gibson went to fish. Gibson got one salmon-trout. Joseph and Reuben Fields arrived with two deer. Shields and La Page came back with them. The latter had not found his horse. Frazier reported that the captain's riding horses and a mule had wandered off towards the quawmash flats. Cruzatte brought some mushrooms which Capt. Lewis found insipid. Labiche came in with a deer.

---

[1] Lolo Fork, Idaho, not to be confused with Lolo Creek, Montana.

JUNE 20.   Reuben Fields killed a brown bear. Labiche and Cruzatte returned late evening with a deer. The fishermen caught seven salmon-trout. As the game is scarce, we determined to move down to the quawmash flats to endeavor to lay in another stock of meat for the mountains. Bratton's horse is missing.

JUNE 21.   We left the Fields brothers with Sgt. Gass to hunt at this camp until our return. We collected the horses and retreated to the flats. One of Thompson's horses is sick, and Cruzatte's horse snagged himself so badly that we fear he will be of no further service. Some Indians returned with three horses and the mule we had lost in the mountains. We sent four hunters ahead to hunt at the flats. Shields got a deer.

JUNE 22.   All the hunters were sent out. They killed eight deer and three bears. We dispatched Whitehouse to the [Clearwater] river near our camp on Collin's Creek to get some salmon which we understand the natives are now catching. We gave him some beads to trade which Capt. Clark unexpectedly found in a waist-coat pocket. John Potts' leg is inflamed and is very painful. We apply a poultice of roots. Neither Shannon, Drouillard nor Whitehouse have returned this evening. Collins killed a black bear.

JUNE 23.   Frazier and Weiser were sent to the Indians who brought back our four horses, and who are camped near us. They are to prevail upon them to remain a day or two longer before crossing the mountains. If the Indians persist in going on, Frazier, Weiser and the three men left at the hunting camp, i.e., Sgt. Gass and the Fields brothers, are to go with them and mark the trail as far as Traveler's Rest, where they are to remain until we join them. Drouillard, Shannon and Whitehouse returned this afternoon, but Colter is still out. The former brought three Indians who promise to go with us as far as the Falls of the Missouri. We will pay them two guns for this service. We therefore secured our horses near camp so as to make an early start in the morning. We have an abundance of strawberries at this place.

JUNE 24.   We set out to cross the mountains accompanied by three guides. Colter had killed a bear, then joined us, but the bear was poor – and far off, so we did not send for it. At Collins' Creek we found Frazier – the other men had gone on. On Fish Creek we found Sgt. Gass and Peter Weiser and the Indians – who had tired of waiting. Reuben and Joseph Fields had killed a small deer which they gave to the Indians, and had gone on to Hungry Creek in order to hunt for us. The Indians, to assure good weather, set the pine trees on fire.

JUNE 25.   We set out early, but one of the guides claimed to be sick – generally the prelude to abandoning an enterprize. We left them, and they promised to overtake us. At 11 a.m. we arrived at the branch of Hungry Creek where we found the Fields brothers. We dined, and the guides came up. Capt. Lewis gave the sick Indian a buffalo robe – he having no other covering but an elk-skin without the hair. Drouillard and Shields fortunately recovered their horses which had been lost on Hungry Creek.

JUNE 26. We set out at 6 a.m. and reached our deposit of goods left on the top of the snowy mountain. It was found untouched. We breakfasted and then reloaded our goods. We set off and ascended and descended several lofty heights, but kept to the dividing ridge. Late in the evening we reached a fine spring with an abundance of good grass for the horses. One of our guides lost two of his horses, but found them, and rejoined us a little after dark. Capt. Clark is tormented with a violent headache. The snow had melted considerably.

JUNE 27. We started out early and continued along the dividing ridge for nine miles to our camp of September 17th, last year. We are surrounded by tremendous mountains covered with snow as far as the eye can reach. We continued our march, ascending and descending steep mountains to a place where we camped which had a little grass. We have traveled twenty-eight miles without relieving the horses of their packs, nor they having had much food. Our meat being gone, we issued a pint of bear's oil to each mess, which the men mixed with their boiled roots. John Pott's leg is better and gives him little pain.

JUNE 28. We collected our horses which look gaunt this morning. We went along the ridge, our guide being extremely sagacious in finding the old summer trail. About 11 a.m. we arrived at an untimbered side of a mountain where we found the abundance of grass the guide had promised. As it was a long way to the next grass, we determined to remain here all night. We melted snow for the water we need.

JUNE 29. We dispatched Drouillard and Reuben Fields to go to the warm [Lolo] springs ahead to hunt, then we set out early. We were on the heights for five miles, then descended to Glade Creek and bid adieu to the snow. Near the creek we found a deer which our hunters had left for us. This was a fortunate find, for our bear's oil was exhausted and we were reduced to roots without salt. At noon we halted to graze the horses. After we had started on again, we found that we had left one of our pack horses and one of Capt. Lewis' riding horses behind. We sent Joseph Fields and John Colter back in search of them. We continued on to Lolo springs where we arrived in the early evening. We then sent out several hunters. All, except

Drouillard and Reuben Fields, returned unsuccessful. Late in the evening Colter and Joseph Fields arrived with the lost horses – and brought a deer. At these springs the Indians have prepared a bath by stopping the warm stream with stones and gravel. The men took a warm and refreshing bath.

JUNE 30. Drouillard and Joseph Fields went ahead to hunt. As we were preparing to set out, a deer came to the lick at the springs and Reuben Fields killed it. We went on down Lolo Creek and nooned at the same spot we had on September 12th last year. While here, Shields killed a deer. In descending the steep side of a hill, Capt. Lewis' horse slipped and the captain fell off backwards. Both horse and man slid forty feet down the hill, but fortunately both were unhurt. After dinner, Shields walked down and killed another deer, and we picked up three others which Drouillard had killed – making six taken today. A little before sunset we arrived at our old encampment of Traveler's Rest on the south side of Lolo Creek a little above its entrance with Clark's [Bitterroot] River. We intend to remain here two days to rest our horses and ourselves, and make the final arrangements for dividing our party. Our horses have stood the hard journey surprisingly well and need only a few days rest to restore them perfectly.

JULY 1, 1806. We sent out all the hunters except John Shields who is at work repairing the guns. Capt. Lewis and Capt. Clark now formed the following plan of future operation:

Capt. Lewis, with George Drouillard, Silas Goodrich, Joseph Fields, Reuben Fields, Patrick Gass, John Thompson, Hugh McNeal, Robert Frazier and William Werner are to go by the most direct route to the Great Falls of the Missouri, and there leave Thompson, McNeal and Goodrich to prepare wagons to transport the canoes and cached baggage over the portage around the falls. This party is to take seventeen horses with them. After leaving the three men on the Missouri, Capt. Lewis, with Drouillard, Joseph and Reuben Fields, are to ascend Maria's River to explore the country to ascertain if any branch of that river lies as far north as latitude 50°. They are then to return and rejoin the canoe party at the mouth of Maria's River.

The balance of the men are to proceed with Capt. Clark to the fork of the Beaverhead River to recover our cache of articles and canoes left there. From hence, Sgt. Ordway with John Colter, John Collins, Peter Cruzatte, Baptiste La Page, Joseph Whitehouse, Peter Weiser, Thomas P. Howard, Alexander Willard and John Potts are to descend the Beaverhead, Jefferson, and Missouri with the canoes.

Capt. Clark with Sgt. Nathaniel Pryor, William Bratton, Hugh Hall,

George Gibson, Francois Labiche, John Shields, George Shannon, Richard Windsor, York, Toussaint Charbonneau, Sacagawea and Baptiste Charbonneau will proceed overland to the upper Yellowstone River to its nearest approach to the Three Forks of the Missouri. On the Yellowstone, he will build a canoe and descend the Yellowstone to its junction with the Missouri, leaving Sgt. Pryor, Windsor and Shannon with the horses to go by land with them to the Mandan Nation.

These arrangements being made, the party was informed, and they prepared themselves accordingly. Our hunters meanwhile had killed thirteen deer in fine order. We had the venison sliced and exposed on poles to the sun to dry. As Windsor had burst his gun near its muzzle a few days since, Shields had cut the end off. Now in good order, this was exchanged with the Indian guide for the one he had been given. The Indian was much pleased with the exchange for the gun shoots very well. The guides express the wish to return to their nation, but have agreed to accompany Capt. Lewis to the Falls of the Missouri.

JULY 2. The hunters with Collins brought in two deer. John Shields completed the repair of the guns by evening. Goodrich and McNeal both are unwell with the pox they had contacted from the Chinook women. They will go to the falls where they can rest and use mercury freely. Our best hunters will be divided among the various parties so as to provide provisions for them. We gave the second gun and some powder and balls to our guides agreeable to our promise. We have dried the greater part of the venison, as we do not expect to find much game on our march. Every man has filled his powder horn, and they have a sufficiency of ammunition for any event. The Indians and our men amused themselves by running foot and horse races.

25

The Party Takes Different Routes

JULY 3.   The hunters brought in three deer, and we gave the Indians half of it. Capt. Lewis took leave of his worthy friend and companion, Capt. Clark, and the men who are to go with the latter. Capt. Lewis could not avoid feeling concern, though he hopes the separation is only momentary, so with Sgt. Gass, Drouillard, Joseph Fields, Reuben Fields, Frazier, Thompson, Werner, Goodrich, McNeal and five Indians, his party started to the north. They crossed Clark's [Bitterroot] River on rafts two miles below the confluence with its east fork [Hellgate] and proceeded up the latter river until they camped on a creek [Grant's Creek].

Capt. Clark and his party of twenty-three people and fifty horses set out at 8 a.m. and proceeded south on the west side of Clark's [Bitterroot] River some thirty-six miles, and encamped at a large creek where tolerable food was found for the horses. Labiche killed a deer. John Potts is unwell from riding a hard trotting horse. Capt. Clark gave him a pill of opium which relieved him.

JULY 4.   Capt. Lewis sent out Drouillard and the Fields brothers to hunt, but they found nothing. He smoked a pipe with the Indians who now leave us, they having pointed out the way. We set out, and after five miles we entered the mountains through a narrow pass and came to the [Blackfoot] river where we camped at evening.

Capt. Clark dispatched three hunters to set out early to kill some meat. By 7 a.m. we had collected our horses and set out. We proceeded up the valley. The hunters joined us with two deer. At noon we dined on a fat saddle of venison and roots in celebration of this July 4th. In crossing several creeks our goods got wet. We came to the road we had passed down last fall, and camped on the west fork [Nez Perce] of the river. Two men went out to hunt, while three went to search for a ford to cross the river. The hunters killed four deer today.

JULY 5.   Capt. Lewis and party set out at 6 a.m. and followed up the [Blackfoot] river. We crossed a river which we named for Werner [Clearwater], one of our men. We camped in a cove after making thirty-one miles.

Capt. Clark sent Labiche after a buck he had killed last evening, and went with three men to look at the ford. Shannon took a good course across the river, and the rest followed him, but some of Capt. Clark's goods got wet. Shannon and Cruzatte each killed a deer, and John Shields got a female bighorn sheep. Shannon left his tomahawk at the place he had killed his deer, and was sent back to look for it and then join us on the east side of the mountains. Shields went ahead to hunt. After drying our goods, we left at 4:30 p.m., and crossed the mountains into a valley where we overtook Shields. He had found a good road which will shorten the distance. Shannon came in, having found his tomahawk; hunters brought in two deer.

JULY 6.   Capt. Lewis and party set out a little after sunrise and passed through an extensive plain. Our hunters overtook us with a deer. We camped on a creek where there is much beaver sign.

Capt. Clark's horses were scattered, and the party could not get off until 9 a.m. We ascended the mountain and crossed the divide at a pass [Gibbon's] which is used by the Indians and buffalo. Shields killed a hare. Sacagawea informed us she had been in this country before, and that we were on the branch of the [Wisdom] river, and that when we reached the plains we would see a gap in the mountains in the direction of the cached goods and canoes. As we were descending, a violent storm came up, and we formed a solid column to protect us as best we could. After the storm passed, we went on to a small creek where there was timber. We camped and made a large fire to dry ourselves.

JULY 7.   Capt. Lewis set out at 7 a.m. Later, the hunters killed three deer and a fawn. Reuben Fields wounded a moose near our camp which worried Scannon very much. We passed the dividing ridge of a pass [Lewis & Clark's Pass]. We then followed down a creek where we camped for the night. Drouillard caught two beaver and shot a third which bit his knee very badly.

Capt. Clark sent his men in every direction to search for the scattered horses. By 6 a.m. they were all brought in but nine. Six men were sent to look for them. They went a great distance but returned by 10 a.m., saying they could not be found. They thought that the Indians may have stolen them during the night, as the very best horses were missing. Sgt. Ordway, Shannon, Gibson, Collins and Labiche were left to search towards the mountains. At 10:30 a.m. the party left, and proceeded through a rich, open valley, and arrived at a boiling spring. Sgt. Pryor and John Shields each put a piece of meat in the boiling springs to cook. After letting the horses graze for an hour, we went on and later camped at some beautiful springs which fall into Willard's [Grasshopper] Creek. We set a sentinel and hobbled the horses. Meanwhile, Ordway and his party found the nine horses traveling on an Indian road. They turned them back and camped at our last night's camp after carefully hobbling the horses.

JULY 8.   Capt. Lewis set out at 6 a.m. and later crossed Dearborn's River

– then struck north for the upper waters of the Medicine [Sun] River in order to secure buffalo skins for the expedition, and meat for the three men who are to be left at the caches near the Falls of the Missouri. Reuben Fields killed a buck and an antelope, and Joseph Fields saw two buffalo at some distance. We are rejoiced at finding ourselves on the plains of the Missouri which abound in game. We camped near a large island where Capt. Lewis killed a large white wolf.

Capt. Clark's party set out at 8 a.m., going down Willard's creek, and then headed for Shoshoni Cove near the two forks of the Beaverhead River. When we reached there in the evening, the tobacco chewers with the party could hardly take time to unpack their horses before they were off to the cache. Upon opening them, we found every article safe. We gave the tobacco users about two feet of a roll, saving some to send down to the men with Capt. Lewis' party. The canoes were all safe except the largest one which had a large hole in one side and was split in the bow. Shields killed an antelope.

Sgt. Ordway and his party set out early with the recovered horses and struck the trail of Capt. Clark's men. They paused at the hot springs and found already cooked the piece of venison that Pryor and Shields had placed there. Having ridden for some forty miles, they camped after hobbling the horses and dined on an antelope's head Capt. Clark's party had dropped.

July 9.   Capt. Lewis set out early, but it began to rain. So we halted at some old Indian lodges until the rain had passed – and then set out, wet to the skin. Joseph Fields killed a very fine, fat buffalo on which we dined, carrying the best of the meat on our horses for the later use.

Capt. Clark's party was occupied in raising and repairing the canoes. We found the tin and nails had been taken off by the Indians. At 10 a.m. Sgt. Ordway and his men arrived with the lost horses. We divided the loads, some of which will be sent in the canoes, and some will be taken by the main party to the Yellowstone. Sacagawea brought a plant, the roots of which the natives eat. Shields and Collins each killed a deer this morning. The day is cold and windy, so the canoes soon dried out.

July 10.   Capt. Lewis continued on down the south-west bank of the Medicine River. In the evening we fell in with a few elk of which Capt. Lewis and Reuben Fields killed three. Sgt. Gass went with the pack horses to encamp at the first timber. Frazier stayed to skin the elk. Drouillard killed a large brown bear. It was dark by the time we butchered the elk and bear, but we loaded the horses with the best of the meat and continued until we joined Sgt. Gass at 9 p.m. Sgt. Gass and Thompson had been chased by a grizzly bear but their horses enabled them to keep out of its reach.

Capt. Clark had all the canoes loaded and put into the water. The horses were packed with what few articles we are to take overland. After breakfast we all set out at the same time. Sgt. Ordway, John Colter, Peter Cruzatte, Baptiste La Page, Joseph Whitehouse, Peter Weiser, Thomas P. Howard, Alexander Willard and John Potts took the canoes down the Beaverhead River.

Capt. Clark, Sgt. Nathaniel Pryor, William Bratton, Hugh Hall, George Gibson, Francois Labiche, John Shields, George Shannon, Richard Windsor, York, Toussaint Charbonneau, Sacagawea and Pomp followed downstream on the horses. At noon both parties came together. Sgt. Ordway felt the canoes could now come as fast as the horses, for the river is now wider and deeper. Therefore, Capt. Clark determined to put all the baggage in the canoes, and go himself in a canoe to the Three Forks. Sgt. Pryor and six of the men were to bring down the horses, and if possible, to camp with us every night. After dinner we all set out and arrived at the same camp where we had been on August 11th, last year. Collins killed a goose.

July 11.   Capt. Lewis sent his hunters down the Medicine River to hunt elk, and then proceeded with the balance of the party to the White Bear Islands on the Missouri. The buffalo are mating and are keeping up a continual roar. Some of our horses were not acquainted with the buffalo, and are much alarmed with them. We joined the hunters, and they are to kill a supply of buffalo for the men who are to be left at this place. The hunters killed eleven, and we brought in a large quantity of meat. We needed the hides to build some bull-boats, and for gear and shelter. We intend to rest our horses before setting out for the Maria's River journey.

Capt. Clark sent four of his best hunters [he had: Gibson, Labiche, Shields, Shannon, Colter and Collins] in two canoes to proceed a few miles ahead of us to hunt. At 8 a.m. we overtook one canoe with a deer which Collins had killed. At noon we passed Sgt. Pryor's horse party near a point of rock called the Beaver's Head. The wind came up, which made our progress slow. At 7 p.m. we camped at the entrance of the Wisdom River. Here we found a bayonet and a canoe we had left here last year. We were joined by Gibson and Colter who had been sent ahead to hunt.

July 12.   Capt. Lewis' party completed the bull-boats by 10 a.m. At this time two of the men who had been sent for the horses returned with only seven of them. The remaining ten of the best horses were not to be found. Two men were sent on horseback to search for them. At noon, Werner returned with three. Sgt. Gass did not return until 3 p.m., not having found any. Joseph Fields and Drouillard were now sent to search for them and Fields returned unsuccessful. Drouillard stayed out all night. Meanwhile we transported our baggage to the opposite side of the Missouri in our bull-boats which we found answered better than we had expected. We swam our horses over, and camped at sunset.

Capt. Clark's party made oars, drew the nails out of the sides of the old canoe, and then set out at 7 a.m. Sgt. Pryor and his horse party had passed on down. The wind arose and it was difficult to keep the canoes midstream. A sudden puff blew Capt. Clark's canoe under an overhanging limb, and Howard was caught and injured. At 3 p.m. Willard and Collins overtook us with two deer they had killed. Collins caught two beaver this evening.

JULY 13.   Capt. Lewis set Sgt. Gass, Frazier, Goodrich, McNeal, Thompson and Werner at work to complete the gear for the horses. We opened the cache and found the bearskins entirely destroyed by water as well as Capt. Lewis' collection of plant specimens. The papers and charts of the Missouri fortunately ecaped damage. Most of the medicines were lost beyond recovery. We are concerned about Drouillard who has not yet returned.

Capt. Clark and party proceeded to the entrance of the Madison River where we found Sgt. Pryor and party with the horses. His men had killed a deer and a grizzly bear. We drove the horses over to the entrance of the Gallatin River to feed. All the baggage of the land party was taken out of the canoes and then Sgt. Ordway with Colter, Collins, Cruzatte, Frazier, Goodrich, La Page, Whitehouse, Weiser, Willard and Potts set out to join Capt. Lewis and his party at our former White Bear Island camp. Capt. Clark gave them a letter to deliver to Capt. Lewis. Capt. Clark's party now consisted of Sgt. Pryor, Shields, Shannon, Bratton, Labiche, Windsor, Hall, Gibson, Charbonneau, Sacagawea, Pomp and York with forty-nine horses and a colt. At 5 p.m. we set out from the Three Forks of the Missouri, proceeded easterly and camped on the banks of the Gallatin. Gibson killed an otter, and Willard killed two deer this morning, which was put into the canoes except enough for our supper. Sacagawea has been of great service as a pilot. She recommends taking a gap in the mountains [Bozeman Pass] which we shall cross to reach the upper waters of the Yellowstone River.

JULY 14.   Capt. Lewis had our old wagon wheels dug up for the portage, and we found them in good order. The frame of the iron boat had not suffered materially. We sliced the meat thin and exposed it to the sun to dry, and the roots were pounded into meal for Capt. Lewis' proposed journey. The old cache was too damp to deposit Capt. Lewis' trunks, so he sent them over to the large island and had them put on a high scaffold and covered them with skins so that the canoe party coming down could find them. Drouillard has not returned.

Capt. Clark sent Shields ahead to hunt. At an early hour we set out with the overland party. Sacagawea guided us towards [Bridger Pass] a low plain where we nooned. We overtook Shields who had killed a large, fat buck. After dinner we struck an old buffalo road and followed it to the commencement of the [Bozeman] pass where we encamped. Deer are abundant here – Shannon, Shields and Pryor each got one.

Sgt. Ordway and his party proceeded down the Missouri. Colter killed two beaver. The wind became so high that we could not proceed, so Collins and Colter went hunting. Later the wind lulled, so we moved down the river and camped. Willard killed a deer. Collins did not join us this evening.

JULY 15. Capt. Lewis sent McNeal to the lower end of the portage to learn the condition of the cache and the white pirogue we had left there. The other men are drying meat, dressing skins and preparing for the reception of the canoe party. At 1 p.m. Drouillard – much to our relief – returned without the horses. He is satisfied they were stolen by a party of Indians. We are so happy for his safe return that we have given little thought to the lost seven horses. We have ten horses remaining. We shall leave four with the portage party, and Capt. Lewis will take six on his tour. Therefore, Capt. Lewis will leave three of the men he had intended to take with him: Sgt. Gass, Frazier and Werner, and have them stay with the canoe party. Only Drouillard, and the Fields brothers will go with him. McNeal had a scrape with a grizzly bear. He broke his musket over the head of the bear and then climbed a willow tree. The bear waited until evening before he left him, and then McNeal ventured down, recovered his horse, and returned to camp. These bears are so ferocious that it seems the hand of Providence has been wonderfully in our favor, or some of us would have long since fallen to their ferocity. Scannon, as we are, is tormented by the mosquitoes.

Capt. Clark's party set out over the gap, then following a buffalo road, reached the Yellowstone River at 2 p.m. After a delay to give the horses time to feed, and allowing ourselves time to cook and eat dinner, we proceeded down the Yellowstone on a buffalo road. At Shield's River, which we named after our John Shields, we crossed, and then went on to a large bottom where we camped. The horses' feet are sore, but they are otherwise sound and in good spirits. We can find no timber sufficiently large for a canoe which will carry more than three men. Such a small one would not serve our purpose.

Sgt. Ordway's canoe party proceeded very well and overtook Collins who had killed three deer. At 9 a.m. we halted for breakfast and Collins killed a buck while Cruzatte got an antelope. John Colter killed a panther and a deer. In the evening we camped near the Gates of the Mountains.

JULY 16. Capt. Lewis got his horses collected by 10 a.m. and set out.

Drouillard and Reuben Fields took the horses to the lower side of the Medicine [Sun] River while Capt. Lewis and Joseph Fields went with the baggage down the Missouri to the mouth of the Medicine in a canoe made of buffalo skins. Having all arrived, we saddled the horses and rode down to the forty-seven foot falls, where Capt. Lewis made a sketch while dinner was being prepared. Afterwards, we rode to the Great Falls where we arrived at sunset.

Capt. Clark on the Yellowstone, sent Labiche to hunt. Our horses having wandered, this detained us much later than common. We set out at 9 a.m. Soon afterwards, we saw a buffalo and killed it. We saved the flesh and made pads of the skin to put on our horses' sore feet. We went on, and after dinner Labiche joined us. The current of the Yellowstone is too rapid for skin-boats, and we cannot find trees large enough to build a large canoe. We therefore continued by horseback down the river.

Sgt. Ordway and his canoe party started early. Collins got a large beaver. We gathered pitch from pine trees to use on the canoes. Collins killed two mountain sheep. We continued, and camped below Ordway's River.

Sgt. Gass with Frazier and Werner now joined Goodrich, Thompson and McNeal. All continued to repair the wagons so as to have them ready to portage the canoes down beyond the falls when Ordway's canoe party arrives. Capt. Lewis had left orders with us to wait for him at the mouth of Maria's River until September 1st. He wrote that if his life was preserved he expected to meet us on August 5th. Then we would all drop down to the mouth of the Yellowstone River to await Capt. Clark's overland party.

JULY 17.   Capt. Lewis, after making a drawing of the falls, set out for the upper Maria's River across the treeless plains. At 5 p.m. they arrived at the [Teton] river where he, Drouillard and the Fields brothers camped. Here they found a wounded buffalo which indicated that Indians were about. The three men reconnoitered for Indian sign, but could make no discovery of them. They brought in two beaver and a deer.

Capt. Clark and his party continued by horseback down the Yellowstone, looking enroute for large trees to build a canoe. Shannon killed a deer.

Sgt. Ordway went on with the canoe party. Collins and Colter skinned the two mountain sheep and saved the hides and bones so they could be taken back to the States. A high wind detained us which gave Cruzatte the opportunity to kill two big-horn sheep – and Colter a deer. Towards evening the wind abated, so we passed down over the rapids with safety, and then encamped.

Sgt. Gass and his party waited at the upper end of the portage road.

JULY 18.   Capt. Lewis continued his route north over open plains filled with buffalo and game. At 6 p.m. they reached the Maria's River above the highest point that had been explored in June of last year. Capt. Lewis directed Drouillard, who was with him on the previous exploration, and Joseph Fields to drop down to the point of the former highest ascent, to see if any important streams flow into Maria's River between there and here. Capt. Lewis and Reuben Fields meanwhile kept a strict lookout over the horses and camp.

At Capt. Clark's camp on the Yellowstone, Charbonneau was thrown from his horse and was bruised. Enroute, we found quantities of ripe currants of excellent flavor. We saw a smoke signal which we think was raised by the [Crow] Indians. We dined on a buck which Shields had killed. After allowing the horses to feed, we set out at 4 p.m., and afterwards camped on an island. Shields killed a buffalo. Gibson, in attempting to mount his horse, fell and ran a snag into his thigh. Capt. Clark dressed Gibson's very bad wound.

Sgt. Ordway's canoe party proceeded on with the gentle current. About noon, Collins killed three deer. We camped a little below a [Smith's] river.

Sgt. Gass from the upper portage, went with three men to the lower end to examine the pirogue and cache left there. Everything was safe, and they took some tobacco from the cache, then covered it over again and returned to the upper portage camp.

JULY 19.   Capt. Lewis sent Drouillard and Joseph Fields down the Maria's River and they went as far as the party had ascended the previous year, and then returned at noon. They killed eight deer and two antelope enroute. After dinner, the party went twenty miles up the river and camped.

Capt. Clark rose early and dressed Gibson's wound. We concluded not to take Gibson in a litter, for he found he was as comfortable on a gentle horse as he was lying down. John Shields was directed to follow the river and search for a large tree, and also to hunt for wild ginger to make a poultice for Gibson's wound. He joined us at dinner with neither, but brought two fat bucks. After dinner we went on, but Gibson's thigh became so painful he could no longer sit on a horse after two and one-half hours riding. Sgt. Pryor with another man waited with Gibson under the shade of a tree until a campsite could be found. Capt. Clark and Shields searched for the best site where there were the largest trees, and Pryor brought Gibson to the camp selected. Charbonneau reported he had seen Indians on the highlands.

Sgt. Ordway's canoe party continued on while his hunters killed four buffalo and a deer. They halted to take the meat aboard, then went on. At 3 p.m. they arrived at the White Bear Island camp where they found Sgt. Gass and his five men. The whole party hauled the boats out of the water to dry in preparation for their portage.

JULY 20.   Capt. Lewis continued up the Maria's River, noting the side creeks and the soil. They traveled up some twenty-eight miles and camped on a bottom.

Capt. Clark sent Pryor and Shields – both good judges of timber – to go down the river to see if any larger trees could be found – and to return by noon. Labiche, Charbonneau and Hugh Hall were sent to bring the skin and flesh of the elk Labiche had killed the evening before. Pryor and Shields returned and informed us that there were no better trees below than those here. Capt. Clark then decided to have two canoes made. We have three axes, so the men set about to fell trees. Sgt. Pryor dressed some skins to make himself some clothes. Gibson's wound looks better. We shall let the horses rest a few days, after which Sgt. Pryor, Shannon and Windsor will take them overland to the Mandan nation. The men are dressing skins to make clothes, for they are nearly naked. Shields killed a deer, Shannon a buffalo, and York an elk. We dried most of the buffalo meat.

Sgt. Ordway and his men, now combined with Sgt. Gass' party, put the tongues in the wagons. Some of the men are dressing skins. Towards evening, we harnessed the horses to the wagons and found that they would drag them along. We are tormented with mosquitoes which abound here.

JULY 21.   Capt. Lewis set out early and proceeded up the Maria's River. The horses' feet are sore and travel is therefore slow. This afternoon they traveled up the northern [Cut Bank] branch, and determined to pursue it to its most northern point. At evening they camped under a cliff.

Capt. Clark's party discovered that twenty-four, or half of the horses were missing. Shannon, Bratton and Charbonneau were sent to hunt them. Though they searched both up and down the river, they returned unsuccessful. The men are at work on the canoes and one is nearly finished. Gibson's wound is beginning to heal. We are apprehensive that Indians have stolen the horses.

The Ordway-Gass party also had trouble with their horses – they lost all of theirs today. We got two canoes started on the portage along with considerable baggage. We use buffalo dung as a smudge to try to ward off the troublesome mosquitoes and flies. We lay with the canoes all night.

JULY 22.   Capt. Lewis set out early up the Cut Bank fork and continued for twenty-four miles. They nooned to let the horses rest and graze. They then went 12 miles further where a clump of cottonwood trees were found and camped. Capt. Lewis made celestial observations to determine this northern spot. The base of the Rocky Mountains can be seen about ten miles to the south-west. Capt. Lewis therefore determined it was unnecessary to proceed further north. They wounded a buffalo this evening but the horses were too worn to pursue it.

Capt. Clark sent Sgt. Pryor and Charbonneau in search of the horses and they returned at 3 p.m., having seen neither horses nor tracks of them. Pryor, Shannon, Charbonneau and Bratton then circled the camp at some distance around in search of tracks. As the plains are hard and dry, no tracks could be found. Labiche, an excellent tracker, is to search tomorrow to find what route the horses had taken.

Sgt. Ordway sent out a search party of eight men to look for his four missing horses. Two were found down near the Great Falls. We hitched these up to two canoes and went about five miles when a axle-tree broke. We made another, and started out with the two other canoes, and then made camp. Sgt. Gass and five men came up late from hunting the two missing horses. They had three buffalo and an antelope.

JULY 23.   Capt. Lewis dispatched Drouillard and Joseph Fields to hunt and observe the bearings of the river. They returned and reported that there was no game in this area. They also reported that they had seen an Indian camp recently abandoned, and suspect there are Indians somewhere on the main branch of the Maria's which they will avoid on their return route.

Capt. Clark found that during the night the wolves had come into camp and had devoured most of the dried meat which was on a scaffold. Labiche, Sgt. Pryor and Windsor went out early to track. Sgt. Pryor found a moccasin and a small piece of robe which had the appearance of having been worn only a few hours before. We are satisfied that Indians stole the horses and are lurking about to take the rest. Labiche informed us that he saw the tracks of the horses leading down the river and judged that they were going very fast. The men finished the canoes, and are now making oars and poles. Shields and Labiche went after buffalo. Capt. Clark gave instructions to Sgt. Pryor, along with a letter to Mr. Heney, the North West trader who visits the Mandans. He directed that Pryor, Shannon and Windsor take the remaining horses to the Mandans. Shields and Labiche killed three buffalo, and we saved as much of the meat as we could carry. The two canoes were lashed together, and everything is fixed for our departure tomorrow. Gibson is now recovered.

The Ordway-Gass party harnessed the horses and set out on the portage road with two canoes – one large, and one a small one. Peter Weiser cut his hand with a knife and had to ride in one of the canoes. Collins went ahead to Willow Creek to get some game for us. We arrived at the creek at sunset with the two canoes and considerable baggage and then camped. We got three buffalo.

26

Exploration and Rejoining

JULY 24. Capt. Lewis tried to make observations, but it was so clouded and rainy all day that he decided to remain another day. The hunters have no success in this locality. We still have a few roots left, which with some pigeons, served as food today.

Capt. Clark and party set out in the two canoes. They are 28 feet long; 16 to 18 inches deep, and 16 to 24 inches wide. We proceeded well and went to a large island to wait for Sgt. Pryor and his horse party to put them across to the east side of the river. At a small creek [Cannon] we met Pryor, Shannon and Windsor. Sgt. Pryor informed us that when the loose horses saw buffalo, they would pursue the buffalo, and that it was impossible for two men to handle the herd. Hugh Hall, who cannot swim, expressed a willingness to go with Sgt. Pryor and his men by land. As Hall was without clothes, Capt. Clark gave him one of his two remaining shirts, a pair of leggings and three pairs of moccasins, which equipped him completely. The rest of the party proceeded in the canoes down the rapid stream until we came to some islands. Here Capt. Clark killed a fat buck, Shields killed a deer, and York killed a buffalo bull. We have an abundance of the best of meat.

Sgt. Ordway and party returned to the head of the portage and brought the two remaining canoes down to Willow Creek. The other men meanwhile had taken one canoe to the foot of the portage. Sgt. Gass was unwell and stayed at Willow Creek with Peter Weiser.

JULY 25. Capt. Lewis was detained by continual cloudy weather. He sent Drouillard and Joseph Fields to hunt near the Maria's River, while he and Reuben Fields attempted to make celestial observations. Reuben killed nine pigeons. Late in the evening Drouillard and Joseph Fields returned with a buck. We are determined to start back tomorrow.

Capt. Clark and his party set out in the canoes and proceeded well for three hours. We saw a large herd of buffalo and Shields killed two fat deer. We went on until 4 p.m. when we arrived at a remarkable rock [Pompey's Pillar]. Capt. Clark ascended the rock which is two hundred feet high. He inscribed his name and date on the rock. Later, the party continued down the Yellowstone and killed two big-horned sheep which were recovered by some of the men. We camped below the entrance of Shannon's [Bull Mountain] Creek.

Sgt. Ordway's party proceeded on to Portage Creek where camp was made. Here two men were left – one to hunt, and one to cook – while the others returned to Willow Creek to bring down the canoes aided by the horses. Collins had killed a buffalo and a badger. Sgt. Gass was better and helped with the portage. By night time we had four canoes safe at Portage Creek.

JULY 26.   Capt. Lewis said adieu to "Camp Disappointment" as he called it, for the continued rains had made observations nearly impossible. At 9 a.m. they set out and took a southerly route over the open plains. After nooning, Capt. Lewis and the Fields brothers kept to the hills while Drouillard followed the valley of a creek they were on. Capt. Lewis discovered an assemblege of thirty horses, and with his spy-glass, saw several Indians on an eminence who appeared to be watching Drouillard. This was an unpleasant sight, and Capt. Lewis resolved to make the best of a bad situation, and approach the Indians in a friendly manner. He calculated their number to be about thirty men. To run would convince them we were enemies. Besides, Drouillard was separated from us, and not being apprised of the Indians, probably would fall as a sacrifice to them if we ran. Joseph Fields displayed the flag, and we advanced towards them, having agreed that we expected trouble and that these Indians might attempt to rob us. We met, and the Indians asked to smoke with us, but we told them that our man below, Drouillard, had the pipe. One of the Indians, with Reuben Fields, went to bring in Drouillard. It now appeared that there were only eight of them, and as it was getting late, Capt. Lewis proposed that we all go to the creek and camp, which we did, joining Reuben Fields and Drouillard. During the evening we had much conversation, and we explained why we were here. Capt. Lewis told them that if they would go with us to the Missouri, he would give them ten horses and some tobacco. As we settled down to sleep, Capt. Lewis took the first watch and the Indians went to sleep. At 11:30 p.m. he awakened Reuben Fields to take the watch and told him that if any Indians left the camp to awaken us all, for he apprehended that they would attempt to steal our horses. This being done, Capt. Lewis fell into a profound sleep and did not wake until a noise awoke him at daylight.

Capt. Clark and party proceeded down the Yellowstone in the canoes and arrived at the mouth of the Big Horn River. Capt. Clark and Labiche walked up this river some seven miles to explore and take measurements, after which they returned to camp. Shields meanwhile had killed two buffalo and three elk.

Sgt. Ordway and the canoe party sent Colter and Potts to take the

canoes down the rapids to where the pirogue and cache were located. Eight
of the men returned to Willow Creek and started to bring down the large
canoe over the portage. Cruzatte killed a buffalo. All the canoes were
brought down to the end of the portage and we went into camp. We opened
the cache and loaded its contents into the white pirogue. Everything was
safe and in good condition.

Sgt. Pryor with Windsor, Hall and Shannon, arrived at a creek where
there was good grass to graze the horses. Here they remained all night.
While asleep, Pryor was bitten by a wolf, which also made an attempt to
seize Windsor. Shannon was awakened and shot the wolf.

JULY 27. At Capt. Lewis' camp the Indians arose and crowded around
the fire. Joseph Fields, who was on post, had laid his gun down near where
Reuben Fields was sleeping. One of the Indians slipped behind and took the
guns of the Fields brothers unperceived, while two others advanced and
seized the guns of Capt. Lewis and Drouillard. Joseph Fields seeing this,
and looking for his gun, saw an Indian running away with both his and
Reuben's guns. Reuben jumped up and both ran after the Indian and overtook him. As they wrested for the guns, Reuben Fields stabbed the Indian
through the heart. The Indian ran a few steps and then dropped dead.
Drouillard recovered his gun and the noise awakened Capt. Lewis, who
finding his gun gone, drew his pistol on the Indian running away with it.
The Fields brothers came up and were taking aim to fire to shoot the running Indian. Capt. Lewis ordered them not to fire. By now, the other Indians were attempting to drive off the horses. Our three men followed so
closely that the Indians left twelve of their own horses, but continued to
drive off one of our own. Capt. Lewis called out that he would shoot, and
as he raised his gun, one of the Indians jumped behind a rock and spoke to
another. Capt. Lewis shot him in the belly. He fell, but raised himself
enough to fire at Capt. Lewis. Not having his shot-pouch, Lewis could not
reload, so he retired towards camp. Here he was met by Drouillard – leaving the Fields brothers to pursue the Indians. They returned with four of
their horses – losing only one of our own. As there was no time to be lost, we
mounted and took a south-east direction. We pushed our horses as hard as
they would go. Fortunately the Indian horses were fresh and very good.
After going some sixty-five miles, we halted for an hour and a half to refresh the horses. We then went seventeen miles more, killed a buffalo and
stopped for two hours. We then rode on until 2 a.m., and at last laid ourselves down to rest, much fatigued.

Capt. Clark set out early and the party proceeded very well. We passed
a creek which we named for Labiche [Sarpy Creek]. Our men killed four

buffalo and we had breakfast. When we passed the Big Horn River we took our last view of the Rocky Mountains in whose tremendous chains we have been since the 1st of May. At sunset we camped, and Capt. Clark shot an elk. Shields killed a deer and an antelope which our party needs to make clothes.

Sgt. Ordway's party hauled out the white pirogue and repaired it. Sgt. Gass and Willard set out with the horses, loaded with meat, for the mouth of Maria's River. At noon, Sgt. Ordway, with Goodrich, McNeal, Frazier, Thompson, Werner, Colter, Collins, Cruzatte, La Page, Whitehouse, Weiser and Potts set out with the white pirogue and five canoes. We went on down the rapid water quickly and made a camp on the south side. Frazier killed a buffalo. Sgt. Gass and Willard camped on the [Teton] river.

Up on the Yellowstone, Sgt. Pryor discovered that all of his horses had been stolen during the night by the Indians. He, Windsor, Shannon and Hall walked some ten miles without finding them, and then returned to camp. They packed the baggage on their backs and headed for the Yellowstone River which they reached at Pompey's Pillar, the big rock which Capt. Clark had named. Here Shannon killed a buffalo and the men proceeded to build a bull-boat from the hide. They decided to make two bull-boats in the event an accident should happen and all would be lost if they were in only one.

JULY 28.   Capt. Lewis, Drouillard and the Fields brothers were sore from the long and hard ride yesterday, but they soon resumed riding, for they had reason to believe that the Indians were trying to overtake them. They decided that if they were attacked they would tie the horses together, and they would stand and defend themselves or else sell their lives as dearly as they could. As they neared the Missouri, they heard the reports of rifles, and upon arriving on its banks, they had the unspeakable joy of seeing the canoes with Sgt. Ordway's party coming down the river. The parties joined, and loaded the baggage that Capt. Lewis had. They threw the saddles in the Missouri and gave the horses a final discharge by setting them free. All embarked in the canoes and proceeded down the river to the principal cache which we proceeded to open. We found it had caved in and much of the contents were injured. The gun-powder, corn flour, pork and salt had sustained little loss, but the parched meal was nearly spoiled. Having no time to air the furs and baggage belonging to the men, we loaded them, and slipped down to the point to take on the articles that had been buried in several small caches there. These we found in good order, and recovered everything including the blacksmith's tools, except three traps belonging to Drouillard. Here Sgt. Gass and Willard joined us with the horses at 1 p.m. We abandoned the horses and all now went by canoes over to the island at the entrance of Maria's River. Here we launched the large red pirogue, but she was so much decayed, and we had no means to fix her. So we took out the nails and other ironwork, and left our old craft here on the upper Missouri. We now re-embarked in the small white pirogue and the five canoes and descended the Missouri about fifteen miles where we camped, surrounded by game. Howard had killed two deer earlier, so Capt. Lewis, Drouillard and the Fields brothers dined well after being on short rations for so long.

Capt. Clark and party set out at daylight and glided down the now calm Yellowstone. We passed many creeks and some cliffs that contained strata of coal. We camped on the upper end of a small island. Shields killed two deer and Labiche killed an antelope for the hides. Beaver are not abundant at this place, but there are many signs of them.

JULY 29. The party on the Missouri had a bad night as it rained, and they had no shelter. It continued raining all day so we could not dry ourselves nor our baggage. Joseph and Reuben Fields, Collins and Colter took two small canoes to hunt. They are to get as many elk as possible for the hides to cover our canoes and furnish us with shelter. The rest of the party set out early, and as the current is strong, we proceeded rapidly down stream. On our way we killed nine big-horn sheep. We preserved the skeletons of two females and one male. The flesh is extremely tender and well flavored. The Missouri is now so muddy we can hardly drink it. Frazier got an elk.

Capt. Clark and party set out early but the rain was straight ahead so we made but little way. We camped on an island opposite the mouth of the Tongue River.

JULY 30. Capt. Lewis and party set out down the Missouri. The men were anxious to get on, and they rowed with the strong current, so we went at the rate of about seven miles an hour. We got some more big-horn sheep which we prepared to carry to the United States. At evening we arrived at an island about two miles above Goodrich's Island. It rained all day. Sgt. Ordway and Willard killed a grizzly bear.

Capt. Clark's party set out early and at twelve miles arrived at the commencement of some shoals. We had to let the canoes down by hand for fear of them striking the rocks and becoming split. We have come 694 miles, and this is the worst place on the entire route. At twenty miles we passed a less dangerous rapid, and as a violent storm approached, we took shelter in an old Indian lodge. After the storm passed, we proceeded to the [Powder] river and camped near by. Gibson is so recovered that he walked out this morning and killed an antelope.

Sgt. Pryor, Shannon, Hall and Windsor continued down the Yellowstone in their bull-boats.

JULY 31. Capt. Lewis' party proceeded in the rain. At 9 a.m. we fell in with a large herd of elk and our party killed fifteen of them. We took the skins. Having come some seventy miles, we camped at some old Indian lodges which, with the elk skins, gave us good shelter from the rains which continued since last night. Joseph Fields killed an ibex [mountain goat].

Capt. Clark and party were disturbed by the herds of buffalo which were about all night. One gang swam the river and we were afraid that they would cross over our canoes. However, we set out as usual, and passed through a mountainous country into a land of extensive plains. Having made sixty-six miles, we camped for the night.

AUGUST 1, 1806. Capt. Lewis and party set out in the rain. At 9 a.m. we saw a large bear swimming in the river, and as he landed, Capt. Lewis and Drouillard shot him. We took the bear on board the pirogue and continued on. At 11 a.m. we passed the entrance of the Musselshell River. At 1 p.m. we arrived at a bottom where there were several spacious lodges. As the rain continued, we stopped here to endeavor to dry the skins of the big-horn sheep before they spoil. We had fires built in the lodges and hung the skins to dry. Collins caught a beaver.

Capt. Clark's party proceeded in the rain in the open canoe with no covering. After a disagreeable day, at evening we camped on an island.

AUGUST 2. Capt. Lewis remained at the lodges all day to give the men and baggage an opportunity to dry, for today was a fine day. We put the powder, parched meal and every article which needed drying, exposed to the sun. The Fields brothers went hunting, and they got several deer. By evening the baggage was dry and we repacked it in readiness to set out early in the morning.

Capt. Clark and his canoe party of Shields, Gibson, Bratton, Labiche, Charbonneau, Sacagawea, Pomp and York set out. The river now is divided by many islands and sand bars, and is less rapid. We camped on "Joseph Field's Creek" which he had discovered last year [now Charbonneau's Creek].

AUGUST 3. Capt. Lewis and party set out at 6 a.m., as we are all anxious to reach the mouth of the Yellowstone River where we expect to join with Capt. Clark and party. At noon we passed the canoe of Colter and Collins who are on shore hunting. We hailed, but got no answer, so we proceeded on and shortly afterwards, overtook the Fields brothers who had gone out to hunt yesterday. They had killed twenty-five deer. We did not halt to

dine as usual, having decided that in the future the party would cook on
the preceding evening, sufficient to serve us for the next day. By this means
we will forward our journey at least twelve to fifteen more miles a day. We
camped this evening near our camp of the 12th of May 1805. Drouillard
killed a doe and the Fields brothers arrived after dark with two bucks.
Collins and Colter did not overtake us this evening.

Capt. Clark's party continued down the Yellowstone and came to a large
herd of big-horn sheep. We landed, and Labiche killed a ram which we
loaded and took as a specimen. Bratton skinned him and saved the head,
horns and feet. At 8 a.m. we arrived at the junction of the Missouri and
Yellowstone rivers and formed a camp at the same point where we had
camped on the 26th of August last year. We unloaded the canoes and exposed every article to dry.

AUGUST 4.   Capt. Lewis set out at 4 a.m. He permitted Willard and Ordway to hunt in place of the Fields brothers. At 3 p.m. we arrived at the
mouth of the Milk River where we halted for a few minutes, then camped
at evening a few miles below it. Colter and Collins have not yet overtaken
us. Sgt. Ordway and Willard did not join us until midnight. They got
caught on a sawyer in the dark, and Willard was thrown overboard. For
tunately he could swim.

Capt. Clark and party were so troubled by mosquitoes that we decided to
move to a more eligible place lower down the river – and where buffalo are
more plentiful. Capt. Clark left a note for Capt. Lewis informing him of
our change of plans, and the note was stuck on a pole and placed on the
point. At 5 p.m. we went on, and later encamped on a sand bar. Pomp is so
bitten by mosquitoes that his face is much puffed and swollen.

AUGUST 5.   Capt. Lewis decided to wait here for Colter and Collins. They
did not arrive, so we concluded they had passed us after dark on the 3rd, as
Sgt. Ordway would have done last night had not the sentinel halted him.
At noon we set out again and continued until late in the evening when we
camped. The Fields brothers killed two large bears this evening.

Capt. Clark's party found that the sand bar was not less free of mosquitoes than the point, so we moved on down to a more wind swept location
which blew away the mosquitoes. We killed some deer and bears and dried a
quantity of the meat. The Fields brothers had preceded us to hunt.

AUGUST 6.   Capt. Lewis' party were drenched by a storm last night. We
could hardly get the canoes loaded before they were filled with water. We
set out early and descended about ten miles below Porcupine River when
the wind became so violent that we had to lay by until 4 p.m. We then

descended the river about five miles below our encampment of May 1st, 1805, where we halted for the night. The Fields brothers had gone ahead this afternoon and we did not overtake them.

Capt. Clark's party was drenched by the same storm. As we were about to set out, Labiche shot a large female big-horn which we skinned, and then went on again. The wind blew hard and we had to go into camp. The men are busy dressing skins except one man who went with Capt. Clark to hunt on a bottom. They got seven deer. The game here is very tame.

AUGUST 7. Capt. Lewis and party set out early in the rain, hoping to reach the Yellowstone River, distant some sixty-five miles. The current forwarded us and the men applied the oars, so we went at a good rate. We saw a number of buffalo, elk and bear, but did not detain to take any of them. We overtook the Fields brothers who had killed two large silver-grey bears. At 4 p.m. we arrived at the mouth of the Yellowstone and found the remnants of the note left by Capt. Clark – informing us of his reasons for dropping further down the Missouri. We found traced in the sand: "W.C., A FEW MILES FURTHER DOWN THE RIVER ON THE RIGHT HAND SIDE." Capt. Lewis now left a note for Colter and Collins – we then embarked and descended the river. About seven miles below we saw some meat hanging on a pole. Sgt. Ordway examined it, and saw tracks of men which appeared to have been made today. A fire was still burning. He found a Chinook hat which the men recognized as one belonging to Gibson. From these signs we concluded that Capt. Clark's party could not be far away. We went on until dark without finding them, and were compelled to camp, after coming some one hundred miles today.

Capt. Clark's party delayed until 11 a.m. when we reloaded and dropped down the river. At 6 p.m. we landed on a sand bar. The wind came up and it was cold and clear. Not a mosquito to be seen! A most joyful circumstance to all the party.

AUGUST 8. Capt. Lewis set out early, and aided by the current and the oars, we made good speed until 10 a.m. when we arrived at the White Earth River. Not finding Capt. Clark here, we were at a loss to conjecture what had happened to them. Therefore we landed and began to calk and repair the canoes – as well as to prepare some skins for clothing. Since leaving the Rocky Mountains we have had no time to make clothing, and the men are nearly naked. Drouillard killed two deer this evening.

Capt. Clark directed Shields and Gibson to hunt. At 8 a.m., Sgt. Pryor, Windsor and Hall arrived. They had come down the Yellowstone and Missouri in two canoes made of buffalo hides. They had found the note at the junction of the Missouri which Capt. Clark had left for Capt. Lewis. Concluding that Capt. Lewis had passed, Pryor took the note and brought it with him. However, we expect that Capt. Lewis will be certain of our passing by the sign we left in the sand – and by seeing our abandoned camp on the point. Sgt. Pryor was so anxious to overtake us this morning that he left his saddle bags which contained all his papers. Bratton went back with him to search for them. Pryor's hand, which had been bitten by the wolf, has nearly recovered. Shannon went to hunt in the bottom. Shields and Gibson returned with the skins and flesh of three deer. They were directed to take one of Sgt. Pryor's bull-boats and go down to the next bottom to hunt until we arrive this evening. Our object is to procure as many skins as possible to trade with the Mandans for corn and beans. As we now have no horses nor merchandise, our only resort is skins for making trade. After dark, Sgt. Pryor and Bratton returned with the lost saddle bags.

AUGUST 9.   Capt. Lewis sent Reuben and Joseph Fields to the White Earth River to search for Capt. Clark and party. The day was fair, so the men are all engaged in making clothes and dressing skins. In the evening the Fields brothers returned, having seen no appearance of Capt. Clark's party. Colter and Collins have not yet overtaken us and we fear some misfortune has happened to them, for their previous fidelity and orderly deportment induces us to believe they would not intentionally delay. The pirogue is not dry enough for repairing. We have no pitch, and will therefore be compelled to use charcoal and tallow.

Capt. Clark and party went on down six miles to the camp of Shields and Gibson. They had killed five deer. Here we took breakfast. Capt. Clark walked ashore and killed three deer. Sacagawea brought Capt. Clark some gooseberries and currants which are well flavored.

AUGUST 10.   The party with Capt. Lewis worked at repairing the pirogue and canoes which were finished by 2 p.m. The other men were hunting and making leather clothes until it started to rain – which put an end to the skin dressing. We therefore reloaded the boats and descended as far as the White Earth River where we went into camp.

Capt. Clark finished his sketches of the Yellowstone River country. Shields killed a black-tailed deer and an antelope. Some of the men dug the roots of what our Frenchmen called the pomme-blanche (white-apple). These tubers are excellent and we cook them with our meat.

AUGUST 11.   Capt. Lewis' party set out early as we wished to arrive at the Burnt Hills – the northernmost bend of the Missouri. We needed to take the altitude of this important location. The men plied the oars and we went on rapidly, but we arrived at twenty minutes after noon, and the sun's meridian was therefore lost. We saw some elk, and Capt. Lewis and Peter Cruzatte went to hunt them. In going through the thick willows by different routes, Capt. Lewis was in the act of firing, when a bullet struck him through the left thigh about an inch below his hip joint. The ball missed the bone, but cut across his buttocks into the right thigh. As Capt. Lewis was dressed in brown leather, and Cruzatte could not see well, he had shot Capt. Lewis, mistaking him for an elk. Capt. Lewis called to Cruzatte several times, but received no answer, and now supposed he may have been shot by an Indian. Capt. Lewis made his way back to the pirogue. He told the men he was shot by an Indian, and that Cruzatte might have fallen into their hands. The party made preparations for an Indian assault. In this state of suspense, he waited until the men had returned with Cruzatte, and they reported that there were no Indians about. Capt. Lewis did not believe that Cruzatte had shot him intentionally, but that when he did not answer, Cruzatte was anxious to conceal his knowledge of having done so. With the assistance of Sgt. Gass, Capt. Lewis' clothes were removed, and the wound dressed by putting lint into the bullet holes. The wound is so situated that Capt. Lewis can not move without great pain, and he had to give up the idea of making celestial observations here. Joseph Fields killed an elk, and then we went on – Capt. Lewis lying in the pirogue. We found a note from Capt. Clark stating that he was below and confirming the information that all of the horses had been stolen from Sgt. Pryor. This puts an end to our hopes of obtaining some Sioux chiefs to accompany us to the United States.

Capt. Clark delayed on a sand bar to dry the elk meat in the sun. About noon we set out again. At 2 p.m. we observed a canoe, which upon joining us, we found manned by two men from the Illinois – Joseph Dickson and Forest Handcock.[1] They informed us that they were on a trapping expedi-

---

1 Joseph Dickson (often, but incorrectly, rendered Dixon), was born January 13, 1775, in Pennsylvania. In 1802 he settled and trapped on the American Bottom, Illinois, across the Mississippi from St. Louis.

Forest Handcock (usually spelled Hancock; I use the form taken from his signature in the Missouri Hist. Soc. Coll.) was perhaps raised in Boonesborough, Kentucky, but later lived in Maysville. He probably was a Ranger under Simon Kenton. He came to Missouri with Daniel Boone in 1799 and lived near the latter at Boone's Lick, Missouri.

Both Dickson and Handcock built a pirogue and went up the Missouri in the summer of 1804. They wintered in a cave built near present Sioux City, Iowa. In the spring of 1805 they proceeded up the Missouri and apparently joined Charles Courtin's trapping party for protection. The Teton Sioux robbed them of most all their merchandise and furs. Dickson was wounded, and the white men barely preserved

tion to the Yellowstone, and had left the Illinois in the summer of 1804, and had wintered with the Teton Sioux in 1805 in company of one Coartony or Ceautoin [Charles Courtin ?] who had brought goods to trade. The Tetons had robbed him of the greater part of his goods, and had wounded Dickson in the leg with a hard wad. They informed us that they had met our party under Cpl. Warfington who had on board the keel boat an Arikara chief. They had also met Pierre Dorion, Robert McClellan and several other traders on their way up the Missouri. As these were the first white men we had seen since April 13th, 1805, we were anxious for news. However, they went on up the river, and we dropped down a way and then camped.

AUGUST 12. The party with Capt. Lewis set out early, being anxious to overtake Capt. Clark. At 8 a.m. we came to the camp of Dickson and Handcock who informed us that they had passed Capt. Clark's party at noon yesterday. We gave them a file and some powder and lead, and a description of the best beaver countries above. We visited for an hour and a half when we were joined by John Colter and John Collins who had been separated from us since August 3rd. They were well and no accident had occurred, but they were delayed because they thought our party was behind them. We are greatly relieved that they are back with us. Capt. Lewis' wounds are stiff and sore. Mr. Dickson and Handcock decided to remain with us, so we all dropped down the river where we found Capt. Clark and his party. We joined them at 1 p.m., and had the pleasure of finding them all well.

Meantime, Shannon discovered that he had left his tomahawk back at last night's camp. He and Gibson went back to look for it. The whole party

their lives. They passed the winter of 1805-06 with the Sioux, and in the spring of 1806, reached the Mandans.

That summer they trapped on the Missouri, working their way upstream and on August 11, 1806, met Captain Clark and his men returning from the Pacific. A few days later they had influenced John Colter to join them on a trapping venture. After a dispute with Dickson, the partnership dissolved after six weeks, and Handcock and Colter returned to winter with the Mandans. Dickson remained alone, probably on Clark's Fork of the Yellowstone, and trapped and wintered there.

Dickson made his way to St. Louis by the summer of 1807; disposed of his furs, and retired from the mountains forever. He settled his family in Sangamon County, Illinois, and died in 1844 at the home of a daughter in Morgan County, Illinois.

Handcock left the Mandans in the spring of 1807 and was soon hired by Manuel Lisa as a trapper. John Colter and George Drouillard were with this same party. Later, Handcock returned to St. Louis and Boone's Lick, Missouri. James, *Three Years among the Indians;* Harris, *John Colter;* Hafen, *Mountain Men,* vol. 3, p. 71, and additional data from Dr. Frank H. Dickson.

went on to a large bottom to hunt and wait until Shannon and Gibson returned. Shields and Labiche hunted deer. Shannon and Gibson arrived at 2 p.m., having found the tomahawk. One of the bull-boats got a hole punched in her, which the men patched up successfully. We are all together again which gives us all extreme satisfaction. Capt. Clark examined Capt. Lewis' wounds and was relieved to think they would be well in twenty days or so. We do not blame Cruzatte, who is near sighted and has the use of but one eye, as he has been an attentive and industrious man in whom we have placed the greatest confidence during our entire journey. At 3 p.m. we proceeded together, having left the bull-boats on the bank as we now have ample canoe space. We camped near Charbonneau's Creek on a large sand point. Capt. Clark dressed and washed Capt. Lewis' wounds.

THE FIGHT ON THE MARIA'S RIVER, JULY 27, 1806
From a painting by Olaf C. Seltzer, painted by the site of the skirmish.
Courtesy of Thomas Gilcrease Institute, Tulsa, Oklahoma.

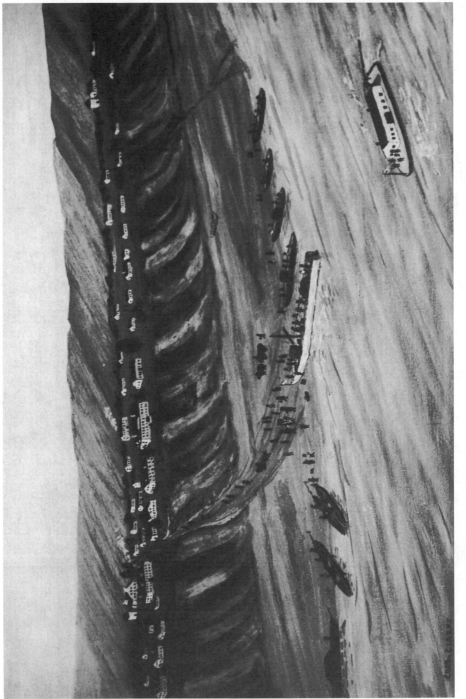

THE ARRIVAL OF LEWIS AND CLARK AT ST. LOUIS, SEPTEMBER 23, 1806
From a painting, based on historical research, made for this work by Charles G. Clarke.

27

The Little Missouri to White River

AUGUST 13. With all hands on board, we set out at sunrise. We passed the entrance of the Little Missouri at 8 a.m., and arrived at the Miry River, having made eighty-six miles. Drouillard wounded an elk, and then we went on. We camped opposite a deserted Gros Ventre village.

AUGUST 14. We set out at sunrise. When we were opposite the grand Minnitaree village we saw a number of natives, so we landed. The principal chief and the people are extremely pleased to see us. After a short delay, we proceeded to Black Cat's Mandan village. We dispatched Charbonneau back to the Minnitaree village with an invitation for them to visit us, and Drouillard went down to the lower Mandan village to ask Mr. René Jessaume to come up and interpret for us. He arrived, and through him we spoke to the chiefs, inviting some of them to accompany us to the United States. After the council, we crossed to the opposite side of the Missouri to camp in a central position — and a place where we would also be clear of mosquitoes. The chiefs promised us some corn, and Sgt. Gass and two men accompanied one to his village. They soon returned loaded with corn, beans and squashes. Several chiefs came over, and Capt. Clark counciled with them. The chiefs declined to go with us for fear of the Sioux Indians below. Capt. Lewis fainted while Capt. Clark was dressing his wound, but was soon revived again.

AUGUST 15. Capt. Clark again spoke to the chiefs in regard to visiting the United States. They offered a young man of bad character, and in fact, at the time had in his possession Gibson's knife, which he had stolen. We informed the chief of this, and the man delivered up the knife with a meek apology. Capt. Clark reproached the chiefs for offering such a man to see and hear the words of the Great Father — and they hung their heads in shame. Charbonneau informed us that Little Crow, a second chief, wanted to go with us, so Capt. Clark walked to his village to talk with him.

John Colter expressed the wish to join Mr. Dickson and Mr. Handcock on their hunt to trap the shores of the Yellowstone and Missouri. As this offer was an advantage for Colter, and his services could now be dispensed with, the captains were disposed to be of service to one of our party who had performed his duty as well as John Colter had done. We agreed to allow him to go, provided no one else of the party would ask for similar permission. All the men agreed to this, and they wished Colter every success. We all gave him some powder and lead and several other small articles which would be useful on his expedition.

Charbonneau learned that our backs had scarcely been turned on Cameah-wait and his friendly band of Shoshoni last fall when they had been attacked by two parties of Minnitarees and had been completely routed. He also informed us that the Mandans and the Arikara had nearly come to blows during our absence to the Pacific.

AUGUST 16. John Colter left early to go back up the Missouri with his new-found friends. The example of this man shows how easily man can be weaned from the habits of civilized life to the ruder, but scarcely less fascinating life and manners of the woods. Colter had been absent for over two years from the frontiers, and might naturally be presumed to have some anxiety, or some curiosity at least, to return to his friends and country; yet, at the moment when he is approaching the frontiers, he was tempted by a hunting scheme to give up these delightful prospects, and go back without the least reluctance to the solitude of the woods.

The Mandans had offered to give us some corn, and sending Sgt. Pryor for it, we found they had given us a greater quantity than our canoes could carry. We thanked the chief and took only six loads. We presented the swivel gun to Le Borgne — the one-eyed chief. As it cannot be fired from the small pirogue we now have, and therefore is no longer useful to us, we thought that by this present we might engage this powerful chief to our country's interest. Le Borgne had it conveyed to his village with great pomp. Capt. Clark walked up to the village and found that "Big White," or Shahaka as he is properly called, had consented to accompany us if we would agree to take his wife and son, and also Mr. René Jessaume and his two children along. This we were obliged to agree to do. We learned that the fine corn mill we had given these Mandans in 1804, had been broken up in order for them to procure pieces of iron, and as a pounder for marrow bones.[1]

AUGUST 17. The principal chiefs of the Minnitaree came to bid us farewell, and as none of them would go with us, Charbonneau, Sacagawea and Pomp took their leave of us. We offered to take them with us, but Charbonneau said he had no chance of making a livelihood below, and that he preferred living among the Indians. Charbonneau has been very serviceable to us, and his wife, Sacagawea, was particularly useful among the Shoshoni. Indeed, she has borne the fatigues of a long route, encumbered with an infant,

---

[1] Coues, *New Light*, v. I, p. 329.

who is now only nineteen months old. We therefore paid Charbonneau his wages of $500.33, including the price of a horse and a lodge purchased of him. Capt. Clark offered to take little Pomp, but as he had not yet been weaned, his parents observed that one year from now he would be sufficiently old enough to leave his mother, and Charbonneau would then bring him down to Capt. Clark to raise and educate. To this Capt. Clark agreed [and later did]. We gave Charbonneau the blacksmith's tools and bellows to use among this nation.

We then dropped down to Shahaka's village to take him and his family aboard. There was much crying by the native women. After smoking the pipe and giving some powder and lead, Shahaka announced that he was ready, and was accompanied to our canoes by all the village. After another council we set out and proceeded as far as our old Fort Mandan where we landed. All the buildings except one in the rear had been burned. Only some pickets were standing in front next to the river. We were saddened to see the present condition of our fort where we had spent so many happy hours during the winter of 1804-1805. We then went on to the old Arikara village where we landed.

AUGUST 18. The wind caused the river to be so rough we could not depart until 8 a.m. We sent some hunters ahead, and by a p.m. we overtook them. They had killed three deer which we divided among our Indians and we cooked dinner on a sand-bar. Shahaka pointed out several places enroute where he said his nation had formerly lived. After dinner we proceeded on and camped a little below the entrance of Heart River. After landing, the hunters killed four deer.

AUGUST 19. Capt. Clark directed the hunters to precede us to a bottom to hunt and butcher some meat. The wind blew with violence, so we did not set out until 4 p.m. Capt. Lewis' wounds are healing. We came to the hunters who had killed four elk and twelve deer. We loaded most of the flesh and proceeded on to a sand-bar where we camped. Jessaume let Capt. Clark have a piece of a lodge, and the wives stretched it over some sticks, under which the captains slept dry. The Indians appear satisfied with our party and mode of procedure. We have lashed the small canoes together for safety, but still can make fifty or sixty miles a day in this strong current. The men are all in good spirits.

AUGUST 20. We embarked a little after sunrise. At noon we passed the entrance of the Cannonball River. At evening we camped on a sand-bar. We only made eighty-one miles as the water was rough, and the small canoes shipped water which required a man to constantly bail them out. We note a great change in the Missouri – where once were sand-bars, the current now passed – and vice-versa. Capt. Clark took time to write a letter to Charbonneau to be sent up by the first traders we meet. He wrote: [2]

> I was so much engaged with getting Shahaka to come along with us that I did not have as much time to talk as I had intended. You have been with us a long time and have conducted yourself in such a manner as to gain my friendship. Your woman, Sacagawea, deserved a greater reward than we had it in our power to give. As to your son, my little boy "Pomp"; you well know my fondness for him, and my anxiety to take and raise him as my own child. I once more tell you to bring your son Baptiste (Pomp) to me. I will educate him and treat him as my own child. If you will come, I will give you land, horses, cows and hogs. If you wish to visit your friends in Montreal, that can be made possible. If you will bring your son, your wife Janey (Sacagawea), had best come along with you to take care of the boy until I get him.
>
> With anxious expectations of seeing my little dancing boy, Baptiste, I shall remain, your friend,   WILLIAM CLARK.

AUGUST 21.   Capt. Clark directed Sgt. Ordway to proceed to where there were ash trees growing, and to cut enough to make two oars which we need. Our men put their guns in perfect order as we are now in Sioux country. We set out at 5 a.m. and overtook Sgt. Ordway with the ash wood. At 8 a.m. we met three Frenchmen coming up the river. They proved to be Francois Rivet, Grenier (Grienyea) and one other man from the Arikara. Two of them, Rivet and Grenier, had wintered with us at the Mandans in 1804-5. They informed us that they were enroute to the Mandans, and intended to return to the Illinois this fall. The other, quite a young lad, who formerly had belonged with the North West Company of traders, wished to return with us. The captains consented, and he was taken aboard in one of the canoes to ply an oar. Rivet and Grenier had neither powder nor lead, so we gave them some. [They probably took Clark's letter up to Charbonneau.] After a delay of an hour, we parted from them, and we proceeded on. At 11:30 a.m. we arrived in view of the upper Arikara village. We saluted them and the natives were rejoiced to see us, and took us by the hand. Capt. Clark held a council with the chiefs and again explained the advantages of peace and trade among the nations, and cautioned them to treat the traders well. After smoking, some medals

---

[2] Paraphrased from a long letter appearing in Thwaites, v. 7, p. 329. Also in Jackson, *op. cit.,* p. 315.

were given, and we parted the best of friends. We dropped down to the first village where Capt. Clark repeated the good advice he had given above. After these long conferences where much diplomacy was required, Capt. Clark returned to the boats and went to bed. Here a Frenchman, Joseph Garreau,[3] an interpreter who had lived among the Arikara, and had also done service for the captains in 1804, joined us to go to St. Louis.

AUGUST 22.   It rained all last night and all our bedding was wet. The interpreter, Mr. Garreau, informed Capt. Clark that he had been speaking with the Arikara chiefs, who had assured him that they had no intention of going with us until the chief who had gone down with Cpl. Warfington last year, had been returned. At this nation we found Rokey [Ross] who had been one of our engagés as high as the Mandans [on the upstream voyage of 1804]. He had spent all his wages, and requested to return with us. We agreed to give him a passage down. Capt. Clark directed that two guns be fired as a salute, and then we proceeded on, and passed the Grand River and landed to dry our bedding, robes, etc. All were wet and some were spoiled. Five hunters were sent ahead, and at 6 p.m. we proceeded to their camp, where we all encamped. They had not killed anything. Capt. Lewis is recovering fast, and walked a little today for the first time.

AUGUST 23.   We set out early, but at 10 a.m. the wind became so strong that we were obliged to put ashore and wait until 3 p.m. Soon after landing, John Shields and the Fields brothers went on down to the next bottom to hunt until our arrival. At 3 p.m. we went on, and landed at the bottom. The hunters had killed three elk and three deer. We went on, and at dark we camped on a sand-bar where the mosquitoes were not so troublesome. Capt. Lewis is recovering – the hole in his buttocks where the bullet passed out, is closed and is nearly well. The hole where the bullet entered discharges very well.

AUGUST 24.   We set out at sunrise and proceeded on until 2 p.m., when the wind arose. We lay by until 5 p.m. when we went on again. We camped above an old trading post, four miles above our camping place of October 1st, 1804. The Sioux have hunted here, so now there is very little game about. We sent out a hunter, but he returned having killed nothing.

AUGUST 25.   Before sunrise we sent Shields, Collins, Shannon and the Fields brothers ahead in two small canoes to hunt on Pania Island until we came along. We set out at the usual time and proceeded very well. At 8

---

[3] Joseph Garreau, identified as both a Frenchman and a Spaniard. His name is also spelled Garout, Garaut, Garon, etc. He was still with the Arikara in 1807. Thwaites, v. I, pp. 7, 272.

a.m. we came to the mouth of the Cheyenne River and made a meridian observation. We sent three hunters to hunt its bottom until noon. They returned with two deer, and at noon we went on. We came to Pania Island and met Shields and Collins. They had killed two deer. We camped below our encampment of September 29, 1804, and here Drouillard killed a deer. Joseph and Reuben Fields and Shannon did not join us this evening which caused us to encamp earlier than usual.

AUGUST 26.   Shannon and the Fields brothers arrived at sunrise and we set out. At 8 a.m. we passed the place where the Teton Sioux attempted to rob us in September 1804. We suspect they are now camped up on the Teton River. We were on guard – all arms in perfect order – for we are determined to bear no insults from this band of Sioux. Capt. Lewis is on the mend and walks a little. He feels the wound where the ball entered is sufficiently healed so that Capt. Clark can remove the tent which he had placed over it. We did not pause to cook today because of the Sioux, so we made sixty miles.

AUGUST 27.   We set off before sunrise and went on to Tylor's River and landed on a sand bar. We sent out hunters as our meat is now exhausted. The hunters returned in three hours empty handed, so we went on. At 1 p.m. we halted in the Big Bend, and killed a fat buck which was very timely. At 6 p.m. we heard the bellowing of buffalo. We sent five men to hunt and they returned with two buffalo cows and one bull and a calf. We camped on the lower end of an island. Capt. Lewis took a longer walk than he had the strength to undergo. He hurt himself very much, which caused him to remain very unwell all night.

AUGUST 28.   We sent Reuben and Joseph Fields to hunt for mule deer and antelope, neither of which we have skins nor skeletons of. They are to go down to the place where we had camped on the 16th and 17th of September 1804. We also sent Drouillard and Labiche ahead with the same instructions. At noon we landed at our former campsite and formed a new camp. We sent out Sgt. Pryor, Shields, Gibson, Willard and Collins to hunt in the plains up Corvus Creek. We sent Bratton and Frazier to hunt for the barking-squirrel [prairie dog], and all were to kill some magpies if they should see any. Several of the men and the wives of the interpreter, Jessaume, and the Mandan Chief, Shahaka, went to the plum bushes and gathered a large quantity of well flavored plums.

At 3 p.m. Drouillard and Labiche returned with a deer of the common kind. In the evening the rest of the hunters returned without any species of the animals we were in want of. We procured two barking squirrels. Therefore we directed Shannon and Collins to leave early tomorrow to hunt one side of the river, while Labiche and Willard are to hunt the other. Reuben Fields is to proceed slowly in a small canoe down the river to take in anything the hunters might kill. The balance of the men are dressing skins to make clothes for themselves and our party.

AUGUST 29. The hunters, agreeable to orders given last night, went on. We sent two hunters to get some barking squirrels, but they returned saying none were to be seen. The other men have completed dressing the skins, so we set out at 10 a.m. At noon we were joined by Labiche, Shannon and Willard. They got two common deer, but no mule deer or antelope. Capt. Clark directed Drouillard to hunt on the south-west side of the river. We then proceeded on until we landed on an island. Capt. Clark and several of the men went in pursuit of buffalo. They killed two bulls, which at this season are very poor. Capt. Clark ascended an eminence from which he had a view of the plains filled with immense herds of buffalo. After dinner we went on down to the camp of the Fields brothers and Collins, and camped a little below our encampment of September 13, 1804. None of the hunters got either a black-tailed deer nor an antelope, but they did get a porcupine and common deer. Drouillard joined us at 10 p.m. We saved all the buffalo horns we can find to take home, as they make excellent knife and fork handles.

AUGUST 30 Capt. Lewis is mending slowly. Joseph Fields was left behind when we set out, so Capt. Clark directed Reuben Fields and Shannon to proceed slowly until Joseph comes along. Capt. Clark took three hunters and walked ashore. They got two fat elk, which were loaded in the canoes. While we were thus delayed two hours, the men gathered plums and then we proceeded to the place where we are to wait for the Fields brothers and Shannon. With the aid of the spy-glass, we saw several men on horseback which proved to be Indians. We landed and immediately twenty Indians were discovered on an eminence on the opposite side of the river. Then we saw eighty or ninety Indians come out of the woods about a fourth mile below us. They fired their guns as a salute, which we returned, but were at a loss to determine of what tribe they were. Capt. Clark took Cruzatte, Labiche and Jessaume, who could speak Omaha, to converse with them. We found they were Tetons of the same band that had attempted to rob and detain us in the fall of 1804, and with whom we nearly came to blows. Capt. Clark told them they had been deaf to our councils and that they had abused white people since, such as Charles Courtin and Joseph Dickson in the winter of 1805. Capt. Clark told them to return to their camp, and not cross to our side of the river, for if they did, we would certainly kill them. Capt. Clark and the three interpreters returned to our camp and we inspected our arms. The main part of the Indians set out for their camp, but seven of them halted on the top of a hill and yelled insults at us. They told us to come across and they would kill us all, etc., of which we paid no notice. All this time we were extremely anxious for the arrival of Shannon and the Fields brothers who were behind. To our great joy they hove in sight at 6 p.m. We then set out and steered towards the shore where the seven Indians were. This move put them in some agitation as to our motives, but we then proceeded on down some six miles where we camped on a large sand bar in the middle of the river. Our hunters killed nine prairie dogs. We put two sentinels on guard. During the night it began to rain, and the wind blew so hard that the cables of two of the canoes broke, and the canoes were blown to the opposite shore. In these boats were Sgt. Pryor, Weiser, Willard and the Indian party. Sgt. Ordway and six men went over to help them return, which was accomplished by 2 a.m. The whole party was reassembled and we waited in the rain for daylight.

AUGUST 31.   We examined our arms and proceeded with a wind in our favor. The men rowed hard all day and we did not take time out to cook. At different times we saw several Indians on the hills, but at length lost sight of them. We camped a little below our encampment of September 5, 1804, having come some seventy miles.

28

The Home Stretch

SEPTEMBER 1, 1806. We all set out at the usual hour. Shortly afterwards, Reuben Fields, Joseph Fields, and George Shannon were landed on an island to hunt deer. We went on past the Niobrara River where we encountered nine Indians who beckoned us to land. We took them to be a war party of the Tetons and paid no attention to them. As the Fields brothers and Shannon were behind, we landed on an open, commanding position out of sight of the Indians to wait until our men came up. About fifteen minutes later, several guns were fired by the Indians, which we feared were at our men behind. Capt. Clark called out fifteen men who ran up to cover them if possible, let the number of Indians be what they might. Capt. Lewis hobbled up the bank and formed the remainder of the men in a defensive position. Capt. Clark's party proceeded some 250 yards when we saw the canoe with our men in the distance – and the Indians were where we had left them. The Indians informed us they were Yanktons and one of our Frenchmen knew one of them to be the brother of young Pierre Dorion's wife. We then invited them to the canoes to smoke. We asked if any of their chiefs had gone down the river with Mr. Dorion, and they answered that their Great Chief and many of their brave men had gone down with him to visit the President. We gave them some ribbons and a bushel of corn. John Shields gave them a pair of excellent leggings. The Fields brothers and Shannon having joined us, we took leave of this party of Yanktons. At 2 p.m. we arrived opposite the ancient fortifications, and we set our men to hunt on both sides of the island. Labiche killed an elk while Capt. Clark walked on the shore of the river. At Bonhomme Island we brought two years together on the 1st of September of 1804 and 1806. After we were all together again, we went on down to a large sand bar opposite the bluff where we had previously met the Yanktons in council, and here our old flag-pole was still standing as we had left it two years before.

SEPTEMBER 2. We passed the Jacques [James] River at 8 a.m. and later saw the remains of Robert McClellan's house which had been built since we had passed up. The wind came up against us, so we were obliged to lay by here nearly all day. Capt. Clark went out with eight men to hunt buffalo. They got two in good order, and each man carried as much as he could of the meat back to the canoes. At sunset we proceeded to a sand bar below where we hoped to be free from the mosquitoes which harbor around the wooded banks of the shores. We killed two turkeys which were much admired by the Indians, as they were the first that they had ever seen or tasted. Capt. Lewis is mending fast.

SEPTEMBER 3.   The wind blew hard last night and the sand sifted over us in a very disagreeable manner. It lulled a little, so we set out; passed the Vermillion River, and at 4:30 p.m. we spied two canoes with eighteen men aboard. As we came alongside, we were met by Mr. James Aird, a trader with the Sioux. He received the captains with every mark of friendship. Our first inquiry was after our President Jefferson, our friends, and the state of the politics of the country. Mr. Aird gave us as much information as he could. Soon after we landed, a violent thunder storm and rain came up, which continued until 10 p.m. Capt. Lewis is well enough to walk with ease. Capt. Clark talked with Mr. Aird in his tent until late in the evening, and obtained additional news of our country.

SEPTEMBER 4.   Mr. Aird generously presented every man of our party with enough tobacco to last us for the rest of our voyage, and insisted upon our accepting a barrel of flour. We found this very agreeable, although we still have a little flour left from our deposit made at the mouth of Maria's River. All we could give in return was about six bushels of corn. At 8 a.m. we set out, and at noon we came to Floyd's Bluff. Capt. Lewis, Capt. Clark and several of the men ascended the bluff to the grave of our late Sgt. Charles Floyd. We found the grave had been opened by the Indians. We covered it over again, and after paying our last respects, we returned to the canoes. We went on to the sand bar where we had camped from the 12th to the 20th of August 1804. Here we laid out every article to dry, for all the skins and bedding were wet. Each man was issued a cup of flour. All now being dry, we loaded the canoes for an early departure tomorrow.

SEPTEMBER 5.   The mosquitoes were so bad last night that the party were already in the canoes, so we set out at daylight. We proceeded on very well, though the river became more narrow and crooked, and is filled with snags and sawyers. Capt. Lewis is still in a convalescent state. We saw no game worth killing — only pelicans, geese, ducks, eagles, etc. We made seventy-three miles.

SEPTEMBER 6.   We set out early, and at the Great-Cut-Off we saw a herd of elk. We landed and sent out several hunters to get some, but they were very wild and ran off, so the hunters returned without killing any. Capt. Clark sent two canoes ahead with hunters to search on the bottoms below.

After a short delay, we went on and soon met one of the trading boats of Mr. Auguste Chouteau; this one under the charge of Mr. Henry Delauney, with twelve Frenchmen. We purchased a gallon of whiskey from him, promising to pay Mr. Chouteau at St. Louis (which he later would not accept). We gave each man a dram which is the first they have tasted since July 4th, 1805. Several men, including Sgt. Ordway, exchanged their leather shirts for linen ones, and beaver skins for course hats. At 1 p.m. we set out. They gave us a salute from a swivel they had, which we returned with our rifles. We went on three miles and came to our hunters. They had not killed anything. At five miles more we overtook the canoe of our other hunters with Shannon in it – the two Fields brothers being in the woods behind. We landed on a sand bar and delayed, waiting for the Fields brothers. We sent out three men to hunt. The Fields brothers did not join us, and Capt. Clark thinks they are below. Our Indians are getting weary of the journey and the children cry, etc.

SEPTEMBER 7.   We left Sgt. Ordway and his canoe and four men to wait for the Fields brothers until noon, and then they are to proceed. We agreed that should we overtake the hunters we would fire a gun which would be a signal to come on. We had proceeded only eight miles by water – though the direct line distance was only about a mile, when we found the hunters and took them on board. We fired the gun as a signal for Sgt. Ordway to proceed. We went to a bottom where we came to – and sent out the hunters. They killed three elk and we sent out some men for the meat on which, with some catfish, we cooked and dined. Sgt. Ordway and his men came up, and after taking a sumptuous dinner, we all set out at 4 p.m., and at dusk we encamped on a sand bar about two miles below our encampment of August 4th, 1804.

SEPTEMBER 8.   We set out very early and at 11 a.m. we came to the Council Bluffs. The captains walked up the bluff to examine the situation and country more particularly as a possible site for a fort or trading post. We then re-embarked, and as the men were anxious to reach the River Platte today, they plied the oars diligently. We made seventy-eight miles when we arrived at our old Catfish Camp where we had stayed on July 22-24, 1804. This place is twelve miles above the Platte. Enroute, George Gibson killed a deer from his canoe.

SEPTEMBER 9.   At 8 a.m. we passed the mouth of the River Platte. Late in the evening we arrived at the Bald-pated Prairie and camped opposite our camp of the 16th and 17th of July 1804, having made seventy-three miles today. Capt. Lewis has entirely recovered. His wounds are healed up and he can walk, even run, nearly as well as ever, though the parts are still tender.

SEPTEMBER 10. We set out very early and proceeded on very well. We met Mr. Alexander Lafrost and three Frenchmen who were up from St. Louis to trade on the River Platte. He was very friendly and we accepted a bottle of whiskey for the men. After a delay of a half hour, we went on about three miles, when we met a large pirogue with seven men from St. Louis in charge of Mr. La Croix, enroute to trade with the Omaha. We made a few inquiries and then proceeded through a very bad part of the river crowded with snags, sawyers and sand bars. Great caution is required to steer clear of all these obstructions in the present low state of the water. One of our men killed a racoon which is of great interest to our Indians.

SEPTEMBER 11. We set out at sunrise and proceeded very well. At 3 p.m. we halted a little above the Nodaway River to kill some game. The six hunters brought in two deer and a turkey. We then went on and camped on an island below the Nodaway. Drouillard killed a deer.

SEPTEMBER 12. We set out at our usual time at sunrise. At about seven miles we met two pirogues from St. Louis. One belonged to Mr. Chouteau, bound for the Platte, while the other was going trapping as high as the Omaha. Here we met one of our Frenchmen who had accompanied us in 1804 as high as the Mandans [Joseph Collin ?]. He informed us that Mr. Robert McClellan was a few miles below. We saw a man on shore who was one of Mr. McClellan's party, and we took him on board and proceeded on until we met Mr. McClellan with his twelve men. With him was Mr. Joseph Gravelines [Gravelein], the Arikara interpreter, whom we had sent down with an Arikara chief and Cpl. Warfington in the spring of 1805. We examined their instructions and found that Mr. Gravelines was ordered to the Arikara nation with a speech from the President of the United States to that nation, and some presents which had been given to the Arikara chief who had visited, and unfortunately had died, in Washington. He was also instructed to make every inquiry after the Lewis and Clark party – no intelligence having been received from us for a long time, and they were beginning to be concerned about us. They had heard that we were all killed, and that the Spaniards held us captive in their mines, etc. Mr. Pierre Dorion, Sr., was also present, and had been instructed to accompany Mr. Gravelines, and through his influence, pass him and his presents through the Teton Sioux. Likewise, Mr. Dorion was instructed to make inquiries after us.

The evening being wet and cloudy, we concluded to lay by all night. Mr. McClellan, whom the captains had known before when he was a scout in Wayne's army in 1794-95, was very polite, and gave us all the news. We sent two canoes with five hunters ahead. Some of the men exchanged robes for shirts, and were treated in the best possible manner by the McClellan party.

SEPTEMBER 13. We arose early and Mr. McClellan gave each man a dram, and a little after sunrise we set out. We landed at the camp of the five hunters whom we had sent ahead, but they had killed nothing. As the wind was high and there were many snags below, we concluded to lay by, and sent the small canoes a short distance ahead to hunt. Capt. Clark felt unwell and had some chocolate made, which Mr. McClellan had presented to us, after which he found great relief. At 11 a.m. we went on, and came up with the hunters who had killed four deer and a turkey. We delayed here until 5 p.m., when the hunters all joined us, then we proceeded down a few miles and encamped. George Shannon left his horn, pouch with powder and ball, and a knife at the last stop and did not think of them until tonight.

SEPTEMBER 14. We set out early. This is that part of the Missouri where the Kansas Indians resort to robbing the traders passing up the river. They have the custom of examining everything in the pirogues, and taking what they want. It is probable they may want to take these liberties with us. This we will not allow, and at the smallest insult we shall fire on them. At 2 p.m. we met three large boats bound for the Yanktons and the Omaha; the property of Mr. La Croix, Mr. Aiten and Mr. Chouteau of St. Louis. Their men received us with friendship and pressed on us some whiskey, biscuit, pork and onions. These men are much afraid of meeting with the Kansas Indians. We killed five deer today. George Gibson got one from his canoe. Our party received a dram after we camped, and we sang songs in the greatest harmony until 11 p.m.

SEPTEMBER 15. We set out early and, after passing the Kansas River, Capt. Lewis and Capt. Clark landed to ascend a hill which appeared to have a commanding situation for a fort. The men gathered pawpaws which are now ripe and we are very fond of them. Joseph and Reuben Fields with Shannon, went hunting and brought back a fine, fat elk. We camped a little below Hay Cabin Creek. We notice the heat now, having been for so long in the cooler, northern climate.

SEPTEMBER 16. We set out early, but as the day was extremely hot, the men rowed but little. At 10 a.m. we met a large trading pirogue bound for the Pawnees. We remained a short time with them. At 11 a.m. we met young Mr. Joseph Robidoux with a large boat of six oars and two canoes, and some twenty Frenchmen. We examined his license to trade which appeared doubtful, and the captains cautioned him against degrading the

American government in the eyes of the Indians. We camped on an island a little above our encampment of June 16 and 17, 1804.

SEPTEMBER 17.   We set out early as usual. At 11 a.m. we met Capt. John McClallan ascending in a large boat. He had 15 men with him. He was somewhat astonished to see us, and was rejoiced at our return. He informed us that we had long since been given up by the people of the United States, and almost forgotten, though President Jefferson yet had hopes for us. He gave us some biscuit, chocolate, sugar and whiskey, for which our party was in want. We gave him in return a barrel of corn. He informed us he was going to trade, through the Pawnees, with the Spaniards for silver and gold. We sent five hunters ahead to the Grand River where we will meet them tomorrow morning. Last night one of our men [Goodrich?] caught a large catfish which weighed nearly one hundred pounds. We camped with Mr. McClallan and his party.

SEPTEMBER 18.   We took our leave of Capt. McClallan and proceeded on to the Grand River where we met our five hunters. They had killed nothing. At 10 a.m. we landed to gather pawpaws to eat with our biscuit, as we are entirely out of any other sort of provisions. The men appear perfectly happy, and say they can live on pawpaws if need be. John Potts complains of one of his eyes being sunburned. We are constantly exposed to the bright light and reflections from the water and have no cover. George Shannon also complains of sunburn and sore eyes. We camped near the Mine River.

SEPTEMBER 19.   We set out early and the men plied their oars, so we descended with great velocity. We stopped only once for pawpaws as the party is anxious to reach the settlements. Our party is afflicted with sore eyes. Three of them have eyes so inflamed as to be extremely painful.

SEPTEMBER 20.   We left adrift the two canoes which had been built high up on the Yellowstone, and divided the men into the other canoes, for some of them are unable to row because of their sore eyes. At noon we met a canoe containing five Frenchmen bound for the Osage nation. We saw some cows on the river bank which was a joyful sight, and the men raised a shout at the pleasure of seeing this image of civilization and domestic life. We came to the little French village of La Charette, where we landed and were very politely received. Every person expressed pleasure at our safe return, and admitted astonishment in seeing us. On our arrival we fired a salute, which was returned by five trading boats moored there. The traders furnished us with beef, flour and pork, which gave us a very agreeable supper. We remained in La Charette overnight. The French residents gave us some milk.

SEPTEMBER 21. We collected our men, for several of them had accepted an invitation by the citizens, and had visited their families. At 7:30 a.m. we set out, and after passing several boats, at 4 p.m. we arrived in sight of St. Charles. The party rejoiced at the sight of this hospitable village, and plied their oars with great dexterity, so we were soon opposite the town. This being Sunday, we observed a number of ladies and gentlemen walking along the bank. We saluted the town with three rounds, and landed at the lower part of the town where we were met by a great number of the citizens. We found them extremely polite and they seemed to vie with each other in being generous. Mr. Quirie [1] undertook to supply our party with provisions. This civility detained us overnight, for most of the party got refreshments and quarters in town.

SEPTEMBER 22. As it rained hard all morning, and our party was all sheltered in the houses of these hospitable people, we did not think it proper to proceed until the rain was over. At 10 a.m. it ceased raining, and we collected our party and proceeded on down to Fort Bellefontaine. We were kindly received by Col. Thomas Hunt and Lieut. George Peter of this place, who gave us a salute of seventeen guns and a hearty welcome. Most of our party was quartered in the cantonement over night.

SEPTEMBER 23. We rose early and took the Mundan chief, Shahaka, to the public store to furnish him with some clothes, etc. After breakfast, we descended the Mississippi and landed at River du Bois to view the camp where we had wintered in 1803-1804. Here we found a widow woman [2] whom we had left here, and who now had a plantation under tolerable way since we have been on our expedition. We delayed a short time and then crossed over the Mississippi, where at about noon we arrived at St. Louis. The party fired their guns as a salute, and we landed opposite the center of the town. We were dressed entirely in buck-skin except for the linen shirts the men had bought from the traders just previously.

We unloaded the canoes and carried the baggage up to the store rooms of Major William Christy. The party is considerably rejoiced that we have the expedition completed. We looked for boarding in town, and wait for our pay. We then intend to return to our native homes to see our parents and families once more, as we have been so long from them. The captains accepted the invitation of Mr. Pierre Chouteau to stay at his house.

SEPTEMBER 24. The captains rose early and commenced to write letters to the President, George Rogers Clark, Gen. Wm. H. Harrison and Char-

---

[1] Probably Mr. Mackey Wherry, who was at that time sheriff of St. Charles.

[2] Perhaps Mrs. Cane, the former washer woman for the men at Camp du Bois.

bonneau. We sent the first of these letters by Drouillard across the river to Cahokia where the post has been detained to receive them. After dinner the captains went to a store to purchase some goods and engage a tailor to make them some clothes.

SEPTEMBER 25.   While the captains were busy with their reports and letters, the men sunned and dried all of the goods and articles. They were then stored at the warehouse of Mr. Caddy Chouteau. The captains paid some formal visits to the gentlemen of St. Louis, who entertained us in the evening with a dinner and a ball.

The horns and skeletons of the big-horn sheep, along with the robes, grizzly bear skins, barking squirrels, mule deer skins, Clatsop hats, Indian baskets, etc., were packed and sent to Washington. Capt. Lewis advised President Jefferson by letter that the expedition had, in obedience to orders, crossed the continent and had sufficiently explored the interior, to have discovered the navigable headwaters of the Missouri and Columbia rivers by the most practical route. He gave a resumé of the trip, but noted that he would soon give a more full report in person. However, he would be necessarily delayed some days to settle with, and discharge the men who had accompanied him on the voyage of discovery. He will bring the Mandan Chief, Shahaka, and with respect to the exertions and services rendered by his worthy friend, Capt. Clark, he cannot say too much. He noted that if any credit be due to the success of the arduous enterprise in which we have been engaged, that Capt. Clark, equally with himself, is entitled to the consideration of yourself and the country.

Finis

The men were paid off and discharged on October 10, 1806, and for most of them it was the end of the adventure. They drifted back to their families and friends. Some married and settled on farms. Others returned to the mountains in the employ of the fur traders who were now anxious to penetrate the newly discovered, rich beaver streams on the headwaters of the Missouri and Yellowstone. Capt. Clark promptly returned his commission in the army. The discharge given to William Bratton is typical of that given the others:

St. Louis, Oct. 10, 1806.

To whom it may concern: Know ye, that the bearer, William Bratton, private in a Corps destined for the discovery of the interior of the continent of North America, having faithfully discharged his duty in said capacity so long as his services have been necessary to complete the objects of a voyage to the Pacific Ocean, is in virtue of the authority vested in me by the President of the United States, hereby discharged from the military service of the said States; and as a tribute justly due the merits of the said William Bratton, I with cheerfulness declare that the ample support which he gave under every difficulty, the manly firmness which he evinced on every necessary occasion, and the fortitude with which he bore the fatigues and painful sufferings incident to that long voyage, entitles him to my highest confidence and sincere thanks; while it eminently recommends him to the consideration and respect of his fellow citizens.   MERIWETHER LEWIS, CAPT.

1st U.S. Regt. Inftry.

I certify that the within named William Bratton has received from me all arrears of pay, clothing and rations due him by the United States from the date of his enlistment to the present date.

Oct. 10, 1806.   MERIWETHER LEWIS, CAPT.

1st U.S. Regt. Inftry.[1]

---

[1] Thwaites, v. 7, p. 344.

Unfortunately not much more can be added to the lives of the men who comprised the expedition than has been given in the brief biographies in the preceding "Roster." The main hope for additional data may be in the discovery of Sgt. Pryor's journal, the Robert Frazier journal, and the original manuscript journal of Patrick Gass. As indicated in my roster, there is the promise of further information yet to be discovered by genealogical research.

Among the obscure records of the fur traders there is the report of David Thompson[2] of one Charles Courtin, or Courter, a Canadian who had sworn allegiance to the United States in order to ascend the Missouri in 1805. In July 1807, Courtin and his party of forty-two Americans were in the Columbia River basin among the Flatheads. Two of these members are stated to have been former members of the Lewis and Clark Expedition. They could have been two men of the return party of 1805, and perhaps Francois Rivet was one. Phillipe Degie, who was not a regular member, could be the other.

It can easily be imagined that for many of the men the return to civilian life was a difficult time of adjustment. After their exciting return they must have been acclaimed and fêted, and this in itself was a complete change from their former woodsman lives, and from the privations they had just come through. Then as today, men have had a problem in adjusting to sudden fame and adulation, and not everyone can successfully take it in stride. We can understand then, if a few of these men fell by the wayside.

For most of them however, it was an experience passed, with a future to be met. Like hundreds of other citizens about them, they fitted into the routine pattern of earning a living, marrying and raising families.

Capt. Lewis and Mr. Clark arrived in Frankfort, Ken-

---

2 Coues, *New Light*, p. 674 note; Jackson, p. 437, n. 3.

tucky, about the 18th of November 1806, accompanied by
Mr. Chouteau and Chief Shahaka, his family and interpreter, René Jessaume. A party of Osages also went along.
They all went on to Washington, except citizen William
Clark. He visited his brothers in Louisville, and then went
on to Virginia to woo Julia Hancock. Clark was not interested in the gala receptions given in Washington on January 10 and 14, 1807, in honor of the expedition's trium-
phant return, so Capt. Lewis attended these affairs without
his companion, William Clark.

Early in 1807, Lewis was appointed Governor of Upper
Louisiana, and Clark was appointed Brigadier General of
the Louisiana Militia. They soon had their hands full of
political problems in the new Territory. There was the
Aaron Burr conspiracy for which ex-member Robert
Frazier had been uncovering alarming evidence of treason,
and was a witness at the trial.

Governor Lewis stepped into a tangled mess. The original French settlers had problems with the influx of American settlers. There were uncertainties and confusion with
the French, Spanish and American land titles. The bitter
antagonism of the jealous Secretary of the Territory, Frederick Bates, was of no help. The Indians did not like the
treaties they had signed, the traders did not like any regula-
tion whatever, and the British were keeping the fires alive
under all. The War Department began to protest Capt.
Lewis' drafts, and it was more than Governor Lewis could
handle. In the end he set off for Washington to try to get
the matters straightened out.

On March 9, 1807, the authorization for the land warrants promised by Congress was received, and the following
men signed a receipt for the bounty:[3]

---

[3] See Jackson, p. 380, for a more complete account of the disposition of the land
warrants.

Nathaniel Pryor
John Collins
Joseph Fields
George Gibson
Francois Labiche
George Shannon
Richard Windsor
Joseph Whitehouse
Patrick Gass
John Colter
Reuben Fields

Thomas P. Howard
Hugh McNeal
John Potts
Peter M. Weiser
William Bratton
Pierre Cruzatte
Robert Frazier
Hugh Hall
John Shields
John B. Thompson
Alexander H. Willard

It may be assumed that these twenty-two men were present in St. Louis at the time. The others were scattered over the country and had to sign, or have Governor Lewis sign for them, at a later time.

Eventually the expenses of the expedition were totaled. There was the extra pay, the land grants and a hundred other charges added to the costs. It was finally estimated at a cost of $38,722.25 which depended on how certain charges were construed as actual costs or incidental charges to the expedition. Were the costs of transporting and entertaining the Indians in Washington a proper charge to the expedition? So the stated figure is as good as any, and certainly not an unreasonable amount for the value received.

Inevitably the scandal mongers had to have their say. They have tried to imply that there was a secret romance between Clark and Sacagawea, and that Clark left descendants among the Flatheads and other tribes. As to the first charge, there is no question that Clark felt sorry for the hard life of Sacagawea, and he respected her. So did everyone else. He certainly tried to help her children have a better life, but beyond that there is no proof of any romance whatsoever. As to the descendants, the men were normal and the native women were willing. But why Clark should be singled out as the only parent among the whole party can only be because he was now a famous name. Scandal is only of interest and is repeated if it can be attached to the names of celebrities.

It is sometimes inferred that the skirmish which Capt. Lewis had with the Blackfoot Indians up on the Cut Bank River was the cause of the bitter animosity which the Blackfoot carried on against the white traders for so many years that followed. Manuel Lisa later learned from the Blackfoot themselves that they felt the actions of their men justified the retribution that Capt. Lewis and his men inflicted upon them, and that they got what was to be expected in an unsuccessful raid.

And then there are those inferences that Capt. Lewis was the commander while Clark was only an adjutant. Of course this is technically true, but there is no evidence that the commanders nor any of the men ever drew such a distinction. The equality of command is abundantly clear throughout the expedition. The remarkable fact is that there never was a recorded occasion, during or after the expedition, when the leaders did not work together in complete appreciation for each other's abilities. This is the more remarkable for both captains were opposites in temperament. Lewis was better schooled but showed several instances of short-tempered impulsive actions. Clark was usually firm and unruffled. Though there is no intimation of it, Lewis in his wounded and painful condition, must have been annoyed when Clark kept dropping down the Missouri when it had been agreed that they would rendezvous at the mouth of the Yellowstone. Furthermore, the men must have been inclined to turn to the warm and friendly Clark, rather than to the more aloof and unapproachable Lewis. These were conditions which normally bring about jealousy and dissension, particularly as they saw each other day in and day out for over two years. Their loyalty and friendship to each other under all conditions is one of the classic friendships in all recorded history.

The same loyalty is evident among the men. In their journals they are silent, or at most, extremely discreet, about mentioning any of the unpleasant things such as punishments and dismissals. One can read between the lines and find suggestions of cases where the men got on each other's nerves. We are hardly told that John Robertson was dismissed from the party, and no reason is given, but it seems clear that he was a trouble maker and did not fit in with the other men. He was dismissed – without comment. We learn there were a few quarrels such as the one between Drouillard and Colter over leading a spare horse. No one tells us what really motivated it, for to them it was unimportant. Knowing human nature, these things would normally have happened.

In answer to those who might construe that the captains' friendship and loyalty to each other was only a bearing assumed to see the expedition through, and that they subdued their inner feelings with a bold front for the sake of example – there remains the final test. The expedition was now an accomplished fact and former promises could have been conveniently forgotten, particularly as there was so much opposition from the War Department against William Clark.

When Secretary of War Dearborn, proposed that the enlisted men should receive 320 acres of government land as an extra bonus; that Clark should get 1000 acres; while Lewis was to receive 1600 acres, Lewis rebelled. To the very end in Lewis' steadfast conviction, they had been in equal command and had shared equal responsibilities, and each should receive the same reward. To the credit of official Washington it is recorded that they got the point, and each leader was awarded the same amount – 1600 acres. Yes, both were true to their dying days, and such respect and friendship are rare and unique in human relations.

And this loyalty prevailed among the enlisted men. Loyalty to each other, loyalty to their captains and loyalty to their country by opening up a vast new country and in bending every effort to bring the expedition's purpose to its successful close. For this they should be remembered and honored. A good place to start would be for enlightened state governments to restore the original names of the rivers and creeks which were named for the members of the expedition.

Bibliography

Bibliography

Abel, Annie Heloise (ed.) *Chardon's Journal at Fort Clark, 1834-1839.* Pierre, So. Dak: Department of History, 1932.

Ardery, Mrs. Wm. Breckenridge, *Kentucky Court and other Records.* 2 vols., Lexington, Ky: 1932.

Bakeless, John, *Lewis and Clark; Partners in Discovery.* New York: William Morrow & Co., 1947.

Beard, J. Howard, "Medical Observations and Practices of Lewis and Clark," in *Scientific Monthly,* May 1925, vol. 20, pp. 506-26.

Biddle, Nicholas (ed.), *History of the Expedition under the Command of Captains Lewis and Clark, to the Sources of the Missouri, thence across the Rocky Mountains and down the River Columbia to the Pacific Ocean. Performed during the years 1804-5-6. By order of the Government of the United States. Prepared for the Press by Paul Allen, esquire.* 2 vols. Philadelphia: Bradford and Inskeep, 1814.

Billon, Frederic L., *Annals of St. Louis in its Territorial Days from 1804 to 1821.* St. Louis: 1888.

Brackenridge, H.M., *Journal of a Voyage up the River Missouri, 1811.* Reprinted in *Early Western Travels,* vol. 6. Cleveland: Arthur H. Clark Co., 1904.

Bradbury, John, *Bradbury's Travels in the Interior of America, 1809-1811.* Reprinted in *Early Western Travels,* vol. 5. Cleveland: Arthur H. Clark Co., 1904.

Bryan, Wm. S., and Robert Rose, *History of the Pioneer Families of the Missouri.* St. Louis: 1876. Reprinted, Columbia, Mo: Lucas Brothers, 1935.

Cartlidge, Anna Margaret, *Children and Grandchildren of William and Abadiah (Davis) Floyd.* Baltimore: 1966.

Chittenden, Hiram M., *The American Fur Trade of the Far West.* Elmira, N.Y: Wilson-Erickson, 1935.

Coues, Elliott (ed.), *History of the Expedition of Lewis and Clark . . .* (Coues edition of the Biddle 1814 edition). 4 vols. New York: Francis P. Harper, 1893.

Coues, Elliott (ed.), *New Light on the Early History of the Greater Northwest: the Manuscript Journals of Alexander Henry and of David Thompson.* 3 vols. New York: Francis P. Harper, 1897.

Coues, Elliott (ed.), *The Expeditions of Zebulon Montgomery Pike to the Headwaters of the Mississippi River, through Louisiana Territory, and in New Spain during the years 1805-6-7.* 3 vols. New York: Francis P. Harper, 1895.

Crawford, Helen, "Sakakawea," in *North Dakota Historical Quarterly,* April 1927.

Criswell, Elijah Harry, "Lewis and Clark; Linguistic Pioneers," in *University of Missouri Studies* (Columbia), vol. 15, no. 2, 1940.

De Voto, Bernard, *Journals of Lewis and Clark.* Boston: Houghton Mifflin Co., 1953.

Dillon, Richard, *Meriwether Lewis.* New York: Putnam, 1965.

Drumm, Stella M. (ed.), *Luttig's Journal of a Fur Trading Expedition on the Upper Missouri, 1812-1813.* St. Louis: Missouri Historical Society, 1920.

Dye, Eva Emery, *The Conquest: The True Story of Lewis and Clark.* Chicago: A. C. McClurg & Co., 1902.

Floyd, N.J., *Biographical Genealogies of Virginia-Kentucky Floyd Families.* Baltimore: 1912.

Forrest, Earle E., "Patrick Gass, Carpenter of the Lewis and Clark Expedition," in *Bulletin of the Missouri Historical Society,* July 1948, vol. 4, pp. 217-22.

Forrest, Earle E., *Patrick Gass, Lewis and Clark's Last Man.* Independence, Pennsylvania: Mrs. A. M. Painter, privately printed, 1950.

Gass, Patrick, *A Journal of the Voyages and Travels of a Corps of Discovery, under the command of Capt. Lewis and Capt. Clarke of the Army of the United States, from the mouth of the River Missouri through the interior parts of North America to the Pacific Ocean, during the years 1804, 1805 & 1806. Containing an authentic relation of the most interesting transactions during the expedition, – a description of the country, – an account of its inhabitants, soil, climate, curiosities and vegetable and animal productions.* Edited by David McKeehan. Pittsburgh: McKeehan, 1807.

Hafen, LeRoy R. (ed.) *The Mountain Men and the Fur Trade of the Far West,* vols. 1-7. Glendale, Calif: The Arthur H. Clark Co., 1965-1969.

Harris, Burton, *John Colter, his years in the Rockies.* New York: Scribner's, 1952.

Hebard, Grace Raymond, *Sacajawea, a guide and interpreter of the Lewis and Clark Expedition, with an account of the travels of Toussaint Charboneau, and of Jean Baptiste, the expedition papoose.* Glendale, Calif: Arthur H. Clark Co., 1933; reprinted 1957, 1967.

Heitman, Francis B. (comp.), *Historical Register and Dictionary of the United States Army.* 2 vols. Washington: Government Printing Office, 1903.

Hosmer, James K. (ed.), *The Expedition of Lewis and Clark.* Chicago: A. C. McClurg & Co., 1903.

Hosmer, James K. (ed.), *Gass's Journal of the Lewis and Clark Expedition.* Chicago, A. C. McClurg & Co., 1904.

Jackson, Donald (ed.), *Letters of the Lewis and Clark Expedition with related documents, 1783-1854.* Urbana: University of Illinois Press, 1962.

Jacob, John G., *The life and times of Patrick Gass, now sole survivor of the overland expedition to the Pacific, under Lewis and Clark, in 1804-5-6.* Wellsburg, Va: Jacob & Smith, 1859.

James, Edwin, *An Account of an expedition from Pittsburgh to the Rocky Mountains, performed in the years 1819 and 1820.* 2 vols. Philadelphia: 1823. Reprinted in *Early Western Travels,* vols. XIV-XVII. Cleveland: Arthur H. Clark Co., 1904.

James, Gen. Thomas, *Three years among the Indians and Mexicans.* Edited by Walter B. Douglas. St. Louis: Missouri Historical Society, 1916.

McClung, Quantrille D. (comp.), *Carson-Bent-Boggs Genealogy.* Denver: Denver Public Library, 1962.

McDermott, John Francis (ed.), *The French in the Mississippi Valley.* Urbana: University of Illinois Press, 1965.

Maloney, Alice B., "Alexander Carson, Wilhamot Freeman," in *Oregon Historical Society Quarterly,* vol. XXXIX, March 1938, pp. 16-21.

Meaney, Edmond S., "Doctor Saugrain helped Lewis and Clark," in *Washington Historical Quarterly,* vol. 22, 1931, pp. 295-311.

Nasatir, A.P. (ed.), *Before Lewis and Clark.* 2 vols. St. Louis: Joseph Desloge Fund Publication, 1954.

Osgood, Ernest Staples (ed.), *The Field Notes of Captain William Clark.* New Haven: Yale University Press, 1964.

Parker, Rev. Samuel, *Journal of an exploring tour beyond the Rocky Mountains . . . in the years 1835, 36, 37.*   Ithaca, N.Y: 1838.

Phelps, Dawson A., "The tragic death of Meriwether Lewis," in *William and Mary Quarterly,* July 1956, ser. 3, v. 13, pp. 305-18.

Pollard, Lancaster, *Lewis and Clark at Seaside.*   Seaside, Oregon: Chamber of Commerce, 1945.

Powers, H.C., "Equipment of the Lewis and Clark exploring expedition," in *Proceedings* of the Academy of Science and Letters, Sioux City: 1903-4.

Quaife, Milo M. (ed.), *The journals of Captain Meriwether Lewis and Sergeant John Ordway kept on the expedition of western exploration 1803-1806.*   Madison, Wisconsin: 1916.   Reprinted by the Wisconsin Historical Society, 1965.

Reid, Russell, *Sakakawea, the Bird Woman.*   State Historical Society of North Dakota, 1950.

Robinson, Doane, "The medical adventures of Lewis and Clark," in *So. Dakota Historical Collections,* vol. 12, 1924, pp. 53-66.

Russell, Carl P., *Firearms, Traps & Tools of the Mountain Men.*   New York: Alfred A. Knopf, 1967.

Sabin, Edwin Legrand, *Kit Carson Days, 1809-1868.*   New York: Press of the Pioneers, 1935.

Shields, John A. (ed.), *Shields Family, 1600-1780.*   Seymor, Indiana: n.d.

Skarsten, M.O., *George Drouillard, Hunter and Interpreter for Lewis and Clark.*   Glendale, Calif: Arthur H. Clark Co., 1964.

Skarsten, M.O., "George Drouillard," in *Mountain Men and the Fur Trade of the Far West;* vol. IV, pp. 69-82.   Glendale, Calif: Arthur H. Clark Co., 1966.

Stanley, L.L., "Medicine and surgery of the Lewis and Clark Expedition," in *Medical Journal and Record,* no. 127, 1928.

Stoddard, Amos, *Sketches Historical and Descriptive of Louisiana.*   Phila: Mathew Carey, 1812.

Tabeau, Pierre Antoine, *Tabeau's Narrative of Loisel's expedition to the Upper Missouri.* Edited by Annie Heloise Abel.   Norman, Oklahoma: University of Oklahoma Press, 1939.

Thwaites, Reuben Gold (ed.), *Original journals of the Lewis and Clark expedition, 1804-1806, printed from the original manuscripts in the library of the American Philosophical Society and by direction of its com-*

mittee on historical documents, together with manuscript material of Lewis and Clark from other sources — now for the first time published in full and exactly as written. 8 vols. New York: Dodd, Mead & Co., 1904-1905. Reprinted N.Y., 1959.

Vinton, Stallo, *John Colter.* New York: E. Eberstadt, 1926.

Weiser, Rev. Frederick S., *The Weiser Family.* John Conrad Weiser Family Assn., 1960.

Wheeler, Olin D., *The Trail of Lewis and Clark.* New York: G. Putnam & Sons., 1904. Reprint, 1926.

Wilkes, Charles, U.S.N., *Narrative of the United States Exploring Expedition, 1838-1839-1840-1841-1842.* 6 vols. Philadelphia: Lee & Blanchard, 1845.

Index

Index

Prepared by Anna Marie and Everett G. Hager